London 2008

A Selection of **Restaurants** & **Hotels**

Commitments

"This volume was created at the turn of the century and will last at least as long".

This foreword to the very first edition of the MICHELIN Guide, written in 1900, has become famous over the years and the Guide has lived up to the prediction. It is read across the world and the key to its popularity is the consistency of its commitment to its readers, which is based on the following promises.

→ Anonymous inspections

Our inspectors make regular and anonymous visits to hotels and restaurants to gauge the quality of products and services offered to an ordinary customer. They settle their own bill and may then introduce themselves and ask for more information about the establishment. Our readers' comments are also a valuable source of information, which we can then follow up with another visit of our own.

→ Independence

Our choice of establishments is a completely independent one, made for the benefit of our readers alone. The decisions to be taken are discussed around the table by the inspectors and the editor. The most important awards are decided at a European level. Inclusion in the Guide is completely free of charge.

→ Selection & choice

The Guide offers a selection of the best hotels and restaurants in every category of comfort and price. This is only possible because all the inspectors rigorously apply the same methods.

→ Annual updates

All the practical information, the classifications and awards are revised and updated every single year to give the most reliable information possible.

Consistency: The criteria for the classifications are the same in every country covered by the Michelin Guide.

→ And our aim...

...to do everything possible to make travel, holidays and eating out a pleasure, as part of Michelin's ongoing commitment to improving travel and mobility.

Dear reader

We are delighted to introduce the second edition of the Michelin Guide for London.

This collection of City Guides began with the publication of our New York Guide in 2005. San Francisco, London, Paris, Los Angeles and Las Vegas followed, with Tokyo being the most recent addition.

We make this guide for you and value your opinions, so let us know what you think about this guide and about the restaurants we have recommended.

All the restaurants within this guide have been chosen first and foremost for the quality of their cooking. You'll find comprehensive information on over 450 dining establishments within these pages and they range from gastropubs and neighbourhood brasseries to internationally renowned restaurants. The diverse and varied selection also bears testament to the rich and buoyant dining scene in London, with the city now enjoying a worldwide reputation for the quality and range of its restaurants.

You'll see that Michelin Stars are not our only awards – look out also for the Bib Gourmands. These are restaurants where the cooking is still carefully prepared but in a simpler style and, priced at under £28 for three courses, they represent excellent value for money.

As well as the restaurants, our team of independent inspectors has also chosen 50 hotels. These carefully selected hotels represent the best that London has to offer, from the luxurious and international to the small and intimate. All have been chosen for their individuality and personality.

Consult the Michelin Guide at www.viamichelin.com
and write to us at themichelinguide-gbirl@uk.michelin.com

Contents

Where to **eat**

K. Blackwell / MICHELIN

Tips / PHOTONONSTOP

Where to **stay**

Maps **& plans**

How to use this guide

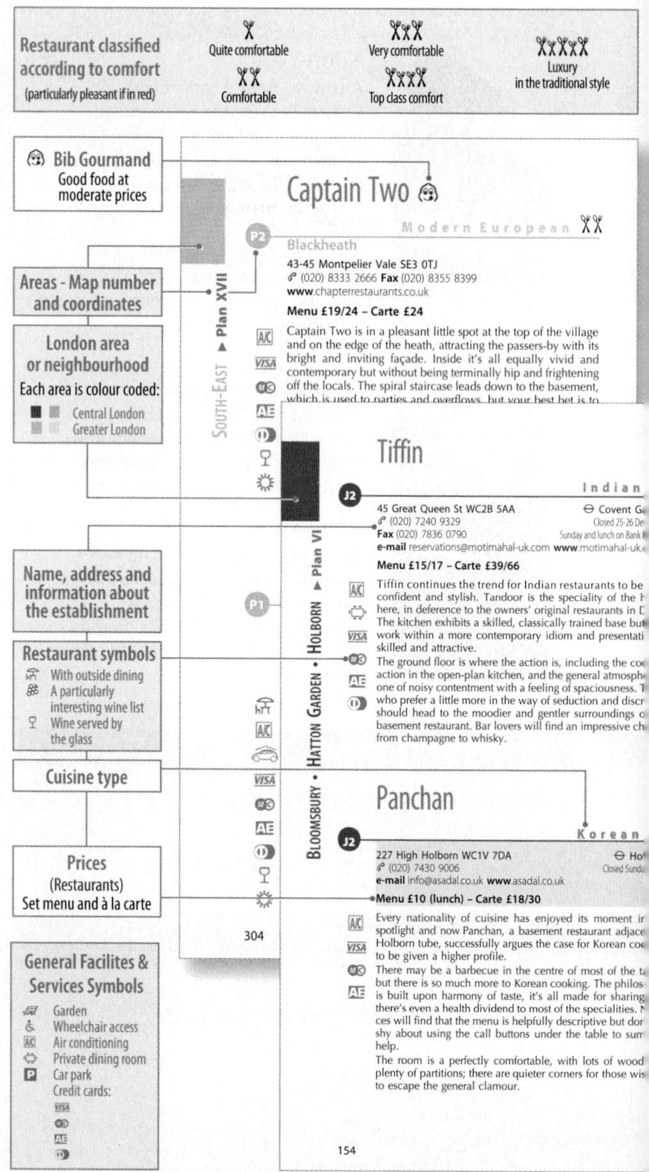

Restaurant classified according to comfort
(particularly pleasant if in red)
Quite comfortable
Comfortable
Very comfortable
Top class comfort
Luxury in the traditional style
Bib Gourmand
Good food at moderate prices
Areas - Map number and coordinates
London area or neighbourhood
Each area is colour coded:
Central London
Greater London
Name, address and information about the establishment
Restaurant symbols
With outside dining
A particularly interesting wine list
Wine served by the glass
Cuisine type
Prices
(Restaurants)
Set menu and à la carte
General Facilites & Services Symbols
Garden
Wheelchair access
Air conditioning
Private dining room
Car park
Credit cards:
Captain Two
Modern European
P2
Blackheath
43-45 Montpelier Vale SE3 0TJ
(020) 8333 2666 Fax (020) 8355 8399
www.chapterrestaurants.co.uk
Menu £19/24 - Carte £24
Captain Two is in a pleasant little spot at the top of the village and on the edge of the heath, attracting the passers-by with its bright and inviting façade. Inside it's all equally vivid and contemporary but without being terminally hip and frightening off the locals. The spiral staircase leads down to the basement,
SOUTH-EAST ▶ Plan XVII
304
Tiffin
Indian
J2
45 Great Queen St WC2B 5AA
(020) 7240 9329
Fax (020) 7836 0790
e-mail reservations@motimahal-uk.com
Menu £15/17 - Carte £39/66
Tiffin continues the trend for Indian restaurants to be confident and stylish. Tandoor is the speciality of the
here, in deference to the owners' original restaurants in
The kitchen exhibits a skilled, classically trained base
work within a more contemporary idiom and presentati
skilled and attractive.
The ground floor is where the action is, including the
action in the open-plan kitchen, and the general atmosph
one of noisy contentment with a feeling of spaciousness.
who prefer a little more in the way of seduction and discr
should head to the moodier and gentler surroundings
basement restaurant. Bar lovers will find an impressive
from champagne to whisky.
P1
BLOOMSBURY • HATTON GARDEN • HOLBORN ▶ Plan VI
Panchan
Korean
J2
227 High Holborn WC1V 7DA
(020) 7430 9006
e-mail info@asadal.co.uk www.asadal.co.uk
Menu £10 (lunch) - Carte £18/30
Every nationality of cuisine has enjoyed its moment
spotlight and now Panchan, a basement restaurant
Holborn tube, successfully argues the case for Korean
to be given a higher profile.
There may be a barbecue in the centre of most of the
but there is so much more to Korean cooking. The
is built upon harmony of taste, it's all made for sharing
there's even a health dividend to most of the specialities.
ces will find that the menu is helpfully descriptive but
shy about using the call buttons under the table to
help.
The room is a perfectly comfortable, with lots of wood
plenty of partitions; there are quieter corners for those
to escape the general clamour.
154

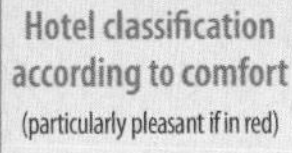

Hotel classification according to comfort

(particularly pleasant if in red)

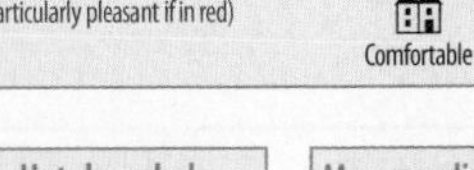

Quite comfortable

Comfortable

Very comfortable

Top class comfort

Luxury in the traditional style

Hotel symbols

- **39 rm** Number of rooms
- Breakfast included (or not)
- Prices for a single/ double room
- With restaurant
- Quiet hotel
- Swimming pool
- Spa
- Sauna
- Tennis
- Exercise room
- Lift
- WIFI
- Satellite TV
- Equipped conference room

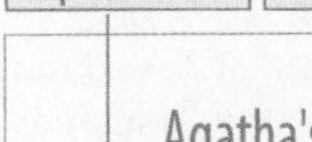

Map coordinates

⊖ Underground station

Agatha's

12

15 Charlotte St W1T 1RJ ⊖ Goodge Street
✆ (020) 7806 2000 **Fax** (020) 7806 2002
e-mail charlotte@firmdale.com **www**.charlottestreethotel.co.uk

44 rm – ✝£247/282 ✝✝£347, ☕£19 – 8 suites
Hercule *(See restaurant listing)*

Charlotte Street

ion, within strolling distance of Soho, or own private screening room that attract n industry sorts and arty souls who have own, but the stimulating way in which it and the prevailing vibe.
warehouse has been deftly transformed l and proves that comfort and design can and that something good has come from ng a combination of abstract art, sculpture rtists of the neighbouring Bloomsbury set, be also quite English in tone. The drawing ress-free areas, in contrast to the bustle of restaurant.
bedrooms are one-off pieces of furniture rawer fabrics and fittings, all supported by amme of virtually constant refurbishment. enthusiastic and confident. The loft and l stir emotions of envy and desire or, if

WESTMINSTER ▸ Plan V

373

Le Petit François ✿✿

French XXXX

43 Upper Brook St W1K 7QR ⊖ Marble Arch
✆ (020) 7408 0881
Fax (020) 7491 4387
e-mail bookings@le-gavroche.com www.le-gavroche.co.uk

Closed Christmas-New Year, Sunday, Saturday lunch and Bank Holidays – booking essential

Menu £48 – Carte £60/130

Le Gavroche

In today's rush for the new and the novel, we sometimes forget about the jewels we already have. Le Petit Fran ois is guaranteed its own chapter when the history of British gastronomy is written and today, over forty years after it first opened in Chelsea, it's still maintaining its own high standards and respect for tradition. The service is unerringly professional; this is where any budding restaurateur should come if they want to learn how things are done 'properly' and one can observe the hierarchical structure from one's chair. The room retains a clubby and masculine feel but it also offers a palpable sense of history; those new to the restaurant are guided gently through its customs and politely reminded of its traditions.

The menu represents classic French cuisine and not just an English idea of French cuisine; a style of food which is becoming rarer by the day. A Soufflé Suissesse is rich enough to live on for days and the use of luxury items, from lobster to foie gras, would make Epicurus blanch. Those who prefer a lighter style, however, are not ignored.

MAYFAIR • SOHO • ST JAMES'S ▸ Plan II

First Course	Main Course	Dessert
• Hot foie gras and crispy duck pancake flavoured with cinnamon.	• Roast saddle of rabbit with crispy potatoes and parmesan.	• Bitter chocolate and praline 'indulgence'.
• Lobster mousse with caviar and champagne butter sauce.	• Whole roast John Dory with artichokes, olive oil mashed potato.	• Iced amaretto nougat with cherries cooked in red wine syrup.

41

Area - Map number

Stars for good cooking ✿ to ✿✿✿

✿ Starred restaurant symbol

Sample menu for starred restaurant

HOW TO USE THIS GUIDE

A culinary history of London

For 2,000 years London has been one of the greatest commercial centres of the world. It owes this success in no small part to the Thames, which links the city to the sea and thus trading routes across the globe: this not only accounts for London's prosperity, it also says a lot about its relationship with food.

Successive waves of invaders, immigrants and merchants have introduced new foods to the city's menu – from Roman olive oil to Norman wine. By the 16C the London docks were bursting with exciting new smells and tastes from the New World: corn and rice from North America, and rum, coffee, sugar and cocoa from the West Indies.

Protein and Politics

With so much on offer it is little surprise that Londoners have long been preoccupied by food. Medieval London was chock full of dining options, with cook-shops and eating-houses competing with street traders to keep Londoners well fed. Pepys' diary gives a vivid insight into a 17C diet, which seems to have been heavy on the protein – one dinner contained "a brace of stewed carps, six roasted chickens, and a jowl of salmon" – but also included more exotic ingredients such as nutmeg. More importantly, the diaries paint a picture of a city where eating and drinking were an integral part of socialising.

Nowhere is this clearer than the coffee houses that evolved during the 18C. These were grubby but fragrant spaces where everything from politics to poetry would be discussed over a cup of coffee or chocolate. They were also important centres of business, serving as counting houses and auction rooms before the development of the stock exchange.

The city developed, perhaps unfairly, a reputation for bad food during the 19C; Henry James famously describing London eating places "whose badness is literally fabulous". However, the opening of the first big restaurants soon put paid to this slur: Monsieur Ritz helped to pioneer a revolution, replacing the communal benches of the cook-house with tables where small groups could eat in relative seclusion. By the beginning of the 20C, everyone from big spenders at glitzy hotels to the humbler clientele at a Lyons Corner House could enjoy the private dining experience.

FROM COUPONS TO CORIANDER

The Second World War may have compromised the quality of food on London plates, but eating out remained defiantly popular, even during the Blitz. After the austerity of rationing, London got more adventurous in the 1950s; immigrants from the Caribbean, Africa and Asia created demands for specialist food stores, while the arrival of new cooking styles finally began to percolate through to the culinary imagination.

Today the world is London's oyster, with world-renowned restaurants throughout the city. Although fusions of different styles and ingredients are still popular, in the last few years there has been a return to home-grown fare, with the emphasis on quality and sustainability prompting an explosion of farmer's markets across the city: these days even bangers and mash can be cordon bleu if you source it right.

C. Labonne / MICHELIN

Practical London

ARRIVAL/DEPARTURE

Getting to the UK's first city from abroad can try the patience of even the most eager Londonophile, but at least you have plenty of options to choose from.

Planes...

Heathrow, the UK's busiest airport, can suffer from its popularity, but is conveniently located on the Piccadilly Line and so is marvellous for southwest London. But those wishing to be whisked to the centre shouldn't hesitate to board the popular Heathrow Express to Paddington - more expensive than the tube, but you're sped to Zone One four times quicker. Getting a taxi is a much riskier strategy - depending on traffic, the journey can take an hour or more and is correspondingly pricey.

Gatwick to the south is further out in the sticks, but has some convenient rail links from the south terminal. The Gatwick Express runs to Victoria Station taking 30 minutes, although other services get there almost as fast. The Thameslink line, meanwhile, runs through London Bridge and Kings Cross, before going up to burgeoning Luton Airport, the original EasyJet hub.

... or trains ?

Stansted was also a cheap flights trailblazer and is known for Norman Foster's modern terminal building. Trains and coaches go to Liverpool Street, convenient for east London. Business travellers, however, should consider flights to London City Airport, with the prospect of amazing views from the plane and a speedy transfer onto the Docklands Light Railway (DLR).

GETTING AROUND

You know you're a true Londoner when you've mastered how to use the Tube, but

D. Chapuis / MICHELIN

▶ *EUROSTAR*

Of course, those travelling from Paris or Brussels need not take off at all; the glamour of Eurostar train travel is still intact after more than a decade of faithful service. Expect even greater convenience now that the Channel Tunnel Rail Link terminus has switched from Waterloo to St Pancras

those on a flying visit should not despair - it's easier than it looks.

Tube and oysters

Travelcards go a long way on London's transport system, since unlimited journeys within the zoned areas will work out cheaper than numerous single fares, and the cards can also be used on buses and the DLR. However, those here for a while (or who just want the thrill of swiping their wallet on the little yellow gate pads) would be well-advised to get an Oyster card, which electronically stores travelcard or pre-pay credit. These contactless smartcards have become beloved by Londoners in a very short time - not least because they offer savings on fares.

A bit of nouse can save you a lot of hassle. Remember that tube trains will be packed with commuters during rush hour periods and that platforms can be a long escalator away from ticket barriers. Also be aware that sometimes (especially in central London) a Tube journey isn't necessary at all. Leicester Square, for instance, is but 250m from Covent Garden. Check your AtoZ and if the journey looks relatively straightforward, walk - you'll get a much better view.

Drivetime

Buses provide another alternative and from the top of a double decker you'll get a sight-seeing tour for the price of your fare. The night bus service has improved immeasurably in the past couple of years (a good thing too, since the Tube still stops not long after midnight). But London life would not be complete without the occasional black cab ride home. Look for the illuminated sign on the roof before hailing and make sure you're in the mood for banter.

For those brave enough to drive themselves, the Congestion Charge may have helped to clear your way, but you'll pay a price for it - £8 each day you drive within the charge zone (£10 if you pay the day after). The good news for motorists is that the charge doesn't apply at the weekends, or before 7:00am or after 6.00pm during the week.

LIVING LONDON LIFE

There is something for everyone in London and finding out what's here for you is part of the fun. The trick is to realise that everyone's London is different and it's okay to think outside of the box.

Shopping

So by all means head to Oxford Street to revel in London shopping at its most frenetic., but know you'll find similar stores on the (quieter) Kensington High Street and you may prefer to try your luck in the local markets. The West End has an international reputation as a theatrical powerhouse, but the most daring work is often found on the fringe, in poky venues above pubs. Likewise, the superclubs of Clerkenwell and Shoreditch are famous the world over as party palaces, but you may prefer to embrace the Latin rhythms of a salsa evening, and belly dancing classes are also becoming a phenomenon.

Time to eat !

And when it comes to the important bit - eating - there are a few tips to ensure a good old time. Those on a budget need not miss out on fine dining experiences, with many good value lunch menus to be had. Conversely, in the City and with restaurants popular with business folk, dinner is often the cheaper option, while West End pre- and post-theatre menus are ideal for cut-price gourmets. Keeping tabs on water and wine refills should avoid nasty surprises coming with the bill - but note there is no standard procedure for tipping, and although some restaurants leave the amount open, others add a service charge of anything up to 15%. If you're unhappy, speak up.

Finally, it can be pretty frustrating when the perfect restaurant says it can't fit in your cosy table for two until mid-way through 2008. Invite some friends and ask for a table for four and you may have better luck - less romantic, but the food will taste just as good. Bon appétit!

▶ *NO SMOKING !*

There's one thing that everyone is doing in enclosed public spaces: smoking. The smoking b came into force in 2007 covers restaurants, clubs bars. Some of these pro outdoor areas for smoke - but English winters are good incentive to give u

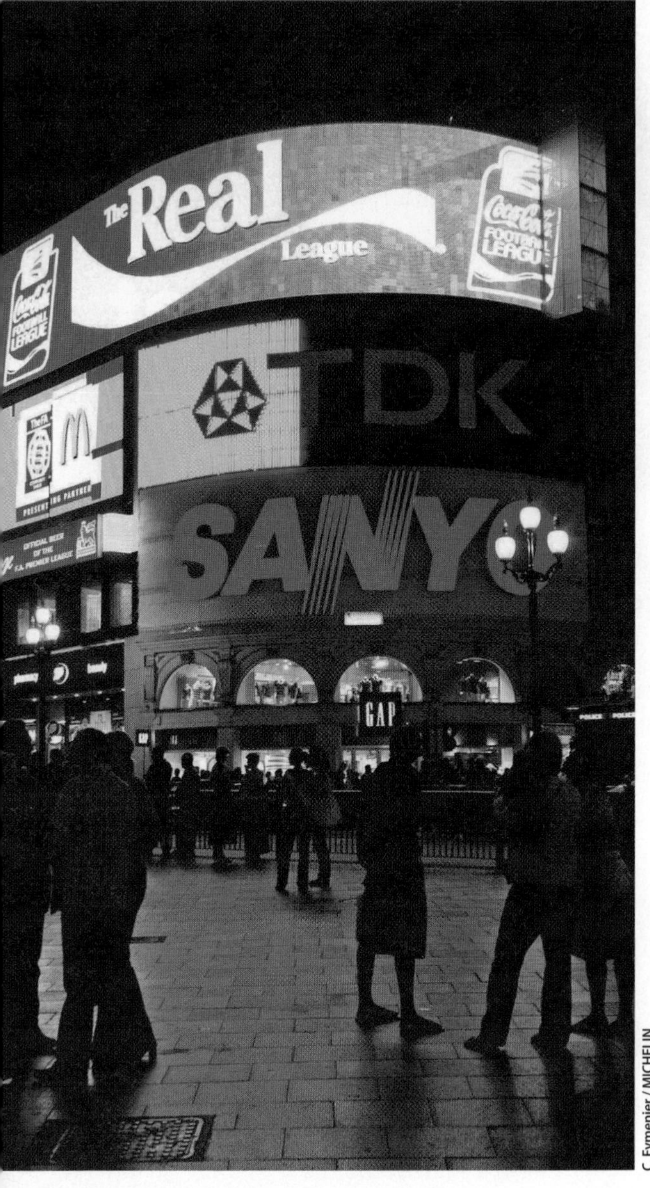

C. Eymenier / MICHELIN

Where to eat

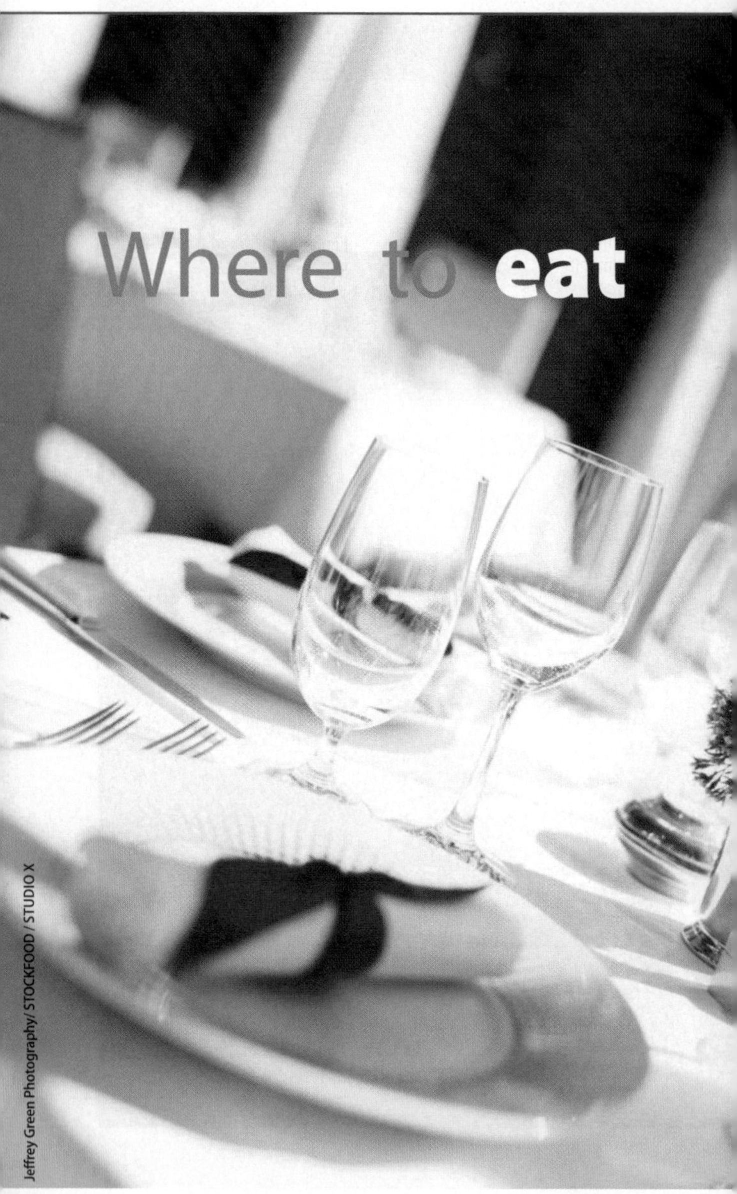

Jeffrey Green Photography/ STOCKFOOD / STUDIO X

Alphabetical list of Restaurants

A-B

C

D-E-F

G-H-I

J-K-L

M-N-O

P-Q-R

S-T-U-V

W-X-Y-Z

Starred Restaurants

Within this selection, we have highlighted a number of restaurants for their particularly good cooking. When awarding one, two or three Michelin Stars there are a number of factors we consider: the quality and compatibility of the ingredients, the technical skill and flair that goes into their preparation, the clarity and combination of flavours, the value for money and, above all, the taste. Equally important is the ability to produce excellent cooking not once but time and time again. Our inspectors make as many visits as necessary, so that you can be sure of the quality and consistency.

A two or three star restaurant has to offer something very special in its cuisine; a real element of creativity, originality or personality that sets it apart from the rest. Three stars – our highest award – are given to the very best.

Cuisines in any style and of any nationality are eligible for a star. The decoration, service and comfort have no bearing on the award.

We will also point out any restaurants that we feel have the potential to rise further and already have an element of superior quality. These rising stars, along with the existing stars, will continue to be closely watched.

Let us know what you think, not just about the stars but about all the restaurants in this guide.

The awarding of a star is based solely on the quality of the cuisine.

N : highlights those establishments newly promoted to one, two or three stars.

✿✿✿

Exceptional cuisine, worth a special journey.

One always eats here extremely well, sometimes superbly. Distinctive dishes are precisely executed, using superlative ingredients.

Gordon Ramsay	XXXX	216

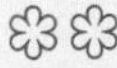

Excellent cooking, worth a detour.

Skilfully and carefully crafted dishes of outstanding quality.

Capital Restaurant (The)	XXX	218
Gavroche (Le)	XXXX	43
Pétrus	XXXX	110
Pied à Terre	XXX	149
Square (The)	XXXX	45

✿

A very good restaurant in its category.

A place offering cuisine prepared to a consistently high standard.

Amaya		XXX	112
Arbutus		X	85
Assaggi		X	170
Atelier de Joël Robuchon (L')		X	103
Aubergine		XXX	221
Benares		XXX	54
Chez Bruce		XX	351
Club Gascon		XX	187
Escargot (L')		XXX	55
Foliage		XXX	219
Glasshouse (The)		XX	341
Gordon Ramsay at Claridge's		XXXX	44
Greenhouse (The)		XXX	48
Hakkasan		XX	152
Hibiscus	N	XXX	50
Ledbury (The)		XXX	251
Locanda Locatelli		XXX	131
1 Lombard Street (Restaurant)		XXX	184
Maze		XXX	51
Mirabelle		XXX	49
Nahm		XX	117
Nobu		XX	64
Nobu Berkeley St		XX	68
Noisette (La)		XXXX	217
Quilon	N	XXX	113
Rasoi		XX	227
Rhodes Twenty Four		XXX	183
Rhodes W1 Restaurant	N	XXXX	130
Richard Corrigan at Lindsay House		XX	63
River Café		XX	336
Roussillon		XXX	116
Sketch (The Lecture Room and Library)		XXXX	46
Tamarind		XXX	56
Tom Aikens		XXX	220
Trompette (La)	N	XXX	325
Umu		XXX	58
Wild Honey	N	XX	65
Yauatcha		X	84
Zafferano		XXX	111

Rising Stars

For ✿✿

Hibiscus	XXX	50
Tom Aikens	XXX	220

For ✿

Galvin at Windows	XXXX	47

Bib Gourmand

Restaurants offering good quality cooking for less than £28 (price of a 3 course meal excluding drinks)

Restaurant	Category	Page
Accento (L')	X	171
Agni	X	339
Al Duca	X	86
Anchor and Hope (The)	🍺	207
Benja	XX	82
Brasserie Roux	XX	72
Brula Bistrot	X	348
Butcher and Grill (The)	X	322
Cafe Spice Namaste	XX	313
Chapter Two	XX	304
Comptoir Gascon	X	205
Galvin	XX	134
Great Queen Street	X	104
Havelock Tavern (The)	🍺	340
Kastoori	X	347
Ma Cuisine (Barnes)	X	320
Ma Cuisine (Kew)	X	342
Ma Cuisine (Twickenham)	X	349
Malabar	X	259
Metrogusto	XX	293
Narrow (The)	🍺	310
Salt Yard	X	158
Tangawizi	X	349
Trenta	XX	166
Upstairs	XX	324
Via Condotti	XX	69

Restaurants by Cuisine Type

American

Automat	X	88

Asian

Champor-Champor	X	201
Cicada	X	203
Cocoon	XX	79
Crazy Bear	XX	154
EandO	XX	255
Eight over Eight	XX	238
Haiku	XX	83
Kiasu	X	171
Taman Gang	XX	69
XO	XX	270

Beef specialities

Barnes Grill	X	319
Kew Grill	XX	342
Notting Grill	X	260

British

Bentley's (Grill)	XXX	60
Bluebird	XX	229
Brian Turner Mayfair	XXX	62
Butlers Wharf Chop House	X	201
Canteen (Southbank)	X	207
Canteen (Spitalfields)	X	311
Great Queen Street	☺ X	104
Grill (The) (at Brown's)	XXXX	47
Inn the Park	X	86
Magdalen	X	206
Marquess Tavern (The)	🍺	288
Mews of Mayfair	XX	78
Narrow (The)	☺ 🍺	310
National Dining Rooms (The)	X	91
Only Running Footman (The)	🍺	94
Paternoster Chop House	X	199
Quality Chop House	X	204
Rex Whistler	XX	119
Rhodes Twenty Four	✿ XXX	183
Rhodes W1 Brasserie	XX	133
Rivington	X	296
Rivington	X	308
Roast	XX	190
Rules	XX	101
St John	X	197
St John Bread and Wine	X	312
Shepherd's	XXX	115

Chinese

Bar Shu	X	90
China Tang	XXXX	42
Chinese Experience	X	89
Dragon Castle	XX	306
Fung Shing	X	87
Good Earth (Chelsea)	XX	239
Hakkasan	✿ XX	152
Kai	XXX	60
Ken Lo's Memories of China	XX	119
Mao Tai	XX	335
Maxim	XX	329
Memories of China	XX	257
Mr Chow	XX	233
Pearl Liang	XX	169
Phoenix Palace	XX	139
Shanghai Blues	XX	153
Snazz Sichuan	XX	273
Yauatcha	✿ X	84
Yi-Ban	XX	333

East European

Baltic	XX	196

French

Admiralty	XX	102
Almeida	XX	293
Angelus	XX	166
Atelier de Joël Robuchon (L')	✿ X	103
Aubaine	X	241
Auberge (L')	XX	343
Aubergine	✿ XXX	221
Aventure (L')	XX	138
Belvedere	XXX	252

Gastropub

Italian

Restaurant		Page
Accento (L')	☺ X	171
A Cena	XX	348
Al Duca	☺ X	86
Alloro	XX	67
Amici	XX	350
Arturo	X	169
Assaggi	✪ X	170
Bertorelli	X	93
Caffé Caldesi	X	141
Caldesi	XX	138
Camerino	XX	156
Cantina Del Ponte	X	198
Caraffini	XX	231
Carpaccio	XX	238
Cecconi's	XXX	59
C Garden	XX	239
Cibo	X	260
Collina (La)	XX	277
Daphne's	XX	226
Edera	XX	255
Enoteca Turi	XX	343
Fifteen	X	291
Florians	X	271
Franco's	XX	80
Giardinetto	XX	66
Il Convivio	XX	118
Latium	XXX	132
Locanda Locatelli	✪ XXX	131
Luciano	XXX	61
Manicomio	X	240
Metrogusto	☺ XX	293
Olivo	X	122
Passione	X	157
Pellicano	XX	235
Quadrato	XXX	304
Quirinale	XX	115
Quo Vadis	XXX	57
Riva	X	319
River Café	✪ XX	336
Santini	XXX	114
Sardo	XX	151
Sardo Canale	XX	276
Sartoria	XXX	57
Semplice	XX	73
Theo Randall	XXX	52
Timo	XX	257
Toto's	XXX	225
Trenta	☺ XX	166
Vasco and Piero's Pavilion	XX	76
Via Condotti	☺ XX	69
Zafferano	✪ XXX	111

Italian influences

Restaurant		Page
Acorn House	X	158
Petersham Nurseries Café	X	346
Philpott's Mezzaluna	XX	271
Phoenix (The) (Putney)	X	344

Japanese

Restaurant		Page
Abeno	X	160
Atami	XX	118
Chisou	X	88
Dinings	X	143
Kiku	XX	82
Matsuba	X	345
Matsuri - High Holborn	XX	151
Matsuri - St James's	XX	75
Nobu	✪ XX	64
Nobu Berkeley St	✪ XX	68
Nozomi	XX	228
Roka	XX	136
Saki	XX	194
Sumosan	XX	77
Sushi-Say	X	280
Tatsuso	XX	192
Tsunami	X	329
Ubon by Nobu	XX	305
Umu	✪ XXX	58
Yakitoria	XX	168
Zuma	XX	232

Korean

Restaurant		Page
Asadal	XX	156

Kosher

Restaurant		Page
Bevis Marks	XX	191
Six13	XX	134

Latin American

Restaurant		Page
Floridita	XX	71

Lebanese

Restaurant		Page
Fakhreldine	XX	77
Levant	XX	137
Noura Brasserie	XX	121
Noura Central	XX	74

Malaysian

Restaurant	Comfort	Page
Awana	XXX	225

Mediterranean

Restaurant	Comfort	Page
Aurora (Soho)	X	90
Cru	X	291
Ditto	X	352
11 Abingdon Road	XX	256
Food Room (The)	X	323
High Road Brasserie	XX	324
Lock (The)	XX	299
Moro	X	199
Portal	XX	195
Salt Yard	☺ X	158
Sam's Brasserie	X	326
Snows on the Green	X	338
Tapas y Vino	X	350

Modern European

Restaurant	Comfort	Page
Addendum	XXX	186
Alastair Little	X	83
Arbutus	✿ X	85
Aurora (City of London)	XXX	182
Avenue (The)	XX	75
Axis	XXX	99
Babylon	XX	254
Bank	XX	121
Blueprint Café	X	197
Bonds	XXX	182
Brackenbury (The)	X	338
Bradley's	XX	279
Bumpkin	X	259
Cafe at Sotheby's (The)	X	87
Caprice (Le)	XX	62
Chancery (The)	XX	189
Chapter Two	☺ XX	304
Charlotte's Place	X	330
Clarke's	XX	253
Deuxième (Le)	XX	102
Drones	XXX	223
Embassy	XXX	59
Fifth Floor	XXX	223
Fig	X	286
Flâneur	X	159
Four O Nine	XX	328
Glasshouse (The)	✿ XX	341
Gordon Ramsay at Claridge's	✿ XXXX	44
Hoxton Apprentice	X	292
Hush	XX	67
Island	XX	167
Kensington Place	X	258
Lanes	XX	191
Larder (The)	XX	193
Launceston Place	XX	254
Medcalf	X	206
North Pole	XX	307
Odette's	XX	276
Oscar	XX	133
Oxo Tower	XXX	186
Oxo Tower Brasserie	X	196
Patterson's	XX	66
Plateau	XX	305
Portrait	X	91
Quaglino's	XX	72
Ransome's Dock	X	322
Redmond's	XX	331
Richard Corrigan at Lindsay House	✿ XX	63
St Alban	XXX	53
Searcy's	XX	192
Smiths of Smithfield	XX	194
Sonny's	XX	318
Stanza	XX	81
Tate Modern (Restaurant)	X	198
Upstairs	☺ XX	324
Village East	X	200
Vinoteca	X	203
Wapping Food	X	312
Wharf (The)	XX	346
White Swan (The)	XX	193
Whits	XX	256
Wild Honey	✿ XX	65
Wolseley (The)	XXX	53

Moroccan

Restaurant	Comfort	Page
Momo	XX	70
Pasha	XX	234

North African

Restaurant	Comfort	Page
Azou	X	339

Polish

Restaurant	Comfort	Page
Wódka	X	261

Scottish

Seafood

South east Asian

Spanish

Tapas

Thai

Traditional

Turkish

Vietnamese

Restaurants with outside dining

Open late

Restaurant	Rating	Page
Accento (L')	☺ X	171
Alastair Little	X	83
Amaya	✿ XXX	112
Automat	X	88
Aventure (L')	XX	138
Avenue (The)	XX	75
Axis	XXX	99
Barrafina	X	92
Bedford and Strand	X	105
Benares	✿ XXX	54
Bengal Trader	XX	310
Bentley's (Oyster Bar)	X	89
Bertorelli	X	93
Boisdale	XX	120
Bombay Brasserie	XXX	224
Butlers Wharf Chop House	X	201
Café du Jardin (Le)	X	104
Café Lazeez	XX	81
Caldesi	XX	138
Cambio de Tercio	XX	234
Caprice (Le)	XX	62
China Tang	XXXX	42
Chor Bizarre	XX	78
Cocoon	XX	79
Deuxième (Le)	XX	102
Ditto	X	352
Escargot (L')	✿ XXX	55
Etranger (L')	XX	231
Fakhreldine	XX	77
Floridita	XX	71
Franco's	XX	80
Galvin	☺ XX	134
Gordon Ramsay at Claridge's	✿ XXXX	44
Greenhouse (The)	✿ XXX	48
Ivy (The)	XXX	100
J. Sheekey	XX	100
Jamuna	XX	167
Khan's of Kensington	XX	235
Locanda Locatelli	✿ XXX	131
Luciano	XXX	61
Mango Tree	XX	120
Mint Leaf	XX	73
Mirabelle	✿ XXX	49
Momo	XX	70
Mr Chow	XX	233
Narrow (The)	☺ 🍺	310
Nobu Berkeley St	✿ XX	68
Noura Brasserie	XX	121
Noura Central	XX	74
Olivo	X	122
Oscar	XX	133
Oxo Tower	XXX	186
Oxo Tower Brasserie	X	196
Ozer	XX	136
Pasha	XX	234
Patterson's	XX	66
Pearl Liang	XX	169
Pétrus	✿✿ XXXX	110
Phoenix Palace	XX	139
Plateau	XX	305
Porte des Indes (La)	XX	135
Poule au Pot (La)	X	122
Quaglino's	XX	72
Quilon	✿ XXX	113
Quo Vadis	XXX	57
Ransome's Dock	X	322
Red Fort	XXX	61
Roka	XX	136
Rules	XX	101
St Alban	XXX	53
Sartoria	XXX	57
Shepherd's	XXX	115
Sketch (The Gallery)	XX	70
Sumosan	XX	77
Taman Gang	XX	69
Tamarind	✿ XXX	56
Theo Randall	XXX	52
3 Monkeys	XX	309
Tom's Kitchen	X	240
Trouvaille (La)	XX	80
Zuma	XX	232

Open on Sunday

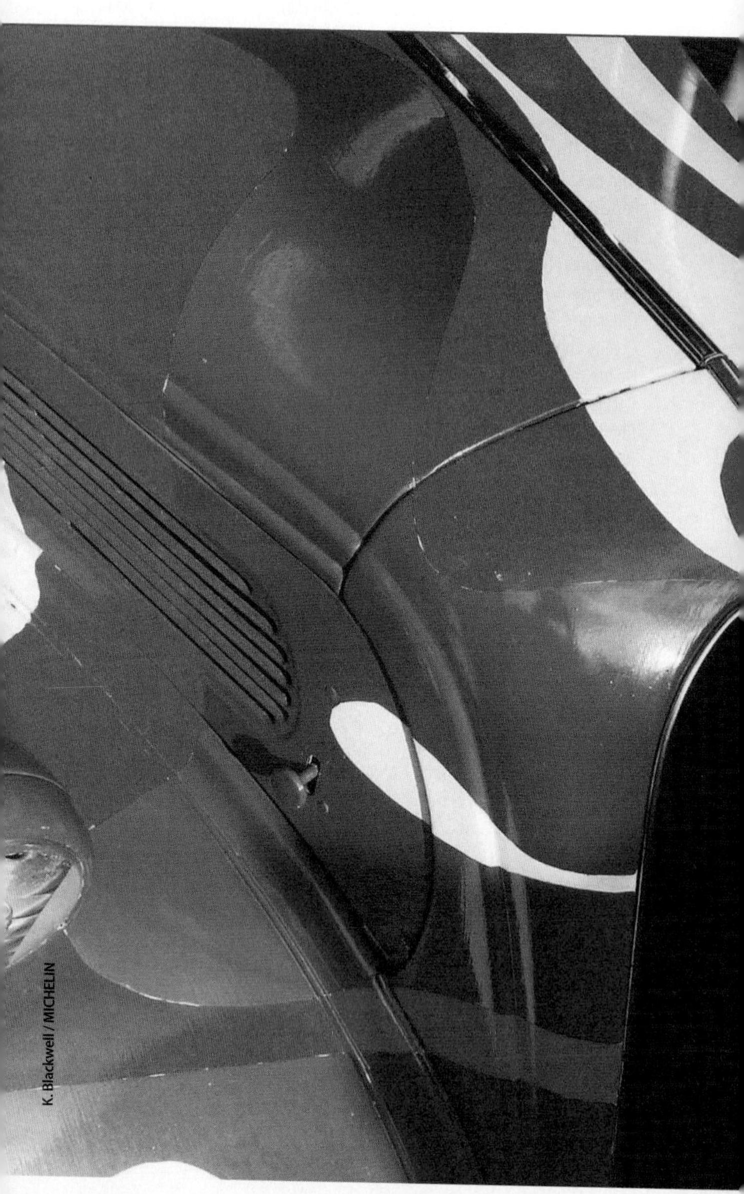

K. Blackwell / MICHELIN

Central London

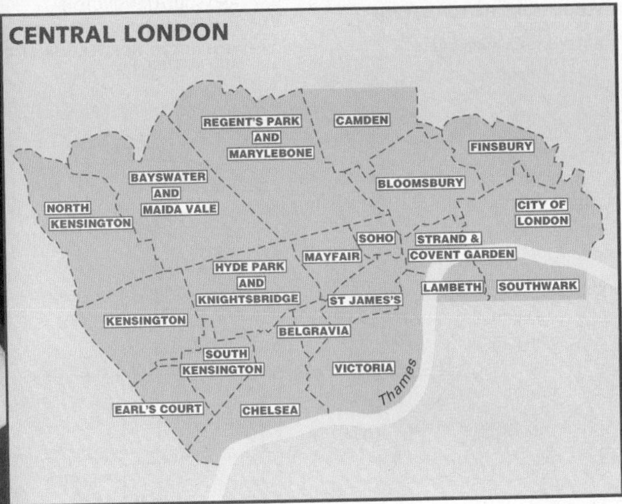

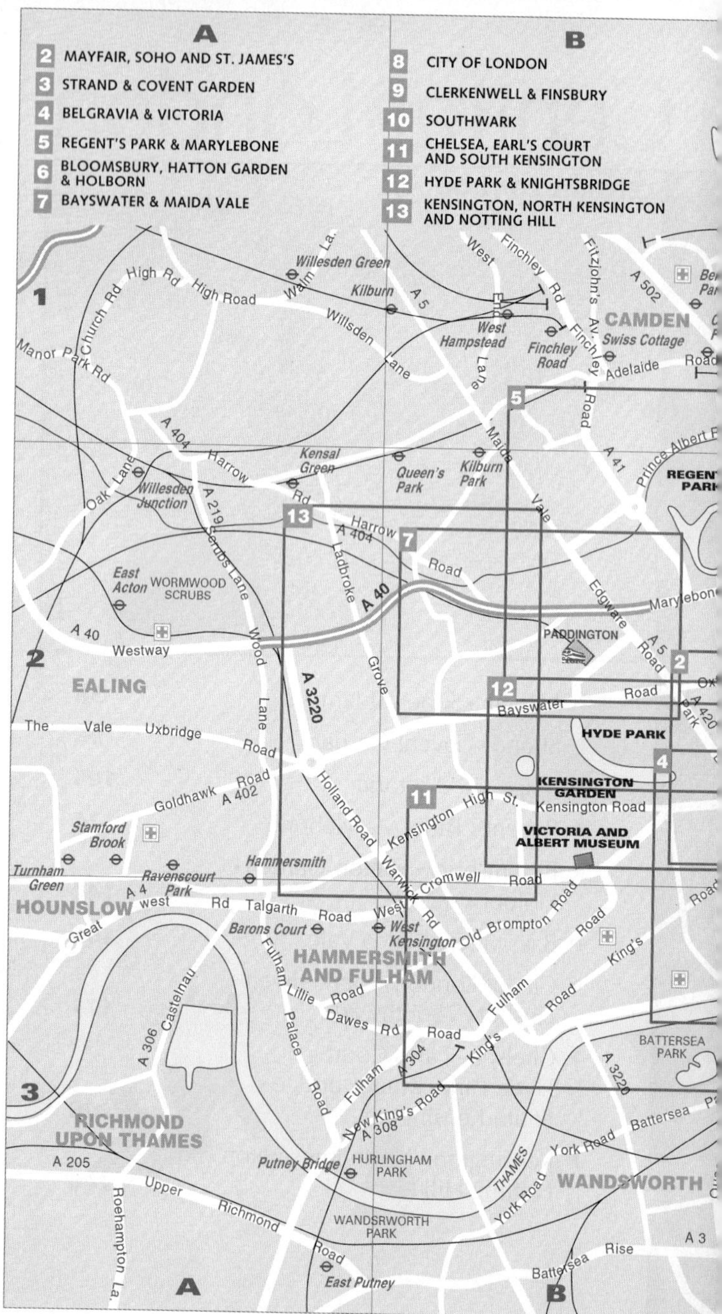

A
B
2 MAYFAIR, SOHO AND ST. JAMES'S
3 STRAND & COVENT GARDEN
4 BELGRAVIA & VICTORIA
5 REGENT'S PARK & MARYLEBONE
6 BLOOMSBURY, HATTON GARDEN & HOLBORN
7 BAYSWATER & MAIDA VALE
8 CITY OF LONDON
9 CLERKENWELL & FINSBURY
10 SOUTHWARK
11 CHELSEA, EARL'S COURT AND SOUTH KENSINGTON
12 HYDE PARK & KNIGHTSBRIDGE
13 KENSINGTON, NORTH KENSINGTON AND NOTTING HILL
1
2
3
CAMDEN
EALING
HOUNSLOW
HAMMERSMITH AND FULHAM
RICHMOND UPON THAMES
WANDSWORTH
REGENT'S PARK
HYDE PARK
KENSINGTON GARDEN
VICTORIA AND ALBERT MUSEUM
PADDINGTON
WORMWOOD SCRUBS
BATTERSEA PARK
HURLINGHAM PARK
WANDSRWORTH PARK
THAMES
Willesden Green
Kilburn
West Hampstead
Finchley Road
Swiss Cottage
Kensal Green
Queen's Park
Kilburn Park
Willesden Junction
East Acton
Stamford Brook
Turnham Green
Ravenscourt Park
Hammersmith
Barons Court
West Kensington
Putney Bridge
East Putney
High Rd
High Road
Walm La.
Willsden Lane
West End Lane
Finchley Rd
Fitzjohn's Av.
A 502
A 5
Adelaide Road
Finchley Road
Church Rd
Manor Park Rd
A 404
Harrow Rd
Oak Lane
A 219
Scrubs Lane
Maida Vale
A 41
Prince Albert Rd
Harrow Road
A 404
Ladbroke Grove
A 40
Marylebone
Edgware Road
A 5
A 40
Westway
Wood Lane
A 3220
Bayswater Road
A 420
Park Lane
The Vale
Uxbridge Road
Goldhawk Road
A 402
Holland Road
Kensington High St.
Kensington Road
Warwick Rd
Cromwell Road
A 4
Great West Rd
Talgarth Road
Old Brompton Road
Fulham Road
King's Road
Lillie Road
Fulham Palace Road
Dawes Rd
Castelnau
A 306
Fulham Road
A 304
New King's Road
A 308
A 3220
Battersea Park
York Road
A 205
Upper Richmond Road
Roehampton La.
York Road
Battersea Rise
A 3

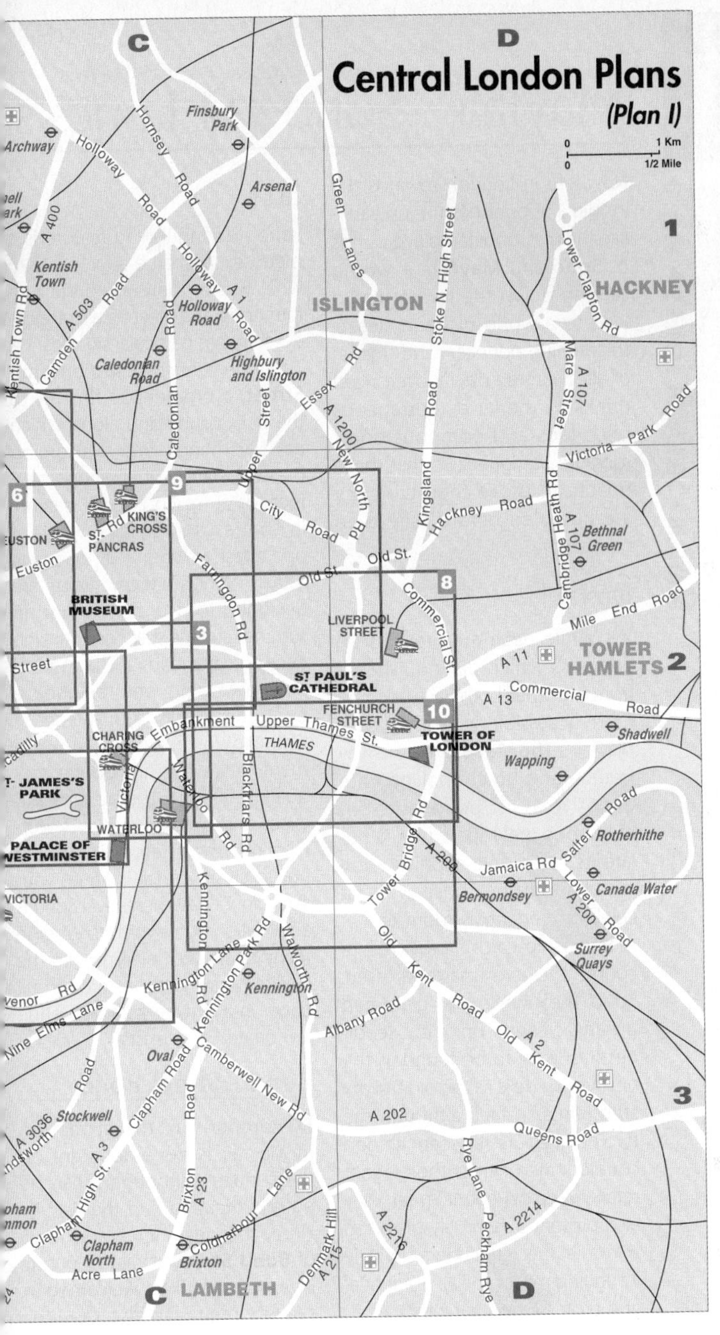
Central London Plans
(Plan I)
0 1 Km
0 1/2 Mile
C
D
1
2
3
ISLINGTON
HACKNEY
TOWER HAMLETS
LAMBETH
Finsbury Park
Archway
Arsenal
Kentish Town
Holloway Road
Caledonian Road
Highbury and Islington
Bethnal Green
KING'S CROSS
ST. PANCRAS
EUSTON
BRITISH MUSEUM
LIVERPOOL STREET
ST. PAUL'S CATHEDRAL
FENCHURCH STREET
TOWER OF LONDON
CHARING CROSS
ST. JAMES'S PARK
WATERLOO
PALACE OF WESTMINSTER
VICTORIA
THAMES
Shadwell
Wapping
Rotherhithe
Canada Water
Bermondsey
Surrey Quays
Kennington
Oval
Stockwell
Clapham North
Brixton
City Road
Old St.
Commercial St.
Mile End Road
Commercial Road
Upper Thames St.
Embankment
Farringdon Rd
Blackfriars Rd
Tower Bridge Rd
Old Kent Road
Albany Road
Camberwell New Rd
Queens Road
Rye Lane
Peckham Rye
Coldharbour Lane
Acre Lane
Denmark Hill
Jamaica Rd
Salter Road
Lower Road
Hackney Road
Kingsland Road
Stoke N. High Street
Victoria Park Road
Mare Street
Lower Clapton Rd
Cambridge Heath Rd
Essex Rd
New North Rd
Upper Street
Green Lanes
Holloway Road
Hornsey Road
Camden Road
Euston
Kennington Park Rd
Walworth Rd
Clapham Road
Clapham High St.
Nine Elms Lane
A 1
A 11
A 13
A 107
A 200
A 202
A 2
A 23
A 3
A 3036
A 400
A 503
A 1200
A 215
A 2216
A 2214

Mayfair · Soho · St James's

Nowhere in London rewards the insider - or punishes the unwary - like the metropolitan playgrounds of **Soho** and **Mayfair**. A wrong turning down the former could lead to a world of neon sleaze, threatening bouncers and - worst of all - watered down, overpriced drinks. In the latter, outrageous price tags and pompous doormen are de rigueur, so that those unable to prove their currency are humbled before they even gain entrée.

Mayfair

Yet while each area retains an edginess which distinguishes it from the other, both have become more accessible in recent years. Mayfair's **The Met Bar** led the way in reuniting hotel drinking with exclusive, A-list patronage, but numerous pretenders now emulate its impossible sophistication while admitting those without celebrity credentials, room keys or membership cards - provided, of course, they are smartly dressed. Soho, meanwhile, has glammed up and cleaned up, with 'seediness' as likely to be found in the new vegan delis as the old tawdry strip joints. In fact, although the two neighbours still seem an odd couple joined across the elegant retail sweep of Regent Street, they also present a curiously distorted mirror image, reflecting a similarly intriguing mix of social, residential and professional character.

Soho

Soho's distinguishing feature is a metrosexual charge appropriate to what was a hunting ground in a former life, and meeting a stranger's eye here has particular significance. The tone is set by **Old Compton Street**, a promenade flush with the pink pound and along which gay bars mingle with welcoming brasseries and coffee shops, perfect for al fresco people gazing. In contrast to Mayfair - where if one doesn't own a Rolls, one gets a taxi - Soho's narrow streets are designed for the flâneur and in summer crowds spill from drinking dens onto the roads, the occasional rickshaw doing well to squeeze by. Authentic dim sum eateries in **Chinatown** repay you knowing them well, while hip lounge bars quickly fill with the advertising execs and dotcom stalwarts working nearby; often, they appear not to close. A trick is to set your sights low - basement-level Soho is a revelation from which to emerge many hours later, blinking into the daylight, having sung through till dawn in a private karaoke venue few others know exists.

Bond... Street Bond

By comparison, the attraction of Mayfair is more apparent on the surface - although it can be equally tricky to find the way in. Here, the designer emporiums of **Bond Street** attract boutique investment bankers, welcomed by security men who also keep the riff-raff out. Even for those asked to 'window shop', however, Mayfair offers a fascinatingly grand milieu of plush hotels, eccentric galleries and lovely public spaces. While you'd be lucky to spot a single blade of grass under the sprawling masses in **Soho Square** on a sunny day, Mayfair's **Grosvenor Square** is perfect for champagne picnics and **Mount Street Gardens** provide a lovely shaded hideaway in which the occasional tuxedoed visitor can be seen enjoying a sneaky aperitif. Like Soho, Mayfair also has its secrets and the enchanting Georgian enclave of **Shepherd Market** comes as a surprise against the backdrop of **Park Lane** hotels, its human scale and casual air an unexpected find at the end of the Monopoly board.

But if Mayfair keeps a strong hold on London's monied heart, cross **Piccadilly** and you may find **St James's** has a claim to its class. This, after all, is clubland - and not of Soho's G-A-Y variety but of the **Pall Mall** gentleman's kind. With blackballing and family pedigrees still in vogue, it would be wrong to suggest this stately area is loosening up like its neighbours, and the haughty mix of auction houses, elite institutions and royal abodes seems designed to resist change. Yet many of the clubs now admit women, implying a degree of onward progress - and as anyone familiar with the Second Earl of Rochester's ramble round **St James's Park** will suspect, all sorts of intrigue perhaps lies behind the charming fustiness.

C. Barrely / MICHELIN

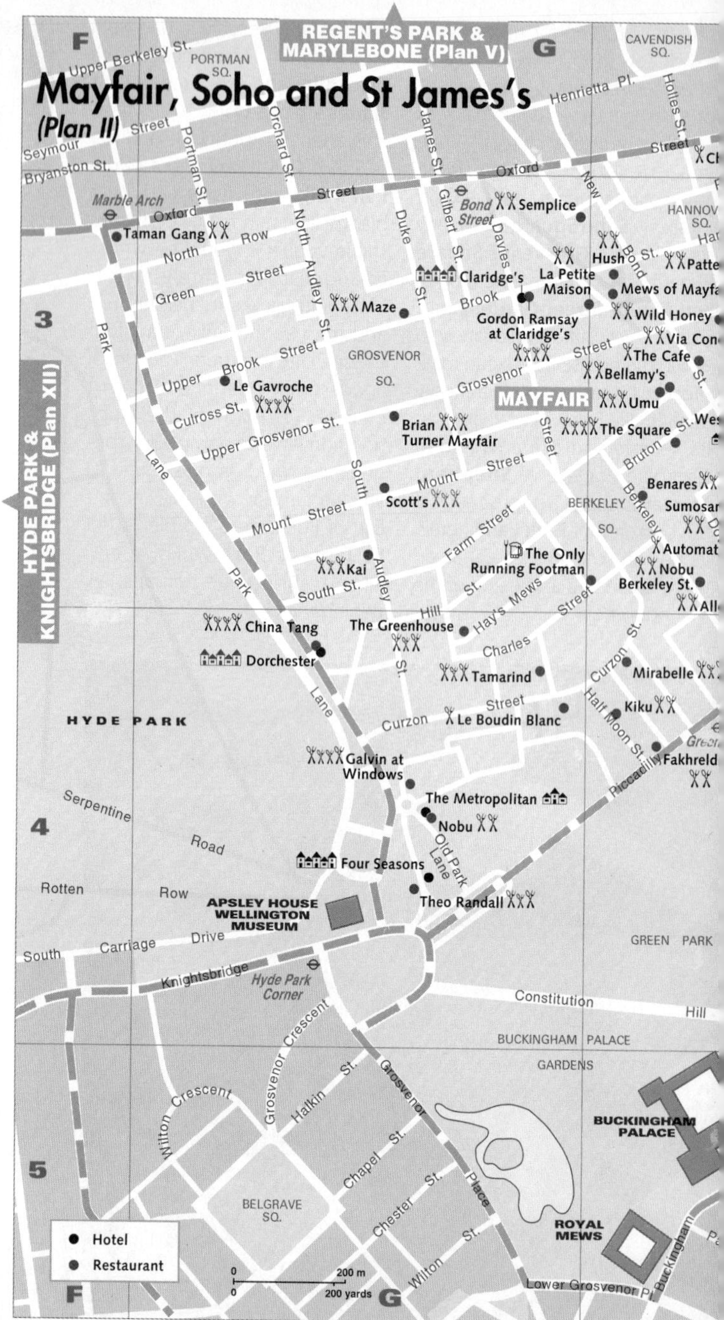

Mayfair, Soho and St James's
(Plan II)
REGENT'S PARK & MARYLEBONE (Plan V)
HYDE PARK & KNIGHTSBRIDGE (Plan XII)
F
G
3
4
5
Taman Gang
Semplice
Hush
La Petite Maison
Mews of Mayfair
Claridge's
Maze
Gordon Ramsay at Claridge's
Wild Honey
Via Con
The Cafe
Bellamy's
Umu
Le Gavroche
Brian Turner Mayfair
The Square
Benares
Sumosan
Scott's
The Only Running Footman
Automat
Nobu Berkeley St.
Kai
China Tang
Dorchester
The Greenhouse
Tamarind
Mirabelle
Kiku
Le Boudin Blanc
Fakhreldine
Galvin at Windows
The Metropolitan
Nobu
Four Seasons
Theo Randall
MAYFAIR
GROSVENOR SQ.
BERKELEY SQ.
PORTMAN SQ.
CAVENDISH SQ.
HANNOVER SQ.
HYDE PARK
GREEN PARK
BUCKINGHAM PALACE GARDENS
BUCKINGHAM PALACE
ROYAL MEWS
BELGRAVE SQ.
APSLEY HOUSE WELLINGTON MUSEUM
Marble Arch
Bond Street
Hyde Park Corner
Oxford Street
Upper Berkeley St.
Seymour Street
Bryanston St.
Portman St.
Orchard St.
North Audley St.
Duke St.
James St.
Gilbert St.
Davies St.
New Bond St.
Henrietta Pl.
Holles St.
North Row
Green Street
Upper Brook Street
Brook Street
Culross St.
Upper Grosvenor St.
Grosvenor Street
Mount Street
South Audley St.
Farm Street
South St.
Hill Street
Hay's Mews
Charles St.
Curzon Street
Curzon St.
Half Moon St.
Piccadilly
Bruton St.
Berkeley St.
Park Lane
Old Park Lane
Serpentine Road
Rotten Row
South Carriage Drive
Knightsbridge
Constitution Hill
Grosvenor Crescent
Wilton Crescent
Halkin St.
Grosvenor Place
Chapel St.
Chester St.
Wilton St.
Lower Grosvenor Pl.
Buckingham
Hotel
Restaurant
0 200 m
0 200 yards

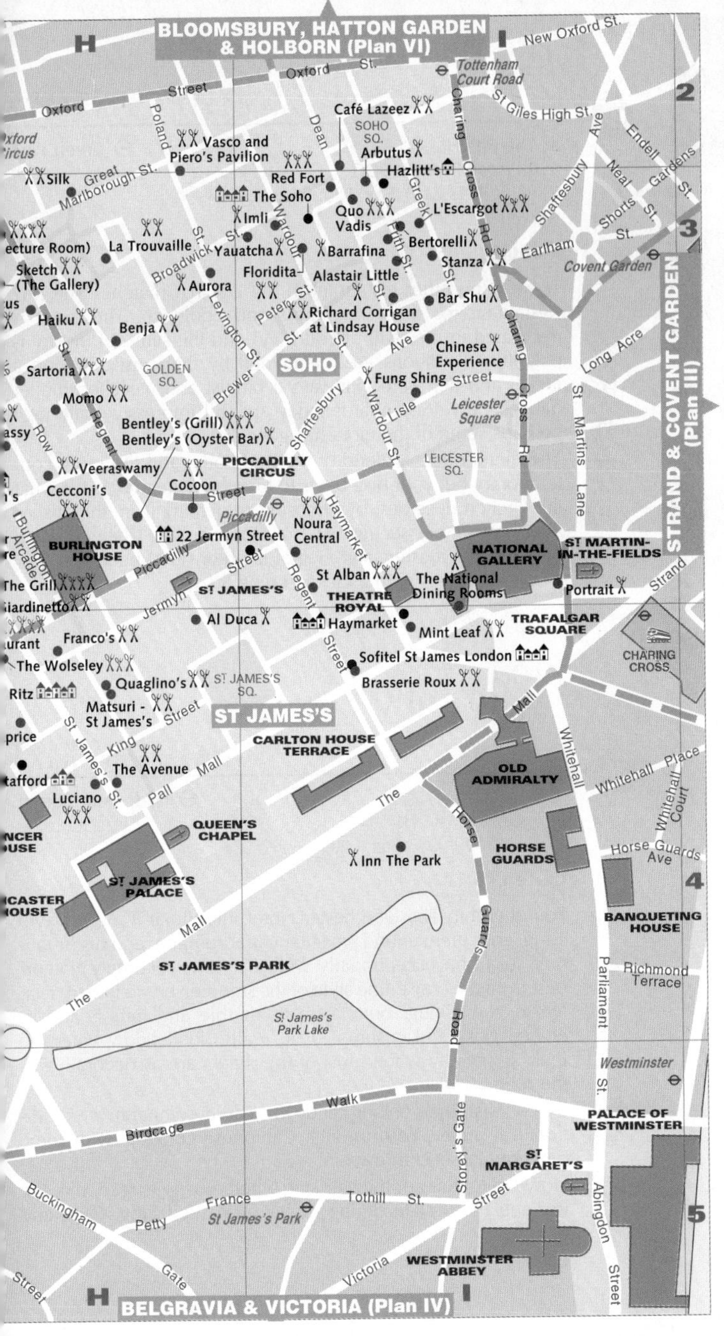
BLOOMSBURY, HATTON GARDEN & HOLBORN (Plan VI)
H
I
2
3
4
5
New Oxford St.
Oxford St.
Oxford Street
Tottenham Court Road
St Giles High St.
Café Lazeez
SOHO SQ.
Vasco and Piero's Pavilion
Arbutus
Hazlitt's
Silk
Great Marlborough St.
Red Fort
The Soho
Quo Vadis
L'Escargot
Imli
Yauatcha
Barrafina
Bertorelli
La Trouvaille
Sketch (The Gallery)
Aurora
Floridita
Alastair Little
Stanza
Bar Shu
Haiku
Benja
Richard Corrigan at Lindsay House
Chinese Experience
Sartoria
GOLDEN SQ.
SOHO
Fung Shing
Momo
Bentley's (Grill)
Bentley's (Oyster Bar)
Leicester Square
LEICESTER SQ.
PICCADILLY CIRCUS
Veeraswamy
Cecconi's
Cocoon
Noura Central
22 Jermyn Street
BURLINGTON HOUSE
Burlington Arcade
NATIONAL GALLERY
ST MARTIN-IN-THE-FIELDS
St Alban
The National Dining Rooms
Portrait
ST JAMES'S
THEATRE ROYAL Haymarket
Al Duca
Mint Leaf
TRAFALGAR SQUARE
Franco's
The Wolseley
Sofitel St James London
CHARING CROSS
Quaglino's
ST JAMES'S SQ.
Brasserie Roux
Ritz
Matsuri - St James's
ST JAMES'S
CARLTON HOUSE TERRACE
The Avenue
OLD ADMIRALTY
Luciano
QUEEN'S CHAPEL
Inn The Park
HORSE GUARDS
ST JAMES'S PALACE
BANQUETING HOUSE
ST JAMES'S PARK
St James's Park Lake
Westminster
PALACE OF WESTMINSTER
ST MARGARET'S
St James's Park
WESTMINSTER ABBEY
STRAND & COVENT GARDEN (Plan III)
Covent Garden
Long Acre
Whitehall
Horse Guards Road
Birdcage Walk
Tothill St.
Victoria Street
BELGRAVIA & VICTORIA (Plan IV)

The Ritz Restaurant

H4 **Traditional** XXXXX

at The Ritz H.,
150 Piccadilly W1V 9DG
(020) 7493 8181 **Fax** (020) 7493 2687
www.theritzlondon.com

⊖ Green Park

Menu £38/65 – Carte £47/74 s

There is no other restaurant in the UK that matches The Ritz Restaurant for sheer lavishness and opulence. The room is decorated in the style of Louis XVI and the sense of history is palpable. Traditions are maintained by their insistence on a jacket and tie; there is always a pianist and weekend dinner dances. Service standards today are still impressive, although perhaps some of the gloss has gone.

The menu offers a blend of the traditional and the more contemporary but your best bet is to turn the page and go for what the kitchen does best by choosing something from the 'dishes always available' section, such as Dover Sole or Chateaubriand or, from the 'roasting spit', leg of lamb or rib of beef. The only way to follow is with a classic crêpe Suzette.

China Tang

G4 **Chinese** XXXX

at Dorchester H.,
Park Lane W1A 2HJ
(020) 7629 9988 **Fax** (020) 7629 9595

⊖ Hyde Park Corner
Closed 25 December

Carte £40/120

Found within The Dorchester Hotel, the titular Tang is David Tang, entrepreneur and jet-setter extraordinaire, and his restaurant suits him exceptionally well. It's all exceedingly glamorous, from the cruise-line style of the stunning bar to the art deco feel of the dining room, with its marble and murals and its etched glass and cushions. You really don't know where to look, especially when most of the diners are as decorative as the room.

By contrast, the cooking tends to tread a comparatively traditional, if pricey, path through Cantonese cooking, with some modern elements thrown in.

How could you not love a place where poetry is recited in the loo and the private dining rooms are called Ping, Pang and Pong?

Le Gavroche ✿✿

French XXXX

G3

43 Upper Brook St W1K 7QR
✆ (020) 7408 0881
Fax (020) 7491 4387
e-mail bookings@le-gavroche.com **www**.le-gavroche.co.uk

⊖ Marble Arch
Closed Christmas-New Year, Sunday, Saturday lunch and Bank Holidays – booking essential

Menu £48 – Carte £60/130

A/C VISA MC AE

Le Gavroche

In today's rush for the new and the novel, we sometimes forget about the jewels we already have. Le Gavroche is guaranteed its own chapter when the history of British gastronomy is written and, over forty years after it first opened in Chelsea, it's still maintaining its own high standards and respect for tradition.

The service is unerringly professional; this is where any budding restaurateur should come if they want to learn how things are done 'properly' and one can observe the hierarchical structure from one's chair. The room retains a clubby and masculine feel but it also offers a palpable sense of history; those new to the restaurant are guided gently through its customs and politely reminded of its traditions.

The menu represents classic French cuisine and not just an English idea of French cuisine; a style of food which is becoming rarer by the day. A Soufflé Suissesse is rich enough to live on for days and the use of luxury items, from lobster to foie gras, would make Epicurus blanch. Those who prefer a lighter style, however, are not ignored.

First Course

- Hot foie gras and crispy duck pancake flavoured with cinnamon.
- Lobster mousse with caviar and champagne butter sauce.

Main Course

- Roast saddle of rabbit with crispy potatoes and parmesan.
- Whole roast John Dory with artichokes, olive oil mashed potato.

Dessert

- Bitter chocolate and praline 'indulgence'.
- Iced amaretto nougat with cherries cooked in red wine syrup.

Gordon Ramsay at Claridge's

Modern European

G3

Brook St W1K 4HR ⊖ Bond Street

(020) 7499 0099 **Fax** (020) 7499 3099 Booking essential

e-mail reservations@gordonramsay.com **www**.gordonramsay.com

Menu £30/65

Of all the restaurants within the Gordon Ramsay Empire, this is probably the hardest one at which to get a table at the time you want. This may have something to do with his name being in the title, but it is, in fact, Mark Sargeant who has been running the kitchen here since it 'reopened' in 2001. His cooking continues to develop and reveals a growing confidence; his dishes look appetising rather than pretty and there is a pronounced vigour to the flavours. There is also a noticeable increase in the amount of seasonal produce he uses and many ingredients have their place of origin or supplier name-checked on the menu, such as Cromer crab, Isle of Skye scallops, Loch Duart salmon and Casterbridge beef.

The lavish, art deco room is a stunning backdrop to all this food. It manages to be absolutely fashionable yet, at the same time, utterly respectful of the traditions of Claridge's. The huge hierarchical brigade of multi-national staff also ensure an absence of stuffiness by being willing to stop and chat with their guests.

First Course

- Persillade of rabbit with vegetables à la Grecque, grain mustard vinaigrette.
- Ravioli of lobster and salmon poached in lemongrass bisque.

Main Course

- Roast John Dory with sautéed langoustines, artichokes and fennel cream.
- Loin of venison, parsnip fondant and juniper sauce.

Dessert

- Lemon meringue with mascarpone ice cream and summer berries.
- Tarte Tatin with pecan and maple ice cream.

The Square ✿✿

French ✗✗✗✗

H3

6-10 Bruton St W1J 6PU
✆ (020) 7495 7100
Fax (020) 7495 7150
e-mail info@squarerestaurant.com **www**.squarerestaurant.com

⊖ Green Park
Closed 25 December, 1 January and lunch Saturday, Sunday and Bank Holidays

Menu £30/65

The Square

You can't see into the restaurant from outside any more which has added to the intimacy, and the bar area feels a little more structured and permanent. That apart, things at The Square are all reassuringly familiar and help explain why the restaurant remains so popular. Philip Howard's cooking is thoughtful, defined and honest. He has an innate understanding of what goes with what and will always return to his classical background but, at the same time, he is always striving to develop his cuisine. The menu changes completely five times a year and dishes display a dextrous balance of flavours and textures, as well as an understanding of when to leave alone. All those little extras you're given are prepared with equal care and the cheeseboard further showcases their serious sourcing and is well worth leaving room for. The wine list matches the food in its range and depth.

The comfort levels are just right and the service is never too intrusive, for here they understand that diners come for enjoyment, not worship.

First Course

- Sautéed langoustines with parmesan gnocchi and truffle.
- Salad of ox tongue and Jabugo ham with pickled vegetables and salt beef sandwich.

Main Course

- Herb-crusted saddle of lamb with shallot purée and rosemary.
- Steamed brill with crushed Jersey potatoes, sea kale and herbs.

Dessert

- Brillat-Savarin cheesecake with gooseberry and elderflower.
- Truffled honey parfait with roasted pear.

Sketch (The Lecture Room & Library) ✿✿

French XXXX

H3

First Floor, 9 Conduit St W1S 2XG — Oxford Street
(0870) 7774 488
Fax (0870) 7774 400
www.sketch.uk.com

Closed 25-30 December, Sunday, Monday, Saturday lunch and Bank Holidays – booking essential

Menu £35/65 – Carte £70/131

A/C VISA MC AE

Skertch

Imagine what an 18th century London house is going to look like inside, then think again. Sketch is the brainchild of Mourad Mazouz who, along with French super-chef Pierre Gagnaire, has created a work of animated art, full of energy and vitality. There's nothing rough or unfinished here. The Lecture Room & Library is the 'serious dining' part of the operation and is ablaze with colour, rich in fabric, spirited in atmosphere and determined in its aspirations.

When the food starts to arrive you'll realise just how understated those menu headings are. In fact, even before you get to the main dishes, you'll be surrounded by a plethora of bowls, dishes and plates and an array of treats to arouse your taste buds. The sheer ambition of the cooking is something to behold; this is seriously labour-intensive, highly elaborate and very skilled cooking where most dishes are made up of a number of components. The pricing and the prices can be a little bewildering-there may be over £30 difference between the prices of some starters-so the best way forward is to take the plunge and go for the Tasting Menu.

First Course

- Langoustines 'addressed in five ways'.
- Scallops and shellfish.

Main Course

- Lamb from Limousin.
- Assiette of duck

Dessert

- Pierre Gagnaire's Grand dessert.
- Lemon macaroon.

The Grill

British XXXX

H3

at Brown's H., ⊖ Green Park
Albemarle St W1S 4BP
✆ (020) 7518 4004 **Fax** (020) 7518 4064

Menu £30 – Carte £48/54

A/C VISA MC AE

Think Brown's, think Britain; there's a daily roast, a carving trolley, game in season and perennial favourites like potted shrimps, beef Wellington and plates of smoked salmon. And where else can you still get a mixed grill these days? Look hard enough at the menu, though, and you might also see the odd word like ballotine, beignet or burrata, proving that the kitchen does occasionally look beyond our shores.

Brown's opened in 1880 and was the first hotel in London to offer its guests their own dining room. The wood panelling, clubby feel, suited clientele and old-school style service may all shout 'establishment,'but the recent addition of Hubertus Hohenlohe prints add a thoroughly contemporary edge.

Galvin at Windows

French XXXX

G4

at London Hilton H., ⊖ Hyde Park Corner
22 Park Lane W1K 1BE
Closed Saturday lunch and Sunday dinner
✆ (020) 7208 4021
www.galvinatwindows.com

Menu £29/75 – Carte £60/75

A/C VISA MC AE

London restaurants don't really do views so Galvin at Windows has a serious advantage by being 28 floors up in the Hilton Hotel; the raised central section of the restaurant and the huge windows ensure that, on a clear day, everyone can see for miles. This is a comfortable and elegantly dressed restaurant; it can be somewhat 'corporate' in its feel at lunch but the atmosphere and clientele are a little more glamorous at dinner and that's when the adjacent cocktail bar really comes into its own. The kitchen offers intricate and thoughtful cooking, where flavours are quite robust and the ingredients of excellent quality. Dishes may not always be the sum of their parts but the diligence and ambition of the kitchen is tangible.

The Greenhouse ✿

G4 — Innovative XXX

27a Hay's Mews W1J 5NY
✆ (020) 7499 3331
Fax (020) 7499 5368
e-mail reservations@greenhouserestaurant.co.uk
www.greenhouserestaurant.co.uk

⊖ Hyde Park Corner
Closed 24 December-5 January, Saturday lunch, Sunday and Bank Holidays

Menu £29/60

The Greenhouse

This Greenhouse is a decidedly smart and elegant affair which comes without the haughty culture. Since its opening in the 1970s it has always taken its food seriously and there has been a line of highly talented chefs at the helm. The incumbent head man, Antonin Bonnet, offers an innovative selection of elaborately presented dishes, all underpinned with sound French culinary techniques. So along with the occasional Asian note, the odd little nuance or unexpected combination comes the reassurance that the blend works because the ingredient is understood. There are dishes specifically made for two, a seasonal truffle menu and a tasting menu. The millefeuille desserts are a house speciality. The wine list is also an impressive work, with all points covered, including a varied choice by the glass. The room is as well-groomed as the customers and is broken up into sections so that it never feels too big. Glass screens, a leaf motif and assorted red hues combine to create pleasingly graceful surroundings. The service is detailed and polished but not entirely bereft of personality.

First Course

- Scottish langoustines with pea, coconut and Moroccan mint.
- Slow-cooked tuna loin with smoked soy sauce.

Main Course

- Roast veal chop with baby carrots and rosemary honey.
- Saddle of venison with pear chutney and celeriac tagliatelle.

Dessert

- 'Carré Dubuffet' chocolate biscuit with praline ice cream.
- Roast apricots with toasted bread ice cream and lychee syrup.

Mirabelle ✿

French XXX

H4

56 Curzon St W1J 8PA
⊖ Green Park
✆ (020) 7499 4636 **Fax** (020) 7499 5449
Closed 26 December
e-mail sales@whitestarline.org.uk **www**.whitestarline.org.uk

Menu £23 – Carte £33/55

Mirabelle

The Mirabelle's great strength is that it doesn't try to reinvent anything: it knows what it does and does it very well, which is why this long-standing restaurant has a loyal following.

The franglais on the menu is perfectly apt here, as the cooking is born of the two countries, although France is the dominant partner in the relationship. The upside of a menu that remains largely unchanged is that dishes have been perfected over time and are executed with aplomb. There's extensive choice for both fish lovers and carnivores, ingredients come from the luxury end of the food chain and the richness of the cooking adds to the feeling of indulgence. Omelette Arnold Bennett, foie gras parfait and braised pig's trotter are among the antidotes to many of today's more waist conscious offerings. The lemon tart comes gloriously unembellished.

The long bar and pianist set the mood even before you reach the restaurant, which is a model of comfort and elegance. It is also big enough to ensure that no single table can dominate proceedings.

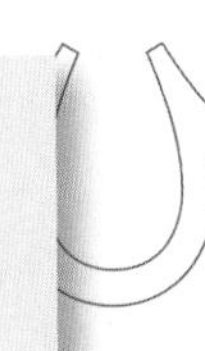

First Course

- Parfait of foie gras with truffles en gelée.
- Vinaigrette of leeks and white asparagus with truffles.

Main Course

- Caramelised wing of skate with winkles and beurre noisette.
- Roast venison à la forestière.

Dessert

- Tarte Tatin with cinnamon.
- Lemon tart.

Hibiscus ✿

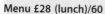

H3 **Innovative** XXX

29 Maddox St W1S 2PA
(020) 7629 2999
www.hibiscusrestaurant.co.uk

Menu £28 (lunch)/60

Oxford Circus
Closed 10 days Christmas - New Year, 1 week August, Saturday, Sunday and Bank Holiday Mondays

A/C

VISA

AE

Michelin

How it usually goes is that a chef proves himself in the cauldron that is the London restaurant scene, then moves out a few years later so he can lower his blood pressure by looking at green fields from his kitchen window. Claude Bosi, however, has done the reverse: he ran a very successful restaurant in the charming Shropshire town of Ludlow but has now packed up, moved to London, and Mayfair to boot, and is setting himself against the big boys. What is even more unusual in the capital - nay, almost unheard of - is that said restaurant is a brand new, purpose built establishment; but this has enabled some of the features of the Ludlow Hibiscus, like the oak wood panelling, and the Welsh slate walls, to be incorporated into the stylish new brown and green design. 'From Ludlow to London with love' is their slogan, and the dishes and the produce follow suit, so you might well find Shropshire rose veal or Elwy valley lamb on the menu, and since Bosi's combinations of ingredients remain as inventive as ever, your ice cream might well taste of Earl Grey tea, and your venison might come with smoked chocolate, cabbage and pear.

First Course

- Foie gras ice cream with brioche emulsion, balsamic vinegar caramel.
- Carpaccio of pollock with black radish, truffle & almond oil vinaigrette.

Main Course

- Roast rack of Shropshire veal with goat's cheese and anchovy jus.
- Choux Farci of Welsh lamb with foie gras, almond & anchovy jus.

Dessert

- Iced sweet olive oil parfait, date sauce, caramelised chickpeas.
- Chocolate tart with Indonesian basil ice cream.

Maze ✿

Innovative XXX

G3

10-13 Grosvenor Sq W1K 6JP ⊖ Bond Street
(020) 7107 0000 **Fax** (020) 7107 0001
e-mail maze@gordonramsay.com **www**.gordonramsay.com

Carte £41/55

Gordon Ramsay Holdings

The name may suggest something baffling or secretive but dining at Maze is a relatively straightforward affair: just order five or six dishes per person from a choice of around 20 or go straight for the tasting menu. What you'll discover is dishes that are innovative but also exquisitely put together, balanced and precise. The size of the plates makes sharing a little pointless but there is enough variety and choice on offer to satisfy the most fastidious of eater. The chef, Jason Atherton, uses a French base to which he adds the occasional Asian or even Italian note, while other creations exude a certain culinary playfulness. The wine list is comprehensive but the undecided may prefer to let the helpful sommelier choose a wine flight - a trio of glasses to match your food.

The stylish David Rockwell space copes well with being busy and you may have more luck getting in if you're prepared to sit at the counter. The large, well-briefed brigade are always more than willing to offer guidance.

First Course

- Cornish crab mayonnaise with avocado, sweetcorn sorbet and caviar.
- Honey and soy roasted quail with foie gras and spiced pear chutney.

Main Course

- Butter poached chicken with maple skin and smoked mussel bread sauce.
- Roasted rack of lamb with braised shoulder and onions.

Dessert

- Coconut panna cotta with black olive caramel.
- Chocolate moelleux with pistachio sabayon.

Scott's

G3 **Seafood** XXX

20 Mount St W1K 2HE
(020) 7495 7309 **Fax** (020) 7647 6327
www.scotts-restaurant.com

Closed 25-26 December, 1 January and August Bank holiday

Carte £45/67

Scott's is a genuine institution. It opened in the 1850s, moved to its current site in the 1960s and is a byword for seafood and oysters. It was revamped and reborn in 2006 by its new owners, Caprice holdings, who have made it once again the epitome of fashion.

The menu is a flurry of headings from Crustacea and Mollusc to Smoked Fish and Fish on the Bone. The quality of the seafood and shellfish from across the UK is first rate and the kitchen knows not to interfere too much when it's this fresh. The mark-ups on the wines are kept minimal. They've also managed the clever trick of making something traditional seem new: the oak panelling is juxtaposed with artwork from Young British Artists. The front room, with the oyster bar, is more casual in style than the back.

Theo Randall

G4 **Italian** XXX

at InterContinental H.,
1 Hamilton Place, Park Lane
W1J 7QY
(020) 7318 8747
www.theorandall.com

⊖ Hyde Park Corner
Closed 25-26 December, Saturday lunch, Sunday dinner and Bank Holidays

Menu £23 (weekday lunch) – Carte £34/48

The InterContinental Hotel may seem an unlikely destination for the former Head Chef of the River Café. The hotel, however, was re-launched in 2007 after a major refit and Theo Randall has his name above the door of the big, swanky ground floor restaurant. Intimate lighting, some stylistic flourishes and chatty service save it from Park Lane functionality.

Those familiar with his alma mater will recognise the cakes on the counter, the menu of rustic and seasonal Italian dishes and the focus on the best ingredients available – the carpaccio with parmesan, for example, is well worth trying. The wood fired oven is used effectively in dishes like turbot on the bone with oregano and pigeon on bruschetta with lentils.

The Wolseley

Modern European XXX

H4

160 Piccadilly W1J 9EB
☎ (020) 7499 6996
Fax (020) 7499 6888
www.thewolseley.com

⊖ Green Park
Closed 25 December, 1 January, August Bank Holiday and dinner 24 and 31 December – booking essential

Carte £26/70

The Wolseley may have only opened in 2003 but it has already earned iconic status thanks to its décor, celebrity following and smooth service. Its owners, Chris Corbin and Jeremy King, have created a restaurant in the style of a grand European café, all pillars, arches and marble.

Open from breakfast until late, the flexible menu offers everything from Austrian and French classics to British staples, so the daily special could be coq au vin or Lancashire hot pot. Pastries come from the Viennoiserie and lunch merges into afternoon tea. So, one table could be tucking into Beluga caviar or a dozen oysters while their neighbours enjoy a salt beef sandwich or eggs Benedict. The large clock reminds you that there are probably others waiting for your table.

AC VISA MC AE

St Alban

Modern European XXX

I3

4-12 Regent St SW1Y 4PE
☎ (020) 7499 8558 **Fax** (020) 7499 6888
e-mail info@stalban.net **www**.stalban.net

Closed 25-26 December and 1 January

Carte £29/41

Restaurant goers rarely ventured to this end of Regent Street but the celebrated restaurateurs Jeremy King and Chris Corbin changed all that with the opening of St Alban. It's a large open-plan affair with back lit walls and curved seating arranged in modular form which provide surprising levels of comfort and privacy. As expected, service is slick, swift and informative.

The cooking calls itself 'contemporary European' which means you'll find dishes and ingredients mostly from France, Italy, Spain and Portugal, but without one wholly dominating. Cooking is sunny and rustic, with the flavours to the fore.

Vegetables and pizza are roasted in their own wood fired oven and their charcoal grill makes any dish 'a la plancha' worth ordering.

AC VISA MC AE

Benares ✿

H3 — Indian XXX

12a Berkeley Square House
W1J 6BS
✆ (020) 7629 8886 **Fax** (020) 7499 2430
www.benaresrestaurant.com

⊖ Green Park
Closed 25-26 December, 1 January, and Bank Holidays

Menu £30 – Carte £34/68

Benares

The further away from the entrance you stand, the more impressive the whole façade seems and, from the middle of Berkeley Square, Benares looks like a very suitable neighbour for those classic car showrooms. That feeling is enhanced as you are led up the stairs from the reception area and deposited in the stylish bar, with its water pools and moody lighting. The restaurant, meanwhile, is good-looking, comfortable and bustling.

It is named after the Holy city on the Ganges and is under the control of Atul Kochhar. His culinary training was with the Oberoi Hotel group but he has been in London now for over a decade. His travels across India have given him an appreciation of all styles of Indian food, from classic restaurant dishes to traditional domestic cooking and even street food. The preparation keeps faith with conventional methods but his spice mixes show a deft touch and his flavours are always nicely balanced. It is in the presentation where his more modern approach is most obvious and this undoubtedly adds to the appeal of his dishes.

First Course

- Soft shell crab with squid salad.
- Chicken tikka with foie gras and smoked duck breast.

Main Course

- Seared sea bass in coconut milk and curry leaf sauce.
- Tandoori roasted monkfish with coriander and ginger sauce.

Dessert

- Pistachio and star anise mousse with rum raisins.
- Trio of kulfi.

L'Escargot ✿

French XXX

13

48 Greek St W1D 4EF ⊖ Tottenham Court Road
(020) 7437 2679 **Fax** (020) 7437 0790
e-mail sales@whitestarline.org.uk **www**.lescargotrestaurant.co.uk

Menu £18 – Carte £28/30

L'Escargot

L'Escargot is one of the most celebrated restaurant names in London. It was opened in the 1920s by George Gaudin – that's him above the window – and the snail can always be found on the menu in one guise or another. It may not be packing them in like it used to but remains a dependable destination and can boast of having two restaurants under one roof.

The ground floor is the more animated and fun, especially early evening thanks to the pre theatre menu. Its warm yellows and mirrors give it a brasserie feel and the kitchen produces robust and satisfying dishes like rump of beef or calves liver. Upstairs in the Picasso Room the pace is altogether more sedate and better suited to those after either privacy or secrecy. The service here is also more formal and the room more comfortable - the collection of lithographs and ceramics that give the room its name is very impressive. Here, the cooking has a greater degree of elaboration and uses more luxury ingredients, so expect seared scallops, smoked foie gras and roasted lobster, plenty of little extras and a bigger bill.

First Course

- Tian of crab with shrimp and avocado, citrus mayonnaise.
- Smoked foie gras with apple and cinnamon purée.

Main Course

- Roast rump of lamb with an onion purée.
- John Dory with oxtail, potato and chive risotto.

Dessert

- Raspberry soufflé with raspberry and lime sauce.
- Vanilla panna cotta with rhubarb ripple ice cream.

Tamarind ✿

G4 **Indian** XXX

20 Queen St W1J 5PR
(020) 7629 3561
Fax (020) 7499 5034
e-mail manager@tamarindrestaurant.com
www.tamarindrestaurant.com

Green Park
Closed 25-26 December, 1 January and lunch Saturday and Bank Holidays

Menu £22/52 – Carte £35/59

Tamarind

At Tamarind, the starting point for the kitchen is the Moghul cooking of the North West and the tandoor oven, but the success of this restaurant is that it appeals to traditionalists as well as those who like to see some personality on the plate. The cooking also reflects the ambitions of the chef and his evolving style will appeal to those who prefer a lighter style of food, whatever its nationality. Common to all the dishes, though, are good quality raw ingredients, deft spicing, enticing presentation and assured flavours.

They have also managed to take an unpromising subterranean location and turn it into an advantage. Descending the stairs adds to a sense of secrecy and exclusiveness and the room has an atmosphere of sophistication to it, as you would expect from a Mayfair address. Fortunately that mood remains light and friendly, helped along by an efficient team of staff under the supervision of plenty of suited lieutenants. Those with an interest in cooking should ask for one of the tables close to the large kitchen window.

First Course

- Salad leaves with melon, plums and kumquats in pine nut dressing.
- Grilled scallops with green, pink and black peppercorns, roasted peppers and fenugreek.

Main Course

- Grilled chicken in creamed tomatoes, fenugreek, ginger and honey.
- Leg of lamb with cinnamon, rose petals and ground spices finished in the tandoor.

Dessert

- White chocolate and cardamom mousse with a ginger semi-freddo.
- Basmati rice in flavoured milks, raisins and stewed apricots.

Sartoria

Italian XXX

H3

20 Savile Row W1S 3PR
⊖ Green Park
Closed 24-28 December, 1 January and Sunday

(020) 7534 7000
Fax (020) 7534 7070
e-mail sartoriareservations@danddlondon.com
www.danddlondon.com

Menu £25 – Carte £35

Too many restaurants seem to have been just plonked down anywhere but the elegantly dressed and appropriately Italian Sartoria was clearly designed with its locality in mind, in this case Savile Row. The street's proud history and traditions of bespoke tailoring come playfully celebrated in the decoration – and even the bill comes pinned to a cushion. It's also quite a stylish affair, with a warm and inviting glow. Several tables come with sofa-style seating and standard lamps adjacent and all tables offer plenty of elbow room.

The menu is extensive, clearly laid out and covers most of the regions of Italy. The kitchen displays a lightness of touch and dishes come attractively presented. The wine list offers a decent selection by the glass.

Quo Vadis

Italian XXX

I3

26-29 Dean St W1D 3LL
⊖ Tottenham Court Road
Closed 24-25 December, 1 January, Saturday lunch and Sunday

(020) 7437 9585
Fax (020) 7734 7593
e-mail sales@whitestarline.org.uk **www**.whitestarline.org.uk

Menu £18 – Carte £25/31

Quo Vadis, dominating Dean Street with its red neon sign, black exterior and stained glass windows, has always looked very appealing to the passer-by. It's one of the oldest buildings in Soho, was once home to Karl Marx and has been a restaurant since the 1930s.

Today, it still offers a palpable sense of history, in contrast to the shoutier restaurants of this parish. Marco Pierre White has respected the heritage of the restaurant by sticking with a predominately Italian menu. With it comes a collection of classical and more contemporary interpretations of dishes from across the country, as well as the occasional French influence. There's a decent value theatre menu and the best tables are the corner booths.

Umu ✿

H3 — Japanese XXX

14-16 Bruton Pl W1J 6LX
(020) 7499 8881
Fax (020) 7499 5120
e-mail enquiries@umurestaurant.com **www**.umurestaurant.com

Bond Street
Closed Christmas, 2 weeks August, Saturday lunch, Sunday and Bank Holidays

Menu £21 – Carte £34/73

A/C VISA MC AE

Umu

Umu is the nearest thing London has to an authentic Kaiseki restaurant. The novice diner will find the plethora of menus a little overwhelming but for the full experience just choose one of the eight Kaiseki Selections. Derived from the Kyoto tea ceremony, this involves a series of tantalizing and delicate dishes. These don't come cheap but then the seasonal ingredients are of the highest quality, making the experience more authentic. Flavours are subtle, the contrast in textures of the different courses is important and one should take time to appreciate the intricate presentation and the aroma of soups. This kind of eating cannot be rushed which is why you have the table for the duration and cannot be hurried out. Those who prefer to do their own thing, however, will find plenty of appealing dishes on the à la carte which continues the theme of blending the traditional with the more contemporary. The sushi section is divided helpfully between the 'classic' and the 'modern'.

Consider one of the counter seats for a fuller experience and don't be afraid of asking questions as the staff know their stuff.

First Course

- Sweet shrimp with sake jelly and caviar.
- Salmon salad with deep-fried tofu flakes and ponzu dressing.

Main Course

- Grilled toro teriyaki, yuzu citrus flavoured grated radish, wasabi.
- Wagyu beef with Japanese mustard and wasabi.

Dessert

- White miso ice cream.
- Chilled green tea soup with pumpkin ice cream.

Embassy

Modern European XXX

H3

29 Old Burlington St W1S 3AN
(020) 7851 0956
Fax (020) 7734 3224
e-mail embassy@embassylondon.com **www**.embassylondon.com

Green Park
Closed Sunday, Monday and Bank Holidays – dinner only

Menu £40 – Carte £27/58

A fashionable restaurant in the middle of Old Burlington Street may sound a little unlikely but Embassy sits there rather confidently. The buzzy nightclub downstairs is on the circuit for an assortment of celebrities on lists A to C but the restaurant, found on the ground floor, is no mere addendum to the club and has become a destination in its own right.

A large bar, with plenty of brown leather seating, leads up to the dining area which comes decorated in stylish creams with well-spaced tables. Floor to ceiling windows and a pavement terrace give it extra appeal in the summer. The menu is that of a classically trained kitchen and features a fair share of extravagant ingredients, used with flair and understanding.

A/C VISA MC AE

Cecconi's

Italian XXX

H3

5a Burlington Gdns W1S 3EP
(020) 7434 1500 **Fax** (020) 7434 2020
e-mail giacomo@cecconis.co.uk **www**.cecconis.com

Green Park
Closed 25 December

Carte £28/48

Those who longingly look back at those halcyon days of excess that were the 1980s will no doubt have fond memories of Cecconi's for it certainly captured the zeitgeist of the era. After a number of re-launches over the years, the restaurant appears to have finally found the right combination and in July 2005 it reopened under the ownership of Nick Jones, known for his Soho House clubs.

There remains an air of exclusivity about the place but now it comes with a little more playfulness and a little less brashness. The kitchen starts by offering breakfast then a cleverly balanced all-day menu to appeal to everyone, from those just wanting a *cichetti* or tapas-style lunch to those after a plate of pasta or something substantial.

A/C VISA MC AE

Kai

G3 **Chinese** XXX

65 South Audley St
W1K 2QU
(020) 7493 8988 **Fax** (020) 7493 1456
e-mail kai@kaimayfair.com **www**.kaimayfair.com

⊖ Hyde Park Corner
Closed 25-26 December and 1 January – booking essential

Menu £22 – Carte £38/91

A/C VISA MC AE

If you get any strange looks from fellow diners it'll be because you've got their favourite table and they've turned up without booking. Kai is a very 'Mayfair' Chinese restaurant: it's all marble and glass and very swish.

Spread over two floors, you'll find most of the action's on the ground floor, which includes the occasional harpist and a strangely hypnotic fish tank.

There's no faulting the enthusiasm of the staff, supervised by the very charming manageress who knows all her regulars. All the dishes come exotically titled and you'll find a balanced blend of the classic and the more adventurous. You have to give five day's notice to the kitchen (and your bank manager) if you want the *Buddha jumps over the wall* soup.

Bentley's (Grill)

H3 **British** XXX

11-15 Swallow St W1B 4DG
(020) 7734 4756
www.bentleysoysterbarandgrill.co.uk

⊖ Piccadilly Circus
Closed 25-26 December

Carte £34/49

A/C VISA MC AE

The beloved institution called Bentley's continues to enjoy its new lease of life, following a complete revamp in 2005. The green neon sign is still outside but the upstairs dining room now has a contemporary feel with leather chairs, fabric covered walls and paintings of boats and fish for those who haven't twigged what's on the menu. One thing that hasn't changed is the clubby feel and the preponderance of suited male customers.

Seafood remains the draw here with fish on the bone dissected at the table something of a house speciality. Much of the produce comes from St Ives and Looe in Cornwall and its freshness is palpable. Dover and Lemon sole feature strongly, as do oysters and soups whilst the breads and beef remind you that owner Richard Corrigan is Irish.

Red Fort

Indian XXX

I3

77 Dean St W1D 3SH
✆ (020) 7437 2525
Fax (020) 7434 0721
e-mail info@redfort.co.uk **www**.redfort.co.uk

⊖ Tottenham Court Road
Closed lunch Saturday, Sunday and Bank Holidays

Carte £35/45

The Red Fort is now one of the daddies of the Soho scene. Although the delightful doorman is sadly no longer outside and the dimly-lit, throbbing basement bar, Akbar, has become quite a hit, the cooking fortunately continues to hit the spot. It follows the 300 year old traditions of the Mughal court; there are plenty of dishes which, on closer inspection, reveal themselves to be familiar constructions, but there is also plenty of originality here: try lamb chops with pomegranate or whole quail dishes. The accompanying breads are particularly good.
The dining room is well-dressed and divided into two – the far room is best and here they use sandstone, mosaics, Indian art and a water feature in homage to Lal Quila, the Red Fort in Delhi.

Luciano

Italian XXX

H4

72-73 St James's St SW1A 1PH
✆ (020) 7408 1440
e-mail info@lucianorestaurant.co.uk **www**.lucianorestaurant.co.uk

⊖ Green Park
Closed Sunday

Menu £22 – Carte £25/49 s

Marco Pierre White goes back to his Italian roots in this restaurant, named after his son. The Man may not, sadly, be cooking any longer but he has put together a good team who deliver satisfyingly wholesome Italian classics, from a balanced and appealing menu.
The ubiquitous David Collins has designed a space which fits effortlessly into the gracious surroundings of St James's. The art deco bar is a favoured local spot for lunch, but descend a few steps and you'll find yourself in the elegant dining room, where the art comes courtesy of Marco's own collection.
Staff may bicker amongst themselves but are the embodiment of politeness at your table and the kitchen delivers the promise of the menu at the correct pace.

Brian Turner Mayfair

G3 — British XXX

at Millennium Mayfair H.,
44 Grosvenor Sq W1K 2HP
(020) 7596 3444 **Fax** (020) 7596 3443
e-mail turner.mayfair@mill-cop.com **www**.brianturneronline.co.uk

⊖ Bond Street
Closed 25-26 December, Saturday lunch and Sunday

Menu £29 – Carte £38/65

VISA MC AE

In the corner of the lobby of the Millennium Mayfair hotel, with its striking 18th century façade overlooking Grosvenor Square, you'll find the entrance to this spacious 80-seater restaurant, named in honour of the proud Yorkshireman who is known to many through his television appearances.

The menu showcases his love and respect for British food, especially in the decidedly homespun puddings, but he also offers his own interpretation of more contemporary cooking. The room has a fresh and luminous feel and tries to break up its capaciousness through raised sections which offer slightly more privacy. Service is obliging and professional and the place has enough of its own personality to stand out from its hotel surroundings.

Le Caprice

H4 — Modern European XX

Arlington House, Arlington St
SW1A 1RJ
(020) 7629 2239
Fax (020) 7493 9040
e-mail reservation@le-caprice.co.uk **www**.le-caprice.co.uk

⊖ Green Park
Closed 24-26 December, 1 January and August Bank Holiday – Sunday brunch

Carte £35/50

A/C VISA MC AE

When a restaurant is described as an "institution" one thinks of somewhere stuffy, old and probably a little smelly. For more than 25 years Le Caprice has proved that a clubby, senior restaurant can actually be warm, fun and feverishly fashionable. The only anachronism here is the cover charge. The pianist and the long bar add a hint of old New York while the black and white décor and David Bailey photographs give it a certain timelessness. The position and size of your table will depend on the extent of your celebrity or patronage but the service is commendably democratic.

Easy-eating is the order of the day and the appealing menu has everything from eggs Benedict to rump of veal. The Caesar salad and salmon fishcakes are a permanent fixture.

Richard Corrigan at Lindsay House ✿

Modern European XX

13

21 Romilly St W1D 5AF
(020) 7439 0450
Fax (020) 7437 7349
e-mail richardcorrigan@lindsayhouse.co.uk
www.lindsayhouse.co.uk

⊖ Leicester Square
Closed 25, 26 December, 1 January, Saturday lunch and Sunday

Menu £56 (dinner) – Carte lunch £31/52

A/C
VISA
MC
AE

Richard Corrigan at Lindsay House

There are all sorts of temptations behind closed doors in Soho, apparently. Lindsay House has always looked very inviting – it's a handsome four storey 18C house – and you have to ring the doorbell to be let in, which just adds to those feelings of exclusivity mixed with the promise of sinful transgression. Now it is even more welcoming inside because it has been given a wash and brush up, and the new fabrics on the walls have added a fresher feel. Diners are still divided between the two cosy dining rooms, which just adds to the general intimacy and staff play their part in this by consciously never over-crowding the rooms with personnel.

Richard Corrigan has his name above the door but, apart from the soda bread and oysters, there is less evidence of his Irish roots on the menu than in previous years. That said, the kitchen is far from timid or unclear about what it does, which is bold flavours and confident presentation. There is an unambiguous modernity to the cooking but without recourse to unusual combinations.

First Course

- Ballotine of foie gras with parfait of duck liver, hazelnuts.
- Ham hock terrine with piccalilli.

Main Course

- Pan-roast halibut with langoustine ravioli and samphire.
- Baked sea trout with peas, baby gem, bacon and mint.

Dessert

- Peanut parfait with caramelised banana and praline ice cream.
- Apple clafoutis with vanilla ice cream.

Nobu ✿

G4

Japanese XX

at The Metropolitan H.,
19 Old Park Lane W1Y 4LB
✆ (020) 7447 4747 **Fax** (020) 7447 4749
e-mail confirmations@noburestaurants.com
www.noburestaurants.com

⊖ Hyde Park Corner
Closed 25-26 December and 1 January – booking essential

Menu £25/70 – Carte £44/52

A/C VISA MC AE

Nobu

Of all the hybrid cuisines out there few can be as unusual in its origins as Nobu. Nobu Matsuhisa, the founder and inspiration, found it difficult to find Japanese ingredients when working in Peru as a young man so substituted them with local produce. The result became this highly original mix of styles, with the delicacy and poise of Japanese food given a jolt by the more robust flavours of South America. There are branches all over the world but London's do seem to maintain their levels of consistency more than others. The staff have an exemplary knowledge of the menu and offer sound advice. Whilst regulars barely look at the menu, the novice will recognise a number of dishes, such as black cod with miso, that have become standards on the menus of all the imitators that have sprung up in recent years. For a restaurant with such a glamorous reputation, the surroundings and levels of comfort are relatively understated but appropriately minimalist, while the decibel levels are at the party end of the spectrum.

First Course
- Lobster ceviche
- Yellowtail tartar with caviar.

Main Course
- Black cod with miso.
- Rock shrimp tempura with ponzu.

Dessert
- Chocolate bento box, green tea ice cream.
- Vanilla rice pudding with sake sorbet and rice cracker.

Wild Honey ✿

Modern European XX

H3

12 St George St W1S 2FB
✆ (020) 7758 9160
e-mail info@wildhoneyrestaurant.co.uk
www.wildhoneyrestaurant.co.uk

⊖ Oxford Circus
Closed 25-26 December and 1 January

Menu £16 (lunch) – Carte £30/36

A/C VISA MC AE

Michelin

Arbutus opened in 2006 to universal praise from the critical herd and so, fourteen months later, comes Anthony Demetre and Will Smith's second venture. The chosen venue of Mayfair is a world away from Soho, however, and mere yards away from some swanky addresses, so Wild Honey was never going to be a straight copy. This was once the Drones Club and the heaviest front door in London and the wood panelling inside both add to that clubby feel. If its extra privacy you want then try reserving one of the booths. The banquettes encourage a tad more table loitering and, while the artwork is lively, the atmosphere is a little more subdued and less frenzied than at its Soho sister.

The kitchen wisely adopts the 'if it ain't broke' formula by sticking to the principles of Arbutus. That means easy-to-eat, understated, gimmick-free food, where an inspired combination of ingredients is used to bring out the flavours, and where prices are kept low by using more unusual cuts. The wine list also offers an admirable inventory of wines by the carafe. It looks like they've done it again.

First Course

- Warm smoked eel with fig jam and raw vegetable salad.
- Corned beef with toast and green vegetables.

Main Course

- Shin of veal with tomato and carrots.
- Halibut with peas, broad beans, samphire and crushed potatoes.

Dessert

- Wild honey ice cream with crushed honeycomb.
- Roast greengages with soft nougat ice cream.

Giardinetto

H3 **Italian** XX

39-40 Albemarle St W1S 4TE
☎ (020) 7493 7091
Fax (020) 7493 7096
e-mail info@giardinetto.co.uk **www**.giardinetto.co.uk

⊖ Green Park
Closed 22 December-6 January, Saturday lunch, Sunday and Bank Holidays

Carte £17/49

This is one of those restaurants that just feels right the minute you enter. Diners are greeted like old friends and the place is stylishly kitted out with plenty of chrome and glass but is still warm and inviting. It comes divided into three, with the front section the busiest, the rear section the quietest and upstairs favoured by the regulars. The service is self assured and detailed.

The chef owner hails from Genoa and this is evident in his cooking. Aromatic herbs, richly flavoured vegetables, wild plants and simple presentation all give Ligurian cooking its distinctive personality and are all evident here. Dishes are precisely timed and textures nicely balanced. The wine list is exclusively Italian, with a huge array by the glass.

A/C VISA MC AE

Patterson's

H3 **Modern European** XX

4 Mill St W1S 2AX
☎ (020) 7499 1308
Fax (020) 7491 2122
e-mail info@pattersonsrestaurant.com
www.pattersonsrestaurant.com

⊖ Oxford Street
Closed 25-26 December, Sunday, Saturday lunch and Bank Holidays

Menu £20/40 – Carte £40/44

Mayfair is not perhaps the most obvious place in which to find that most admirable, and sadly these days all too rare type of establishment: the family restaurant.

Patterson's is the most genuine of family affairs with parents, son and daughter all involved with the day-to-day running of this modern, comfortable eatery on this narrow little street. The décor is stylishly understated and the menu offers up a selection of precisely executed and decoratively presented dishes. Lunchtime sees a well-priced set menu alongside the à la carte, which features a choice of five dishes per course. Service is swift and smooth for those on a time schedule but dinner on the whole is an altogether more languorous affair.

A/C VISA MC AE

Alloro

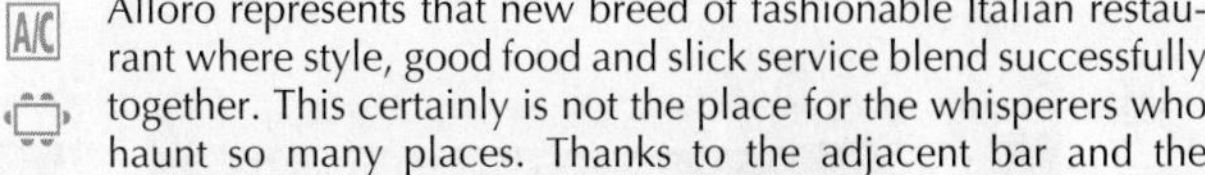

Italian XX

H3

19-20 Dover St W1S 4LU
⊖ Green Park
✆ (020) 7495 4768
Closed Easter, 25 December, Saturday lunch, Sunday and Bank Holidays
Fax (020) 7629 5348
e-mail alloro@hotmail.co.uk **www**.alloro-restaurant.com

Menu £29/34

Alloro represents that new breed of fashionable Italian restaurant where style, good food and slick service blend successfully together. This certainly is not the place for the whisperers who haunt so many places. Thanks to the adjacent bar and the principle of osmosis, the atmosphere here is always pretty exuberant.

Lunchtimes are popular with dealers of both the art and wheeler variety while dinner draws a typically metropolitan mix of types, all attracted by both the warm styling of the room and the modernity of the menu. Cooking has a slight Northern Italian attitude and the pasta dishes will no doubt be one of the highlights of your meal. The waiting staff carry out their duties with a confident swagger.

Hush

Modern European XX

H3

8 Lancashire Court, Brook St
W1S 1EY
⊖ Bond Street
Booking essential
✆ (020) 7659 1500 **Fax** (020) 7659 1501
e-mail info@hush.co.uk **www**.hush.co.uk

Carte £31/47

The setting is delightful - in the courtyard of a charming mews – and the outside terrace must surely be one of the places to be on a summer's day. You'll easily forget you're in the heart of the city. Hush indeed.

The brasserie on the ground floor is the mainstay of this surprisingly large operation and is quite a perky little number. The vibe is cool with a hint of flirtatiousness in the air. The menu reads like a comprehensive guide to modern European brasserie dining. Those who prefer their dining to be a little more exclusive should head upstairs to Le Club: the more formal room where the menu is altogether more your classic French. You'll also find the rather swanky cocktail lounge on this floor.

Nobu Berkeley St ✿

H3

Japanese XX

15 Berkeley St W1J 8DY
(020) 7290 9222
Fax (020) 7290 9223
e-mail nobuberkeley@noburestaurants.com
www.noburestaurants.com

⊖ Green Park
Closed 25-26 December, 1 January, lunch Saturday and Sunday

Menu £25/60 – Carte £33/49

Nobu

It's vast and always packed to the gunnels but you can still walk past without really noticing the place. It's only the doorman and the backed up Bentleys on Berkeley Street that tell you something's going on here.

Nobu Berkeley St has almost superseded the original in the Metropolitan Hotel in the amount of media coverage of departing/arriving celebrities and there is no doubt that this is a glamorous restaurant for glamorous people. More commendably, it shows that star-studded restaurants and good food do not have to be mutually exclusive. The menu lay out can be a little confusing to the neophyte or to the forgetful. The modern Japanese food is divided into a number of differing sections but the best thing is to order anything that takes your fancy and wait until the waiter tells you that you've got enough. Just make sure you've got something from the wood oven, a speciality of this 'branch' of this international brand.

The ground floor bar is now a destination in itself but upstairs is where the real action is.

First Course
- Yellowtail sashimi with jalapeño.
- Seafood ceviche.

Main Course
- Anti-Cucho rib-eye beef.
- Duck breast with wasabi salsa.

Dessert
- Yuzu tart.
- Chocolate bento box.

Via Condotti

Italian XX

H3

23 Conduit St W1S 2XS
(020) 7493 7050
Fax (020) 7409 7985
e-mail info@viacondotti.co.uk **www**.viacondotti.co.uk

Oxford Circus
Closed 25 December, Sunday and Bank Holidays

Menu £25/28

Via Condotti is not only an Italian translation of Conduit Street but is itself an equally glamorous shopper's paradise in Rome. The restaurant is warm and inviting, with colourful posters and comfortable leather seats. It's busier at lunchtimes and the upstairs room is used as an overflow which is a shame as it's the nicer of the two.

The menu delivers what it promises. That means generously sized dishes from across Italy, with the occasional twist. The Italian breads and olives may get the taste buds going but many of the ingredients are sourced from within the UK and there's an appealing earthiness to the cooking. The raviolis are particularly good, as are the set prices, even when you add the occasional vegetable side dish. You'll leave feeling satisfied.

A/C VISA MC AE

Taman Gang

Asian XX

F3

141 Park Lane W1K 7AA
(020) 7518 3160 **Fax** (020) 7518 3161
e-mail info@tamangang.com **www**.tamangang.com

Marble Arch
Closed Sunday – dinner only

Menu £55/75

As with many of today's fashionable hotspots, the casual passer-by will barely know it is there. The understated entrance to Taman Gang leads down to the moodily lit basement restaurant that's been added to the circuit of the bold and the beautiful. Split into various levels and decorated with silks, mahogany and stone, the place gets gradually busier and noisier as the night progresses. The cooking, though, is of a far better standard that one would expect from such a consciously fashionable place, although it does come at a price. The kitchen takes its cue from a number of South East Asian countries but adds its own original touches; the desserts are particularly modern. The loos are a triumph of style over practicality.

A/C VISA MC AE

Sketch (The Gallery)

H3 **International** XX

9 Conduit St W1S 2XG
(0870) 777 4488
Fax (0870) 777 4400
e-mail info@sketch.uk.com **www**.sketch.uk.com

Oxford Street
Closed 25-26 December, 1 January, Sunday and Bank Holidays – booking essential – dinner only

Carte £34/53

Art and food have been linked since bison first appeared in Palaeolithic cave drawings. The Gallery at Sketch just connects the two in more of a 21st century sort of way. During the day it's an art gallery, with regularly changing exhibitions featuring mostly video art thanks to the projectors and the huge white space. In the evening it transforms itself into a lively brasserie, with the videos still dancing around the walls.

France provides the starting point for the cooking but along the way it picks up influences from Italy to Japan which seems to suit the international crowd. It doesn't come cheap but that's the price for exclusivity.

For a more languorous, less frenzied affair, head upstairs to The Lecture Room & Library.

Momo

H3 **Moroccan** XX

25 Heddon St W1B 4BH
(020) 7434 4040
Fax (020) 7287 0404
e-mail info@momoresto.com **www**.momoresto.com

Oxford Circus
Closed 24-26 and 31 December, 1 January and Sunday

Menu £18/45 – Carte £29/52

Momo is one of those places that are perennially busy and it's easy to see why. Tucked away on a little side street, it's kitted out like a souk, with window screens and hanging lanterns, but it also comes with a soundtrack.

The candlelight and the low slung tables add to the exotic romance of the room, although adoring couples may find intimacy curtailed by the close proximity of the neighbouring table. It's much more fun to come in a group and spend some time in the hip surroundings and the happening bar, admiring all the beautiful people who fill the place on a nightly basis. The food is predominantly Moroccan, with pastilla, couscous and tagines all there, although there are other more contemporary Maghrebian choices available.

La Petite Maison

G3 **French** XX

54 Brooks Mews W1K 4EG — ⊖ Bond Street
(020) 7495 4774 — Closed Sunday
e-mail info@lpmlondon.co.uk **www**.lpmlondon.co.uk

Carte £35/50

Packed from the moment it opened in June 2007, La Petite Maison brings a little piece of Nice to Mayfair; French Mediterranean cooking and its sunny bounty of artichokes, lemons, olives, peppers and tomatoes have clearly caught the prevailing fashion for healthy eating.

'Food is served to help yourself' it proclaims, which translates as 'you may want to share,' but you don't have to, as the dishes are of normal size. However, with over 20 starters including pissaladière, sardines and squid, it may be worth ordering a few. The whole roast black-leg chicken with foie gras has proved a hit, as have the fish main courses. As one would expect, there's plenty of rosé on the wine list. Their slogan is 'Tous célèbres ici', which means all-year tans and good tailoring.

Floridita

I3 **Latin American** 

100 Wardour St — ⊖ Tottenham Court Road
W1F 0TN — Closed 24-26 December,
(020) 7314 4000 — 1 January and Sunday – dinner only
Fax (020) 7314 4040
www.floriditalondon.com

Carte £32/61

Not so much a meal out, more your full Cuban Spectacular - just head downstairs for vibrant cocktails, fiery food and a little salsa. The name and concept pay homage to Havana's legendary bar of the same name, the birthplace of the daiquiri and favoured haunt of Ernest Hemingway.

An impressive cocktail list, live music and dancing prove to be a contagious combination and, thanks to the swivel chairs, even those eating will find the rhythm hard to resist.

The food lends a predictably modern edge to some rustic dishes but keeps flavours authentic and crosses the wider Latin America countries in search of inspiration. But, this is all about the buzz and the great atmosphere and, as such, means coming here for partying and general merrymaking.

Brasserie Roux

French XX

I4

8 Pall Mall SW1Y 5NG — Piccadilly Circus

(020) 7968 2900 **Fax** (020) 7747 2251

e-mail h3144-fb4@accor.com **www**.sofitelstjames.com

Menu £20/25 – Carte £26/35

The term 'brasserie' does not really prepare you for the grandeur of a room that once formed part of a banking hall. Those giant lamps are needed to counter such an enormous ceiling and the leather armchairs and large tables up the ante on the comfort front.

It is a surprise, therefore, to discover there's a weekly changing set menu that's not only keenly priced but also includes two glasses of wine. The 'brasserie' label certainly makes more sense when talking about the food; expect comforting classics like blanquette de veau or baba au rhum alongside terrines and plenty of grilled meats and fish. Add to this some pasta dishes, a few salads and a children's menu and you'll find that there's something for everyone.

Quaglino's

Modern European XX

H4

16 Bury St SW1Y 6AL — Green Park

(020) 7930 6767

Fax (020) 7930 2732

Closed 25-26 December and 1 January – booking essential

e-mail quaglinos@danddlondon.com **www**.quaglinos.co.uk

Carte £25/41

Quaglino's has been around long enough for us to forget what an impact its opening had, back in the early 1990s. The large bar, the sweeping staircase, the cigarette girls and the bustle of a vast, glamorous restaurant really set London's collective pulse racing. Today, the 'scene' may have moved elsewhere but Quaglino's still offers a good night out.

The menu is an appealing mix of brasserie style favourites, with traditional French dishes marked out in red. Grilled meats are done well but the shellfish and seafood are the stars of the show and the kitchen understands the importance of freshness and simplicity. Lunch and early evening set menus are well priced. The bar, with live music, is a great spot for pre or post prandial drinks.

ROEDERE
ndé en 1776

Semplice

Italian XX

G3

10 Blenheim St W1S 1LJ
(020) 7495 1509
Fax (020) 7493 7074
e-mail info@ristorantesemplice.com **www**.ristorantesemplice.com

⊖ Bond Street
Closed Christmas, Easter, Saturday lunch, Sunday and Bank Holidays

Menu £18 (lunch) - Carte £28/38

A/C VISA MC AE

Semplice is hardly the word to describe the unequivocally swish surroundings which the young owners have created by knocking together an old café and chippy. Custom made lacquered ebony, Venetian gold wavy walls and leather seating lend the room warmth and a sense of style. Seating just over fifty, it also feels quite intimate, helped along by the amiable service.

Perhaps semplice applies more to the cooking but, then again, there is considerable craft and no little flair here. The co-owning chef hails from Northern Italy but his influences range across the country and he has found small specialist producers wherever possible. Dishes are delicately textured and confidently presented, accompanied by a wine list that's reasonably priced and exclusively Italian.

Mint Leaf

Indian XX

I4

Suffolk Pl SW1Y 4HX
(020) 7930 9020
Fax (020) 7930 6205
e-mail reservations@mintleafrestaurant.com
www.mintleafrestaurant.com

⊖ Piccadilly Circus
Closed lunch Saturday and Sunday

Menu £15 - Carte £33/40

A/C VISA MC AE

Being surrounded by playhouses has clearly rubbed off because Mint Leaf provides a thoroughly theatrical experience. Just watch your entrance as the stairs down are cloaked in darkness. You'll firstly encounter a long, tenebrous and highly fashionable bar. The dining room beyond splits into five areas, all equal in their moodiness and energised by the constant pulse of lounge music. Don't be alarmed when the staff leave what looks like a catwalk and crouch down at your table – it's their way of offering reassuring service.

In such surroundings one would expect decidedly eclectic Indian food but instead they keep things traditional and grounded, except for the very European desserts. Try the specially created Indian salads at lunch.

Noura Central

I3 **Lebanese** XX

22 Lower Regent St SW1Y 4UJ — ⊖ Piccadilly Circus
(020) 7839 2020 **Fax** (020) 7839 7700
www.noura.co.uk

Menu £18/30 – Carte £20/39

The nearer one got to Piccadilly Circus, the fewer choices of restaurant one usually had. However, Noura Central changed all that when it opened in 2004. This capacious Lebanese restaurant, together with its equally roomy bar, offers a wide selection of Levantine dishes, in richly colourful surroundings. Assorted mezes, charcoal grilled meats, various fish platters and rich, sweet pastries all feature on the extensive menus and provide sufficiently varied choice for all tastes.
The decoration is exuberant and lavish, matched by an atmosphere that's never less than animated, thanks in part to the extensive cocktail list and the decent prices found on the wine list.
The occasional DJ also ensures that the noise levels don't fall below party mode.

Bellamy's

H3 **Traditional** XX

18 Bruton Pl W1J 6LY — ⊖ Bond Street
(020) 7491 2727
Fax (020) 7491 9990
www.bellamysrestaurant.co.uk

Closed Saturday lunch, Sunday, 25 December and Bank Holidays

Menu £29 – Carte £36/53

First find the little mews of Bruton Place, snake through the appetising deli out front, glide through the double doors and you'll find yourself in Bellamy's restaurant.
This is a decidedly clubby little place with a hint of the brasserie about it. It's also perennially full of Mayfair regulars, some of whom are a little more 'Horse and Hounds' and a little less 'Hello'.
Prices here are hard to quantify: there is a very reasonable set menu for under £30 but this comes juxtaposed with £340 for Beluga Caviar. The menu covers an equally broad field with everything from whitebait to foie gras, mixing the English with the French. The scrambled eggs with truffles are ideal for the louche late riser. Puds are more your classic French.

The Avenue

Modern European XX

H4

7-9 St James's St SW1A 1EE
(020) 7321 2111
Fax (020) 7321 2500
e-mail avenue@egami.co.uk **www**.egami.co.uk

⊖ Green Park
Closed 25-26 December, Saturday lunch and Sunday

Menu £22 – Carte £29/48

In contrast to some of the starchier establishments in the street, The Avenue is a loud and confident affair, even though it's been around long enough to be approaching its teenage years. It's easy to spot, thanks to its large billowing flag and it occupies an impressive amount of square footage. White is the predominant colour, although the large artwork which changes three or four times a year tries to compete for your attention.

The kitchen keeps things simple and knows not to mess around too much with the ingredients. Expect satisfying European brasserie favourites where the flavours are pronounced and the choice extensive. The pricing of the lunch time set menu is particularly keen when you consider the neighbourhood.

Matsuri - St James's

Japanese XX

H4

15 Bury St SW1Y 6AL
(020) 7839 1101
Fax (020) 7930 7010
e-mail dine@matsuri-restaurant.com **www**.matsuri-restaurant.com

⊖ Green Park
Closed Christmas and New Year

Menu £35 – Carte £28/71

The façade of this Japanese restaurant may be a little drab but the location - in among the art galleries of Bury Street - explains why lunch is such a busy affair. It is also much nicer all round once you're inside, where you're greeted by a very charming hostess who escorts you downstairs to one of the teppan-yaki tables or, if you're quick, you can grab one of the few seats at the neighbouring sushi bar.

The managers have a tendency to stand around looking important while the service is undertaken by very helpful and earnest waitresses, traditionally kitted out. Once you have chosen from one of the many different menus available, watch the chef at your table slice and dice and your appetite will get going immediately.

Vasco and Piero's Pavilion

H2 **Italian** XX

15 Poland St W1F 8QE
(020) 7437 8774
Fax (020) 7437 0467
e-mail eat@vascosfood.com **www**.vascosfood.com

⊖ Tottenham Court Road
Closed Saturday lunch, Sunday and Bank Holidays – booking essential at lunch

Menu £28 – Carte lunch £26/36

With the expansion of corporate, homogenous chains, family-owned restaurants are something of a rarity these days, especially in Soho. Thank heavens, therefore, for Vasco and Piero's Pavilion which has been in Poland Street since 1989, having first opened in Oxford Street in the 1970s.

The menu still changes twice a day and much of the meat, cheese, vegetables and truffles come from small, family producers back in Umbria. Specialities from the region also include guinea fowl and cured pork, while the home-made pastas are an obvious strength. Dishes come with an appetising simplicity that has been perfected over the years and, for this, the restaurant is rewarded with a very loyal clientele, many of whom don't even need to look at a menu.

Silk

H3 **International** XX

at Courthouse Kempinksi H.,
19-21 Great Marlborough St
W1F 7HL
(020) 7297 5567 **Fax** (020) 7297 5566
www.courthouse-hotel.com

⊖ Oxford Circus
Closed Sunday-Monday – dinner only

Carte £24/36

The Courthouse Kempinski Hotel, so named because it was converted from a former magistrate's court, offers a number of dining options, the most notable being Silk, which is housed in the handsome, oak panelled surroundings of what was once Court Number One. The benches are still there to prove it.

The name not only refers to the QCs who once paced this room but it also, perhaps more tortuously, outlines the culinary identity of the place. The menu follows the 'silk route', taking in Italy, India and Asia. This somewhat bewilderingly varied cooking actually works perfectly satisfactorily, due mostly to the decent ingredients. It's also the perfect menu for friends who can't agree on which nationality of restaurant they fancy.

Fakhreldine

Lebanese XX

H4

85 Piccadilly W1J 7NB ⊖ Green Park
✆ (020) 7493 3424 **Fax** (020) 7495 1977 Closed 24 to 26 December
e-mail info@fakhreldine.co.uk **www**.fakhreldine.co.uk

Menu £19 (lunch) – Carte £26/41

Ascend the marble staircase and you enter into this stylish and urbane Lebanese restaurant which comes with its own smart lounge bar where large sofas provide the perfect spot for pre-dinner cocktails. The restaurant, reinvented by a refurbishment and named after an 18th century Lebanese Prince, benefits from its large picture windows which let in plenty of light, as well as providing great views of Green Park for those with window tables. The stone, oak and muted palate all lend a sensual, contemporary edge to the decoration.

It's not just the meze which blend the traditional with the modern: the Lebanese home cooking is equally fragrant and no less accomplished, with daily changing specials and tasting plates available.

Sumosan

Japanese XX

H3

26 Albemarle St W1S 4HY ⊖ Green Park
✆ (020) 7495 5999 Closed 25-26 December, 1 January and
Fax (020) 7355 1247 lunch Saturday and Sunday – dinner only
e-mail info@sumosan.co.uk **www**.sumosan.com

Menu £23/70 – Carte £33/59

As you would expect from a restaurant on the circuit of fashionable haunts, the outside sign is discreet and the window is covered with a thin gauze to deter passing gawpers.

Inside, it's all fawn – the colour rather than the verb. In fact, the staff do need a little encouragement before they'll offer advice or help with the extensive menu, although many of the regulars do seem to know what they're doing. Lunch is easier to navigate as 'lunch combinations' allow you to create your own menu, but the main à la carte covers four pages and over-ordering is easy. Whilst there are some familiar sounding modern Japanese classics, others exhibit greater originality. Ensure you leave room at the end for some sushi and sashimi, as this is what the kitchen does best.

Mews of Mayfair

British XX

10-11 Lancashire Court, New Bond St W1S 1EY
(020) 7518 9388 **Fax** (020) 7518 9389
www.mewsofmayfair.com

Bond Street
Closed Christmas and New Year and Sunday

Menu £26/40 – Carte £36/54

Look out for the narrow little lane opposite D&G because down there you'll find Mews of Mayfair. This is a bright and pretty first floor restaurant, on a site dating from 1902 which was once used as storage rooms for Savile Row. A cocktail bar occupies the ground floor, with a lounge bar in the basement, but upstairs you'll find the relative serenity of the restaurant. It's nicely decorated with very comfortable cream leather seating and attractive silk embroidered wallpaper.

The atmosphere is far more relaxed than the style suggests, thanks largely to the delightfully enthusiastic service. The kitchen makes good use of produce from across the British Isles but does so in a contemporary, yet restrained, style.

Chor Bizarre

H3

Indian XX

16 Albemarle St W1S 4HW
(020) 7629 9802
Fax (020) 7493 7756
e-mail chorbizarrelondon@oldworldhospitality.com
www.chorbizarre.com

Green Park
Closed 25-26 December, 1 January, Sunday lunch and Bank Holidays

Menu £18 – Carte £24/38

The façade of this Mayfair restaurant is actually quite discreet, which doesn't really prepare you for the exuberance of the interior. Playfully translated as "thieves market", Chor Bizarre offers something a little different and cannot fail to charm. Elaborate and ornate wooden carvings, vivacious colours and an abundance of knick-knackery combine to give the room immense character, appeal and a palpable sense of India.

The menu is equally busy, with full explanations of the differing cooking styles and techniques found across India; the flavoursome dishes of the Northwest frontier are something of a house speciality. Service is suitably enthusiastic and attentive, with plenty of suited managers around to do the supervising.

Cocoon

Asian XX

H3

65 Regent St W1B 4EA
✆ (020) 7494 7600
Fax (020) 7494 7607
www.cocoon-restaurants.com

⊖ Piccadilly Circus
Closed Saturday lunch and Sunday

Carte £35/70

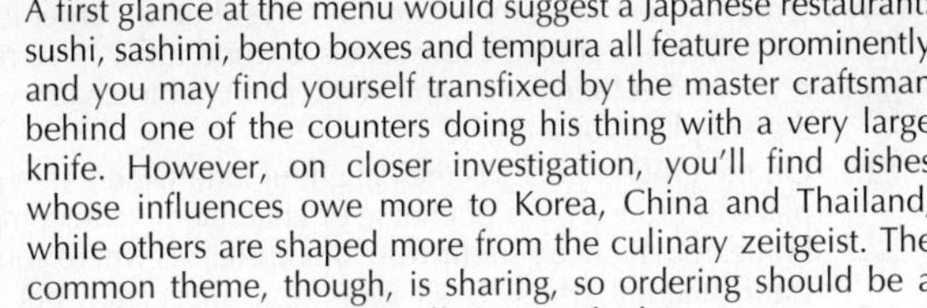

A first glance at the menu would suggest a Japanese restaurant: sushi, sashimi, bento boxes and tempura all feature prominently and you may find yourself transfixed by the master craftsman behind one of the counters doing his thing with a very large knife. However, on closer investigation, you'll find dishes whose influences owe more to Korea, China and Thailand, while others are shaped more from the culinary zeitgeist. The common theme, though, is sharing, so ordering should be a group activity, although staff give good advice.
The place seats 170 but is cleverly divided and the styling and décor are decidedly space-age. Lunches are relatively calm affairs with shoppers in for salads and bento boxes. It all hots up big-time in the evenings.

Veeraswamy

Indian XX

H3

Victory House, 99 Regent St
(entrance on Swallow St)
W1B 4RS
✆ (020) 7734 1401 **Fax** (020) 7439 8434
e-mail veeraswamy@realindianfood.com **www**.realindianfood.com

⊖ Piccadilly Circus
Closed dinner 25 December

Menu £20 – Carte £29/52

Not many Indian restaurants can boast Nehru and Gandhi as former customers but then not many Indian restaurants began life in 1926.

Such longevity may lead you to imagine it has something of an old fashioned feel but Veeraswamy was re-launched in late 2005 as a sleek and contemporary restaurant, while still managing to respect the restaurant's own glorious past. Colour and light are everywhere, from the hanging display of turbans to the coloured glass, silver screens, chandeliers and large picture windows.

Visually enticing choices from across India are showcased, from recipes garnered from palaces and royal courts to humble homes, with many designed for sharing. Veeraswamy looks set to be around for another 80 years.

La Trouvaille

H3 **French** XX

12A Newburgh St W1F 7RR
(020) 7287 8488
Fax (020) 7434 4170
www.latrouvaille.co.uk

Piccadilly Circus
Closed 25 December, Saturday lunch, Sunday and Bank Holidays

Menu £18/33

VISA

It may be just yards from Carnaby Street but its corner location on a narrow cobbled street seems a world away. This really is a very sweet little restaurant which can't fail to charm you. It's a great place for a date.

On the ground floor sits the delightful little wine bar, a perfect place to order a plate of cheese or charcuterie to accompany a bottle from France's southwest. But upstairs is where you'll find the restaurant which is all very fresh and clean, but with a simple, effortless intimacy.

The menus, like the staff, are French, with lunch and pre-theatre representing good value. The fixed price main menu offers plenty of interest but keeps you on your toes with occasional moments of playfulness - much like a good date.

Franco's

H4 **Italian** XX

61 Jermyn St SW1Y 6LX
(020) 7499 2211
Fax (020) 7495 1375
e-mail reserve@francoslondon.com **www**.francoslondon.com

Green Park
Closed 24 December-2 January, Sunday and Bank Holidays – booking essential

Menu £25 (lunch) – Carte £36/45

A/C

VISA

Franco's first opened in the 1940's and, understandably, was beginning to show his age until gracefully withdrawing from the scene for a while, before bursting back at the end of 2005 with a new, fresh image. He then managed the difficult trick of both attracting new admirers and hanging onto the loyalty of existing fans.

The dining room is spread over two floors, with the ground floor the most popular, and the new decoration pays homage to the era of its original opening. The sartorially immaculate regulars have been highly receptive to the new image so booking, especially at lunch, is recommended. The seasonally-biased Italian menu is constantly evolving and the cooking is both bold and generous but refined where it should be.

Café Lazeez

Indian XX

12

21 Dean St W1D 3TN ⊖ Tottenham Court Road
✆ (020) 7434 9393 **Fax** (020) 7434 0022 Closed Sunday lunch
e-mail soho@cafelazeez.com **www**.cafelazeez.com

Carte £27/35

The ground floor bar, attached to the Soho Theatre, is a lively little number and draws quite a crowd, more for its drinks list, no doubt, than the little Indian delicacies that are on offer. If you prefer to do your eating sitting down, then head downstairs for somewhere a tad quieter. Sketches of former Indian prime ministers adorn the brightly coloured walls, service is conscientious and the best tables are the booths by the staircase. The open-plan kitchen exhibits a certain ambition, encouraged by the restaurant's new owners. Several dishes come appealingly presented in earthenware dishes; there's clarity to the flavours and vigour in their construction. The wine list is also not your normal drab affair.

Stanza

Modern European XX

13

97-107 Shaftesbury Ave ⊖ Leicester Square
W1D 5DY Closed Easter, 25 December and Sunday
✆ (020) 7494 3040
www.stanzalondon.com

Menu £19 (dinner) – Carte £23/36

This was once Teatro and so the new name is not a great leap. However, this chef is well versed in British cooking and his menus display a commendable loyalty to ingredients from the British Isles and, as he's from Rochdale, a special affection for more northerly parts, with Cumbrian lamb and cured meats, Morecombe Bay shrimp and chicken and ducks from Reg Johnson all appearing. The cooking is seasonal and although some dishes display a certain intricacy, such as scallops with a pea blancmange and wood-dried ham, the strength lies in the simpler offerings, such as asparagus with hollandaise or fish pie with shrimps and lobster sauce. The restaurant is on the first floor and is quite a smart affair, with a large bar.

Benja

Thai XX

H3

17 Beak St W1F 9RW
(020) 7287 0555
Fax (020) 7287 0056

⊖ Oxford Circus
Closed 25 December, Sunday and lunch Bank Holidays

Carte £19/32

VISA MC AE

Benja means 'five' in Thai and that's the theme: there are five owners, it occupies five floors of a Soho townhouse and there are five colours used. The best room is the eye-catching first floor dining room with its roomy feel and attractive decoration of greens and mirrors and it's also worth sampling the appealing basement bar. The restaurant opened in January 2007 but took a while to find its feet.

The cooking offers an attractive mix of the traditional dishes one expects alongside others of more contemporary sensibilities. So, alongside the Tom Yum soups and mussamun curries, you'll find minced chicken curry puffs and sliced duck breast with herbs and Thai whisky. The service is delightful and unfailingly sweet natured.

Kiku

Japanese XX

H4

17 Half Moon St W1J 7BE
(020) 7499 4208
www.kikurestaurant.co.uk

⊖ Green Park
Closed 25-26 December, Sunday and lunch Bank Holidays

Menu £14/46 s – Carte £28/58 s

A/C VISA MC AE

These days you'll find countless restaurants attempting to 're-interpret' Japanese food but Kiku, a Mayfair stalwart for many years, shows there is a still a demand for tradition. The restaurant feels very bright and fresh, thanks to the minimalist décor of stone and natural wood. There are seats for 50 in the main room but panels break it up and at the back, up a few steps, you'll find the sushi counter.

A plethora of menus is on offer so whether it's just soba noodles, a casserole, sushi or the full kaiseki experience you're after then they've got it covered. As expected, the natural flavours of the ingredients are allowed to come through, there's a fierce adherence to seasonality and importance placed on presentation.

Haiku

H3

Asian XX

15 New Burlington Place
W1S 2HX
(020) 7494 4777
www.haikurestaurant.com

⊖ Oxford Circus
Closed Sunday

Menu £22/50 - Carte £32/54

A/C VISA MC AE

It is not just the concept that was imported from South Africa – the original is in Cape Town – but also much of the stone and wood that decorates this moodily lit restaurant spread over three floors. The bar is downstairs but the ground floor is where the action is, although you never quite forget it's all housed within an office block.

There are about 18 chefs here, from all over the world, which is a clue as to the food. They've given it the frighteningly unspecific name of 'Asian tapas', but then the menu does feature dishes from Japan, China, India and Thailand. Everything is on offer here, from sashimi and tempura to dim sum, tandoori and curry. Just be prepared to share and to accept that some parts will be greater than the sum.

Alastair Little

I3

Modern European X

49 Frith St W1D 5SG
(020) 7734 5183
Fax (020) 7734 5206

⊖ Tottenham Court Road
Closed Sunday, Saturday lunch and Bank Holidays – booking essential

Menu £38/40

A/C VISA MC AE

It may seem an age ago but there was a time when Soho was a place one avoided after dark, unless searching for entertainment altogether more corporeal. The eponymous former owner of this Soho stalwart was not only at the vanguard of the new wave of British chefs in the 1980s, but was also one of those responsible for turning Soho into the diners' delight that we enjoy today.

Alastair Little may no longer be involved in the restaurant but his philosophy - of letting the quality of the ingredients shine through - lives on. The sparseness of the restaurant itself was also ground-breaking in its time and matched the cooking in its rustic simplicity. Twenty years after opening, the place remains as popular as ever.

Yauatcha ✿

13 — Chinese

15 Broadwick St
W1F 0DL

(020) 7494 8888 **Fax** (020) 7494 8889
e-mail mail@yauatcha.com

⊖ Tottenham Court Road
Closed 24-25 December

Carte £20/48

A/C
VISA
MC
AE

Yauatcha

To many, dim sum means a meandering trolley full of steamed dumplings and mysterious Chinese specialities. Yauatcha takes the basic principles of ordering small dishes but gives it a thoroughly modern makeover; hardly surprising, as the owner is Alan Yau, who created the devilishly hip Chinese restaurant, Hakkasan.

It's located beneath Richard Rogers' Ingeni building and comes divided between two floors. The brighter ground floor is ideal for lunch, as it doubles as the tea room (and there are some stunning first-growth teas available). Downstairs, with its twinkling lights and buzzy vibe, is an altogether sexier space, better suited for dinner.

The menu may appear daunting but everything is divided by its method of preparation - so choose whether you want steamed, stir-fried, cheung fun, baked or grilled and then just order plenty to share. Most plates contain three pieces; some, like chicken feet, are quite traditional; others, such as the hugely popular venison puff, are more contemporary creations. Delivery is prompt so you can always order more mid-meal if you've underestimated.

First Course

- Prawn cheung fun; scallop shumai.
- Baked venison puff; salt and pepper quail; King crab dumpling.

Main Course

- Szechuan tea smoked duck with Chinese pancake, kumquat and plum sauce.
- Roast silver cod with baby leek in Chinese honey.

Dessert

- White chocolate with mandarin and kumquat rice pudding.
- Chocolate soufflé with chilli ice cream.

Arbutus ✿

Modern European

13

63-64 Frith St
W1D 3 JW

⊖ Tottenham Court Road
Closed 25-26 December and 1 January

(020) 7734 4545 **Fax** (020) 7287 8624
e-mail info@arbutusrestaurant.co.uk **www**.arbutusrestaurant.co.uk

Menu £16 – Carte £29/35

A/C VISA MC AE

Arbutus

Despite opening back in 2006, Arbutus still feels like Soho's most interesting new restaurant. It just seems to fit Frith Street perfectly and has been understandably packed from day one. Faced with such success, the owners, Will Smith and Anthony Demetre, did the obvious and opened another branch (Wild Honey in Mayfair) but Arbutus, their first born, continues to impress all-comers and influence many.

Its success is down to its food; that means food that's satisfying, fresh and, above all, honest. The kitchen, under the supervision of Demetre, displays a loyalty to the seasons rather than to any particular European country and the menu is printed daily. They also know how to do things properly here, from butchery to braising. Prices are kept low by using less expensive ingredients, such as pollack, pig's cheek or bavette of beef, but then the kitchen goes to work to produce dishes with well defined flavours and harmonious combinations.

Fruit from the arbutus tree is said to be a narcotic; dining at Arbutus can easily become a habit.

First Course

- Braised pig's head with potato purée and caramelised onions.
- Roast butternut squash with girolles, ricotta and grapes.

Main Course

- Bavette of beef with gratin dauphinois, red wine and shallot sauce.
- Saddle of rabbit with shoulder cottage pie.

Dessert

- Vanilla panna cotta with poached rhubarb.
- Floating Island with pink pralines.

Al Duca

H4

Italian

4-5 Duke of York St SW1Y 6LA
Piccadilly Circus
(020) 7839 3090
Closed 25 December, Sunday and Bank Holidays
Fax (020) 7839 4050
e-mail info@alduca-restaurants.co.uk
www.alduca-restaurant.co.uk

Menu £25/27

A/C VISA MC AE

Fresh and invigorating Italian cooking is the draw at Al Duca, nestling among the galleries, outfitters and old pubs of St James's. The set menus offer an appealing mix of dishes, many of which come in a modern, understated way with a nicely balanced simplicity. There's a daily changing pasta and risotto and the kitchen demonstrates a light and confident touch, as well as an obvious appreciation of the ingredients. Furthermore, it represents very good value, especially when you consider the location. Service makes up in efficiency what is lacks in personality.

The crisp terracotta interior of tiles and stone means that noise has a tendency to bounce around the place a little when busy, which it nearly always is - and deservedly so.

Inn the Park

I4

British

St James's Park SW1A 2BJ
Charing Cross
(020) 7451 9999 **Fax** (020) 7451 9998
Closed 25 December
e-mail info@innthepark.com **www**.innthepark.com

Carte £32/52

VISA MC AE

Food miles, sustainability, global warming – we could talk for hours, but Oliver Peyton went and did something. His eco-friendly pavilion blends into the environment wonderfully well - even the roof is covered with grass. It sits in St James's Park, the oldest Royal Park, and, in summer, the views over the lake from the terrace are terrific. It's also open all day and gains extra plaudits for the Britishness of its menu. Asparagus, crab, rabbit, duck, mutton, shrimps - it's a good reminder of what great fresh produce we have in this country. The cooking is also light and wholesome and there is a children's menu of 'real' food. Puds are properly filling and may include treacle tart or apple pie.

The Cafe at Sotheby's

Modern European

H3

34-35 New Bond St W1A 2AA — Bond Street
(020) 7293 5077
Fax (020) 7293 6993
e-mail ken.hall@sothebys.com
www.sothebys.com

Closed last 3 weeks August, 23 December-3 January, Saturday and Sunday – booking essential – lunch only

Carte £29/34 s

VISA MC AE

'Café' is something of a misnomer as this is a thoroughly civilised, comfortable and urbane little spot for morning coffee, lunch or afternoon tea, located within the world famous auction house. It spills into the lobby but the best tables are those against the wall, with the banquette seating. Mirrors and Cecil Beaton photographs lighten the space and the waitresses are a charming and efficient group.

The lunch menu is a short but well balanced affair, mixing the light with the more substantial and dishes are fresh and invigorating, including the popular lobster sandwich, a permanent feature. The wine list is also diminutive but the dozen or so wines are varied and well chosen. Bookings are essential, especially on sale days.

Fung Shing

Chinese

I3

15 Lisle St WC2H 7BE — Leicester Square
(020) 7437 1539
Fax (020) 7734 0284
www.fung.shing.co.uk

Closed 24-26 December and lunch Bank Holidays

Menu £17 – Carte £16/25

A/C VISA MC AE

Chinatown offers a colourful, varied and, to the new visitor, rather bewildering selection of Chinese restaurants. Fung Shing was one of the first to open and remains one of the best.

For a start, it offers bright and well-looked-after surroundings and, by dividing itself into two, manages to create a more personable feel. It also rises above the norm in the service - many of the staff have been around for years and make the effort to know and recognise their regulars.

The main menu features an extensive selection of the tried and tested but those who wish to delve deeper into the mysteries of Cantonese cooking, and to experience some of Fung Shing's more ambitious creations, should head straight for the 'specials' selection.

Chisou

Japanese

H2

4 Princes St W1B 2LE — Oxford Circus
(020) 7629 3931 — Closed Sunday

Menu £15 – Carte £17/55

A/C VISA MC AE

Hanover Square and the surrounding streets are becoming something of a Japanese quarter and Chisou stands out from the crowd with its decidedly smart façade. Inside, it's equally plush, with its clean and fresh theme of slate, glass and polished wood. The high ceiling brightens what is actually quite a small room.

Lunchtimes sees some good value set menus but the kitchen's creativity is more evident in the evening when dishes such as monkfish liver with ponzu merit exploration. Evenings are certainly busier so reservations are advisable. Traditionalists, though, are far from ignored and the sushi bar at the back of the room offers top notch sashimi and sushi. The waitresses provide engaging and very capable service.

Automat

American

H3

33 Dover St W1S 4NF — Green Park
(020) 7499 3033 — Closed 25 December and 1 January
Fax (020) 7499 2682
e-mail info@automat-london.com **www**.automat-london.com

Carte £25/42

A/C VISA MC AE

Automat, an American-style brasserie, comes divided into three: the first section by the entrance is the least enticing as those waiting for tables will stand around near yours; the mid-section comes decked out in the style of a railway carriage and the third is undoubtedly where the action is. The open kitchen and noise bouncing of the white tiles creates quite a buzzy vibe.

The menu could have come direct from NYC. You'll find chowder, cakes of the crab and cheese variety, burgers and steaks, although in portions more European than Stateside. Brunch here is the genuine article. Where the authenticity falls down is in the service which lacks that energetic confidence and relentless efficiency one usually finds across the pond.

Chinese Experience

Chinese

I3

118 Shaftesbury Ave W1D 5EP ⊖ Leicester Square
(020) 7437 0377
e-mail info@chineseexperience.com
www.chineseexperience.com

Menu £15 – Carte £19

A/C VISA MC AE

Those strangely hypnotic and curiously warming neon lights may compete for your attention along the length of Shaftesbury Avenue but Chinese Experience more than holds its own with its shimmering façade of silver and glass. Step into its equally bright and airy interior and you'll find that the distinctly friendly and obliging nature of the staff belies its touristy location.
It's divided into two rooms: the first with bench tables for those communally inclined and the second with individual tables and a simple, crisp décor of white or red walls and calligraphy. The *dim sum* is worthy of note and the menu offers an extensive choice of classics and other dishes of a more individual nature, all served in a fun and buzzy atmosphere.

Bentley's (Oyster Bar)

Seafood

H3

11-15 Swallow St W1B 4DG ⊖ Piccadilly Circus
(020) 7734 4756 Closed 25 December and 1 January
www.bentleysoysterbarandgrill.co.uk

Carte £27/39

A/C VISA MC AE

Once the place where sons took their ageing fathers or bewildered tourists took themselves, but now, following its full make-over, it's attracting an altogether sprightlier group of pescatarians.
The elements remain largely the same: white jacketed staff open native or rock oysters by the bucket load, while others serve smoked salmon, fish pie, Dover sole and assorted seafood dishes. The difference is that the cooking is undertaken with a little more care these days.
The panelled walls, marble topped tables and leather banquettes are also a great improvement and provide highly civilised surroundings in which to indulge. Reservations are not taken for the rather smart place settings up at the bar, so get in early if you want one of these.

Aurora

Mediterranean

H3

49 Lexington St W1F 9AP — Piccadilly Circus
(020) 7494 0514 — Closed Sunday – booking essential

Carte £19/26

Not to be confused with the City restaurant of the same name, this Aurora is a charming and intimate little Soho favourite in one of the mid terrace 18th century houses and whose sense of bohemian independence perfectly reflects the general feel of Lexington Street.

The limited space, closely set tables lit by candles and the pretty little walled garden all conspire to lend an air of secrecy to the place, somewhere the regulars would rather not share with outsiders.

The cooking also takes an uncomplicated and unfussy approach, with the main emphasis being on Mediterranean colours and flavours, although a little Asian influence occasionally slips in. The service is, as you would expect, friendly and well meaning.

Bar Shu

Chinese

I3

28 Frith St W1D 5LF — Leicester Square
(020) 7287 8822 **Fax** (020) 7287 8858 — Closed 25-26 December

Carte £20/25

Bar Shu opened in May 2006 and is detached, both geographically and qualitatively, from the restaurants in Chinatown. Not only is this serious Szechuan cooking but it is also unapologetically authentic.

Those who like their food hot and spicy may have to reset their thermometers. The dishes here pack a ferocious punch and when some are described as 'hot and numbing' you know they're serious. Fantastically named choices such as 'pock marked old woman's beancurd', 'smacked cucumbers' or 'man and wife offal slices' also prove this is no ordinary Chinese restaurant, despite the retro glossy menus with (undeniably helpful) photographs of the dishes.

The restaurant is spread over three floors - avoid the rather dull basement level.

The National Dining Rooms

British

13

Sainsbury Wing, The National Gallery, Trafalgar Sq WC2N 5DN
(020) 7747 2525
e-mail enquiries@thenationaldiningrooms.co.uk
www.thenationaldiningrooms.co.uk

⊖ Charing Cross
Closed Christmas – lunch only and dinner Wednesday

Menu £30

The UK's dismal culinary reputation abroad may be hopelessly outdated but will remain so until overseas visitors see evidence to the contrary. Credit then to Oliver Peyton for opening a restaurant in one of our great popular landmarks - The National Gallery. This Peyton place is on the first floor of the Sainsbury Wing, looking down over Trafalgar Square.

The menu is a decidedly British affair, with carefully sourced ingredients from across our sceptred isle. So, Dorset crab can be followed by Scottish beef and the cheese selection shows off our great repertoire.

Adjacent to the David Collins designed restaurant is a 'bakery', serving up evocative treats like jammy dodgers and fig rolls for those who haven't been to a gallery since that school trip.

Portrait

Modern European 

13

3rd Floor, National Portrait Gallery, St Martin's Pl WC2H 0HE
(020) 7312 2490
Fax (020) 7925 0244
e-mail portrait.restaurant@searcys.co.uk **www**.searcys.co.uk

⊖ Charing Cross
Closed 25-26 December – booking essential – lunch only and dinner Friday and Saturday

Carte £25/46

Thankfully, there are fewer museums and galleries around who assume that visitors seek nothing more than intellectual nourishment and will therefore be happy enough with a stale, overpriced cheese sandwich. Not only is the National Portrait Gallery as splendidly varied and fascinating as ever but it also provides a agreeably bright and modern restaurant, on the top floor of the Ondaatje wing.

The menu features reliable and modern dishes which do far more than merely sustain you through another tour. Wisely the room does not try to compete with the galleries; its minimalist décor soothes the senses and the large curved windows provide great views across the rooftops towards Nelson and the Eye.

Barrafina

Spanish

I3

54 Frith St W1D 4SL — Closed Sunday – bookings not accepted
(020) 7813 8016 **Fax** (020) 7813 8011
e-mail info@barrafina.co.uk **www**.barrafina.co.uk

Carte £19/35

London has been a bit iffy about restaurants that don't take reservations but Barrafina is the likely candidate to buck that trend. This is the newest sibling to the Hart brothers' Fino restaurant and its success is down to its mix of satisfyingly unfussy and authentic tapas and a buzzy atmosphere. Seafood is a speciality and the fish displays an exhilarating freshness; the Jabugo ham is also well worth trying. Four dishes per person is about par and the choice varies from razor clams a la plancha and tuna tartar to grilled chorizo and lamb sweetbreads with capers. Be sure to try one of the sherries.

It all centres around a counter, with seating for 20, so be prepared to talk to your neighbour. That's another thing that's never caught on in the capital.

Le Boudin Blanc

French

G4

5 Trebeck St W1J 7LT — ⊖ Green Park
(020) 7499 3292 **Fax** (020) 7495 6973
e-mail reservations@boudinblanc.co.uk **www**.boudinblanc.co.uk

Menu £15 (lunch) – Carte £28/48

Shepherd Market is true heart of Mayfair, as it was here that the original May fair was held before the area was developed in the 18C into the village-like quarter it is now. The atmosphere may be a little less licentious these days but there's still a certain breeziness in the air and Le Boudin Blanc brings along some Gallic joie de vivre. The place is always busy and there's seating for about 150 but the first floor is marginally less frantic.

The crowds are attracted by authentic and satisfying French classics, from snails and fish soup to confit of duck or beef tartare. Side orders can push up the final bill but there's a good value lunch and early evening menu. If you want more responsive service, try practising your French.

Bertorelli

13

Italian X

11-13 Frith St W1D 4RB ⊖ Tottenham Court Road
✆ (020) 7494 3491 **Fax** (020) 7439 9431 Closed 25-26 December
e-mail bertorelli-soho@groupechezgerard.co.uk
www.santeonline.co.uk

Carte £20/40

Bertorelli restaurants have been around for a while and they offer decent value for their unchallenging Italian food. This Frith Street outlet sits in the heart of Soho and usually has its doors thrown open and its narrow terrace fully occupied.

There's live music from Thursday to Saturday and the room is never less than lively, with the young staff getting more points for artistic impression than technical merit. Tables are quite small, unless you can grab one of the four booths. There's a separate bar upstairs.

They may be owned now by a chain but the word *mama* still appears on the menu to describe the provenance of some dishes. All points are covered, from pizza to pasta, and the cooking is perfectly sound and sensibly priced.

Imli

13

Indian X

167-169 Wardour St ⊖ Tottenham Court Road
W1F 8WR Closed 25 December and 1 January
✆ (020) 7287 4243 **Fax** (020) 7287 4245
e-mail info@imli.co.uk **www**.imli.co.uk

Menu £17 (dinner) – Carte £11/18

Imli comes courtesy of the people behind Tamarind and provides Soho regulars with an easy and accessible Indian restaurant, but one where the food is still prepared with care and attention.

The place may look simple, with paper mats and napkins, but they've clearly had the designers in and there is a certain slickness and sleekness to the room. But you don't come here to while away a whole evening - the atmosphere is pretty hectic and turnover can be swift, which in turn helps keep the prices down.

The menu is divided into three main sections: 'light and refreshing', 'new traditions' and 'signature dishes', with the emphasis firmly on sharing. Those who cannot decide for themselves can ask the kitchen to choose.

The Only Running Footman

H3 — British

5 Charles St. W1J 5DF — ⊖ Green Park
(020) 7499 2988 **Fax** (020) 7491 8162
e-mail info@therunningfootman.biz
www.therunningfootman.biz

Carte £22/30

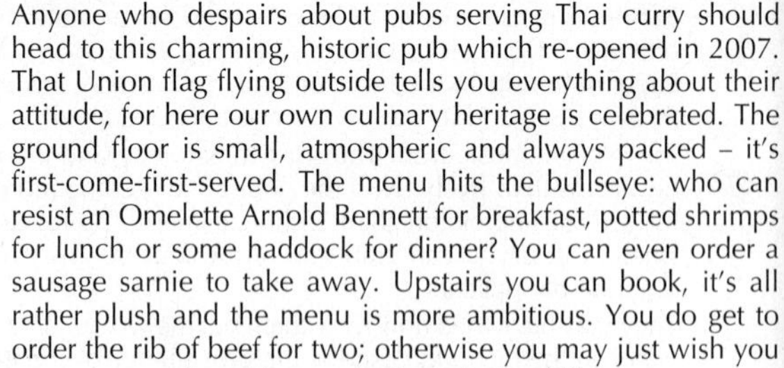

Anyone who despairs about pubs serving Thai curry should head to this charming, historic pub which re-opened in 2007. That Union flag flying outside tells you everything about their attitude, for here our own culinary heritage is celebrated. The ground floor is small, atmospheric and always packed – it's first-come-first-served. The menu hits the bullseye: who can resist an Omelette Arnold Bennett for breakfast, potted shrimps for lunch or some haddock for dinner? You can even order a sausage sarnie to take away. Upstairs you can book, it's all rather plush and the menu is more ambitious. You do get to order the rib of beef for two; otherwise you may just wish you were downstairs with a pork pie and piccalilli.

JUST PEACHY

The famous opera singer Dame Nellie Melba may have spent much of her time in London having dishes named after her, but in fact neither Melba Toast nor Pêche Melba were so called at first. Auguste Escoffier, then maître chef at London's Savoy Hotel, named the former after Marie Ritz, wife of Cesar, before Dame Nellie came to stay. The dessert - delivered to the diva with an ice sculpture of a swan - was originally called Pêche au Cygne.

D. Chapuis / MICHELIN

Strand · Covent Garden

Bang in the middle of theatreland, it's fair to say that **Covent Garden** has always had a flair for the dramatic. The **Royal Opera House** and the **Coliseum** both offer a huge range of opera and ballet, while the numerous theatres play everything from Greek tragedy to the latest musical. If that all sounds a bit too much like hard work then stroll down to **Leicester Square** to catch the latest blockbuster: the red carpets are rolled out for the big film openings most weekends if you fancy a bit of star spotting. If crowds aren't your thing then why not meander down to **Trafalgar Square** – you can take in a bit of art at the **National Gallery**, soak up the splendid vistas down **Whitehall** or simply cross the **Strand** to lean on the banks of the Thames and watch life go by.

The range of entertainment is matched by the dining options. You can large it up at one of the über-fashionable restaurants such as The Ivy on West Street, which has paparazzi permanently stationed outside to snap the latest starlet. Otherwise the streets are lined with eateries to suit every budget – it's worth looking out for special pre and post-theatre deals, specially designed for those in town to catch a show.

A little history...

Covent Garden started life as the kitchen garden to **Westminster Abbey**, pre-shadowing its development as London's most famous market, selling fruit and vegetables, as well as fresh flowers from all over the country. The Italianate piazza was developed in the early 17C by the Earl of Bedford. Given the area's theatrical bent it's little surprise that the designer Inigo Jones was not only a brilliant architect, instrumental in introducing the classical Palladian style to London, but also a talented painter and set builder who collaborated with Shakespeare and Ben Jonson on several court masques.

Although the market moved out to Battersea in the 1970s there are still plenty of reminders of Covent Garden's mercantile past. The covered market, right in the heart of the piazza, is a tempting warren of shops and stalls: in particular the **Apple Market** is devoted entirely to stalls selling everything from designer jewellery to hand-carved toys.

If you're interested in Covent Garden's showbiz past, then check out the often overlooked **St Paul's Church** on **Bedford Street**, better known as the actor's church because of its long association with the theatrical community. The inner walls and garden are lined with memorial plaques to famous personalities – from English lions such as the satirist Samuel Butler to Hollywood greats such as Vivien Leigh. But the drama of Covent Garden isn't confined to the past, nor always contained in the theatres – street performers are a common sight in the piazza, often drawing large crowds for an impromptu show.

The Strand was originally the main artery of London connecting the City and Westminster and is still a busy thoroughfare today. In medieval and Renaissance times it was also one of the most desirable addresses in London, lined with royal palaces whose grounds stretched right down to the river. Although most of these have now disappeared, the Palace of the Savoy lives on as the **Savoy Hotel**, home to many a celebrated visitor, including Oscar Wilde who took up residence at the hotel at the height of his career. **Somerset House**, formerly the registry for births, deaths and marriages, is another grand house that's well worth a visit: today it is home to collections from the Courtauld Institute of Art, acts as a popular venue for live music and in winter the fountain court is transformed into a stunning outdoor ice-rink.

While there are some extremely fine dining options on the Strand itself, if you're on a budget then you might find it worthwhile stepping off the beaten track and exploring some of the quieter streets leading down to the river. And there's no need to stop once you reach the water: boats moored off **Victoria Embankment** provide popular drinking spots and an excellent way to enjoy this vibrant area.

AGE / PHOTONONSTOP

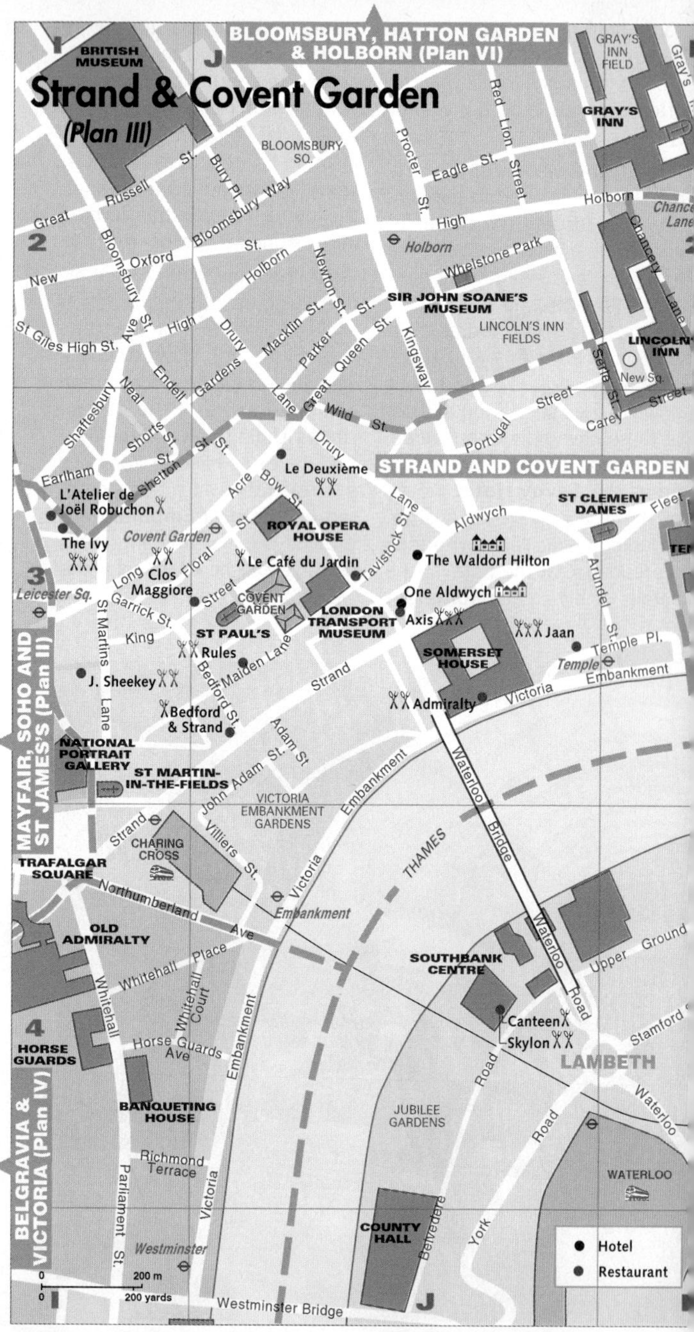
Strand & Covent Garden
(Plan III)
BLOOMSBURY, HATTON GARDEN & HOLBORN (Plan VI)
STRAND AND COVENT GARDEN
MAYFAIR, SOHO AND ST JAMES'S (Plan II)
BELGRAVIA & VICTORIA (Plan IV)
BRITISH MUSEUM
GRAY'S INN FIELD
GRAY'S INN
BLOOMSBURY SQ.
SIR JOHN SOANE'S MUSEUM
LINCOLN'S INN FIELDS
Holborn
Covent Garden
Leicester Sq.
Temple
Embankment
Westminster
Le Deuxième
L'Atelier de Joël Robuchon
The Ivy
Clos Maggiore
Le Café du Jardin
ROYAL OPERA HOUSE
The Waldorf Hilton
One Aldwych
Axis
Jaan
ST CLEMENT DANES
COVENT GARDEN
LONDON TRANSPORT MUSEUM
ST PAUL'S
Rules
J. Sheekey
SOMERSET HOUSE
Admiralty
Bedford & Strand
NATIONAL PORTRAIT GALLERY
ST MARTIN-IN-THE-FIELDS
VICTORIA EMBANKMENT GARDENS
CHARING CROSS
TRAFALGAR SQUARE
THAMES
OLD ADMIRALTY
SOUTHBANK CENTRE
Canteen
Skylon
LAMBETH
HORSE GUARDS
BANQUETING HOUSE
JUBILEE GARDENS
WATERLOO
COUNTY HALL
Hotel
Restaurant
200 m
200 yards

Jaan

Innovative XXX

J3

at Swissôtel The Howard,
Temple Pl WC2R 2PR
(020) 7300 1700 **Fax** (020) 7240 7816
e-mail jaan.london@swissotel.com **www**.swissotel-london.com

⊖ Temple
Closed Saturday lunch, Sunday and bank holidays

Menu £24/38 - Carte £33/49

A/C VISA MC AE

Jaan takes modern French and European cooking and gives it the odd little Asian tweak here and there. The chef certainly comes up with some original dishes so expect red mullet and lobster with coco bean and coconut, caramel coated duck with green tea noodle and, to finish, lychee jelly with mango mousse. The kitchen clearly knows its butchery but there can be a tendency towards over elaboration and perhaps one flavour too far. However, vegetarians will find themselves with something a little different and the Business Lunch is good value, especially in this area.

The restaurant is on the ground floor of the Swissôtel Howard Hotel and what the room lacks in personality it makes up in enthusiastic service and a delightful terrace.

Axis

Modern European XXX

J3

1 Aldwych WC2B 4RH
(020) 7300 0300
Fax (020) 7300 0301
e-mail axis@onealdwych.com **www**.onealdwych.co.uk

⊖ Covent Garden
Closed 24 December-4 January, Easter, Sunday, Saturday lunch and Bank Holidays

Menu £18 - Carte £28/37

A/C VISA MC AE

Axis belongs to One Aldwych Hotel but is marketed as a separate entity and is helped considerably in this by having its own street entrance. You descend spirally from the reception and bar area and come out into a double height space with a vast futuristic mural on one wall and lots of curves and pillars. Noise levels can be a little full-on, especially if there's a large table of business types in from the hotel, but there are quieter sections. The menu offers an unthreatening selection of assorted European-influenced food, with a grill section for those who prefer to keep things simple.

Its proximity to a number of theatres and the popularity of its pre-theatre menus means that the restaurant is already jumping by early evening.

The Ivy

International XXX

13

1-5 West St WC2H 9NQ
(020) 7836 4751
Fax (020) 7240 9333
www.the-ivy.co.uk

⊖ Leicester Square
Closed 24-26 December, 1 January and August Bank Holiday

Carte £30/54

If celebrity is indeed the currency of our age, then this is the Bank of England. On any given day it will have more than its share of those whose business is show, while the snappers will be outside hoping to catch someone with someone else.

However, it would be unfair to class it as merely a glitterati hang-out, for it remains one of the best run restaurants around, with that reassuring hum one finds when the service is choreographed with precision and élan. The menu too has a satisfying balance to appeal to all tastes and appetites with everything from eggs Benedict to foie gras. An actor once said "fame means nothing except a good table in a restaurant"; we mere mortals may find getting in a rather more challenging experience.

J. Sheekey

Seafood XX

13

28-32 St Martin's Court
WC2N 4AL
(020) 7240 2565
Fax (020) 7497 0891
e-mail reservations@j-sheekey.co.uk
www.j-sheeky.co.uk

⊖ Leicester Square
Closed 25-26 December, 1 January and August Bank Holiday – booking essential

Carte £25/51

When one thinks of fashionable restaurants one usually thinks of the glossy and the new but J. Sheekey has been doing its thing since 1896 and its sense of Englishness and links to the theatre still draw a crowd. It helps that they also do fish and seafood rather well, by keeping it all simple. The reassuring sight of potted shrimps, fruits de mer, fishcakes, fish pies and Dover Sole all feature and can be followed by uncomplicated fruit tarts or chocolate puddings so you leave feeling immeasurably satisfied, although a little lighter in the wallet.

There are five sections and if you're a regular or your name's been up in lights, the more choice of table you'll have. Those tables are compact but that just adds to the bonhomie.

Rules

British XX

J3

35 Maiden Lane WC2E 7LB
⊖ Leicester Square
✆ (020) 7836 5314
Closed 4 days Christmas – booking essential
Fax (020) 7497 1081
e-mail info@rules.co.uk **www**.rules.co.uk

Carte £35/53

Such is the transient nature of restaurants that anywhere over 15 years old is referred to as 'well-established'. Rules opened its doors in 1798 and, as London's oldest restaurant, is fully entitled to look down on all those johnny-come-lately's.

It is simply bursting with character and history and its quintessential Englishness is something to behold. Every inch of wall is covered with paintings, cartoons and drawings and its customers, from Charles Dickens to Charlie Chaplin, have always been drawn from the literary and theatrical worlds.

The cooking too celebrates the best of British by specialising in game, often from its own estate on the Pennines, so this is the place for grouse, partridge and pheasant or a great steak and kidney pie.

Clos Maggiore

French XX

I3

33 King St WC2 8JD
⊖ Leicester Square
✆ (020) 7379 9696
Closed 25-26 December, Saturday and Sunday lunch and Bank Holidays
Fax (020) 7379 6767
e-mail enquiries@closmaggiore.com
www.closmaggiore.com

Menu £20 (lunch) – Carte £46/56

Those wanting something more than a stale slice of overpriced pizza have always found Covent Garden to be a little challenging in the restaurant stakes. Fortunately, Clos Maggiore proves that good food and tourist attractions are not always mutually exclusive.

The place certainly has charm and the blossom hanging everywhere adds a romantic touch. The glowing fire warms the winter evenings, while in summer ask for a table in the back room where the glass roof opens.

The menu reads like a Frenchman who lives in the countryside but still likes to travel. The cooking is grounded in sound culinary techniques but occasionally slips in a contemporary twist. Wine here is clearly taken seriously and the list certainly merits careful exploration.

Admiralty

J3

French XX

Somerset House, The Strand WC2R 1LA
(020) 7845 4646
Fax (020) 7845 4658
e-mail info@theadmiraltyrestaurant.com
www.theadmiraltyrestaurant.com

⊖ Temple
Closed 24-27 December, dinner Sunday and Bank Holiday Mondays

Menu £16 – Carte £26/37

VISA MC AE D

There are any number of reasons to visit the magnificent 18C Somerset House, one of them being the restaurant in the south building. The Admiralty acknowledges the palace's link with the Royal Navy in its name and in the ship-shaped chandeliers hanging in the two rooms into which the restaurant is divided. The high ceiling and arched windows ensure plenty of light, although it's a shame the river-side outside terrace is a separate operation. The kitchen has adopted more of a French brasserie style menu these days, with soups, rillettes and terrines featuring alongside some fairly robust main courses like duck confit.

The atmosphere is far more typical of this side of the Channel, thanks to the discreet and well mannered clientele.

Le Deuxième

J3

Modern European XX

65a Long Acre WC2E 9JH
(020) 7379 0033 **Fax** (020) 7379 0066
www.ledeuxieme.com

⊖ Covent Garden
Closed 24-25 December

Menu £16 – Carte £29/30

A/C VISA MC AE

Depending on which direction you've come from, this is either the first, or the last, restaurant in Covent Garden. Either way, it's a world away from the plethora of tourist joints which cover the surrounding streets. For a start, the service is enthusiastic, while the room has a warmth and an unthreatening neutrality. The cooking is also above this neighbourhood's norms. Lunch and pre-theatre menus are a steal and come with sufficient choice. The à la carte, meanwhile, offers a balanced and comprehensive choice -whilst there may be the occasional Asian note, the thrust remains within Europe, with a Franco-Italian emphasis. Expect risotto, gnocchi, foie gras and lemon tart. It shares the same owners as Le Café du Jardin.

L'Atelier de Joël Robuchon ✿

French

13

13-15 West St WC2H 9NE ⊖ Leicester Square
(020) 7010 8600 **Fax** (020) 7010 8601
e-mail info@joelrobuchon.co.uk **www**.joel-robuchon.com

Carte £33/75

L'Atelier de Joël Robuchon

Joël Robuchon's London branch has bedded in effortlessly well. The charming hostesses by the reception show how a warm smile can work wonders and they'll direct you to one of the two restaurants housed in the building. L'Atelier on the ground floor is mostly counter seating with a menu made up of small tasting plates. Upstairs you'll find La Cuisine which is more of a structured operation but still agreeably informal. Here, the menu is more your standard-three-courses, unless you opt for the tasting menu which comes along at a steady pace and gives you a rounded experience of Robuchon's classic repertoire. The black and white décor also contrasts nicely with the colour of the ground floor.

The dishes are poised, delicate and precise and there are thirty-six chefs in the building-most of whom are on view- to ensure the quality remains consistent. French is the major influence but Spain and Italy also feature and there is a clarity, freshness and vitality to all the flavours as well as pleasing textural contrasts.

It may be a world-wide brand but each city has its own idiosyncrasies –the no-booking policy never works in London so it has been scrapped.

First Course

- Fresh mackerel tart with parmesan shavings and olives.
- Egg cocotte topped wth wild mushroom cream.

Main Course

- Free range quail stuffed with foie gras, truffled mashed potatoes.
- Lamb cutlets with fresh thyme.

Dessert

- Araguani chocolate, white chocolate ice cream and Oreo cookie.
- Iced strawberry lollipop, mulled wine marinated cherries.

Le Café du Jardin

J3 **French**

28 Wellington St WC2E 7BD
(020) 7836 8769 **Fax** (020) 7836 4123
e-mail info@lecafedujardin.com **www**.lecafedujardin.com

⊖ Covent Garden
Closed 25-26 December

Menu £16 – Carte £28/34

At around 7.15pm there'll be a flurry of activity, as theatre-goers check the time and all ask for their bills simultaneously. To the outsider this may look like your classic tourist trap found in all theatre districts, with tables being forever pushed together or pulled apart and a 15% service charge added to bills. However, those who have more time and are tempted by the *à la carte* menu will find the cooking undertaken with more skill and care than they expect, accompanied by a thoughtful and considered wine list.

The basement level is the more spacious but the glass framed ground floor is where you'll find most of the action and is clearly the more popular. The staff all work hard to justify that added service charge.

Great Queen Street

J2 **British**

32 Great Queen St WC2B 5AA
(020) 7242 0622
Fax (020) 7404 9582

⊖ Holborn
▶ **Plan VI**
Closed Monday lunch and Sunday – booking essential

Carte £20/30

You can be sure that a team garnered from the Anchor & Hope and St John will know what they're doing and, sure enough, Great Queen Street is doing all the right things. Just about the only sign outside that this is a restaurant is the daily menu posted in the window; the inside is all about pared-down simplicity.

The menu is also a model of understatement; written simply as 'charcuterie and figs', 'potted shrimps' or 'venison pie', the cooking is full-bodied, confident and satisfying and at prices that are laudably low. Dishes such as rib of Hereford beef and seven hour shoulder of lamb are made for sharing and puds like caramel custard continue the British theme. It's always packed, gets very noisy and the amiable service can sometimes struggle to keep up.

Bedford & Strand

Traditional

J3

1a Bedford St WC2E 9HH
(020) 7836 3033
www.bedford-strand.com

Charing Cross
Closed 25-26 and 31 December, 1 January, Saturday lunch, Sunday and Bank Holidays – booking essential

Menu £16 – Carte £24/53

They call themselves a 'wine room and bistro' which neatly sums up both the philosophy and the style of the place - interesting wines, reassuringly familiar food and relaxed surroundings. It's named, American-style, after the cross streets so it's easy to find and the basement location shouldn't be off-putting. The after-work crowd have largely dispersed by 8ish in the evening but it all remains fairly energetic, helped along by a bright and sprightly team. British and Mediterranean comfort food is the feature of the menu, with a choice ranging from fish soup and risotto to cottage pie, with classic deli food served at the bar.

The wine list has been thoughtfully put together and comes accompanied by some sensible pricing.

A PINT OF THE HARD STUFF

At over 300 years old, the Lamb & Flag on Rose Street is the oldest pub in Covent Garden and a great, if busy, place to sup a pint. However, former names hint at a more violent past. The pub used to be known as the Bucket of Blood because of the bare-knuckled fights held there; while the upstairs Dryden room commemorates the poet laureate who, in 1679, was beaten up outside for writing a satire on the king's mistress.

Belgravia · Victoria

Central' is a good word to describe this area. The gentle stucco and harmonious greys of **Belgravia** belie its status as the diplomatic heart of London, with embassies from all over the world lining the streets and squares. While if you follow **Victoria Street** down to **Parliament Square** you're right in the centre of political life in London, and indeed the whole country.

The transport hubs of **Victoria Station** and **Coach Station** provide easy access from airports and mean that Victoria is often the first port of call for visitors to London. **Buckingham Palace**, the queen's official residence, and the "royal peculiar" **Westminster Abbey** are obvious draws for the crowd. Unsurprisingly there are plenty of serviceable eateries and an embarrassment of hotels to cater for the tourists, but step off the well-worn trails and you can enjoy a touch of old world gentility among the cobbled mews and gracious townhouses of Belgravia. As you might expect from such an upmarket area there are a number of excellent restaurants modestly located on the quiet streets. If that's a little tame for your tastes you can always venture down to Westminster, take in the views that Turner and Monet painted, and indulge in gossip with the politicians and hacks at any of the surrounding pubs – all within hearing of the **House of Common's** division bell.

A little history...

The area of Belgravia takes its name from Belgrave Square, which was laid out in the 19C by Thomas Cubitt, at the time London's most prolific builder and developer, and a man with a keen eye for a bargain. A little misleadingly the square is actually named after a village in Cheshire, which forms one of the secondary titles of the landlord, the Duke of Westminster.

Belgravia has been at the cutting edge of fashionable London since it was developed by Cubitt and there's no sign of it slipping off the radar yet. The lavishly porticoed townhouses that now account for some of the most expensive real estate anywhere in the world were originally designed to be the London bases for moneyed families coming to town for "the season". Today the area is relatively quiet but still gently reeking of money. Famous residents include Baroness Thatcher, the actress Joan Collins and Ian Fleming – the creator of James Bond. In many ways the area can be said to perfectly represent the suave secret agent – urbane, impeccably turned out and with an eye for the finer things in life. As you might expect, the shops here are aimed at the high end of the market with exclusive designer boutiques nuzzling up to wallet-busting antiques and interior shops. However, it's not all objets d'art

– even the rich have to eat, and **Elizabeth Street** in particular offers a mouth-watering series of treats for the dedicated gourmet. Stand out shops include the wine and cheese merchants **Jereboams**, bakers **Poilane** and **Baker & Spicer** will cater for all your carbs, greengrocer extraordinaire **Mash** boasts of being a specialist in fruit baskets, while the **Chocolate Society** offers its customers something a little more indulgent.

If Belgravia is notable for its harmonious lines and muted, neutral palate, the same cannot be said of Victoria. The best way to describe the bustling hub of **Victoria Street** is chaotic – both for the volume of traffic and people, and for the jumble of architectural styles. The Victorian mass of the station gives way to the neo-Byzantine façade of **Westminster Cathedral** – then further down to the medieval **Westminster Abbey**, and Pugin's neo-gothic **Houses of Parliament**. However, despite this mish-mash, its proximity to the so-called Westminster Village gives Victoria an undeniable buzz.

If politics is not your thing then take a stroll down the river to Pimlico and **Tate Britain,** which houses the greatest collection of British art in the world. From there you can hop onto the popular ferry service, which uses a specially decorated Damien Hirst boat and goes between the Tate and its younger sister, the **Tate Modern** on **Bankside**.

visitlondon.com / MICHELIN

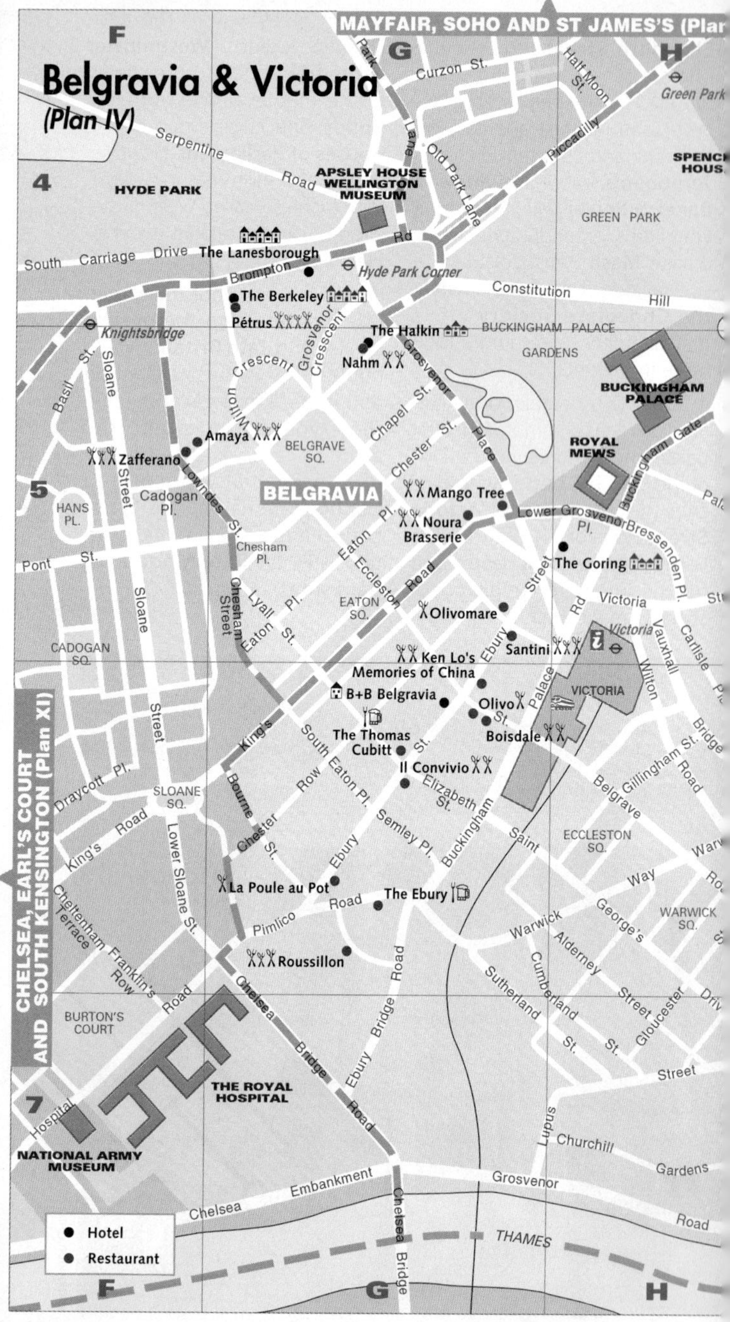
Belgravia & Victoria
(Plan IV)
MAYFAIR, SOHO AND ST JAMES'S (Plan
HYDE PARK
APSLEY HOUSE WELLINGTON MUSEUM
GREEN PARK
The Lanesborough
The Berkeley
Pétrus
The Halkin
Nahm
BUCKINGHAM PALACE GARDENS
BUCKINGHAM PALACE
ROYAL MEWS
Amaya
Zafferano
BELGRAVE SQ.
BELGRAVIA
Mango Tree
Noura Brasserie
The Goring
Olivomare
Santini
Ken Lo's Memories of China
B+B Belgravia
Olivo
The Thomas Cubitt
Boisdale
Il Convivio
VICTORIA
CADOGAN SQ.
SLOANE SQ.
ECCLESTON SQ.
WARWICK SQ.
La Poule au Pot
The Ebury
Roussillon
CHELSEA, EARL'S COURT AND SOUTH KENSINGTON (Plan XI)
BURTON'S COURT
THE ROYAL HOSPITAL
NATIONAL ARMY MUSEUM
THAMES
Hotel
Restaurant

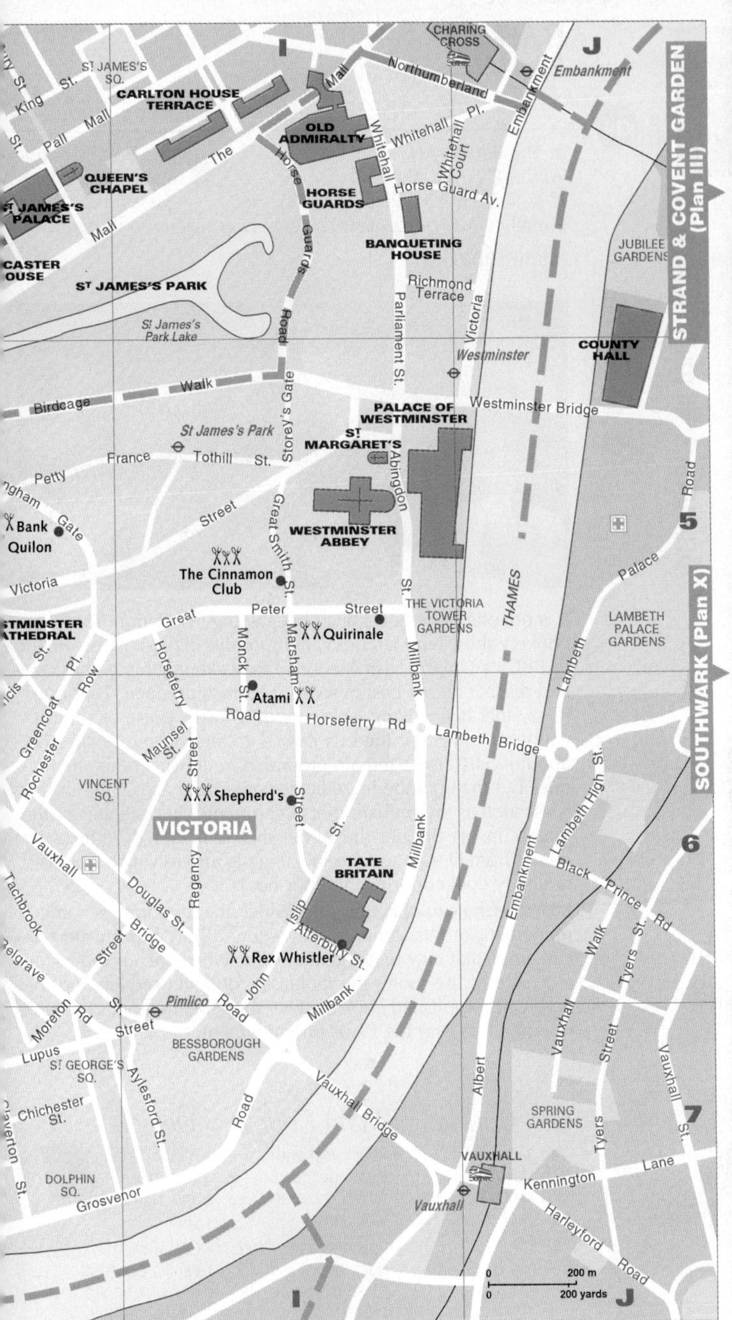
CHARING CROSS
Embankment
ST JAMES'S SQ.
CARLTON HOUSE TERRACE
OLD ADMIRALTY
QUEEN'S CHAPEL
ST JAMES'S PALACE
HORSE GUARDS
BANQUETING HOUSE
ST JAMES'S PARK
St James's Park Lake
STRAND & COVENT GARDEN (Plan III)
JUBILEE GARDENS
COUNTY HALL
Westminster
PALACE OF WESTMINSTER
St James's Park
ST MARGARET'S
WESTMINSTER ABBEY
Bank
Quilon
The Cinnamon Club
Quirinale
Atami
THE VICTORIA TOWER GARDENS
THAMES
LAMBETH PALACE GARDENS
SOUTHWARK (Plan X)
Shepherd's
VINCENT SQ.
VICTORIA
TATE BRITAIN
Rex Whistler
Pimlico
BESSBOROUGH GARDENS
ST GEORGE'S SQ.
SPRING GARDENS
VAUXHALL
Vauxhall
DOLPHIN SQ.
200 m
200 yards

Pétrus ✿✿

G4

French XXXX

at The Berkeley H.,
Wilton Pl SW1X 7RL
✆ (020) 7235 1200 **Fax** (020) 7235 1266
e-mail petrus@marcuswareing.com **www**.marcuswareing.com

⊖ Knightsbridge
Closed 1 week Christmas, Sunday and lunch Saturday

Menu £30/65

Gordon Ramsay Holdings

It is not often one hears of a chef gaining inspiration from a TV cookery show but Marcus Wareing credits his own involvement in BBC2's Great British Menu for reawakening his enthusiasm and respect for the best in seasonal British produce. That is not to say that his cooking lacks any of its usual poise or sophistication; it's just that there is now a greater degree of sincerity about it. His dishes remain grounded in classic French techniques but many of the ingredients come from across the British Isles, such as the rhubarb that accompanies his foie gras or the lobster in his bisque; the turbot that is matched with caviar comes from Dorset and the suckling pig arrives via Norfolk and is slowly cooked for twenty-four hours.

Like the Chateau of Pétrus, after which the restaurant is named, refinement of this standard may equal a lofty bill but no one can argue that they're not getting value when one considers the elegance of the room, the faultlessly obliging service and the highly accomplished cooking. Ever more heartening is the lack of pomposity and the focus on enjoyment.

First Course

- Crab, langoustine and brown shrimp with avocado purée and smoked paprika crouton.
- Breast of quail with Cumbrian bacon.

Main Course

- Roast veal with asparagus, courgette flower salad and veal vinaigrette.
- Poached and glazed duck breast with toasted sesame seeds.

Dessert

- Almond panna cotta with glazed apricots and tonka bean ice cream.
- Custard tart with vanilla poached rhubarb, vanilla ice cream.

Zafferano ✿

Italian ✗✗✗

F5

15 Lowndes St SW1X 9EY
✆ (020) 7235 5800
Fax (020) 7235 1971
www.zafferanorestaurant.com

⊖ Knightsbridge
Closed Christmas-New Year and Bank Holiday lunches

Menu £30/40

Zafferano

The expansion into next door in 2005 not only made this a much nicer and brighter restaurant but is also energised the whole place and gave the kitchen renewed vigour. The sign of any skilled practitioner, whether sportsman, actor or chef, is to make the thing they do appear easy; the cooking here, like much Italian cooking, may look relatively simple on the plate but that simplicity belies the depth of knowledge and real understanding of the ingredients involved. The absolute freshness of those ingredients is a given, the home-made pasta is a real strength and much of the produce can now be bought at their adjacent deli which brings new meaning to the idea of 'takeaway'.

Service is also more enthusiastic and the Mediterranean colours of the room are guaranteed to add a bit of brightness to anyone's day. This is a restaurant with plenty of regulars, some of whom no doubt still insist on their same table, but what they do add is a feeling of togetherness and mutual respect that few restaurants manage to achieve.

First Course

- Linguini with lobster.
- Pan-fried scallops and prawns with saffron vinaigrette.

Main Course

- Salt Marsh lamb with garlic purée and taggiasca olives.
- Chargrilled monkfish with courgettes and sweet chilli.

Dessert

- Fig and almond tart with vanilla ice cream.
- Tiramisu.

Amaya ✿

F5 **Indian** XXX

Halkin Arcade, 19 Motcomb St
SW1X 8JT
⊖ Knightsbridge
(020) 7823 1166 **Fax** (020) 7259 6464
e-mail info@realindianfood.com **www**.realindianfood.com

Menu £16/36 – Carte £37/46

Amaya

Grills and kebabs are the speciality of the house at Amaya, which styles itself a 'bar and grill' and is a decidedly different Indian restaurant. Here, the bigger your party, the better, as the idea is to order a selection of small dishes to share and then finish off with a biryani or curry. The subtly spiced, tender and aromatic kebabs and grills arrive in no particularly order - to ensure they're piping hot - and you'll quickly get into the rhythm. The set menus are perhaps the best way to experience the chef's expertise.

The multi-national staff are all perfectly familiar with the dishes and they offer sensible and helpful advice to those who ask. They are also an enthusiastic bunch which keeps things light. The room is an unusual shape – this was once three boutiques in an otherwise non-descript 'arcade' – with the odd splash of colour. The best tables are in the raised section under the glass roof, where you get a bit of theatre by watching the chefs at their griddle, grill and tandoor stations. There's a large table by the bar for those who arrive without reservations.

First Course

- Scallops griddled and served in a green herb sauce.
- Tandoori smoked chicken tikka with cloves.

Main Course

- Grilled lamb chops with ginger, lime and coriander.
- Kerala chicken curry with star anise, aniseed and coconut.

Dessert

- Lime tart with lime jelly and blueberry compote.
- Grilled mango.

Quilon ✿

Indian XXX

H5

at Crowne Plaza London - St James H.,
41 Buckingham Gate SW1E 6AF
✆ (020) 7821 1899 **Fax** (020) 7233 9597
e-mail info@quilonrestaurant.co.uk **www**.quilon.co.uk

⊖ Victoria
Closed 25 December and Saturday lunch

Menu £18 (lunch) – Carte £34/47

Michelin

The kitchen at Quilon has continued to evolve and develop to the point where it is now responsible for some of the best Indian cooking around. The name refers to the port on the South West coast of India and it is from here that many of the dishes originate, such as masala dosa or tilapia fish wrapped in banana leaf. Indian cooking is just as open to interpretation as any other cuisine, however, and the kitchen is not afraid of a little originality and self expression. All of the cooking, though, displays the chef's enthusiasm for his craft; his dishes are vibrant and balanced, and his seafood specialities are particularly appealing. Spicing is subtle and even handed and the spice room in the kitchen is enormous. Vegetarians will find themselves in clover and there is a bread station in the dining room ensuring not only plentiful, cooked-to-order supplies but also imbuing the room with a wonderful aroma. The staff exhibit a certain gracefulness and have obvious and understandable pride in their restaurant.

First Course

- Crab cakes with curry leaves, ginger and green chillies.
- Fried cauliflower florets tossed with yoghurt.

Main Course

- Chargrilled lobster, prawn, fish and scallops with a mild sauce.
- Spiced black cod.

Dessert

- Spiced chocolate dessert.
- Almond delight.

Santini

G5

Italian XXX

29 Ebury St SW1W 0NZ ⊖ Victoria
✆ (020) 7730 4094 **Fax** (020) 7730 0544
e-mail info@santini-restaurant.com **www**.santini-restaurant.com

Carte £35/55

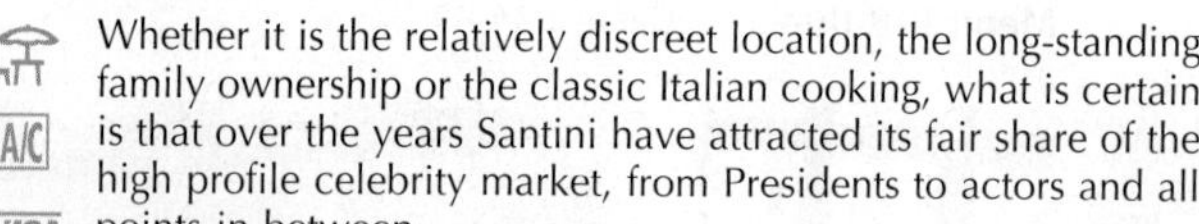

Whether it is the relatively discreet location, the long-standing family ownership or the classic Italian cooking, what is certain is that over the years Santini have attracted its fair share of the high profile celebrity market, from Presidents to actors and all points in between.

The décor is sleek and understated and the service formal and deliberate. A pretty foliage-fringed terrace provides a pleasant spot for alfresco dining for those unafraid or unlikely to be troubled by passing admirers.

The menu keeps it classic with a subtle Venetian accent and the focus rightly falls on the quality of the ingredients. Those whose ambition outweighs their wallet should try the more reasonably priced pre-theatre menu.

The Cinnamon Club

I5

Indian XXX

30-32 Great Smith St ⊖ St James's Park
SW1P 3BU Closed Sunday
✆ (020) 7222 2555 **Fax** (020) 7222 1333
e-mail info@cinnamonclub.com **www**.cinnamonclub.com

Menu £22 – Carte £35/48

Housed within the century old Grade II listed former Westminster Library one finds this stylish and very comfortable Indian restaurant. The main dining room has many of the original features, including the mezzanine floor and parquet flooring, while the bars are certainly worthy of exploration – one is quieter as it's the former reference room of the library and the other screens scenes from Bollywood films. The place has a lively and convivial ambience and provides perfect revenge for anyone who has been shushed in a library. Appropriately, it really does feel clubby.

The kitchen imports many of its ingredients from India but uses modern European techniques to create original and colourful specialities with more than a hint of personality

Shepherd's

British XXX

16

Marsham Court, Marsham St SW1P 4LA
✆ (020) 7834 9552
Fax (020) 7233 6047
e-mail admin@langansrestaurants.co.uk
www.langansrestaurants.co.uk

⊖ Pimlico
Closed Saturday, Sunday and Bank Holidays – booking essential

Menu £33

A good lunch at Shepherd's may explain the apparent somnolent poses of some of our politicians in afternoon debates. This is very much a favoured dining room of the Westminster crowd, who are no doubt attracted by its clubby feel, the degree of privacy offered and the type of cooking that'll gladden the heart of your average Eurosceptic. The set menu lists a veritable who's who of popular British classics, from potted shrimps and Dover sole to rib of beef and calves liver and bacon, supplemented by some brasserie favourites. The service is effortlessly smooth from the well-versed team.

Those seeking a definition of Britishness in all its glory, from food to customer, need look no further.

Quirinale

Italian XX

15

North Court, 1 Great Peter St
SW1P 3LL
✆ (020) 7222 7080 **Fax** (020) 7233 3080
e-mail info@quirinale.co.uk **www**.quirinale.co.uk

⊖ Westminster
Closed August, 1week Christmas, Saturday and Sunday

Carte £28/38

Named after one of the Seven Hills of Rome where the Italian head of state resides, Quirinale lies in the shadow of Parliament. It's easy to miss as the discreet entrance is tucked inside a mansion block entrance. Descend the wide tiled staircase and you'll find yourself in a surprisingly bright and contemporary styled restaurant, where the service is scrupulously slick and the atmosphere discreet.

The chef hails from Brescia but his seasonally-changing menu is all-encompassing, with a few more Sicilian and Neapolitan touches. Pastas are home-made, cooking shows a light touch and the wine list covers all parts. There's a large selection of cheeses that are worth exploring, all sourced from small, artisan suppliers.

Roussillon ✿

G6 — **French** XXX

16 St Barnabas St SW1W 8PE — ⊖ Sloane Square
(020) 7730 5550 — Closed Saturday lunch and Sunday
Fax (020) 7824 8617
e-mail alexis@roussillon.co.uk **www**.roussillon.co.uk

Menu £35/55

VISA

AE

Roussillon

Sourcing and seasonality sum up the philosophy of Roussillon and there's a lesson here for all chefs about the importance of using the best possible produce at the optimum moment. What makes eating here such a pleasure is that chef Alex Gauthier puts as much thought and care into the vegetables as has gone into procuring the meat and fish and, indeed, there is even a vegetable menu that shows how the best of ingredients taste truly of themselves.

As the name suggests, there is a distinct French flavour to the cooking but the rules are universal – don't muck about with the ingredients too much. There is a gracefulness to the cooking but some dishes can also pack quite a punch. The wine list also celebrates Roussillon, Languedoc and the South West of France, as well as Italy and the Old World, but consider also the thoughtfully chosen wine pairings by the glass.

The restaurant has a pleasing neighbourhood feel and has built a loyal following over ten years. The low ceiling adds to the intimacy and the veg-themed art adds some colour.

First Course

- Black truffle risotto, veal jus.
- Steamed sea kale with scallops, langoustine, red chard and hollandaise.

Main Course

- Highland venison with pumpkin, poached pear and celeriac, truffle purée.
- Wild sea bass with cos lettuce, girolle and chanterelles, baby onions.

Dessert

- Louis XV, crunchy praline and chocolate.
- Grand Marnier soufflé with cherry and balsamic infusion.

Nahm ✿

Thai XX

G5

at The Halkin H.,
5 Halkin St SW1X 7DJ
(020) 7333 1234
Fax (020) 7333 1100
e-mail res@nahm.como.bz **www**.halkin.como.bz

Hyde Park Corner
Closed Christmas, Easter, lunch Saturday-Sunday, and Bank Holidays – booking essential

Menu £26/55 - Carte £37/39

Nahm

Nahm is the vision of Australian chef David Thompson and is located within the stylish Halkin Hotel which was one of London's first boutique hotels. Here he presents Thai food based on Royal traditions but also uses some of Britain's best ingredients like game and seafood. His cooking is sophisticated yet easy to eat and showcases the wonderful harmony of Thai cooking that is achieved through combinations of countered and balanced textures and contrasting flavours. The waiting staff are more than willing to offer explanations of the various dishes and advice on the right balance when ordering. The easiest way remains the nahm arharn banquet meal which hands responsibility over to the kitchen. Just be prepared for when the dishes arrive virtually all together. At lunch, there is a simpler single plate style of cooking, based more on the traditions of street food but still carefully prepared.
The room is comfortable and discreet and is decorated with plenty of shiny marble but the drapes do soften it all.

First Course

- Crispy noodles with Asian citron.
- Salad of poached prawns with banana blossoms.

Main Course

- Green curry of crisp sea bass with wild ginger, coconut and pea.
- Stir-fry beef with chilli paste and dried prawns.

Dessert

- Fresh Thai fruits
- Rice dumplings with coconut cream and sesame seed cakes.

Atami

I6 **Japanese** XX

37 Monck St (entrance on Great Peter St) ⊖ Pimlico
SW1P 2BL Closed Saturday lunch and Sunday
✆ (020) 7222 2218 **Fax** (020) 7222 2788
e-mail mail@atami-restaurant.com **www**.atami-restaurant.com

Menu £23 (lunch) – Carte £25/37

A/C VISA MC AE

Named after one of Japan's best known hot spring resorts, Atami is the latest in a line of stylishly decorated Japanese restaurants that have proved very popular over the last few years by mixing the traditional with the decidedly contemporary. The difference is that here prices are a little more down to earth.

The serving team offer the novice expert guidance around the menu and, alongside the *sushi* and *sashimi*, expect to find ingredients of a more European provenance, paired in some unexpected yet delicate combinations.

Bamboo, leather, mirrors, glass and natural woods combine to create a sensual and striking space, illuminated by four large ceiling orbs. The bar is tucked away discreetly but is equally appealing and strangely calming.

Il Convivio

G6 **Italian** XX

143 Ebury St SW1W 9QN ⊖ Sloane Square
✆ (020) 7730 4099 Closed 25 December and Sunday
Fax (020) 7730 4103
e-mail comments@etruscarestaurants.com
www.etruscarestaurants.com

Menu £22 (lunch) – Carte £34

A/C VISA MC AE

You know you're in a serious Italian restaurant when the autumnal truffle season produces specialities on the menu featuring the white truffle - tartufo bianco, the king of truffles. Indeed, there's no denying the quality of the produce here, whether it's the milk-fed lamb, Angus beef or wild sea bass. Pasta is also something of a house speciality and any of the half-dozen choices can be taken as a starter, middle or main course.

Found within an attractive Georgian house, the poet Dante is celebrated in the name and the decoration of the restaurant and lines of his poetry are embossed on the wall. The best place to sit is either at the front, overlooking the street, or right at the back under the retractable roof.

Rex Whistler

British XX

I6

Tate Britain, Millbank SW1P 4RG — ⊖ Pimlico
✆ (020) 7887 8825 — Closed 25 December
Fax (020) 7887 8902 — – booking essential – lunch only
e-mail tate.restaurant@tate.org.uk **www**.tate.org.uk

Carte £31/38

The restaurant may be in the basement of Tate Britain but the views are better than most thanks to the specially commissioned mural by Rex Whistler, "The Expedition in Pursuit of Rare Meats", painted in 1927. It is also a highly civilised haven of tranquillity, in comparison to the more frantic pace found in the neighbouring café.

Just as upstairs celebrates English artists, downstairs does its bit by using mostly home-grown ingredients and offers a choice of both modern British as well as European specialities. The wine list is hugely impressive thanks to the restaurant history of cellaring wine for over thirty years. Commendably, it also offers over sixty half bottles for those wishing to make use of the afternoon.

Ken Lo's Memories of China

Chinese XX

G6

65-69 Ebury St SW1W 0NZ — ⊖ Victoria
✆ (020) 7730 7734 — Closed 25-26 December,
Fax (020) 7730 2992 — Sunday lunch and Bank Holidays
www.memories-of-china.co.uk

Menu £19/30 - Carte £29/35

The restaurant may have changed hands over the years but the late Ken Lo was responsible for putting the place on the map all those years ago and so it's appropriate to find his name still in the title. The restaurant belies its age in its looks. It is bright, modern and quite minimalist in its design but also manages to be warm and welcoming. Chinese script, lattice panels and well dressed tables ensure a sense of comfort and style.

The length of the menu can appear a little bewildering, as can the seemingly eccentric numbering system, but the dishes come carefully prepared. The set menus are often the easier option and take you on a gastronomic tour of China. Service is positive, well marshalled and clued-up.

Boisdale

Scottish XX

G6

15 Eccleston St SW1W 9LX
Victoria
(020) 7730 6922
Closed Christmas and Sunday
Fax (020) 7730 0548
e-mail info@boisdale.co.uk **www**.boisdale.co.uk

Carte £29/48

Those waiting for the day when a Scottish Embassy opens in London can more than make do with Boisdale, for they will be unlikely to find anywhere, outside of Scotland, more Scottish than this. The owner is a proud Macdonald and the Macdonald tartan is everywhere, along with a plethora of prints and paintings. The menu showcases the best of Scotland's fine produce from salmon to game and matured beef.

There is a choice of dining room within this charming Regency town house, from the clubby atmosphere of the Macdonald Bar to the more formal and demure surroundings of the Auld restaurant. In summer the retractable roof makes the Courtyard Garden a popular choice. The one element to break from all things Scottish is the nightly jazz band.

Mango Tree

Thai XX

G5

46 Grosvenor Pl SW1 7EQ
Victoria
(020) 7823 1888
Closed 24-26 December and 1 January
Fax (020) 7838 9275
e-mail info@mangotree.org.uk
www.mangotree.org.uk

Menu £18/40 – Carte £23/51

The mango may be one of the best known of tropical fruits common to South East Asia but those expecting a laid-back beach-hut style Thai restaurant will be in for something of a surprise. This Mango Tree is a decidedly Belgravian affair.

For one thing it's a big, shiny room with contemporary styling that's usually always busy. This can yank up the decibel levels and, as such, makes it a favourite after-work spot, helped in turn by an interesting selection of cocktails. This may not be the place for romantic dinners for two but it is the place to come with a group of friends and the menu is helpfully divided into soups, curries, stir-fries and grills. Vegetarians and vegans are offered plenty of choice with their own dedicated menus.

Bank

Modern European XX

H5

45 Buckingham Gate SW1E 6BS
☎ (020) 7379 9797
Fax (020) 7379 5070
e-mail westres@bankrestaurants.com **www**.bankrestaurants.com

St James's
Closed Saturday lunch, Sunday and Bank Holidays – booking essential at lunch

Carte £29/45

Adjoined to the Crowne Plaza Hotel but with its own street entrance, this branch of Bank is a little less frenzied than the one that used to exist in Aldwych but can, nonetheless, still provide a fun night out. You do first have to get past the Zander Bar, which purports to be the longest bar in the country, and those who find themselves unable to ever pass a bar will find it also has a food menu.

The restaurant itself is a large conservatory affair and looks out onto an attractive Victorian courtyard. The lunchtime clientele can be a little business orientated but is less so in the evenings. You'll find classic, familiar choices alongside more contemporary influences on the extensive à la carte, which is supplemented by a fixed priced option.

A/C VISA MC AE

Noura Brasserie

Lebanese XX

G5

16 Hobart Pl SW1W 0HH
☎ (020) 7235 9444 **Fax** (020) 7235 9244
e-mail noura@noura.co.uk **www**.noura.co.uk

Victoria

Menu £18/60 – Carte £24/39

Having made their name in Paris, the owners set their sights across the Channel and opened their first London restaurant here in Belgravia in 2000. It undoubtedly challenged any preconceptions by being a big, bold and brash room which was both decidedly contemporary and reflective of the zeitgeist. Today, it's as busy as ever, especially with larger tables and parties for whom the surroundings are ideal. Nonetheless, the staff remain stoically immune to the enthusiasm of their customers.

A slightly less formal approach is adopted at lunch, with a keenly priced lunch menu on offer. The main menu is a dazzlingly long affair, with authentic Lebanese delicacies designed for sharing. Those new to it all should try the set menus or selected platters.

A/C VISA MC AE

Olivo

G6 — Italian

21 Eccleston St SW1W 9LX — ⊖ Victoria
(020) 7730 2505 — Closed Bank Holidays,
Fax (020) 7823 5377 — lunch Saturday and Sunday
e-mail maurosanna@oliveto.fsnet.co.uk

Menu £21 – Carte £26/30

All restaurants work best when the owner is present. At Olivo, Mauro not only keeps a steady hand on the tiller but he also ensures that the atmosphere remains bright and welcoming - that's what makes Olivo such an attraction. It still feels like a local restaurant, although some diners are prepared to travel quite some distance to get here, and its twenty year anniversary bears testament to its continued popularity. The rustic décor and the closely set tables within this relatively small space further ensure a highly convivial feel, helped along by a keen team of servers.

The menu and the wine list are both Italian, with subtle hints of Sardinia. The chargrill is a house speciality, dishes are colourful and satisfying and the produce used is top notch.

La Poule au Pot

G6 — French

231 Ebury St SW1W 8UT — ⊖ Sloane Square
(020) 7730 7763 — Closed 25-26 December
Fax (020) 7259 9651

Menu £17 – Carte £27/41

Trends may come, styles may go, but the one constant will always be La Poule au Pot. As Gallic as a Gauloise and as French as a frog's leg, this long-standing favourite, with its exuberant decoration of hanging baskets of dried flowers and assorted horticultural knick-knacks, has been entertaining everyone, from the romantically inclined to groups of friends out for fun, for many years. Somehow all the disparate elements just seem to gel wonderfully well and it's reassuring to know that not everything is fashion led.

It's not just the atmosphere: the classic country cooking is also responsible for drawing the crowds. Expect a selection of rustic favourites from coq au vin to crème brûlée, supplemented by daily specials.

Olivomare

Seafood

G5

10 Lower Belgrave St SW1W 0LJ — ⊖ Victoria
(020) 7730 9022 — Closed Sunday and Bank Holidays

Carte £29/36

A new cog in the local Olivo chain was added in May 2007 with the opening of Olivomare. Seafood is the theme here, with a subtle Sardinian subtext, which means you'll find bottarga, intensely flavoured grey mullet roe, grated on spaghetti; fregola, Sardinia's own version of couscous, with the classic accompaniment of clams and some chilli heat; cassola di pesce, a version of fish soup, and lorighittas - earring-shaped pasta. The pasta dishes are available as a starter or main course, although the individually priced veg and breads can nudge the bill northward.

The decor is minimalistic chic, with snow-blind white and a mural of intertwined fish – stare at this for long enough and apparently you'll see a boat.

The Thomas Cubitt

Gastropub

G6

44 Elizabeth Street SW1W 9PA — ⊖ Sloane Square
(020) 7730 6060 — Closed 24 December-1 January – booking essential
Fax (020) 7730 6055
e-mail reservations@thethomascubitt.co.uk
www.thethomascubitt.co.uk

Menu £25 - Carte £23/40

Welcome to the world of the pub, Belgravia style. Thomas Cubitt was the master builder responsible for the landmark local squares, Eaton and Belgrave, and he would surely have approved of this decidedly handsome establishment.

Regency and Georgian styles have been put to good effect, with oak flooring, panelling and fireplaces, to create a warm and welcoming feel, from the delightful ground floor bar in which to enjoy more casual dining to the charming and more formal upstairs room where the period feel really comes into its own. Here the menu is more structured and features seasonal produce, carefully sourced from across the British Isles, in unfussy and flavoursome dishes. Service also hits the right note in its unobtrusiveness and warmth.

The Ebury

G6 — **Gastropub**

11 Pimlico Rd SW1W 8NA
(020) 7730 6784
Fax (020) 7730 6149
e-mail info@theebury.co.uk
www.theebury.co.uk

⊖ Sloane Square
Closed 25-26 December

Carte £25/30

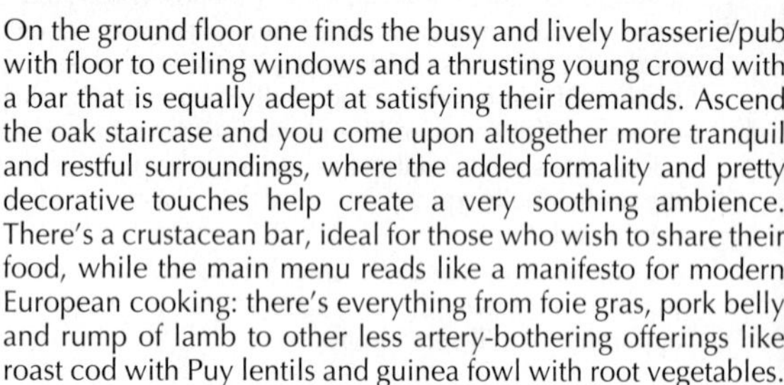

A/C · VISA · MC · AE

On the ground floor one finds the busy and lively brasserie/pub with floor to ceiling windows and a thrusting young crowd with a bar that is equally adept at satisfying their demands. Ascend the oak staircase and you come upon altogether more tranquil and restful surroundings, where the added formality and pretty decorative touches help create a very soothing ambience. There's a crustacean bar, ideal for those who wish to share their food, while the main menu reads like a manifesto for modern European cooking: there's everything from foie gras, pork belly and rump of lamb to other less artery-bothering offerings like roast cod with Puy lentils and guinea fowl with root vegetables. Desserts will be hard to resist.

THE WINTER'S TALE

Recent court battles over Granny Smiths may not have gone The Beatles' way, but the life of artist Yoko Ono was definitely changed for the better by an apple she exhibited in her 1966 show at London's Indica Gallery. The installation (appropriately titled 'apple') caught the attention of a certain John Lennon, who plucked it from its plinth and took a bite. At the time, Ono didn't know Lennon from Adam and was cross - but soon forgave him.

C. Barrely/MICHELIN

Regent's Park · Marylebone

Regent's Park is one of those rare places in London where it is hard to suggest ways in which it could be improved. This lush green expanse, with secret corners that are accessible to all, is imbued with both graceful grandeur and pastoral never-may-care, so that promenading and picnicking go hand in hand. It is much loved and well used - but stroll through the Italianate gardens on a weekday evening and you could almost believe you're in the grounds of your own Tuscan villa, taking a quiet moment to admire the topiary or recline in one of the sequestered pavilions.

Round the outside

Though much pleasure is to be had in a simple sojourn in the rose gardens of the **Inner Circle** or sharing a punnet of strawberries in the northern meadows, more involved activities are also possible. Boating lakes and sports pitches are available for the energetic, while Shakespeare in the **Open Air Theatre** is a reliable inducement to midsummer dreaming. **London Zoo** is also here and in recent years has worked hard to improve enclosures so that the animals are as happy as the visitors. Not to be missed is the view of Lord Snowdon's netted tetrahedral aviary from the **Regent's Canal**, the latter cutting the zoo in two, with horned residents of the **Into Africa** zone gazing curiously at iPod joggers whizzing by on the tow path below.

More than a moated impasse, the fringe-skirting canal is an indication of how the park's surrounds flow out of this urban oasis. To the west, the park's handsome mansions evolve into St John's Wood, an apparent bastion of Englishness but one where the village cricket pitch happens to be **Lords** and local place of worship the **London Central Mosque**. To the east, the white Regency terraces, provide a natural home for estimable institutions, before blending into the street-smart chaos of Camden Town. And, most subtly of all, to the north the park stretches into Primrose Hill, a high-class bohemian enclave with a view of the London skyline that many rate as the capital's best.

A little history...

Perhaps it's no surprise that an area as harmonious and elegant as this did not evolve haphazardly but was meticulously planned. The lease of Marylebone Park, an unprepossessing piece of land that had been used for farming, reverted to the Crown in 1811. The architect John Nash, backed by his patron the Prince Regent, jumped at the chance to design the park and surrounding houses in order to lure the moneyed classes north away from the centre of London. Today **Marylebone Road** is a busy thoroughfare, the skyline punctuated by the verdigrised dome of the **Planetarium**, the Grecian cupola of **St Marylebone Parish Church** and the spiky sputnik of the **BT tower**. It may appear a trifle bleak after the verdant greenery of the park, however, the road is also home to the **Royal Academy of Music** – an excellent place to find cheap or even free concerts of classical favourites and brand new compositions.

Marylebone village

Turn south off the road and you come to the self-consciously styled Marylebone village; the narrow, winding streets are in contrast to the geometric Georgian layout of Regent's Park and in many places still follow the course of the underground Tyburn river, which gives the area its name. Cafés spill out onto the pavement and in summer it has an almost Mediterranean feel: it's certainly a challenge to imagine you're a shout away from the bustle of Oxford Street.

Baker and bread

As ever in London, these moneyed nooks are excellent places to find a bite to eat. There are several good specialist shops, including **La Fromagerie**, which of-fers an eye-opening and mouth-watering array of cheeses. There's also a farmers' market in the **Moxton Street car park,** which takes place on Sundays the whole year round.

If you fancy delving into the area's literary past, head east and onto **Baker Street**, whose most famous resident, Sherlock Holmes, still dominates the area: there's a museum sited aptly enough at 221b Baker Street – although, ironically, the address was as fictional as Holmes until the museum was built there.

C. Eymenier / MICHELIN

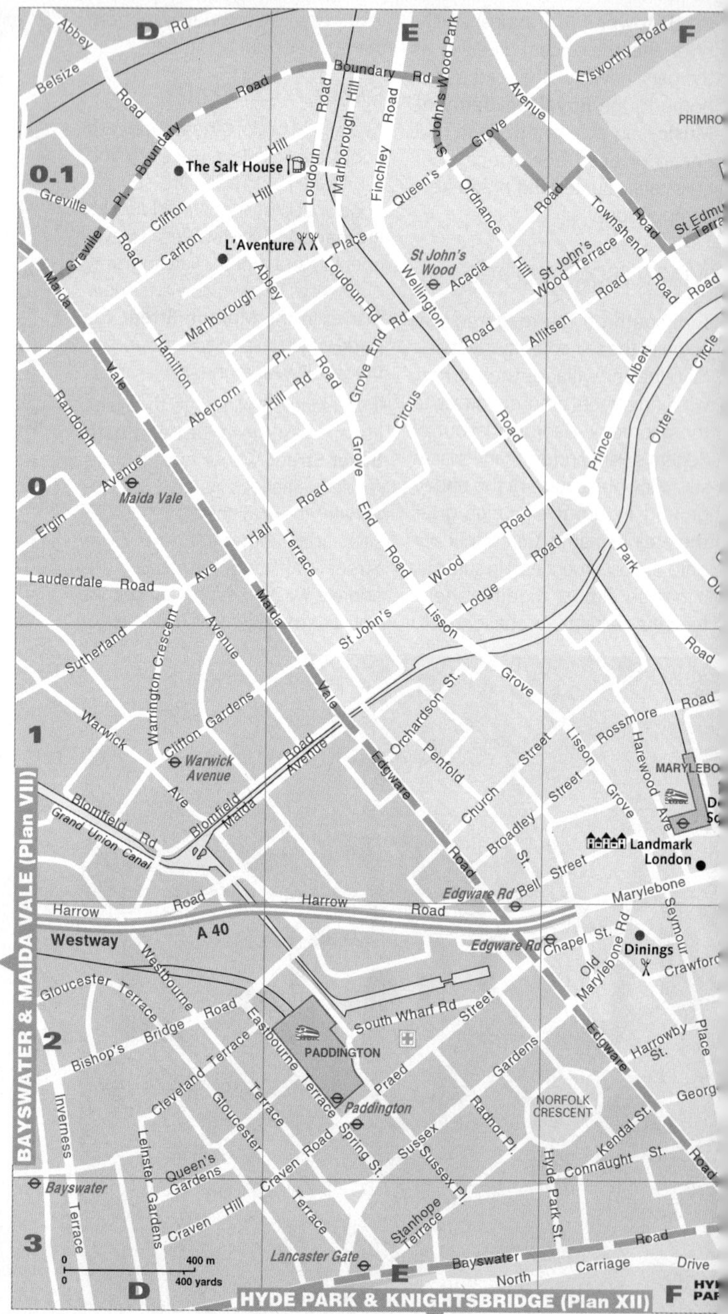

D
E
F
Abbey Rd
Belsize Road
Boundary Road
Boundary Rd
Loudoun Road
Marlborough Hill
Finchley Road
St John's Wood Park
Elsworthy Road
Avenue Road
PRIMROSE
The Salt House
Greville Pl.
Clifton Hill
Carlton Hill
Greville Road
L'Aventure
Queen's Grove
Ordnance Hill
Townshend Road
St Edmund's Terrace
Place
Loudoun Rd
St John's Wood
Wellington Road
Acacia Road
St John's Wood Terrace
Road
Maida Vale
Abbey Road
Marlborough Place
Grove End Rd
Allitsen Road
Albert Road
Circle
Hamilton
Abercorn Pl.
Hill Rd
Circus Road
Outer Circle
Randolph Avenue
Maida Vale
Grove End Road
Prince Albert Road
Elgin Avenue
Hall Road
Terrace
Wood Road
Lodge Road
Park Road
Lauderdale Road
Ave
St John's Wood
Lisson Grove
Sutherland Avenue
Warrington Crescent
Orchardson St.
Clifton Gardens
Warwick Avenue
Penfold Street
Rossmore Road
Harewood Ave
MARYLEBONE
Church Street
Broadley Street
Lisson Grove
Blomfield Rd
Grand Union Canal
Blomfield Road
Maida Avenue
Edgware Road
Landmark London
Bell Street
St.
Edgware Rd
Marylebone Road
Seymour Place
Harrow Road
A 40
Westway
Chapel St.
Old Marylebone Rd
Dinings
Crawford St.
Westbourne Terrace
Gloucester Terrace
Bishop's Bridge Road
Eastbourne Terrace
South Wharf Rd
Street
PADDINGTON
Paddington
Praed Street
Gardens
Harrowby St.
Cleveland Terrace
Gloucester Terrace
Radnor Pl.
NORFOLK CRESCENT
Kendal St.
George St.
Inverness Terrace
Leinster Gardens
Queen's Gardens
Craven Road
Spring St.
Sussex Gardens
Sussex Pl.
Hyde Park St.
Connaught St.
Bayswater
Craven Hill
Terrace
Stanhope Terrace
Lancaster Gate
Bayswater Road
North Carriage Drive
0 400 m
0 400 yards
BAYSWATER & MAIDA VALE (Plan VII)
HYDE PARK & KNIGHTSBRIDGE (Plan XII)

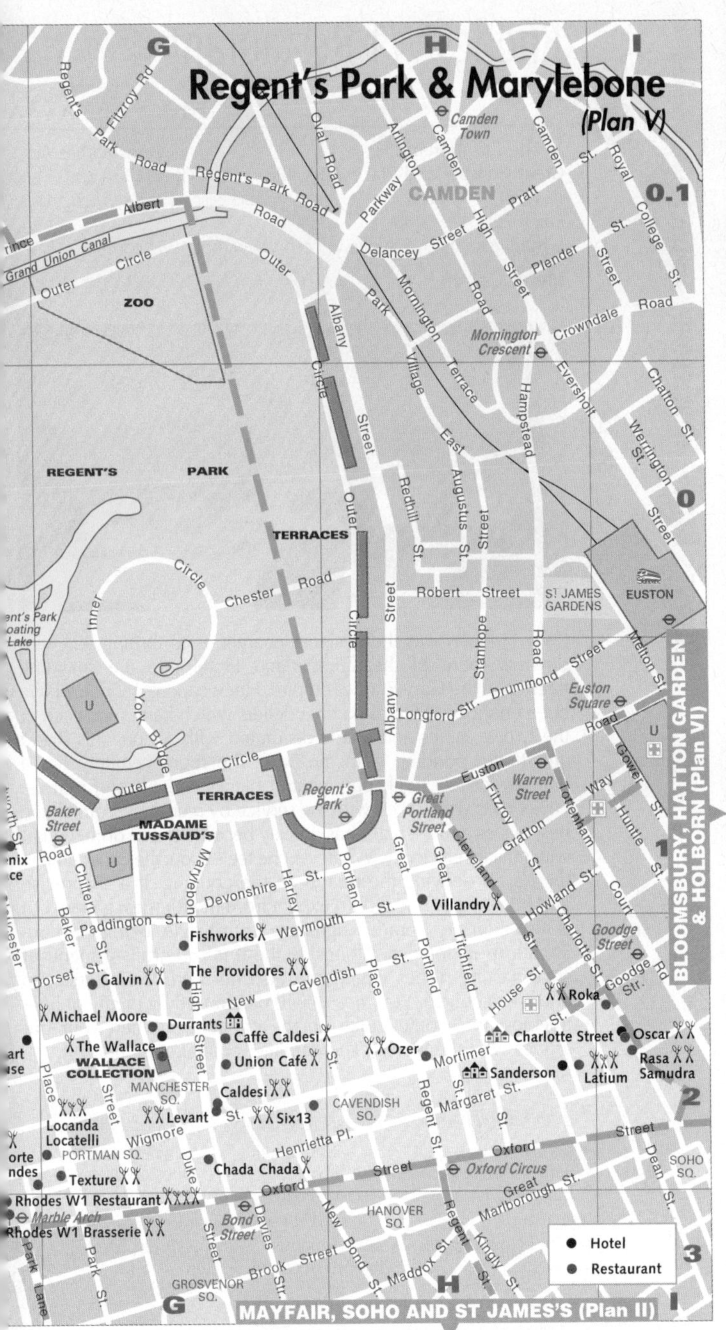
Regent's Park & Marylebone
(Plan V)
REGENT'S PARK
ZOO
CAMDEN
TERRACES
MADAME TUSSAUD'S
WALLACE COLLECTION
EUSTON
BLOOMSBURY, HATTON GARDEN & HOLBORN (Plan VI)
MAYFAIR, SOHO AND ST JAMES'S (Plan II)
Villandry
Fishworks
The Providores
Galvin
Michael Moore
Durrants
Caffè Caldesi
The Wallace
Union Café
Ozer
Roka
Charlotte Street
Oscar
Sanderson
Latium
Rasa Samudra
Caldesi
Levant
Six13
Locanda Locatelli
Chada Chada
Texture
Rhodes W1 Restaurant
Rhodes W1 Brasserie
Hotel
Restaurant

Rhodes W1 Restaurant ✿

F3 **French** XXXX

at The Cumberland H.,
Great Cumberland Place W1A 4RF
✆ (020) 7479 3737
Fax (020) 7479 3888
e-mail restaurant@rhodesw1.com **www**.rhodesw1.com

⊖ Marble Arch
Closed 28 December-5 January, Easter, Sunday, Monday and lunch Saturday

Menu £28/48

VISA MC AE

Michelin

Kelly Hoppen was the designer charged with turning this windowless room of the Cumberland Hotel into the sparkling flagship of the Gary Rhodes empire. Her weapons of choice have been enormous Swarovski chandeliers which hang over each of the twelve tables and chairs decorated with recipes (his Bread and Butter pudding is in the bar). The room certainly has a flamboyant feel, with purples and blacks, velvets and mirrors. Fewer risks were taken with the service by recruiting from all the best places and the team has quickly become a well drilled outfit with military efficiency. Whatever one feels about the environment, there's no denying the quality of the cooking. It is as precise and polished as one would expect from the Rhodes' gallery but is also a far cry from his signature British style, being far more French in its temper. Alongside the *à la carte* runs a menu of small tasting dishes which can also be used, for instance, to add a fish course. Your *gueule* will be amused by plenty of little freebies; just don't choke on the chocolates when your bill arrives with the words 'The damage' emblazoned upon it.

First Course

- Double oyster ragoût with samphire and fresh herbs.
- Suckling pig ravioli with Bramley apple sauce.

Main Course

- Salt roast pigeon with asparagus, cabbage hearts and lemon cumin gravy.
- Poached lobster with summer vegetables.

Dessert

- Caramel chocolate mousse millefeuille with lemon sorbet.
- Iced lemon Chiboust with raspberries.

Locanda Locatelli ✿

Italian XXX

G2

8 Seymour St W1H 7JZ
✆ (020) 7935 9088
Fax (020) 7935 1149
e-mail info@locandalocatelli.com
www.locandalocatelli.com

⊖ Marble Arch
Closed Bank Holidays

Carte £35/56

Locanda Locatelli

Trying to get a table is still tortuous but they have, at least, improved the procedure. Anyway, it proves that Giorgio Locatelli's restaurant remains as popular as ever. The David Collins designed room is certainly appealing, with the best tables being the corner booths, and no detail has been overlooked with the table setting. The team of waiting staff are a young and chirpy lot who carry out their responsibilities very professionally and the clientele are from the more glamorous end of the evolutionary scale. But the main appeal remains the food. The menu changes seasonally and, whilst of outstanding quality, dishes are authentic and rooted in honesty. Specials are described at the table in thick Italian accents and, in typical Italian fashion, focus on the primary ingredients which are kept unmasked and true to themselves. Just remember not to devour too many of the five varieties of bread and home-made grissini that arrives at the start and comes with exceptionally good olive oil. The food is complemented by a wine list of enormous depth, including a comprehensive collection of Barolo.

First Course

- Pan-fried scallops with a saffron vinaigrette and celeriac purée.
- Linguini with langoustine, garlic and chilli.

Main Course

- Roast monkfish with a walnut and caper sauce.
- Veal with Parma ham and sage, baked aubergine.

Dessert

- Amarelli liquorice and chocolate fondant, coffee and mascarpone.
- Wild berry panna cotta with stracciatella ice cream.

Latium

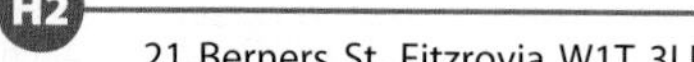

H2 — Italian XXX

21 Berners St, Fitzrovia W1T 3LP
(020) 7323 9123
Fax (020) 7323 3205
e-mail info@latiumrestaurant.com **www**.latiumrestaurant.com

⊖ Oxford Circus
Closed 25 December, Saturday lunch, Sunday, and Bank Holidays

Menu £20/29

A/C VISA MC AE

In contrast to the über trendy Sanderson Hotel opposite, Latium has steadily built up a loyal following by providing surroundings which are less challenging and altogether more down to earth. That is not to say the restaurant is without personality for it has a certain well-groomed, understated chic, but comfort and relaxation are clearly the priorities.

The strength also lies in the service which is executed with a confidence which comes from having pride and belief in your establishment - names and faces of returning customers are remembered. The chef-owner hails from Lazio and his set-price menu offers a balanced selection of specialities which all come with a certain degree of elaboration and top-notch ingredients.

Texture

G2 — Innovative XX

34 Portman Square W1H 7BY
(020) 7224 0028
e-mail info@texture-restaurant.co.uk
www.texture-restaurant.co.uk

⊖ Marble Arch
Closed 22 December-8 January, last 2 weeks August, Sunday and Monday

Menu £26/45

A/C VISA MC AE

The Champagne bar's clearly a main feature as it's claimed all the windows; the restaurant lies behind it and has a sleekness coupled with a bit of Nordic naturalism. Texture opened in 2007 as a partnership between two young alumni of Le Manoir aux Quat'Saisons; the kitchen comes under the aegis of Icelandic Agnar Sverrisson and he's brought some cod with him. For the food, think of a Viking in a dress: it's a bit different, pretty from a distance but surprisingly muscular. An ingredient can be prepared in differing ways to produce contrasting 'textures' and there's no holding back on flavours. It is highly skilled but sometimes the cleverness can appear to take over. The other owner does the wine and his list is exceptional.

Rhodes W1 Brasserie

British XX

F3

at The Cumberland H., ⊖ Marble Arch
Great Cumberland Pl W1A 4RF
✆ (020) 7479 3838 **Fax** (020) 7479 3888
e-mail rhodesw1@thecumberland.co.uk **www**.garyrhodes.com

Carte £25/42

A/C VISA MC AE

From the street entrance look out for the candelabras and keep heading through the bustling bar. The main dining room is a pretty big affair, but panels and glass break it up a little and the staff appear to be able to cope. The cooking takes the brasserie theme and mixes European dishes with a little British twist here and an emphasis there, so, alongside risotto and fish soup, you'll find terrines of ham hock with piccalilli, sausage and mash and an assortment of grilled meats and fish. For dessert, the choice can range from cheesecake and tarts to rice pudding and tiramisu. The kitchen is confident, times things well and offers something to suit everyone. For a less frenetic experience, head to the eponymous chef's more formal restaurant adjacent.

Oscar

Modern European XX

I2

at Charlotte Street H., ⊖ Goodge Street
15 Charlotte St W1T 1RJ — Closed Sunday lunch – booking essential
✆ (020) 7907 4005
Fax (020) 7806 2002
e-mail charlotte@firmdale.com **www**.charlottestreethotel.co.uk

Carte £29/44

A/C VISA MC AE

Charlotte Street always appears to be full of life and the sheer range of restaurants, snack bars and cafes may be the cause or the effect. The unimaginatively, but undeniably accurately, named Charlotte Street Hotel offers up another popular option with their Oscar restaurant. It's located at street level in this fashionable hotel, while its bar fills the front and often spills out onto the pavement.

The place is a wonderfully colourful affair, with murals, stained glass lanterns and striped seating. The pace can be quite frenetic and reminds us all that restaurants are there as places of enjoyment, not worship. Cooking is decidedly modern and dishes come neatly presented. They offer a commendable number of wines by the glass.

Galvin

French XX

G2

66 Baker St W1U 7DN
⊖ Baker Street
(020) 7935 4007
Closed 25-26 December and 1 January
Fax (020) 7486 1735
e-mail info@galvinuk.com **www**.galvinuk.com

Menu £16 – Carte £24/35

Some said a restaurant would never succeed on this site, the 'wrong end' of Baker Street. Well, Galvin opened in September 2005 and there has hardly been a spare table since.

The Galvin brothers proved the doomsayers wrong by pooling their considerable culinary experience and expertise in creating what they describe as a bistrot de luxe. They took as their model the new wave of bistrots modernes and their cooking is a refreshingly uncomplicated celebration of French cuisine and one executed with care and understanding.

The L shaped room also has the character of a Parisian bistro, with wood panelling, slate flooring and large globe lights hanging from the ceiling. You feel that everyone is dining in their favourite restaurant.

Six13

Kosher XX

G2

19 Wigmore St W1H 9LA
⊖ Bond Street
(020) 7629 6133
Closed Jewish Holidays, Friday and Saturday
Fax (020) 7629 6135
e-mail inquiries@six13.com **www**.six13.com

Menu £28 – Carte £28/45

'Kosher fusion' may sound like one of the more unlikely culinary images but that is exactly what is found at Six13. Named after the 613 mitzvoth or commandments, Six13 produces elaborately presented cooking using influences from around the world, but all strictly within the laws of kashrut. The kitchen needs to be both inventive and imaginative in the creation and conception of the dishes and in this it mostly succeeds.

The room is a high-ceilinged, rather smart affair with two large lampshades providing the only real decorative features of any note. Otherwise it's all rather understated, with a bar at one end and tables laid out in long rows. Private functions can be held on the lower ground floor.

La Porte des Indes

F2

Indian XX

32 Bryanston St W1H 7EG ⊖ Marble Arch
(020) 7224 0055 Closed 25-28 December and Saturday lunch
Fax (020) 7224 1144
e-mail london.reservation@laportedesindes.com
www.laportedesindes.com

Menu £15/29 – Carte £28/42

The façade gives little away but step in and you'll be instantly transported to what looks like the set from the latest Bollywood movie. Spread over two floors, La Porte des Indes really is vast and it's decorated in a spectacularly unrestrained display of palm trees, murals and waterfalls. The equally exuberant Jungle Bar is a popular place to kick off the evening.

The menu offers something for everyone, including specialities from Pondicherry and others influenced by French India. Vegetarians are particularly well catered for and cookery demonstrations are held regularly for those wishing to learn more about Indian food. For those after a memento of their meal here, there is a little shop in the entrance lobby.

The Providores

G2

Innovative XX

109 Marylebone High St W1U 4RX ⊖ Bond Street
(020) 7935 6175 Closed Easter and Christmas
Fax (020) 7935 6877
e-mail anyone@theprovidores.co.uk **www**.theprovidores.co.uk

Carte £26/46

'Fusion cooking' too often means 'confusion cooking' as chefs wrestle with unfamiliar ingredients they recently encountered on an exotic holiday. However, New Zealander Peter Gordon was one of the first to showcase what could be achieved with a sound appreciation and understanding of other cuisines. His first floor restaurant, The Providores, displays his original and complex dishes, in a room of decorative simplicity which is reached by fighting through the ever-popular ground floor Tapa Room where globally inspired tapas is served.

The menu may seem full of unusual and unfamiliar sounding ingredients but the keen young staff are more than happy to answer questions. The wine list has some interesting Kiwi selections.

Roka

I2 — **Japanese** XX

37 Charlotte St W1T 1RR — ⊖ Goodge Street
✆ (020) 7580 6464 **Fax** (020) 7580 0220 — Closed 25 December
e-mail info@rokarestaurant.com
www.rokarestaurant.com

Carte £29/36 s

When a restaurant has been designed by a company called 'Super Potato' you can be pretty sure it's going to be all shiny and modern, and Roka doesn't disappoint. The walls are made of glass so expect passers-by to gaze covetously at your lunch and they open up fully in summer (the walls, not the passers-by). There's also a lot of wood, from the tables to the large counter wrapped around the robata grill where the chefs all do their thing in full view. The menus can appear a little bewildering at first so don't be afraid to ask for help. The grill is the main event but it's certainly worth ordering from a variety of sections and the dishes have a robustness that belies their delicate presentation. There's a great bar downstairs.

Ozer

H2 — **Turkish** XX

4-5 Langham Pl, Regent St
W1B 3DG — ⊖ Oxford Circus
✆ (020) 7323 0505 **Fax** (020) 7323 0111
e-mail info@sofra.co.uk **www**.sofra.co.uk

Menu £21 – Carte £15/29

The front section, for cocktails, can take a good pounding in the evenings, especially in the summer when the large windows at the front are thrown open onto Regent Street, and the place is seemingly packed with BBC staff discussing DJ's salaries. If you fight your way through, you'll find yourself in a spacious yet equally frenetic restaurant. It's decorated in very bold colours of red and gold and framed by an ornately modern chandelier. Noise levels remain high, especially when the music is pumped up.
Service makes up in efficiency what it may lack in personality, while the menu offers a full range of fresh and revitalising Turkish food. Fish lovers and vegetarians are particularly well catered for.

Rasa Samudra

Indian XX

I2

5 Charlotte St W1T 1RE
☎ (020) 7637 0222
Fax (020) 7637 0224
www.rasarestaurants.com

⊖ Goodge St
Closed 24 December-1 January and lunch Sunday and Bank Holidays

Menu £23/30 – Carte £13/24

VISA MC AE

So how best to draw attention to yourself when you're competing for business in a street filled with an abundance of restaurants and cafés? Full marks go to Rasa Samudra for painting their façade a shocking shade of pink, which certainly makes them stand out, although intriguingly they have also decided to paint the interior in the same hue. The front room fills up first but go through to the rooms at the back which are far more inviting.

The restaurant is decorated with silks, carvings and assorted Indian ornaments but the food's the main attraction here with the menu divided into two main parts: rich and creamy seafood specialities from Kerala and fragrant vegetarian dishes. Begin your meal by trying typical Keralan tea shop snacks.

Levant

Lebanese XX

G2

Jason Court, 76 Wigmore St
W1U 2SJ
☎ (020) 7224 1111 **Fax** (020) 7486 1216
e-mail info@levant.co.uk **www**.levant.co.uk

⊖ Bond Street

Menu £15/29

A/C VISA

AE

This atmospheric basement restaurant is ideal for entertaining groups of friends - not only are the cocktails as exotic as the low slung, laid-back bar but watching the nightly belly dancing is an activity best appreciated from behind the security of a large table.

The restaurant has turned its basement location into a positive, by decorating the room in a colourful and vibrant manner, with wood carvings, lanterns and the aromatic scent one associates with the mysteries of the Levant.

The Lebanon provides most, but not all, of the inspiration behind the cooking, with the assorted mezes and salads providing the best opportunities for sharing with your fellow diners and, as such, another reason for coming in a group.

Caldesi

Italian XX

G2

15-17 Marylebone Lane W1U 2NE — ⊖ Bond Street
(020) 7935 9226 — Closed Saturday lunch and Sunday
Fax (020) 7935 9228
e-mail tuscan@caldesi.com **www**.caldesi.com

Carte £35/43

There's something reassuring about a restaurant bearing the owner's name, in this case Giancarlo's, who has been here since 1994. The abundance of mirrored panelling makes the room feel larger than it actually is, while the candlelight adds to the general atmosphere of intimacy and warmth. Chairs can be a little uncomfortable for those who have insufficient padding of their own.

Signor Caldesi hails from Tuscany and it is to this region of Italy that the kitchen seeks inspiration, with the appropriately muscular wines to match. The waiters come dressed in black, know what they're doing and deliver chosen dishes promptly. The striking upstairs room used for private parties comes colourfully painted and has its own bar.

L'Aventure

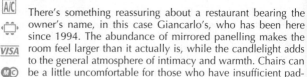

French XX

D0

3 Blenheim Terrace NW8 0EH — ⊖ St John's Wood
(020) 7624 6232 — Closed first week January, Easter, Sunday, Saturday lunch and Bank Holidays
Fax (020) 7625 5548

Menu £19/35

You can just about make out the small neon sign through the foliage which twinkles with fairy lights and frames the delightful little terrace. L'Aventure is as French a restaurant as you can get and has been satisfying St John's Wood regulars since 1979. It is also a very romantic and intimate little restaurant although, if you want to impress your date, you may want to brush up on your linguistic skills as the handwritten menu is all in French. That menu contains all the classics for which our Gallic chums are celebrated, along with others displaying the kitchen's own personality. There are daily specials and all courses are satisfyingly robust.

Booted and suited staff ensure it all runs smoothly, with accents as rich as the pot au chocolat.

Phoenix Palace

Chinese XX

F1

3-5 Glentworth St NW1 5PG ⊖ Baker Street
(020) 7486 3515
Fax (020) 7486 3401
e-mail phoenixpalace@btconnect.com

Menu £18 – Carte £18/26

The unassuming entrance gives few hints as to the enormity of what lies within. Firstly, you walk through a small bar, where the photo wall of fame includes some luminaries as Jackie Chan, Gordon Ramsay and Ken Livingstone. This leads you into the absolutely vast dining room which has a galleried level and seating for well over 200. It's nicely decorated, though, with black lacquer, elaborate Oriental artwork and smartly dressed tables. Service is smooth and personable although, perhaps understandably, it can get a little stretched at times.

The menu can appear a little daunting at first, as dishes are numbered and the count doesn't stop until 218. But it is sensibly subdivided and mixes the recognisable and the more unusual; dishes are confidently prepared and satisfying.

Villandry

French XX

H1

170 Great Portland St W1W 5QB ⊖ Regent's Park
(020) 7631 3131 Closed 25, 31 December,
Fax (020) 7631 3030 1 January and Sunday dinner
e-mail contactus@villandry.com **www**.villandry.com

Carte £29/40

Villandry goes from strength to strength. The shop at the front features fantastic breads and pastries; you can sit in the Charcuterie Bar in amongst the cookbooks and jars; have something from the stir-fry station where you can try your own recipe or grab a smoothie at Villandry Rapide. All this before you even get to the restaurant. Here you'll find a bright, high-ceilinged room with doors opening onto the pavement. It serves appealing French-biased food like mussels, cassoulet and steak tartare; the plat du jour attracts quite a following. There's a separate Oysters and Shellfish section on the menu and a decently priced wine list divided by style. On Saturday, parents can have lunch while the kiddies get a "cookie class".

The Wallace

French

G2

Hertford House, Manchester Sq
W1U 3BN
(020) 7563 9505
e-mail reservations@thewallacerestaurant.com
www.thewallacerestaurant.com

⊖ Bond St
Lunch only

Menu £25 – Carte £29/36

VISA MC AE

Along with the Old Masters, The Wallace Collection is famed for its galleries of 18C French paintings, furniture and porcelain. It's appropriate then that Oliver Peyton's restaurant has an equally Gallic tone. Housed in a delightful glass-roofed courtyard at the rear, with an all-day café to one side, the restaurant offers a comprehensive selection of classic French fare. Terrines are a speciality and come with a large jar of cornichons, cheeses are in good condition and main courses could include everything from escargots to bouillabaisse. For dessert it has to be Tarte Tatin or Baba au rhum. The wine list is also exclusively French and comes with realistic prices. It gets busy, so book - especially on a summer's day.

Michael Moore

International

G2

19 Blandford St W1U 3DH
(020) 7224 1898
Fax (020) 7224 0970
e-mail info@michaelmoorerestaurant.com
www.michaelmoorerestaurant.com

⊖ Baker Street
Closed Christmas-New Year, Saturday lunch, Sunday and Bank Holidays

Menu £19 – Carte £30/45

VISA MC AE

No, it's not that Michael Moore - although the portly American polemicist clearly enjoys his food - but the name of the chef-owner who runs this sweet little neighbourhood restaurant. It seats just 32 so booking is imperative to avoid disappointment. The locals clearly know this as most evenings a procession of interlopers try their luck but find themselves welcomed by smug and contented looks from the regulars at their tables.

The chef has worked in kitchens across the continents and his influences are widespread, hence his description of his cooking as 'global cuisine'. However, all his dishes arrive underpinned by a solidly classical base thanks, no doubt, to his time spent in the kitchens of The Savoy and Dorchester Hotels.

Union Café

International

G2

96 Marylebone Lane W1U 2QA
(020) 7486 4860
Fax (020) 7935 1537
e-mail unioncafe@brinkleys.com **www**.brinkleys.com

⊖ Bond Street
Closed 25-26 December, 1 January and Sunday dinner

Carte £23/32

VISA MC AE

This corner restaurant, with its arched windows and welcoming clamour of contentment, fits seamlessly into the surroundings of this rapidly smartening neighbourhood. Inside, it's all open-plan, with the chefs on view at one end of the room and exposed air conditioning vents overhead. Comforts are all very classless and egalitarian, with uncovered tables and chairs from Van Gogh's bedroom.

The menu represents that section of the culinary zeitgeist where influences range from Thailand to the Med, and those coming in for a post work bowl of pasta are as welcome as those going high on the hog. The young staff come dressed in black T-shirts and make up for any efficiency deficiencies thanks to their sunny dispositions.

Caffé Caldesi

Italian

G2

1st Floor, 118 Marylebone Lane
W1U 2QF
(020) 7935 1144 **Fax** (020) 7935 8832
e-mail people@caldesi.com **www**.caldesi.com

⊖ Bond Street
Closed Christmas, Sunday and Bank Holidays

Carte £29/38

A/C VISA MC AE

This is more than merely a younger sibling to the owner's other restaurant, Caldesi, for this is the sort of place every neighbourhood would love to have on its doorstep. You can pop into the ground floor of this bright converted pub for coffee, snacks or a bottle of wine or go upstairs to the simply furnished restaurant where the cooking is as vibrant as the atmosphere, while service comes with a certain vim. Caldesi may focus more on Tuscany, but here at Caffe Caldesi the influences derive from all parts of Italy but also include some lesser-known recipes and undiscovered treasures.

Those feeling particularly inspired by the experience merely have to go next door to enrol in the cookery school.

Chada Chada

G2 **Thai** X

16-17 Picton Pl W1U 1BP ⊖ Bond Street
✆ (020) 7935 8212 Closed 25 December, 1 January, and Sunday
Fax (020) 7924 2178
e-mail enquiry@chadathai.com **www**.chadathai.com

Menu £13 – Carte £15/29

In Picton Place, just slightly removed from the melee of populist eateries in James Street, sits Chada Chada, a Thai restaurant and offspring of the Battersea original. Its comforts may be modest but it has an appealingly sweet atmosphere, thanks largely to the staff who always appear to have just been told a good joke.

The first half of the restaurant allows you views of the open kitchen and there is a nicely decorated downstairs room which is used more as an overflow. The seats are not overly upholstered but fortunately delivery from the kitchen is fairly swift.

The dishes on the menu are numbered and go all the way up to 112 but are clearly divided. They come authentically prepared, generously proportioned and appropriately priced.

Fishworks

G2 **Seafood** X

89 Marylebone High St W1U 4QW ⊖ Baker Street
✆ (020) 7935 9796 **Fax** (020) 7935 8796 Booking essential
e-mail marylebone@fishworks.co.uk **www**.fishworks.co.uk

Carte £25/49

Following the success of the first outlet in Chiswick, there followed Fishworks Number Two which slotted effortlessly into Marylebone High Street; positively awash with restaurants and cafés these days.

The principle remains the same: the front section is your local fishmonger - for when you're knocking up that little Rick Stein number at home – which, in turn, leads into a bright and simple restaurant, where seafood is the catch of the day. The menu is really quite substantial and your choice of fish can arrive at your table by means of frying or grilling. Along with lobsters, prawns and assorted shellfish, there are platters and oysters and even a separate menu for the kids.

Perhaps we're finally realising we live on an island.

Dinings

F2 **Japanese**

22 Harcourt St. W1H 4HH
(020) 7723 0666
Fax (020) 7723 3222

Marylebone
Closed 2 weeks August, Saturday lunch and Sunday – booking essential

Carte £26/36

The smiling chefs greet you from behind the sushi counter which acts as a prompt to the girls in the basement to rush upstairs and escort you back down below. The idea behind Dinings is to resemble an after-work Japanese izakaya, or pub, and this they achieve. Staff outnumber guests and their service is endearingly sweet, while comfort levels are modest – chairs are built for purpose rather than comfort. The atmosphere is chummy and music loud.

The young owner has come from Nobu-land and the food calls itself 'Japanese tapas'; shorthand for small plates of diligently prepared dishes, similar in style to his alma mater in its mix of traditional and modern, but without the lofty price tag. Puddings are more your classic French.

The Salt House

D0 **Gastropub**

63 Abbey Road, St John's Wood NW8 0AE
(020) 7328 6626
e-mail salthousemail@majol.co.uk **www**.thesalthouse.co.uk

St John's Wood
Closed 25 December

Carte £20/45

First it was The Salt House, then The Abbey Road, then it changed back again to The Salt House. But whatever the name, it has remained a reliable and inviting neighbourhood pub, with cooking that has a sunny, country feel and comes in man-size portions.

The dining room's a few steps down from the bar and overlooks the pleasant semi-enclosed outside terrace and its style is from the relaxed, higgledy-piggledy school. The bill can tot up without you noticing but there's plenty of interest on the menu, whether that's the sea bass cartoccio, the rack of lamb with sweet potatoes or the top-notch quality Scottish beef. There are always assorted pasta dishes available as well as more unusual offerings like rabbit casserole or honey-glazed poussin.

Queen's Head & Artichoke

Gastropub

G3

30-32 Albany St NW1 4EA
(020) 7916 6206
e-mail info@theartichoke.net
www.theartichoke.net

⊖ Great Portland Street
▶ Plan XV

A/C

The location may be just about spot-on: bordering the park to catch the strollers and close enough to the Euston Road to get the office bods. The formula also hits the spot: modern European influenced food mixed with a large selection of 'tapas' in its loosest form. The place is certainly always jumping and the licence can be traced back to good Queen Bess - apparently she loved a bit of artichoke. Today's customers can all enjoy completely differing culinary experiences. One might be having pâté followed by roast lamb, while their partner has chicken satay followed by red duck curry. Tapas is the nebulous term for a huge and appealing mix of small dishes, where the influences take in North Africa, the Middle East, as well as Europe and is offered all day.

ROLL OUT THE BARREL

Horatio Nelson is celebrated by one of London's best-known landmarks; however he was not always treated with such respect. When he fell at the Battle of Trafalgar in 1805, his body was transported back to England preserved in rum or brandy. The story goes that when the ship arrived home the crew had drunk half the spirits from the barrel: although of dubious truth, the tale has given rise to the slang 'tapping the Admiral', for illicit drinking.

Bloomsbury · Hatton Garden · Holborn

From the highs of Senate House and the Centre Point Tower to the lows of the Fleet Valley, this is an area steeped in history. With its gracious streets and tree-lined squares, Bloomsbury is famed for its intellect, and houses such august institutions as the British Museum, RADA and University College. Not to be outdone by its blue-stocking neighbour, Holborn is the city's legal district and home to the **Royal Courts of Justice**: pin-striped lawyers, gowned barristers and even the odd be-wigged judge can all be seen on the narrow streets, many of which feature in Dickens' novels – he lived in the area and there is a museum devoted to his life on **Doughty Street**. Tucked into the north-east corner of Holborn, Hatton Garden may not have as many academic credentials to its name, but as London's jewellery quarter and home to over 300 businesses devoted to the trade, it has more than enough bling to keep up with its bigger neighbours.

The area has a superb array of traditional pubs, some descended from 17C coffee houses, as well as a good selection of bars. It also hosts a wide range of restaurants with something to suit every taste and budget – from student eateries where poets and artists can debate long into the night, to more upmarket establishments suitable for celebrating a big day in court.

A little history...

The land on which Bloomsbury stands was sold in the 13C to William of Blemund: his name, together with 'bury' or manor, survives as the district's name. **Bloomsbury Square** was originally laid out in the 1650s as part of the push to expand London – such squares were designed to function as "little towns" according to the diarist John Evelyn, and Bloomsbury retains that sense of identity today. It's particularly famous for the eponymous 1920s group of artists and writers – the most famous of whom was Virginia Woolf – who were known as much for their tangled love lives as for their fierce intellect and avant-garde ideas.

The British Museum – with art and antiques from around the world and the dazzling space of the Great Court, recently redesigned by Sir Normal Foster – is well worth a visit. You might then wander down to **Russell Square**, overlooked by the art deco Senate House – these days it houses the University of London Library but during the Second World War it acted as the Ministry of Information and was the inspiration for the Ministry of Truth in George Orwell's *1984*.

Meander west down Southampton Row and perhaps linger at **Lincoln's Inn**, one of the four Inns of Court established as centres for learning in the 14thC.

Lincoln's Inn Field, once a popular venue for duels, is now a calm, green space amid the bustle of busy Holborn. From there you might stroll down to **Gough Square** where the house of another famous resident, Dr Johnson, survives and has been restored to its original 18C condition. While the main streets of Holborn are lined with chi chi bars and some of the best tailors outside Savile Row – lawyers have to look the part – the winding backstreets, a legacy of medieval civic planning or lack thereof, are stuffed with sandwich shops, old pubs and eclectic eateries.

Hatton Garden was named after Sir Christopher Hatton, a favourite of Elizabeth I. The story goes that he took a fancy to the gardens of the Bishops of Ely; at first the bishop was reluctant to give up the land but changed his mind after the Queen made him an offer he couldn't refuse. He was paid £10, ten loads of hay and a red rose each year. The rents in Hatton Garden are considerably steeper these days but there are other reminders of the district's past. Strawberries from the gardens are mentioned in Shakespeare's *Richard III*, and a Strawberry Fayre is held every June. Newly-engaged couples wandering dewy-eyed as they shop for engagement rings are a common sight; luckily some of Holborn's finest pubs, many of which offer excellent food as well, are on hand to provide Dutch courage for those parting with their money.

C. Eymenier / MICHELIN

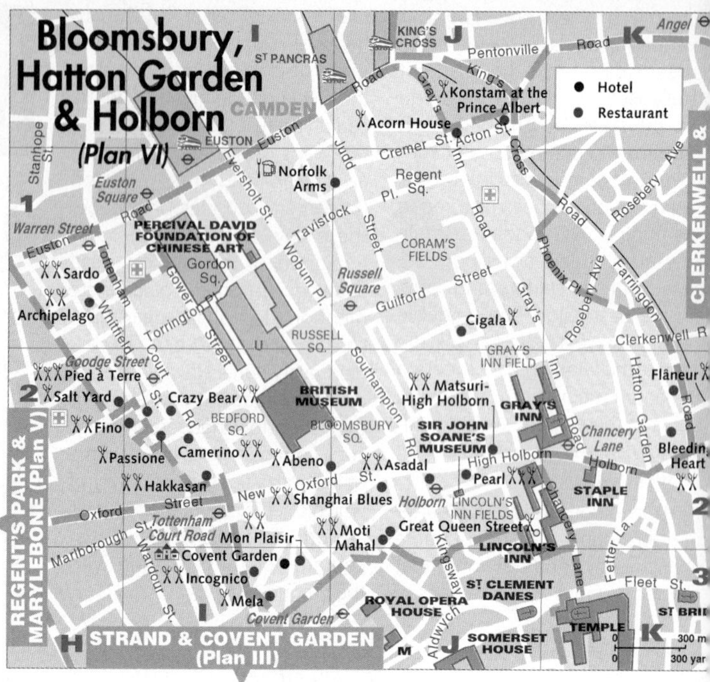

Pearl

J2 **French** XXX

at Renaissance Chancery Court H.,
252 High Holborn WC1V 7EN
(020) 7829 7000
Fax (020) 7829 9889
e-mail info@pearl-restaurant.com **www**.pearl-restaurant.com

⊖ Holborn
Closed last 2 weeks August, Saturday lunch and Sunday

Menu £29/49 – Carte £50

Pearl's a zinger. A room as grand and ornate as this could only have been a banking hall; its name refers to its former life as the Pearl Assurance Building. There is a hotel attached but you're not aware of it. The long catwalk of a bar gets a pasting in the evenings but is being pushed as a lunch spot with small tasting plates, while the pillars, hanging beads and pearls break up what is a very large restaurant. Service copes well and is on the ball.

Jun Tanaka's cooking is French at its core but the influences stretch far and wide and he's not afraid of strong flavours. Dishes come artfully assembled and are made up of several components. The appropriately vast wine list includes 55 choices by the glass.

Pied à Terre ✿✿

Innovative XXX

12

34 Charlotte St W1T 2NH
(020) 7636 1178
Fax (020) 7916 1171
e-mail info@pied-a-terre.co.uk **www**.pied-a-terre.co.uk

Goodge Street
Closed last week December-first week January, Saturday lunch and Sunday

Menu £30/62

Pied à Terre remains the flagship restaurant of Charlotte Street, which is exactly how it should be. When David Moore opened the restaurant in 1991 the area was not exactly known for its food and despite facing challenges and some adversity, including a fire in 2004, his restaurant continues not only to excel but to develop even further.

His co-owner Australian Shane Osborn has an experienced team behind him and his cooking is original and expertly crafted. A classical French foundation underpins it all and his dishes display expert understanding of cooking techniques. Dishes have clearly been perfected 'backstage' over time, so that there are no extraneous elements or jarring flavours, even when the dish appears to be quite elaborate on the plate. This is intelligent and highly consistent cooking.

The restaurant shows how to make the most of somewhat limited space. The main room is the nicer, there's an underused bar upstairs and the atmosphere is discreet but never overly reverential, thanks largely to the experience and thoughtfulness of the front of house team.

First Course

- Seared and poached foie gras with borlotti beans and girolles.
- Carrot and lime marinated scallops with avocado purée and baby carrots.

Main Course

- Steamed halibut with tomato fondue and courgette flower beignet.
- Pan-fried langoustines with apple jelly, celery emulsion and walnut crumb.

Dessert

- Bitter chocolate tart with stout ice cream and macadamia nut cream.
- Baked vanilla cheesecake, poached peach and wild strawberries.

Mon Plaisir

13 — French XX

21 Monmouth St WC2H 9DD — ⊖ Covent Garden
✆ (020) 7836 7243
Fax (020) 7240 4774
e-mail eatafrog@mail.com **www**.monplaisir.co.uk

Closed 25 December-2 January, Saturday lunch, Sunday and Bank Holidays

Menu £17 – Carte £28/34

VISA MC AE

London's oldest French restaurant is also one of its most gloriously unpretentious and individual. If you think the Eurostar transports you to France in an instant, try walking into Mon Plaisir, family run for over fifty years, where cries of 'Bonjour!' greet every arrival.

The walls are decorated with a plethora of posters, pictures and paraphernalia and the bar is from a Lyonnais brothel. Regulars all have their favourite of the numerous interconnecting rooms, all of which ooze unmistakeable Gallic charm.

But this is no themed restaurant. This is as real as the coq au vin or cassolette d'escargots. The fixed price lunch and pre-theatre menus represent excellent value and periodically held evenings featuring a particular region of France are popular events.

Incognico

13 — French XX

117 Shaftesbury Ave
WC2H 8AD — ⊖ Tottenham Court Road
✆ (020) 7836 8866 **Fax** (020) 7240 9525
e-mail incognicorestaurant@gmail.com
www.incognico.com

Closed 1 week Christmas, Sunday and Bank Holidays

Menu £25 – Carte £30/38

A/C VISA MC AE

The smart brasserie look remains largely the same, thanks to its worn-in leather, art deco styling, panelling and neatly laid tables. Table 25, enveloped in an alcove, is still the table of choice for the romantically inclined and the service continues to be well organised. But the main change is the elusiveness of those good value set menus; there is one available but you sometimes have to tease it out of them.

The cooking has a French base but with prominent Italian influences and the menu is heavily supported by daily specials. It's frill-free and confidently executed but those side dishes are needed and can push up the final bill. It still beats all those tourist joints that this part of town attracts hands down.

Sardo

Italian XX

H1

45 Grafton Way W1T 5DQ — ⊖ Warren Street
✆ (020) 7387 2521 — Closed Saturday lunch and Sunday
Fax (020) 7387 2559
e-mail info@sardo-restaurant.com **www**.sardo-restaurant.com

Carte £23/32

A/C VISA MC AE

It's worth booking as Sardo is nearly always full - entirely understandably, as this is the sort of restaurant regulars turn up to on an almost daily basis. The owner, chef and most of the kitchen hail from Sardinia and the island provides most of the influences. The ravioli and speciality pastas are made in-house and the kitchen uses particularly hard wheat imported from small suppliers in Sardinia. The cooking is fresh, unpretentious and uses a lot of char-grilling; the menu is helped out by the daily changing blackboard specials. The wine list also remains faithful as Sardinian wines make up half the list.
The room is neat and tables are simply laid; those at the back are slightly lighter, thanks to the ceiling window.

Matsuri - High Holborn

Japanese XX

J2

Mid City Pl, 71 High Holborn — ⊖ Holborn
WC1V 6EA — Closed 25 December, 1 January, Sunday and Bank Holidays
✆ (020) 7430 1970 **Fax** (020) 7430 1971
e-mail eat@matsuri-restaurant.com
www.matsuri-restaurant.com

Menu £9/20 – Carte £29/42

VISA MC AE

Not unlike the original branch in St James's, this newer member of the group offers you the choice of three restaurants in one: a large, bright main dining room, a stylish sushi bar and, downstairs, an authentic teppan-yaki room. Unlike the more traditional looking St James's, this branch is modern and contemporary in its decoration with a mix of slatted screens, glass and clean, crisp lines.
The clued up team are also on the ball, offering helpful advice to any novices and generally being unerringly courteous.
With such a broad range of dishes and styles of cooking, the menus vary enormously in scope. However, what they all share is the use of exemplary ingredients, skilled craftsmanship and precise presentation.

Hakkasan ✿

12 Chinese XX

8 Hanway Place
W1T 1HD
✆ (020) 7927 7000 **Fax** (020) 7907 1889
e-mail mail@hakkasan.com

⊖ Tottenham Court Road
Closed 24-25 December

Menu £40/55 – Carte £27/90

A/C VISA MC AE

Hakkasan

Hakkasan continues to pull in the crowds for its expertly crafted and innovative Chinese cooking. Laurels, though, are not being rested on and the restaurant understands the importance of constantly striving for improvement. Waiting staff, for example, undergo six weeks of kitchen training before they hit the floor, as dish and ingredient knowledge is paramount and some of the brief menu descriptions require a little verbal elaboration.
The restaurant itself is less intimidated by the bar than was the case in the early days. The area that was once the lounge is now called Ling Ling and is aimed at larger tables and for use by the regulars. The room as a whole still has that sexy, smouldering thing going on.
The kitchen is also still on the money. It's all in the ordering, with some thought and guidance required. The ideal is to aim for a balance of textures and flavours, from the delicacy and sweetness of the silver cod to the tender succulence of the Jasmine tea smoked ribs or the crispness of the duck roll, for example.

First Course

- Crispy duck salad with pomelo, pine nut and shallot.
- Jasmine tea smoked organic pork ribs.

Main Course

- Silver cod with Chinese honey and champagne.
- Braised belly pork claypot with salted fish, baby leek and dried chilli.

Dessert

- Chocolate fondant with passion fruit sorbet.
- Pineapple cannelloni.

Shanghai Blues

Chinese XX

J2

193-197 High Holborn WC1V 7BD ⊖ Holborn
✆ (020) 7404 1668 **Fax** (020) 7404 1448 Closed 25-26 December
e-mail info@shanghaiblues.co.uk
www.shanghaiblues.co.uk

Menu £15/40 – Carte £30/69

A/C

VISA

AE

Another stylish Chinese restaurant arrived in 2005 in the form of Shanghai Blues, housed in the Grade II listed former St Giles library. With seating for 180, the sleek design divides the room into differing spaces, along with a cool bar and mezzanine lounge, and uses hand painted silks, colourful lampshades and Chinese antiques to create a highly original, moody and atmospheric restaurant. The kitchen sticks with the traditional by offering dim sum at lunchtime while in the evening the extensive à la carte menu offers an array of dishes, including regional specialities from Shanghai.

The wine list features a number of floral wines to accompany the food but the list of Chinese teas, including some unusual blends, is well worth considering.

Fino

Spanish XX

I2

33 Charlotte St (entrance on Rathbone St) W1T 1RR ⊖ Goodge Street
Closed Saturday lunch and Sunday
✆ (020) 7813 8010 **Fax** (020) 7813 8011
e-mail info@finorestaurant.com **www**.finorestaurant.com

Carte £45/55

VISA

AE

They don't make it easy on themselves by giving their address as Charlotte Street when, in fact, the discreet entrance to this basement restaurant is actually on Rathbone Street. Perhaps that's the reason why, once you've descended the staircase, you'll find that it has something of a secretive and local vibe. Tapas is the order of the day, although it's all structured slightly more formally than you'd find in Spain and the room itself is decidedly more stylish than you'd expect. Five or six dishes per couple to share should suffice, although set menus are available for the undecided. Try a Sherry or something from the exclusively Spanish wine list. Helpful waitresses are more than willing to offer advice as well as a translation of unfamiliar words.

Crazy Bear

I2 **Asian** XX

26-28 Whitfield St W1T 2RG
(020) 7631 0088
Fax (020) 7631 1188
e-mail enquiries@crazybear-london.co.uk
www.crazybeargroup.co.uk

⊖ Goodge Street
Closed Christmas, Saturday lunch, Sunday and Bank Holidays

Carte £30/40

A/C VISA MC AE

This bear's not just crazy, he's exotic and somewhat mysterious. Even the sign is just a discreet floor mosaic by the door. The dining room on the ground floor is an effervescent fusion of art deco, Asian ornament and cosmopolitan gloss. Downstairs, the idiosyncratic design is given full rein in the ultra trendy bar and is well worth a trip in itself, provided you pass muster on the personal presentation stakes. A hostess is there at the door to greet arrivals and deliver them safely; service is well organised and pleasantly informal.

More sensory challenges come courtesy of the extensive menus which take their influence and inspiration from a number of Asian countries but do so with due respect for the ingredients.

Archipelago

H1 **Innovative** XX

110 Whitfield St W1T 5ED
(020) 7383 3346
Fax (020) 7383 7181
e-mail archipelago@onetel.com **www**.archipelago-restaurant.co.uk

⊖ Goodge Street
Closed Christmas -New Year, Bank Holidays, Saturday lunch and Sunday

Menu £39 – Carte £26/37 s

VISA MC AE

On a rainy night it takes on the atmosphere of a steamy colonial outpost and you half expect a hunter in a pith helmet to walk past your table. This restaurant is certainly not for the squeamish while those of an overly serious disposition may not get it either. 'Eclectic' is an oft-bandied word to describe hybrid cooking but here it's truly merited. Where else can you eat crocodile, zebra, kangaroo or wildebeest? Peacock has also recently appeared and scorpion has made the odd appearance in the past. The cooking itself often takes on an Asian element and the staff are all faultlessly well informed. Every surface is covered in feathers, trinkets and carvings, all for sale, and your local will seem very dull after this.

Bleeding Heart

French XX

K2

Bleeding Heart Yard (off Greville St) ⊖ Farringdon
EC1N 8SJ
Closed Christmas-New Year, Saturday, Sunday and Bank Holidays – booking essential
(020) 7242 8238
Fax (020) 7831 1402
e-mail bookings@bleedingheart.co.uk **www**.bleedingheart.co.uk

Carte £28/37

Head for the luminous hanging heart in the right-hand corner of the atmospheric 17C yard, pass the bustling bistro and terrace, and go downstairs for the full Bleeding Heart experience. You'll find a restaurant that's always busy, especially with those from the City - if you're after a more romantic dinner then come on a Friday night when the suits have long gone.

The attractions for the regulars are the fast-paced service, the French food and the terrific wine list. The menu changes seasonally and has a traditional core, while the cooking is as well practised as the service and the sauces satisfyingly rich. The owners also have their own vineyard in Hawkes Bay and their highly impressive wine list has a bias towards New Zealand and France.

Moti Mahal

Indian XX

J2

45 Great Queen St WC2B 5AA ⊖ Covent Garden
(020) 7240 9329
Closed 25-26 December, Sunday and lunch on Bank Holidays
Fax (020) 7836 0790
e-mail reservations@motimahal-uk.com
www.motimahal-uk.com

Menu £15/17 – Carte £39/66

Moti Mahal continues the trend for Indian restaurants to be big, confident and stylish. Tandoor is the speciality of the house here, in deference to the owners' original restaurants in Delhi. The kitchen exhibits a skilled, classically trained base but they work within a more contemporary idiom and presentation is skilled and attractive.

The ground floor is where the action is, including the cooking action in the open-plan kitchen, and the general atmosphere is one of noisy contentment with a feeling of spaciousness. Those who prefer a little more in the way of seduction and discretion should head to the moodier and gentler surroundings of the basement restaurant. Bar lovers will find an impressive choice, from champagne to whisky.

Asadal

J2 Korean XX

227 High Holborn WC1V 7DA
✆ (020) 7430 9006
e-mail info@asadal.co.uk
www.asadal.co.uk

⊖ Holborn
Closed Sunday lunch

Menu £10 (lunch) – Carte £18/30

A/C VISA MC AE

Every nationality of cuisine has enjoyed its moment in the spotlight and now Asadal, a basement restaurant adjacent to Holborn tube, successfully argues the case for Korean cooking to be given a higher profile.

There may be a barbecue in the centre of most of the tables but there is so much more to Korean cooking. The philosophy is built upon harmony of taste, it's all made for sharing and there's even a health dividend to most of the specialities. Novices will find that the menu is helpfully descriptive but don't be shy about using the call buttons under the table to summon help. The room is a perfectly comfortable, with lots of wood and plenty of partitions; there are quieter corners for those wishing to escape the general clamour.

Camerino

I2 Italian XX

16 Percy St W1T 1DT
✆ (020) 7637 9900
Fax (020) 7637 9696
e-mail info@camerinorestaurant.com
www.camerinorestaurant.com

⊖ Tottenham Court Road
Closed 24 -26 December, Bank Holidays, Saturday lunch and Sunday

Menu £20 – Carte £20/28

A/C VISA MC AE

Thanks to the twin appeal of decent food and wallet-friendly prices, Camerino is always one of the busiest restaurants around these parts, especially before curtain up. It's a colourful place, from the pink neon sign outside to the large red curtains inside that explain the name – Camerino is Italian for 'theatre dressing room'. The personable owner is a constant presence and he ensures that the service remains on the ball.

The à la carte menu offers a comprehensive synopsis of familiar Italian dishes, with a good value set menu running alongside. Home-made pasta is something of a speciality and portions are generous in size, healthy in composition and stout in flavour. Desserts are prepared with particular dexterity.

Passione

I2 — **Italian**

10 Charlotte St
W1T 2LT
✆ (020) 7636 2833
Fax (020) 7636 2889
e-mail liz@passione.co.uk **www**.passione.co.uk

⊖ Tottenham Court Road
Closed Christmas-New Year, Bank Holidays, Saturday lunch and Sunday – booking essential

Carte £40/47

VISA MC AE

Chef-owner Gennaro Contaldo, Jamie Oliver's great mentor, hails originally from Amalfi and it is from the sun-drenched Southern Italian coast that he seeks inspiration for his cooking. The menu offers a wide selection of dishes using the very best fresh and seasonal produce and dishes such as rabbit with rosemary and wild sorrel risotto remain perennial favourites. The restaurant, like the cooking, comes refreshingly free of unnecessary adornment. It is warm, simply decorated and brightly coloured.

In a street offering a plethora of dining options, Passione stands out not just for the quality of the cooking but also for its intimate and relaxed atmosphere. Many clearly agree as it is always busy so reservations are essential.

Cigala

J1 — **Spanish**

54 Lamb's Conduit St WC1N 3LW
✆ (020) 7405 1717
Fax (020) 7242 9949
e-mail tasty@cigala.co.uk **www**.cigala.co.uk

⊖ Holborn
Closed 24-26 December, 1 January and Easter

Menu £18 – Carte £24/37

VISA MC AE

The young chef-owner proves at Cigala that he has genuine passion and understanding of Spanish cooking in all its vibrant colours and sunny flavours. The restaurant itself is simply furnished in a clean, bright style with the large picture windows overlooking the part-pedestrianised street outside. The atmosphere is never less than convivial, especially in the more intimate evenings.

The staff all display a keen willingness to help and advise and the menu is complemented by an exclusively Spanish wine list with some very reasonably priced bottles, as well an impressive selection of Sherries. Lunchtimes represent particularly good value; a tapas menu is served in the basement bar.

Salt Yard

Mediterranean

H2

54 Goodge St W1T 4NA
(020) 7637 0657
Fax (020) 7580 7435
e-mail info@saltyard.co.uk **www**.saltyard.co.uk

⊖ Goodge Street
Closed Sunday, Saturday lunch and Bank Holidays

Carte £18/40

A/C VISA MC AE

The first thing you get is a smiley welcome and then it's a straight choice between the bar-like ground floor or the more traditionally laid out dining room downstairs; the former is usually more fun. You'll then have a few snacks with something from the mostly Italian wine list, work up to ordering some charcuterie and go from there. It's this kind of flexibility, as well as the competitive pricing, that makes this place so appealing. Spanish is obviously the main influence but the kitchen also adds some Italian specialities and these vibrant Mediterranean aromas fill the air in an enticing way. Flavours are punchy, varied and effective while puddings, such as soft chocolate cake with Frangelico ice cream, are prepared with care.

Acorn House

Italian influences

J0

69 Swinton St WC1X 9NT
(020) 7812 1842
www.acornhouserestaurant.com

⊖ King's Cross
Closed 24-31 December, Sunday and Bank Holidays

Carte £27/44

A/C VISA MC AE

Any chef using Peruvian asparagus should be sent to Acorn House. The restaurant is a joint venture between the Terence Higgins and Shoreditch Trusts and is London's first eco-friendly training restaurant.

They buy local and organic, use renewable 'green' electricity, purify their water, compost waste and recycle. They also hope to develop their training of chefs. Not only do they do all that, but the food happens to be rather good too. It's modern European with largely Italian influences and the mentoring chefs have instilled the importance of keeping it simple; portions are generous and the flavours fresh and natural. Pastas are something of a house speciality. How nice also to see staff smiling and seemingly enjoying their work.

Flâneur

Modern European

K2

41 Farringdon Rd EC1M 3JB
(020) 7404 4422 **Fax** (020) 7831 4532
e-mail mail@flaneur.com
www.flaneur.com

⊖ Farringdon
▶ **Plan VI**
Closed 24 December-2 January and Sunday dinner

Menu £25 - Carte £27

This veritable kingdom of foodie heaven shines ever brightly on the otherwise rather non-descript Farringdon Road. Part food-hall, packed to the gunnels with produce ranging from charcuterie and pasta to oils and sauces, and part-restaurant with outsized chairs lending a certain Alice in Wonderland quality, the aroma alone is enough to stimulate the most jaded of taste buds. Lunch can be a little 'on the hoof' but dinner is usually a slightly more relaxed affair as the store quietens.
The menu is tweaked daily to reflect the freshness of the produce and the style is modern European, refreshingly free from unnecessary frills. The wine list, slanted more towards France, reflects what's on the shelves.

Mela

Indian

I3

152-156 Shaftesbury Ave
WC2H 8HL
(020) 7836 8635 **Fax** (020) 7379 0527
e-mail info@melarestaurant.co.uk **www**.melarestaurant.co.uk

⊖ Leicester Square

Menu £30/37 - Carte £28

Decoratively it's light years away from your traditional Indian restaurant. In place of fading flock wallpaper and a sticky carpet come brightly coloured walls, twinkling lights, wood flooring and a general air of freshness and vitality. The resplendently attired staff are also demonstratively proud of their restaurant and display a superior understanding of customer care.

The kitchen takes Indian country cooking as its starting point and, alongside the variety of keenly priced lunch menus, comes a comprehensive à la carte menu helpfully divided into 'traditional', featuring favourites from across India, to 'exotic' which allows the chefs to show off their creativity. Its Shaftesbury Avenue location makes it a popular with theatre-goers.

Konstam at the Prince Albert

J0 **Traditional**

2 Acton St WC1X 9NA
(020) 7833 5040 **Fax** (020) 7833 5045
e-mail princealbert@konstam.co.uk
www.konstam.co.uk

⊖ King's Cross St Pancras
▶ **Plan VI**
Closed 25 December-3 January, Saturday lunch, Sunday and Bank Holidays

Carte £23/32

Gentrification may remain elusive but at least King's Cross now offers somewhere to eat. Oliver Rowe has taken a shabby Victorian pub, named it after his great grandfather and has kept the décor functional, save for a striking ornamental lighting feature.

However, what makes this restaurant so unusual is that the produce is nearly all sourced from within the boundaries of the London transport network. Using local supplies is easy when you're in Devon but Central London throws up its own challenges and you'll spend most of the time wondering where exactly some of the ingredients on your plate came from. The open kitchen means that if curiosity gets the better of you, then the chefs are within questioning range.

Abeno

I2 **Japanese**

47 Museum St
WC1A 1LY
(020) 7405 3211
Fax (020) 7405 3212
e-mail okonomi@abeno.co.uk
www.abeno.co.uk

⊖ Tottenham Court Road
Closed 24-26 and 31 December and 1 January

Menu £10 – Carte £17/35

In among the antiquarian bookshops and art galleries and, conveniently, just yards from the British Museum, sits this modest little restaurant which offers something altogether different, particularly to those who think they know Japanese food.

The speciality here is Okonomi-yaki, a dish which originated in Osaka and which represents their equivalent of fast food. It's a cross between a pancake and a pizza - the latter bearing a similarity in that it is the choice of accompanying filling that gives it the individual flavour. They are prepared at your table which doubles as a hotplate, or teppan, and are satisfyingly filling, although you can choose the size as well as the accompaniments. Novices should not be afraid to ask for advice.

Norfolk Arms

Gastropub

IJ1

Leigh & Sandwich St WC1H 9EP — ⊖ Russell Square
(020) 7388 3937
e-mail info@norfolkarms.co.uk
www.norfolkarms.co.uk

AE VISA MC

A onetime drinkers' paradise, the transformation of The Norfolk Arms to gastropub has been as welcome as it has been absolute. The bench-strewn exterior is beautifully tiled and the inside is just as charming, with ornate ceiling squares, raw plaster walls and tables neatly laid with teacloth napkins. Dried peppers, chillies and strings of onions hang from the walls and light fittings, and cured hams and salami decorate the bar.
On the menu you will find some British dishes, but it's heavily influenced by the Mediterranean and particularly Spain, and dominated by appealingly colourful tapas. Food comes served in ceramic dishes and suits the surroundings perfectly hence the occasional queue. Wines are also chosen carefully.

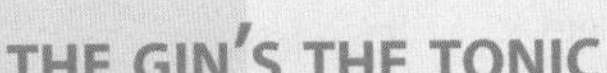

THE GIN'S THE TONIC

Londoners have always been fond of gin as a tipple, as was clear during the Gordon Riots in 1780. The only thing that gave the rampaging mob pause was the destruction of a gin distillery on Holborn Hill: aghast at seeing the spirit go to waste, the rioters threw themselves on the ground and proceeded to get roaring drunk on the flaming liquor. Thankfully these days you're more likely to find your gin served with tonic and a slice of lime.

Bayswater · Maida Vale

As hinterlands to London stations go, the area behind **Paddington** used to be one of the worst. While the railway terminus was fondly regarded for its graceful Brunel spans and association with a certain bear who liked marmalade sandwiches, the surrounding bedsits, derelict goods yards and worse were somewhat less salubrious.

Today, the situation is all change, led by the reclamation of the old canal basin, which has been turned into a mini-Canary Wharf of blue chip HQs set against a modern waterscape. Uncannily convincing human sculptures substitute for a lack of pedestrians outside of business hours - but residential complexes are going up fast and it won't be long till the transformation from seedy to "chi chi" is complete.

The canals

Heading up the basin, the narrow-boat moorings and foliage thicken out as you approach the more established area of Warwick Avenue, popularly known as **Little Venice**. The appellation is a tad fanciful, referring to the intersection of the Regent's and Grand Union Canals, but Londoners have a habit of making the most of such features. Indeed, absent the intrusion of crooning gondoliers, lovely waterside cafes and pubs have a pleasant peacefulness that is all but miraculous considering that, beyond the tree line, the Westway roars past.

Further on and the grand esplanades and chic corners of **Maida Vale** may not claim a Venetian connection, but they do evoke the flavour of a Parisian arrondissement - ironic, considering the area is named after a British victory in the Napoleonic Wars. The ubiquity of purpose-built Edwardian flats makes for a highly distinctive street scene and one of the capital's most well-to-do addresses. Behind the mansion blocks, sequestered communal gardens lie almost entirely hidden from view. Meanwhile, the Institute of Psychoanalysis - one of a scattering of curious facilities that eccentrically colour the suburban character - attempts to probe the secret spaces of the mind.

Ducking and shopping

Duck back under the Westway and you're on **Westbourne Grove**, a perennially hip shopping street claimed by both **Bayswater** and neighbouring **Notting Hill**. But while familiar chain stores begin to outnumber the darling little boutiques as you head towards the eastern district, Bayswater itself has enjoyed something of a resurgence in cool in recent years.

Whose side are you on ?

Though it has long been known for its cosmopolitan nature and convenient location within striking distance of the capital's glamour hotspots, Bayswater used to suffer from its reputation - in estate-agent speak - of being 'the wrong side of the park'. Those who could afford to bought in **Knightsbridge** and **Kensington** to the south, resulting in an odd hodgepodge ghetto north of Hyde Park, a combination of diaspora communities, transient hotel populations and stifling middle classness (this, after all, was where Charles Ryder ached to escape from in *Brideshead Revisited*).

On the up

The bed and breakfasts are still here and the turnover of residents remains relatively high - but those choosing to make Bayswater their home are adding some real jazz. The area first knew it had arrived when Madonna bought a £7 million townhouse at its edge, with her erstwhile producer wunderkind William Orbit close by. Yet it was the revelation that one Mr and Mrs Blair had purchased a post-prime ministerial pile in **Connaught Square** that really put the district on the map.

Their instinct may well be right - Bayswater is a handsome, diverse but neglected corner of London that seems to be on the up. Walking down **Queensway** has always exposed the eavesdropper to a barrage of languages, from Greek to Portuguese to Arabic. Now it is the area itself which is finding its voice.

S. Ollivier / MICHELIN

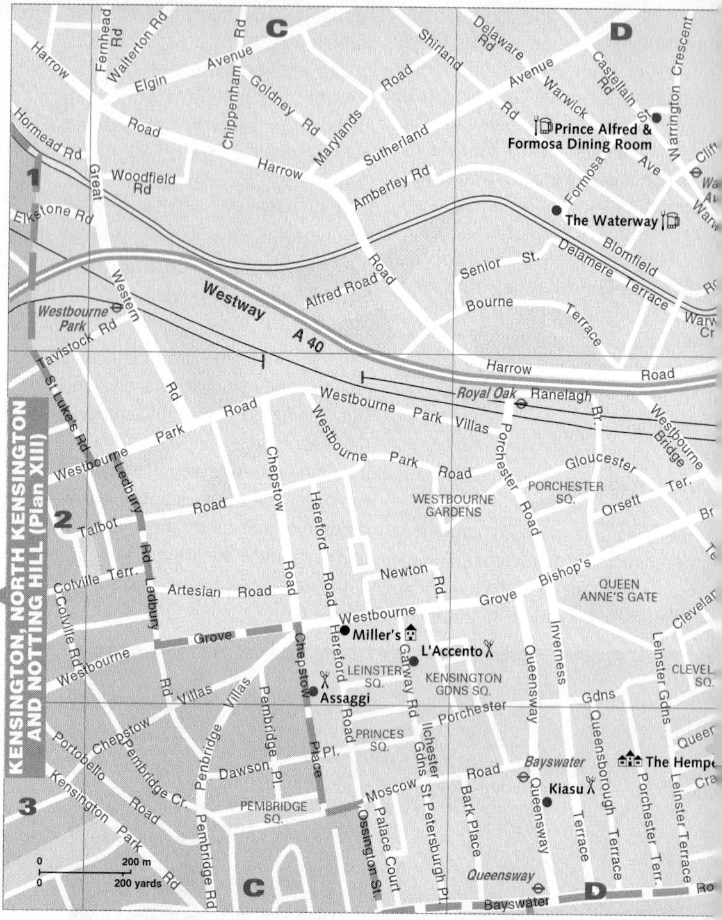

KENSINGTON, NORTH KENSINGTON AND NOTTING HILL (Plan XIII)

C D

1 2 3

Prince Alfred & Formosa Dining Room

The Waterway

Miller's

L'Accento

Assaggi

Kiasu

The Hempel

Harrow Road
Elgin Avenue
Fernhead Rd
Walterton Rd
Chippenham Rd
Goldney Rd
Shirland Road
Delaware Rd
Warwick Avenue
Castellain Rd
Warrington Crescent
Hormead Rd
Woodfield Rd
Great Western Rd
Marylands Road
Sutherland Ave
Amberley Rd
Formosa St.
Elkstone Rd
Blomfield Rd
Delamere Terrace
Senior St.
Alfred Road
Bourne Terrace
Westway A 40
Westbourne Park
Tavistock Rd
St Luke's Rd
Royal Oak
Ranelagh Br.
Westbourne Bridge
Westbourne Park Road
Westbourne Park Villas
Porchester Road
Gloucester Ter.
PORCHESTER SQ.
Orsett Ter.
WESTBOURNE GARDENS
Chepstow Road
Hereford Road
Talbot Road
Ledbury Rd
Colville Terr.
Colville Rd
Artesian Road
Newton Rd.
Bishop's Bridge Road
QUEEN ANNE'S GATE
Westbourne Grove
Cleveland
Garway Rd
KENSINGTON GDNS SQ.
LEINSTER SQ.
Queensway
Inverness Terrace
Leinster Gdns
CLEVELAND SQ.
Westbourne Villas
Pembridge Villas
Pembridge Pl.
Chepstow Place
Porchester Gdns
Queensborough Terrace
Porchester Terr.
Leinster Terrace
Chepstow Villas
Pembridge Cr.
Portobello Road
Kensington Park Rd
Dawson Pl.
PRINCES SQ.
Ilchester Gdns
Bayswater Road
Moscow Road
PEMBRIDGE SQ.
Ossington St.
Palace Court
St Petersburgh Pl.
Bark Place
Queensway
Bayswater
Pembridge Rd

0 200 m
0 200 yards

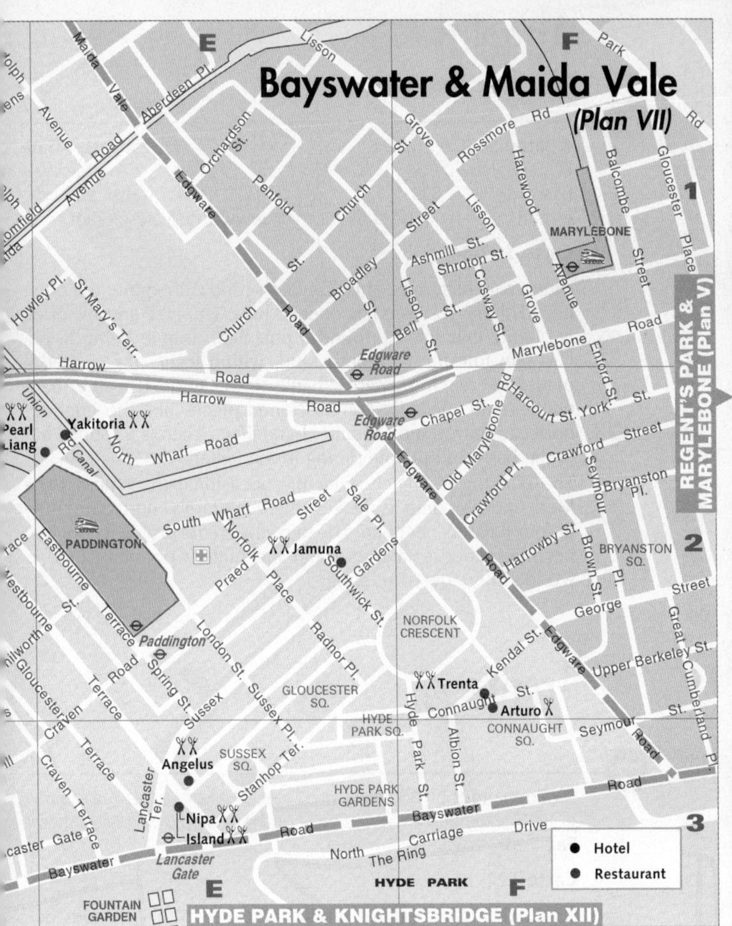

Bayswater & Maida Vale
(Plan VII)
MARYLEBONE
PADDINGTON
Edgware Road
Paddington
Lancaster Gate
Yakitoria
Pearl Liang
Jamuna
Trenta
Arturo
Angelus
Nipa
Island
NORFOLK CRESCENT
GLOUCESTER SQ.
HYDE PARK SQ.
CONNAUGHT SQ.
SUSSEX SQ.
HYDE PARK GARDENS
BRYANSTON SQ.
HYDE PARK
FOUNTAIN GARDEN
Hotel
Restaurant
REGENT'S PARK & MARYLEBONE (Plan V)
HYDE PARK & KNIGHTSBRIDGE (Plan XII)

Angelus

E3

French XX

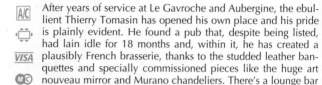

4 Bathurst St W2 2SD
(020) 7402 0083
Fax (020) 7402 5383
e-mail info@angelusrestaurant.co.uk **www**.angelusrestaurant.co.uk

⊖ Lancaster Gate
Closed 25-26 and 31 December, 1 January and Monday

Carte £27/44

After years of service at Le Gavroche and Aubergine, the ebullient Thierry Tomasin has opened his own place and his pride is plainly evident. He found a pub that, despite being listed, had lain idle for 18 months and, within it, he has created a plausibly French brasserie, thanks to the studded leather banquettes and specially commissioned pieces like the huge art nouveau mirror and Murano chandeliers. There's a lounge bar at the back and private dining in the cellar.

The cooking is French, with the occasional foray across the Med, and simplicity is the key; there are rarely more than three or four flavours per plate. The foie gras crème brûlée has swiftly become a house favourite and the buttery pomme purée is wonderfully artery-troubling.

Trenta

F2

Italian XX

30 Connaught St W2 2AF
(020) 7262 9623
Fax (020) 7262 9636

Closed 1-14 January, Sunday, and Bank Holidays – dinner only and lunch Thursday and Friday

Carte £21/26

Let's hope Trenta enjoys similar longevity to the previous occupant of Number Thirty, Al San Vincenzo, for there are clear similarities: a palpable sense of neighbourhood and uncomplicated Italian cooking. There are just 7 tables in the front room, which a gilt framed mirror tries to make feel bigger. Red and cream are the colours, matched by the surprisingly comfy leather chairs. Downstairs has another 5 tables but you don't want to be the first ones down there.

The menu is constantly changing and offers quite a choice - there can be up to ten starters and main courses, all concisely described. Dishes themselves are also appealingly unfussy. The price is commendable and even the £2 cover charge is bearable when one considers the breads and little extras.

Jamuna

Indian XX

E2

38A Southwick St W2 1JQ
✆ (020) 7723 5056
Fax (020) 7706 1870
e-mail info@jamuna.co.uk **www**.jamuna.co.uk

⊖ Edgware Road
Closed 25 December-1 January and lunch Saturday to Sunday

Menu £20 (lunch) - Carte £35/63

Its largely transient population means that Bayswater has never been an area particularly noted for the quality of its restaurants. Jamuna is the latest to try its luck and its distinctly smart looking façade tells you that this is no ordinary Indian restaurant.It's similarly well turned-out inside, with neatly laid tables and modern artwork for sale on the walls, although, curiously, there are no clues in the décor with regard to the nationality of the cooking.

The cooking is more than sound. It has a broad regional base but with few predictable offerings. Dishes, particularly those involving seafood, are vibrant and fresh, display a certain refinement and are full of flavour. The wine list is extensive and thoughtfully put together.

Island

Modern European XX

E3

at Royal Lancaster H.,
Lancaster Terrace W2 2TY
✆ (020) 7551 6070 **Fax** (020) 7551 6071
e-mail eat@islandrestaurant.co.uk **www**.islandrestaurant.co.uk

⊖ Lancaster Gate

Menu £21 - Carte £24/36

The Island in question may be more 'traffic' than 'tropical' but there's no denying they've made the best of an unpromising location. It's actually part of the huge Royal Lancaster Hotel but you wouldn't know it if you approach this large glass structure from the park. Inside it's all very crisp and bright; there's a bar to one side with views of the park (and that traffic) but the atmosphere is relaxed and the staff demonstrate commendable enthusiasm.

The menu tries to appeal to everyone by offering an easy mix of grilled steaks, European brasserie favourites, a bit of Asia here and some American there. So expect everything from crab cakes and burgers to sea bass and risotto, all prepared on view through the hatch into the kitchen.

Yakitoria

E2 Japanese XX

25 Sheldon Sq W2 6EY
(020) 3214 3000
www.yakitoria.co.uk

⊖ Paddington
Closed 24-26 December, 1-2 January, Saturday lunch and Sunday

Menu £35 – Carte £29/43

A/C  VISA MC AE

'Paddington Central' is the imaginative name for this new development next to the station and after all the office blocks now come the restaurants. Yakitoria's owners have several places in Moscow but here they turn more to the US for their take on Japanese food, for it includes aburi sushi and assorted rolls, alongside the Tokyo and Osaki specialities. The Kushi-yaki, or skewers, are something of a house speciality. Bento boxes are available for the local businesses.

The place is big in size, funky in design and lively in atmosphere. The service is enthusiastic and the chefs, in their natty little kimonos, go about their business with vim and vigour. There's direct access from Platform 8 for any sushi-loving commuters.

Nipa

E3 Thai XX

at Royal Lancaster H.,
Lancaster Terrace W2 2TY
(020) 7551 6039 **Fax** (020) 7724 3191
www.niparestaurant.co.uk

⊖ Lancaster Gate
Closed Saturday lunch, Sunday and Bank Holidays

Menu £27/32 – Carte £21/47

A/C VISA  AE 

You'll find Nipa to be a little oasis of calm and hospitality, once you've made it up to the first floor of the Royal Lancaster and sidestepped the businessmen on their laptops in the adjacent lounge. Its teak panelling and ornaments are all imported from Thailand and they've done a convincing job of replicating the original Nipa in Bangkok's Landmark Hotel – if anything, it's even a little smarter.

The menu is comprehensive, with a mix of the recognisable blended with more regional specialities. Dishes are marked 1-3 in chillies for their respective heat, come in decent sizes and the harmonious blend of flavours and textures successfully delivers what the aromas promise. Set menus are at the back and provide a convenient all-round experience.

Pearl Liang

Chinese XX

E2

8 Sheldon Sq., Paddington Central
W2 6EZ
(020) 7289 7000
www.pearlliang.co.uk

⊖ Paddington
Closed 25-26 December

Menu £10 (lunch) – Carte £20/65 s

Paddington Central, to those who don't work in the area, is a newly created office and residential development, best reached via Platform 8 from Paddington Station. One of the first restaurants to open was Pearl Liang, a Chinese restaurant. It's big but comfy, with an eye-catching, specially commissioned painting on one wall.

When the 'neighbourhood' takes off then the generously proportioned dim sum will surely be the local lunch of choice. After 5pm check out the specialities on the à la carte, such as fresh abalone, shark's fin soup or even the pot of 'Buddha Jump over the wall'; there are three balanced set menus as well. From Shanghai dumplings to Szechuan chicken, the choice is extensive. All that's missing is a tad more enthusiasm from the staff.

A/C VISA MC AE

Arturo

Italian X

F2

23 Connaught St W2 2AY
(020) 7706 3388
Fax (020) 7402 9195
e-mail enquiries@arturorestaurant.co.uk
www.arturorestaurant.co.uk

⊖ Marble Arch
Closed 25-26 December, 1 January, Good Friday and Easter Sunday

Menu £17 – Carte £24/33

Connaught Street stands in stark contrast to the rather drab surroundings of nearby Edgware Road and Arturo is a good example of the type of stylish establishment that is starting to crop up in this street. The large glass façade and moody lighting set the tone for the elegant informality within, with its sleek and modern design. The chef looks to two regions of Italy for inspiration, Tuscany and Sicily, and offers classic dishes from these areas alongside those with more original elements. The exclusively Italian wine list has some interesting little gems and the service is slick and attentive.

It retains the intimacy of a friendly, local Italian and may be just the place to appeal to anyone who owns property in Connaught Square.

A/C VISA MC AE

Assaggi ✿

Italian

39 Chepstow Pl, (above Chepstow pub) W2 4TS
(020) 7792 5501
e-mail nipi@assaggi.demon.co.uk
www.assaggi.com

Bayswater
Closed 2 weeks Christmas, Sunday and Bank Holidays – booking essential

Carte £36/48

Assaggi

Good cooking starts with good produce. Nowhere is this more apparent than in Assaggi where the quality of their raw ingredients is never less than superlative. A veal chop will cut like butter, pasta has a lightness and vitality and flakes of pure white halibut will just peel off. There is more than a hint of Sardinia in the cooking, from the carta da musica crisp bread to the pecorino, roasted meats and the respect for vegetables, but what is so appealing is that the dishes arrive with an appetisingly rustic simplicity. Those menu prices that seemed high when you ordered will appear justified when you've finished eating.

You get the impression that everyone here is eating in their favourite restaurant, although its popularity means it's not so secret these days and you'll need to book well in advance. Still, those greeted with kisses from the staff elicit envious looks as this is a place where we all want to belong. It may be above a pub but the tall windows and colour add to the brightness and the acoustics have been recently improved.

First Course

- Tonno alla tartara.
- Tagliolini alle erbe.

Main Course

- Pan-fried calf's liver with sage and onions.
- Fritto Misto.

Dessert

- Dark chocolate flourless cake, white chocolate ice cream.
- Lemon tart.

L'Accento

Italian

C2

16 Garway Rd W2 4NH
(020) 7243 2201
Fax (020) 7243 2201
e-mail laccentorest@aol.com

Bayswater
Closed Sunday and Bank Holidays

Menu £22 - Carte £22/31

L'Accento has been a feature in Garway Road now for seventeen years; it knows exactly what it does and it does it very well. That means earthy and flavoursome Italian cooking, served in casual surroundings at a very decent price. The à la carte offers a rounded trip throughout Italy but it's hard to ignore the right hand side of the menu where the set menu is printed – this also offers some choice and comes at an exceptionally good price. The food is earthy, full of flavour and very satisfying.

The more familiar your face, the better the service you'll get, but whoever you are, you'll find the atmosphere's always convivial. Avoid the duller back room, though, and don't bother asking for that corner table – that's where the owner sits.

Kiasu

Asian

D3

48 Queensway W2 3RY
(020) 7727 8810
Fax (020) 7727 7220

Bayswater

Carte £11/24

Queensway is awash with similar looking restaurants, but when there's one named after the Hokkien Chinese word for 'afraid to be second best' then it must be worth exploring. The owner of Kiasu is Malaysian and the Strait of Malacca, a passageway between the Indian and Pacific oceans, is the inspiration behind his food. That means exotic-sounding specialities like nasi lemak or otak-otak but also dishes from neighbouring countries like Indonesia and Singapore. Some are hot and spicy, others light and fragrant and this is food designed for sharing; as your dishes arrive in no particularly order and the tables are a little small, you may have to do some juggling.

The place is always packed out; it's simply but brightly decorated and good fun.

The Waterway

Gastropub

D1

54 Formosa St W9 2JU ⊖ Warwick Avenue
✆ (020) 7266 3557 **Fax** (020) 7266 3547
e-mail info@thewaterway.co.uk **www**.thewaterway.co.uk

Carte £28/38

A glimpse of sun and we're all outside so praise be for places like The Waterway. Not only does it have a large terrace but its pleasing vista takes in the canal, barges and the church spire beyond, although you'll have to be quick off the mark to get a spot. Spit and sawdust this is not. Instead you'll find quite a swanky affair - all wood and leather, with the staff dressed in black.

The kitchen successfully balances the traditional with the contemporary. So, the 'classics' section on the menu may include moules or burgers and there are barbecues and Sunday roasts, but you'll also find more restauranty food involving sea bass or pork belly. Puds are quite delicate little things, and it's nice to see cheese being taken seriously.

Prince Alfred & Formosa Dining Room

Gastropub

D1

5A Formosa St W9 1EE ⊖ Warwick Avenue
✆ (020) 7286 3287
e-mail princealfred@youngs.co.uk

Menu £10 – Carte £21/31

It is possible, if you're approaching from Warrington Crescent, to find yourself seated in the Formosa Dining Room and be virtually unaware of the pub to which it is attached. This would be a crying shame as the Prince Alfred is a magnificent Grade II listed pub which dates back to 1863. Its most striking feature, along with the etched glass, is the partitions creating individual private booths.

Heritage enthusiasts may shudder at the more contemporary, almost semi-industrial, dining room which has been attached but local diners seemingly have little regard for such sensibilities and just enjoy the space. The very open open-kitchen produces robust gastropub staples with global influences, while the wine lists features over thirty choices by the glass.

S. Ollivier / MICHELIN

City of London · Clerkenwell Finsbury · Southwark

If you're looking for the real London, then this is where it all began. The original square mile was first settled by the Romans nearly 2,000 years ago and today is one of the financial capitals of the world. From the City you can head north to Finsbury to see remnants of the wall that once marked the boundaries of London, and then west to Clerkenwell where a magpie attitude to the past makes this one of the trendiest places to work and play. Alternatively you can cross the river at London Bridge and head over to Southwark. Once the City's poor relative, full of prisons, brothels and gambling dens, today it's enjoying a spectacular resurgence and fast becoming one of the most exciting and vibrant areas of London.

A little history...

The City of London has always been a trading centre. Today it's devoted to the business of money but you can still read signs of a different mercantile past in the street names – **Cheapside** (from the old English for market), **Poultry** and **Pudding Lane**, where the Great Fire of 1666 first started. **Leadenhall Market** offers retail therapy at a less frantic pace: the beautiful covered market stands on the site of a lead-roofed manor house, hence the name, which was owned in the 15C by one Richard Whittington, Lord Mayor of London. Today the cobbled market is full of shops, pubs and even a shoe-shining stand for the city gent or lady in a hurry.

If all this talk of money and shopping seems a little mercenary, then you can always seek sanctuary at the cultural oasis that is the **Barbican Centre**. The brutalist architecture is not to everyone's taste, but with a wide-ranging programme of theatre and music as well as its own cinema there's something to suit everyone. Just down the road is **Smithfield Market**, which has been London's main meat market for over 800 years. It still does a roaring trade in meat and poultry, as well as other foodstuffs. Unsurprisingly this has attracted a fair number of restaurants, which take advantage of the wealth of excellent ingredients right on their doorstep.

The City trend for building ever higher glass skyscrapers has yet to reach Clerkenwell, formerly full of artisans and factories and now occupying an interesting hinterland of decaying 60s tower blocks and reclaimed factory space. Although there's no shortage of offices, workers here are more likely to be sporting the latest designer jeans and trainers than wearing a suit. Graffiti is an overground art form and the labyrinthine streets are stuffed to the gills with gorgeous places to eat and drink, each more self-consciously hip than the last. Although the vibe is anything goes, there's a definite trend for reclaiming the past with flock wallpaper and rescued objects frequently displayed with a touch of knowing irony.

Southwark too is reclaiming its workaday past with **Tate Bankside**, the power station turned art gallery, and the recreated **Globe Theatre** leading the way. While Southwark has a rich tradition of fine pubs and inns – Chaucer's pilgrims set off from the Tabard Inn in Southwark – these days the bars and restaurants are likely to be converted from warehouses or dry docks. The **Borough Market** perfectly encapsulates the Southwark resurgence. There has been a market on this site for nearly 1,000 years; however, in the last few years it has made the jump from a respected wholesale market to a popular destination for weekend shoppers. Alongside excellent, often organic, produce there are also more unusual treats on offer: go to **Scandelicious** for Swedish delicacies, partake of a refreshing drink at **East Teas**, or visit **Dark Sugars** for some dangerously addictive chocolates. The market is open on Fridays and Saturdays but you'll need to get there early to beat the rush and spot top chefs buying in supplies. During the rest of the week **Bedale Street** and **Stoney Street** host a cluster of foody shops offering everything from organic poultry at **Wyndham House** to superb cakes at **Konditor & Cook.**

C. Eymenier / MICHELIN

City of London
(Plan VIII)

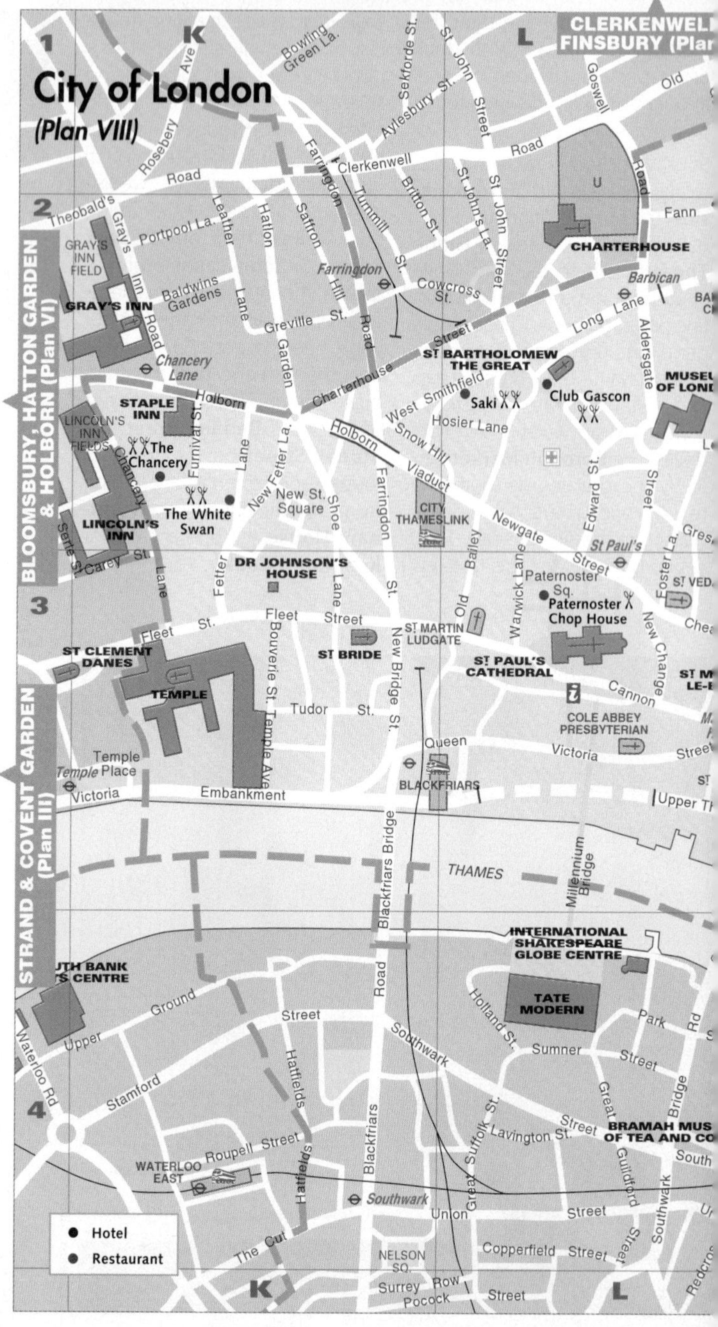

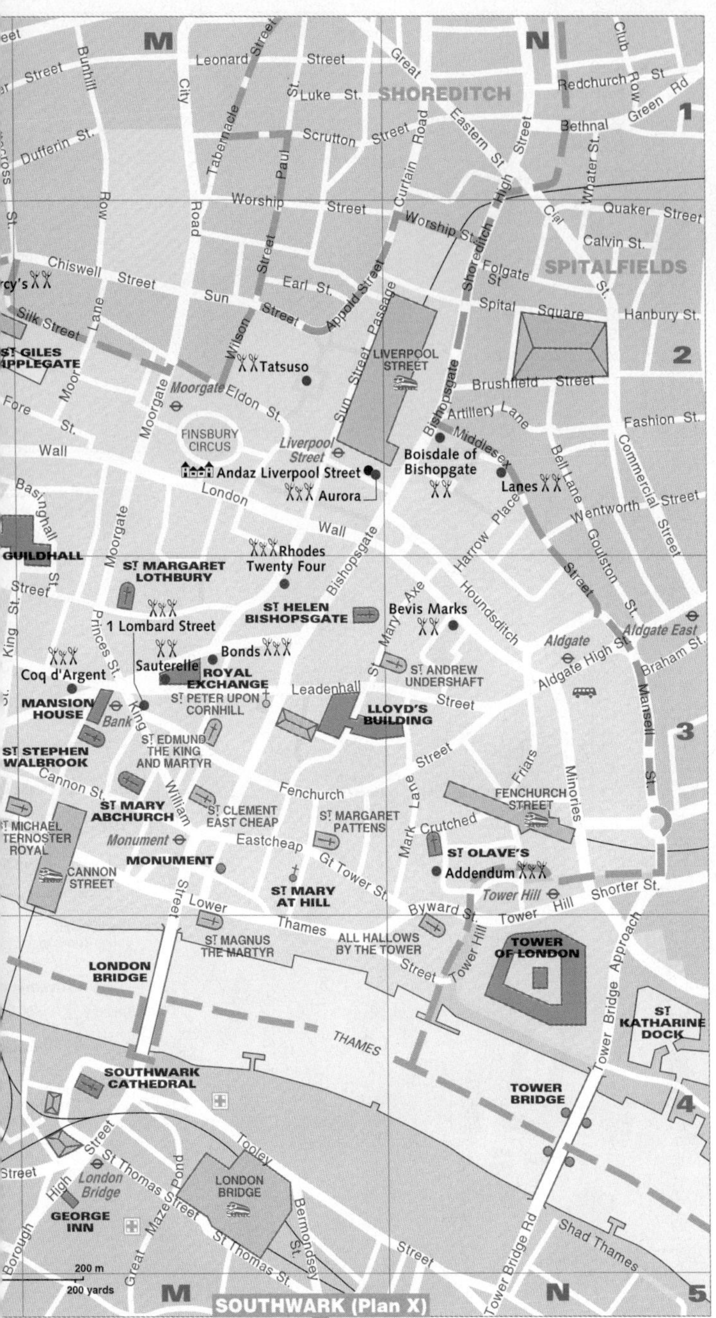
M
N
SHOREDITCH
SPITALFIELDS
Leonard Street
Great Eastern St
St Luke St.
Redchurch St
Club Row
Bethnal Green Rd
Scrutton Street
Tabernacle Street
Paul Street
Curtain Road
Worship Street
Quaker Street
Calvin St.
Folgate St
Spital Square
Hanbury St.
Chiswell Street
Sun Street
Earl St.
Appold Street
Sun Street Passage
Shoreditch High Street
Wilson Street
Silk Street
ST GILES CRIPPLEGATE
Tatsuso
LIVERPOOL STREET
Brushfield Street
Fashion St.
Moorgate
Eldon St.
Moor Lane
Fore St.
Wall
FINSBURY CIRCUS
Liverpool Street
Artillery Lane
Middlesex Street
Bishopsgate
Boisdale of Bishopgate
Andaz Liverpool Street
Aurora
Lanes
London Wall
Basinghall St.
Bell Lane
Commercial Street
Wentworth Street
Goulston St.
GUILDHALL
ST MARGARET LOTHBURY
Rhodes Twenty Four
Harrow Place
Houndsditch
ST HELEN BISHOPSGATE
Bevis Marks
Aldgate
Aldgate East
Aldgate High St.
Braham St.
1 Lombard Street
Princes St.
King St.
Coq d'Argent
Sauterelle
Bonds
ROYAL EXCHANGE
St Mary Axe
ST ANDREW UNDERSHAFT
MANSION HOUSE
Bank
ST PETER UPON CORNHILL
Leadenhall Street
LLOYD'S BUILDING
Mansell St.
ST STEPHEN WALBROOK
ST EDMUND THE KING AND MARTYR
Cannon St.
William St.
Fenchurch Street
Lime Street
Mark Lane
Minories
Jewry
FENCHURCH STREET
ST MARY ABCHURCH
ST CLEMENT EAST CHEAP
ST MARGARET PATTENS
Crutched Friars
ST MICHAEL PATERNOSTER ROYAL
Monument
Eastcheap
ST OLAVE'S
MONUMENT
Addendum
CANNON STREET
Gt Tower St.
Tower Hill
ST MARY AT HILL
Shorter St.
Lower Thames Street
Byward St.
Tower Hill
ST MAGNUS THE MARTYR
ALL HALLOWS BY THE TOWER
TOWER OF LONDON
LONDON BRIDGE
Tower Bridge Approach
ST KATHARINE DOCK
THAMES
SOUTHWARK CATHEDRAL
TOWER BRIDGE
Tooley Street
Borough High Street
London Bridge
St Thomas Street
Maze Pond
LONDON BRIDGE
GEORGE INN
Bermondsey St.
Shad Thames
Tower Bridge Rd
Great Maze Pond
200 m
200 yards
SOUTHWARK (Plan X)
1
2
3
4
5

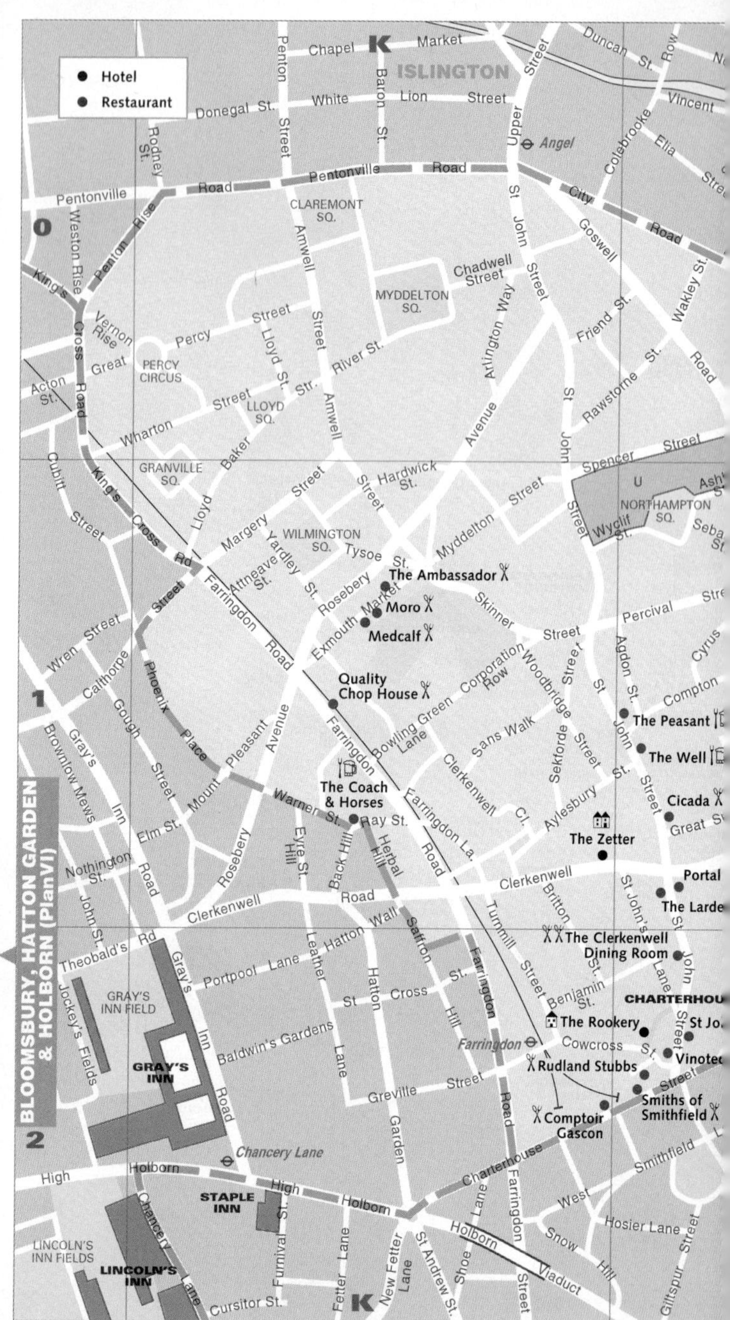

Hotel
Restaurant
ISLINGTON
Chapel Market
White Lion Street
Donegal St.
Penton Street
Baron St.
Rodney St.
Upper Street
Angel
Duncan St.
Vincent
Colebrooke Row
Elia
Pentonville Road
Pentonville
City Road
CLAREMONT SQ.
Goswell Road
Weston Rise
Penton Rise
King's Cross Road
Vernon Rise
Amwell Street
MYDDELTON SQ.
Chadwell Street
Arlington Way
St John Street
Friend St.
Wakley St.
Great Percy Street
PERCY CIRCUS
Lloyd St.
River St.
Acton St.
Lloyd Baker Street
LLOYD SQ.
Wharton Street
Rawstorne St.
Avenue
Spencer Street
GRANVILLE SQ.
Cubitt Street
Hardwick St.
Myddelton Street
NORTHAMPTON SQ.
Wyclif St.
Margery Street
WILMINGTON SQ.
Yardley St.
Tysoe St.
Attneave St.
The Ambassador
Rosebery Avenue
Exmouth Market
Moro
Medcalf
Skinner Street
Percival Street
Farringdon Road
Wren Street
Calthorpe Street
Quality Chop House
Corporation Row
Woodbridge Street
Agdon St.
Compton
Bowling Green Lane
Sans Walk
The Peasant
The Well
Gough Street
Phoenix Place
Gray's Inn Road
Brownlow Mews
Mount Pleasant
Sekforde Street
Clerkenwell Cl.
The Coach & Horses
Warner St.
Ray St.
Cicada
Aylesbury St.
The Zetter
Great S
Elm St.
Nothington St.
John St.
Eyre St. Hill
Back Hill
Herbal Hill
Farringdon La.
Clerkenwell Road
Britton St.
St John's Lane
Portal
The Larder
Theobald's Rd
Hatton Wall
Saffron Hill
Turnmill Street
The Clerkenwell Dining Room
Portpool Lane
Leather Lane
Hatton Garden
St Cross St.
GRAY'S INN FIELD
Jockey's Fields
Benjamin St.
CHARTERHOUSE
The Rookery
Baldwin's Gardens
Farringdon
Cowcross St.
GRAY'S INN
Rudland Stubbs
Greville Street
Smiths of Smithfield
Comptoir Gascon
Charterhouse Street
Chancery Lane
High Holborn
Smithfield
STAPLE INN
Holborn
West Smithfield
Hosier Lane
Holborn Viaduct
Snow Hill
LINCOLN'S INN FIELDS
LINCOLN'S INN
Furnival St.
Fetter Lane
New Fetter Lane
St Andrew St.
Shoe Lane
Farringdon Street
Giltspur Street
Cursitor St.
BLOOMSBURY, HATTON GARDEN & HOLBORN (Plan VI)

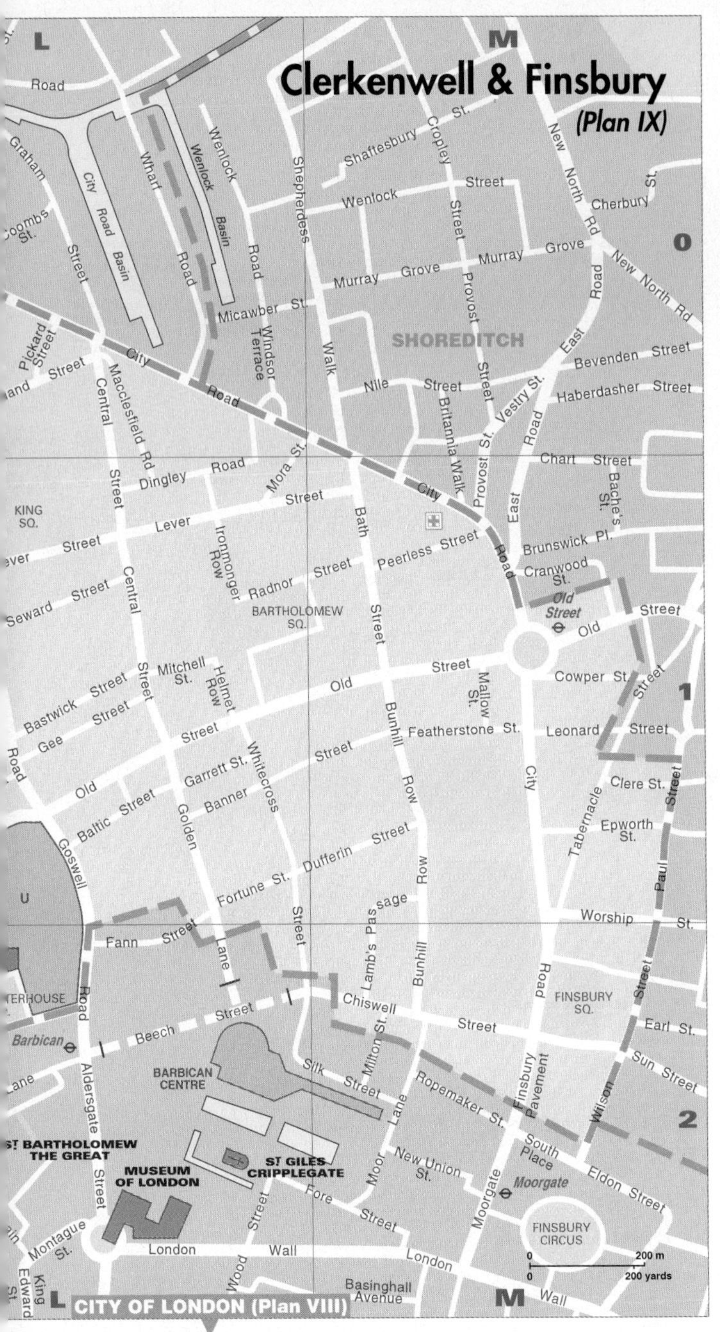
Clerkenwell & Finsbury
(Plan IX)
L
M
O
1
2
SHOREDITCH
KING SQ.
BARTHOLOMEW SQ.
FINSBURY SQ.
FINSBURY CIRCUS
BARBICAN CENTRE
ST BARTHOLOMEW THE GREAT
MUSEUM OF LONDON
ST GILES CRIPPLEGATE
Old Street
Barbican
Moorgate
City Road Basin
Wenlock Basin
Wharf Road
Wenlock Road
Shepherdess Walk
Shaftesbury St.
Cropley St.
Wenlock Street
Murray Grove
Provost Street
New North Rd
Cherbury St.
East Road
Micawber St.
Windsor Terrace
Nile Street
Britannia Walk
Bevenden Street
Haberdasher Street
Vestry St.
Provost St.
Chart Street
Bache's St.
Graham Street
Pickard Street
Macclesfield Rd
Central Street
City Road
Dingley Road
Mora St.
Lever Street
Ironmonger Row
Bath Street
Peerless Street
Brunswick Pl.
Cranwood St.
Radnor Street
Seward Street
Mitchell St.
Helmet Row
Bastwick Street
Gee Street
Old Street
Mallow St.
Cowper St.
Featherstone St.
Leonard Street
Bunhill Row
Garrett St.
Whitecross Street
Banner Street
Baltic Street
Golden Lane
Goswell Road
Clere St.
Tabernacle Street
Epworth St.
Paul Street
Dufferin Street
Fortune St.
Lamb's Passage
Worship St.
Fann Street
Chiswell Street
Beech Street
Earl St.
Sun Street
Aldersgate Street
Silk Street
Milton St.
Ropemaker St.
Moor Lane
Finsbury Pavement
Wilson Street
South Place
Eldon Street
New Union St.
Fore Street
Wood Street
Moorgate
Montague St.
King Edward St.
London Wall
Basinghall Avenue
CITY OF LONDON (Plan VIII)
200 m
200 yards

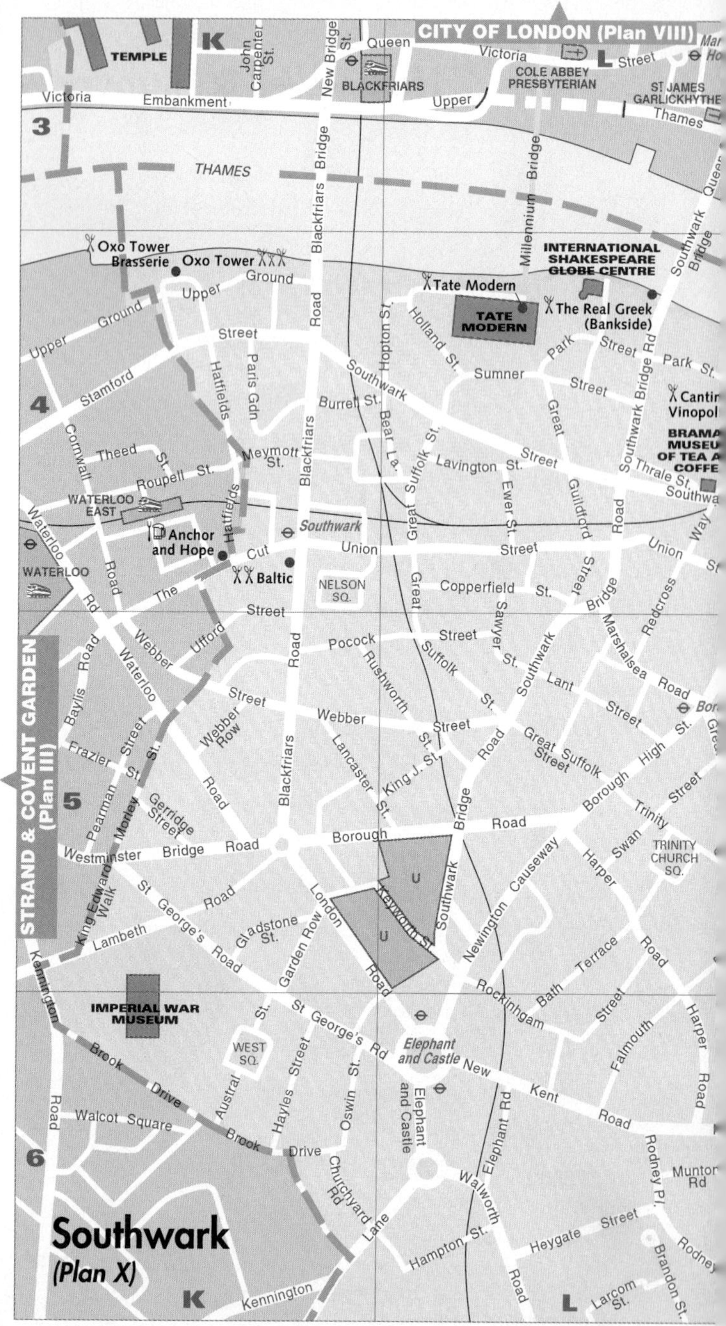
CITY OF LONDON (Plan VIII)
TEMPLE
BLACKFRIARS
COLE ABBEY PRESBYTERIAN
ST JAMES GARLICKHYTHE
THAMES
Oxo Tower Brasserie
Oxo Tower
INTERNATIONAL SHAKESPEARE GLOBE CENTRE
Tate Modern
TATE MODERN
The Real Greek (Bankside)
WATERLOO EAST
Anchor and Hope
Southwark
Baltic
WATERLOO
NELSON SQ.
STRAND & COVENT GARDEN (Plan III)
TRINITY CHURCH SQ.
IMPERIAL WAR MUSEUM
WEST SQ.
Elephant and Castle
Southwark
(Plan X)

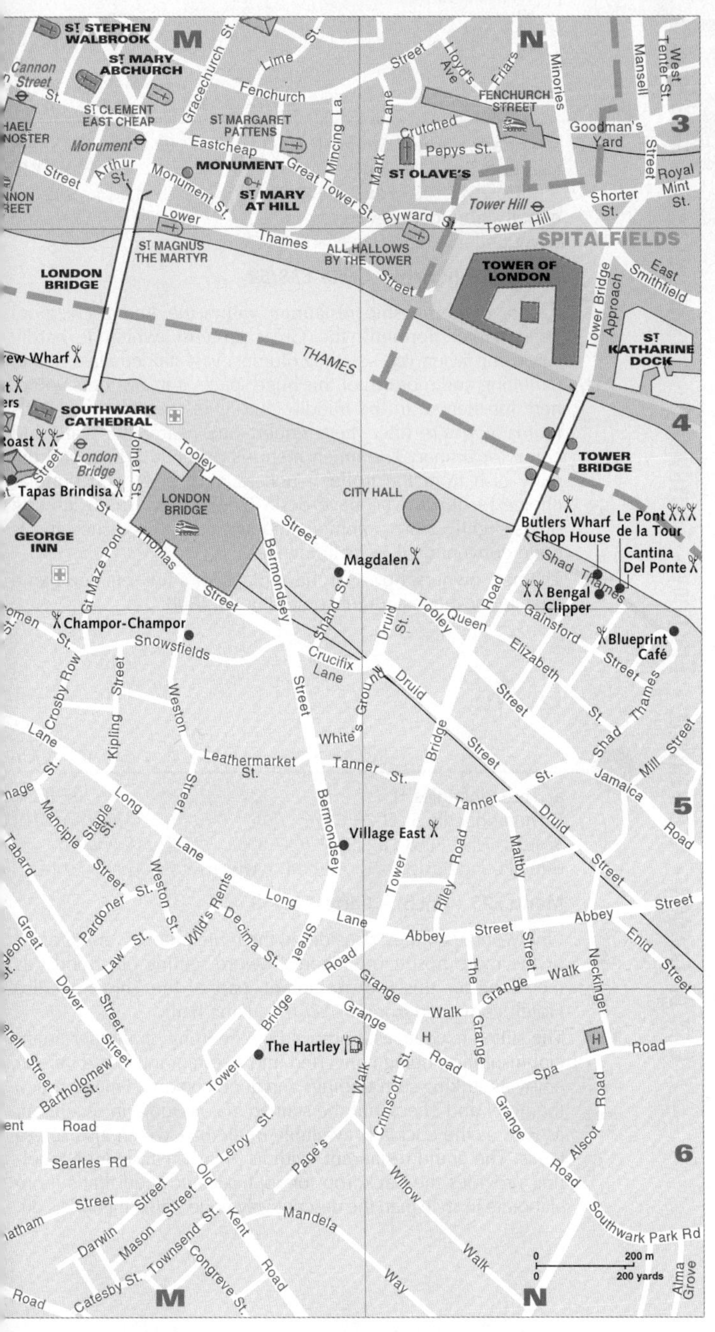

ST STEPHEN WALBROOK
ST MARY ABCHURCH
ST CLEMENT EAST CHEAP
ST MARGARET PATTENS
MONUMENT
ST MARY AT HILL
ST OLAVE'S
FENCHURCH STREET
ST MAGNUS THE MARTYR
ALL HALLOWS BY THE TOWER
LONDON BRIDGE
TOWER OF LONDON
SPITALFIELDS
ST KATHARINE DOCK
THAMES
SOUTHWARK CATHEDRAL
TOWER BRIDGE
CITY HALL
GEORGE INN
Tapas Brindisa
Magdalen
Butlers Wharf Chop House
Le Pont de la Tour
Cantina Del Ponte
Bengal Clipper
Blueprint Café
Champor-Champor
Village East
The Hartley
Tooley Street
Bermondsey Street
Long Lane
Tower Bridge Road
Abbey Street
Grange Road
Old Kent Road
Southwark Park Rd
M
N
3
4
5
6
0 200 m
0 200 yards

Aurora

M2 **Modern European** XXX

at Andaz Liverpool Street H.,
Liverpool St EC2M 7QN
✆ (020) 7618 7000 **Fax** (020) 7618 5035
e-mail aurora.londonliv@andaz.com
www.london.liverpoolstreet.andaz.com

⊖ Liverpool Street
▶ Plan VIII
Closed Saturday, Sunday and Bank Holidays

Menu £28 (lunch) – Carte £38/54

A/C VISA MC AE D

Aurora is the flagship restaurant within the Andaz Liverpool Street Hotel (formerly the Great Eastern), which is hardly surprising when you see the columns, vast stained glass dome, panelling and mosaics of this huge space. If its business you're here for then sit in the middle (the lightest section), but if it's intimacy you're after then request one nearer the wall, and come for dinner. The lunch menu is decently priced and the daily dish from the trolley, such as roast pork, is a popular choice for those who have desks to return to. The à la carte offers slightly more ambitious modern European dishes and is quite conventional in its influences.

The new owners, however, have plans for a full refit and name change for the restaurant some time in 2008.

Bonds

M3 **Modern European** XXX

at Threadneedles H.,
5 Threadneedle St EC2R 8AY
✆ (020) 7657 8088 **Fax** (020) 7657 8089
e-mail bonds@theetongroup.com **www**.theetoncollection.com

⊖ Bank
▶ Plan VIII
Closed Saturday and Sunday

Menu £25 (lunch) – Carte £31/48

A/C VISA MC AE D

One wonders if they considered the more culinary apt 'Stocks' or the more hospitable 'Shares' before settling on 'Bonds' as the name for this City restaurant, part of the Threadneedles Hotel, converted from an 1856 banking hall.

The suited executives, unmoved by the irony of another financial institution being converted into a restaurant, come here to enjoy its striking surroundings and good cooking. Enter through the hotel and check out the stained glass cupola in reception, as well as the cocktails available in the bar, which also serves tapas. The grand restaurant, with its pillars, marble and panelling provides the backdrop for sophisticated food that's more elaborate in style than the descriptively understated menu lets on.

Rhodes Twenty Four ✿

British XXX

M3

24th floor, Tower 42, 25 Old Broad St EC2N 1HQ
✆ (020) 7877 7703
Fax (020) 7877 7788
e-mail reservations@rhodes24.co.uk **www**.rhodes24.co.uk

⊖ Liverpool Street
► **Plan VIII**
Closed Christmas-New Year, Saturday, Sunday and Bank Holidays

Carte £32/58

A/C VISA MC AE

Rhodes Twenty Four

Tower 42 - still the Natwest Tower to some of us, which should please the bank no end – is home to this outpost of the Gary Rhodes empire. Once you're past the airport style security it's up in the blue lift to the 24th floor. The man himself has his office a few floors below so expect to see him occasionally.

Even though it points north eastward, the views are terrific. Book a window table at lunch but if its romance for dinner then try one of the booths on the back wall which are deep, enveloping and slightly raised, giving you intimacy, views and a sense of superiority.

It's the same menu lunch and dinner. Decide on your favoured main ingredient, whether that's eel, salmon, mutton or monkfish and read below the chosen accompaniments. The Rhodes philosophy, if not the hand, is clearly evident in all the dishes: they are largely British, nicely balanced, appetisingly presented and wholly bereft of any extraneous embellishment. They also come in decent portions. The wine list keeps things realistic, although there's a sommeliers section for those pushing the boat out.

First Course

- Seared scallops with mashed potato and shallot mustard sauce.
- Partridge sausage with sweet thyme roasted parsnips and apple sauce.

Main Course

- Steamed mutton and onion suet pudding with buttered carrots.
- Saddle of venison on game toast with sloe gin red cabbage.

Dessert

- Bread and butter pudding.
- Treacle tart with clotted cream ice cream.

1 Lombard Street (Restaurant) ✿

M3

French XXX

1 Lombard St EC3V 9AA
(020) 7929 6611
Fax (020) 7929 6622
e-mail hb@1lombardstreet.com
www.1lombardstreet.com

⊖ Bank
▶ Plan VIII

Closed 22 December- 3 January, Saturday, Sunday and Bank Holidays – booking essential at lunch

Menu £39/45 – Carte £54/62

A/C VISA AE

Those coming to the restaurant at One Lombard Street have always had to pick their way through the crowds at the bar/brasserie at the front and such was the atmosphere that one had to fight the temptation to stay and join the party. The restaurant, in contrast, was an oasis of calm, order and courteousness. There are plans now afoot to relocate the restaurant to the bank adjacent and turn the existing spot into a private dining room.

Wherever the location, Herbert Berger's elaborately presented food will continue to draw a following. This being the City, the tempting menu offers come at dinner; the nine course *dégustation* menu is attractively priced and is the ideal introduction. Specialities for two such as the rib of beef with marrow or the suckling pig with sauerkraut remain a popular choice from the extensive *à la carte* and are skilfully prepared. Menu descriptions are helpfully full and precise so there are no nasty surprises and although his cooking remains classical in its leanings, he is not afraid of using the occasional Oriental twist to add a little oomph.

First Course

- Carpaccio of tuna with Oriental spices, ginger and lime vinaigrette.
- Seared foie gras with sweet and sour endive tart Tatin.

Main Course

- Trio of lamb with sorrel velouté and tomato compote, lamb jus.
- Roast turbot on the bone with woodland mushrooms and lobster essence.

Dessert

- Warm strawberries in Sauternes with crème fraîche sorbet.
- Bitter chocolate pyramid with almond milk granité.

Coq d'Argent

M3 **French** XXX

No.1 Poultry EC2R 8EJ
(020) 7395 5000
Fax (020) 7395 5050
e-mail coqdargent@danddlondon.com
www.danddlondon.com

⊖ Bank
▶ **Plan VIII**
Closed Christmas, Easter, Saturday lunch, Sunday dinner and Bank Holidays – booking essential

Menu £29 – Carte £31/47

Take the lift up to the top of this modern office building and you come out in the middle of a terrace, around which is wrapped the restaurant. Al fresco summer dining really comes into its own here. The bar is also very much a local destination in itself and the popular choice for those after lighter meals or snacks. This being a D&D restaurant, the dining room is slick, stylish and polished and the atmosphere is one of cool sophistication. By contrast, the French cooking is fairly classical; lobster bisque, snails, beef Rossini and assorted tarts all appear and the fruits de mer are a speciality. For the best views, ask for a table by the large picture window; jazz lunches on Sunday provide a more relaxed mood than the midweek power lunches.

Le Pont de la Tour

N4 **French** XXX

36d Shad Thames, Butlers Wharf SE1 2YE
(020) 7403 8403 **Fax** (020) 7940 1835
www.conran.com

⊖ London Bridge
▶ **Plan X**

Menu £25 – Carte £33/57

The regeneration of the River and Butlers Wharf were there for all to see in 1991 when Sir Terence Conran opened Le Pont de la Tour and its glamorous reputation was done no harm when Tony Blair entertained Bill Clinton here in 1997. The elegant room provides diners with terrific views of Tower Bridge and the activity on the river, especially from the delightful terrace, while the menu offers a comprehensive selection of dishes that borrow heavily from France, all served by a well-drilled team.

For those after less formal surroundings, head for the Bar & Grill which specialises in crustaceans and fruits de mer while those wanting something to take home are catered for by an impressive array of produce in the adjacent food store.

Oxo Tower

K4

Modern European XXX

(8th floor), Oxo Tower Wharf, Barge House St SE1 9PH
(020) 7803 3888 **Fax** (020) 7803 3838
www.harveynichols.com

⊖ Southwark
▶ **Plan X**
Closed 24-26 December

Menu £32 – Carte £33/53

Sitting majestically on the top floor of the converted Oxo factory, which has gradually become one of the more recognisable Thames-side landmarks, the Oxo Tower Restaurant is one of the surprisingly few London restaurants able to offer diners a room with a view - in this case a terrific one of the river and beyond.

Fortunately, the elegant surroundings of the interior mean than 'within' is as agreeable as 'without' and the stylish and very comfortable room is complemented by silky smooth and perfectly pitched service. Lunch is a fixed price affair, dinner à la carte, and the modern cooking displays a certain sophistication and creativity, using superior ingredients that are reflected in the price.

Addendum

N3

Modern European XXX

No 1, Seething Lane
EC3N 4AX
(020) 7977 9500
e-mail londonevents@apexhotels.co.uk
www.addendumrestaurant.co.uk

⊖ Fenchurch Street
▶ **Plan VIII**
Closed 20 December -5 January and Bank Holidays

Menu £27 (lunch) – Carte £33/37

The Apex Hotel opened at the end of 2005 and with it came the decidedly smart Addendum restaurant which is located, appropriately enough, at the back. Having its own street entrance certainly helped establish its separate identity from the hotel while the chocolate leather seating, fresh flowers and mirrors contribute to the general atmosphere of style and comfort. As with most places in the city, lunchtimes are for animated deal making while dinners are far quieter affairs.

The cooking is undertaken with precision and elan but is far more robust and earthy than one would expect from such a glossy looking restaurant. The chef also clearly likes his offal and those who share his passion will find the assiette particularly appealing.

Club Gascon ✿

French XX

L2

57 West Smithfield EC1A 9DS
(020) 7796 0600
Fax (020) 7796 0601
e-mail info@clubgascon.com
www.clubgascon.com

⊖ Barbican
▶ **Plan VIII**
Closed 22 December-6 January, 21-24 March, Sunday, Saturday lunch and Bank Holidays – booking essential

Menu £42 – Carte £38/72

A/C
VISA
MC
AE

Club Gascon

In common with several restaurants in the City, this was once a bank - with the marble on the walls to prove it - but it all gets softened up with the big floral displays and mirrors, while the nutty colours give it a contemporary edge. The tables may be close enough for elbow rubbing and eavesdropping on neighbours but the atmosphere remains buzzy and appealing. Much of that is down to the fact that all have come here principally for the food.

Pascal Aussignac's paean to Gascony and the gastronomy of south west France is the attraction. It's not all duck and geese but a love of foie gras certainly helps as it has one of the five sections into which the menu is divided all to itself. Depending on the richness and intensity of certain ingredients, three dishes per person plus a veg and a pud should see you through. Each one of those little plates is elegantly crafted and the kitchen is constantly developing and introducing new and innovative combinations. There is a set menu also available, with suggested wines by the glass.

First Course
- Carpaccio of venison with summer truffle and crispy artichoke.
- Plancha of baby squid with black polenta emulsion.

Main Course
- Pyrenean lamb on vine shoot embers with blinis and trevise.
- Grilled duck foie gras with grapes.

Dessert
- Cherries with yoghurt coulis, almonds and griottes.
- Black truffle chocolate fondant and ice cream.

Sauterelle

French XX

The Royal Exchange EC3V 3LR
(020) 7618 2483
www.conran.com

Bank
▶ **Plan VIII**
Closed Saturday and Sunday

Carte £32/49

Opened in 1565, The Royal Exchange may have been rebuilt twice, most recently in 1842, but today it is one of the great rousing landmarks in the City. Within the Exchange and to complement the Grand Bar and Café, one finds, on its mezzanine level, Sauterelle. It opened in late 2005 and is another in the D&D collection of restaurants.

From its lofty position, Sauterelle (meaning 'grasshopper' in French) provides slick and comfortable surroundings and the well-drilled staff make light of the busy lunchtimes. The menu concentrates on classic bourgeois French cooking, with rillettes, marmites and saucissons to the fore. Expect scallops with Jerusalem artichoke, magret of duck and, to finish, a crème brûlée.

Bengal Clipper

Indian 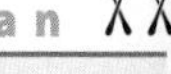

N4

Cardamom Building, Shad Thames, Butlers Wharf SE1 2YR
(020) 7357 9001 **Fax** (020) 7357 9002
e-mail mail@bengalclipper.co.uk **www**.bengalclipper.co.uk

London Bridge
▶ **Plan X**

Carte £13/27

Set among the converted wharves and warehouses by the part of the Thames where cargoes of Indian teas and spices were once traded, you'll find, fittingly enough, Bengal Clipper, a firmly established Indian restaurant whose reputation has been based on reliable cooking and big, bustling surroundings.

The size means that the restaurant is often the chosen venue of larger parties and tables so the atmosphere, particularly in the evenings, is usually fairly hectic, although the smartly kitted out staff are an unflappable lot.

Specialities from all parts of India are showcased, along with several originally conceived dishes which include, in honour of the building in which the restaurant sits, a chicken curry flavoured with cardamom.

The Chancery

Modern European XX

K2

9 Cursitor St EC4A 1LL
(020) 7831 4000
Fax (020) 7831 4002
e-mail reservations@thechancery.co.uk
www.thechancery.co.uk

⊖ Chancery Lane
▶ **Plan VIII**
Closed 22 December-5 January, Saturday and Sunday

Menu £32

A/C VISA MC AE

Surrounded by the law courts, The Chancery, open only during the week, provides the perfect spot for that last meal of freedom or the post-trial celebratory acquittal.
It is the sister restaurant to The Clerkenwell Dining Room and the bright main room benefits from large picture windows and understated decoration. This is the room in which to reserve your table, rather than the basement which can lack something in atmosphere.
Service is sufficiently fleet of foot and efficient to reassure those with an eye on the adjournment. The cooking also comes suitably well-judged and is modern in style but underpinned by a solid understanding of the ingredients. The wine list has some well-chosen bottles under £25.

Skylon

XX

J4

1 Southbank Centre, Belvedere Rd
SE1 8XX
(020) 7654 7800 **Fax** (020) 7654 7801
e-mail skylon@danddlondon.com **www**.skylonrestaurant.co.uk

⊖ Waterloo
▶ **Plan III**

Menu £22/30 – Carte £27/38

A/C VISA MC AE

The dining flagship in the revamped Royal Festival Hall offers a choice: a Grill to one side, with a raised cocktail bar making the most of the river views, and a Restaurant to the other, where things are a little more sedate and a tad more comfortable. This was the first project from D&D London, following their management buy-out of Conran Restaurants, but the 1950s styling and imaginative design makes it a natural addition to the existing portfolio. The Grill offers an easy-to-eat menu, from eggs Benedict to bowls of pasta, as well as pre and post performance menus and something for the kids. The restaurant offers up more ambitious dishes that display a greater degree of complication, finer ingredients and higher prices.

Roast

British XX

The Floral Hall, Borough Market
SE1 1TL
(020) 7940 1300 **Fax** (020) 7940 1301
e-mail info@roast-restaurant.com
www.roast-restaurant.com

⊖ London Bridge
▶ **Plan X**
Closed Sunday dinner

Carte £32/50

The mouth-watering array of gastronomic delights on display in Borough Market cannot fail to entice the senses of the thousands who pass through it. For those who cannot wait to return home with their fresh produce there is now a restaurant at hand that shares the philosophy of the market by using high quality produce with verifiable provenance.

The best of British is celebrated here and that includes hitherto forgotten meats like mutton, which appears to be making something of a comeback. The daily specials are particularly classic, from Beef Wellington to Toad in the Hole.

Located atop Floral Hall, this contemporary restaurant comes with a split level so ask for the brighter, higher one as the lower floor can get somewhat overawed by the bar.

Boisdale of Bishopgate

Scottish XX

Swedeland Court,
202 Bishopgate EC2M 4NR
(020) 7283 1763
Fax (020) 7283 1664
e-mail info@boisdale-city.co.uk **www**.boisdale.co.uk

⊖ Liverpool Street
▶ **Plan VIII**
Closed 25 December, 3 January, Saturday, Sunday and Bank Holidays

Carte £24/49

"My heart's in the highlands, wherever I go" said the Scottish Bard. Homesick Scots longing for a taste of home will find succour at this charming Scottish restaurant which specialises in dishes to gladden the heart, such as haggis, smoked salmon and beef, which is matured for 28 days.

The ground floor is given over to a pleasant Champagne and Oyster Bar but descend to the restaurant and you'll find a cosy and very characterful room, warmly decorated in rich reds with a subtle tartan motif and antique prints. The atmosphere is distinctly clubby and indeed membership is available for their regularly held themed evenings, many of which seemingly appear drink-based. There is also a huge selection of whiskies available.

Bevis Marks

N3 **Kosher** XX

Bevis Marks EC3 5DQ
☎ (020) 7283 2220
Fax (020) 7283 2221
e-mail enquiries@bevismarkstherestaurant.com
www.bevismarkstherestaurant.com

⊖ Aldgate
▶ **Plan VIII**
Closed Saturday, Sunday, Friday dinner and Jewish Holidays

Carte £30/36

The restaurant is, in essence, a recent extension to the Bevis Marks synagogue which opened in 1701 and is the oldest Jewish place of worship in the UK. The glass enclosed space – with a retractable roof - was originally constructed for a festival, after which it was decided to turn it into a restaurant. Look out for the billboard and menu otherwise you'll never find it.

'Innovative kosher' describes the cooking and the choice is fairly extensive. The kitchen not only updates such classics as chicken soup with matzo balls but adds an Asian influence to some dishes like Sichuan duck and Cantonese chicken. Others have more of a European accent such as cassoulet and fettuccine. Wines are well chosen and several are Mevushal.

Lanes

N2 **Modern European** XX

109-117 Middlesex St E1 7JF
☎ (020) 7247 5050
Fax (020) 7247 8071
e-mail info@lanesrestaurant.co.uk
www.lanesrestaurant.co.uk

⊖ Liverpool Street
▶ **Plan VIII**
Closed Saturday lunch, Sunday and Bank Holidays

Carte £33/41

Claustrophobes need not fear its basement location for Lanes benefits from pavement-level windows and a general air of openness and space. The bar is a major attraction, especially at lunchtimes when it offers simpler food for stockbrokers on a deadline, but those after somewhere a little smarter and more comfortable should head through to the main restaurant. It's attractively kitted out, with art for sale on the walls, well-spaced tables with the full napery and enthusiastic service.

Expect colourful and modish European cooking, using good quality produce, much of which is British. Evenings are altogether more sedate affairs, highlighted by the good value supper set menu which runs alongside the à la carte.

Searcy's

Modern European XX

L2

Barbican Centre, Level 2, Silk St
EC2Y 8DS
☎ (020) 7588 3008
Fax (020) 7382 7247
e-mail searcys@barbican.org.uk **www**.searcys.co.uk

⊖ Barbican
▶ **Plan VIII**
Closed 24-26 December, Sunday, Saturday lunch and Bank Holidays

Carte £26/40

A/C VISA MC AE D

In an area of the city where dining options remain rather limited, Searcy's is a more than useful restaurant for those looking for a quick snack before, or after, attending a performance or exhibition at the Barbican. It also offers the added bonus of letting you look out from, rather than at, this iconic architectural project. The picture windows offer views across the water features and city buildings, while the décor of the place is one of stylised utilitarianism.

The team of waiting staff are appreciative of the time considerations many have and so dishes are delivered swiftly and efficiently. The menu features a tried and tested formula of modern cooking, Eurocentric in its influences.

Tatsuso

Japanese XX

M2

32 Broadgate Circle EC2M 2QS
☎ (020) 7638 5863
Fax (020) 7638 5864
e-mail info.tatsuso@btinternet.com

⊖ Liverpool Street
▶ **Plan VIII**
Closed Saturday, Sunday and Bank Holidays – booking essential

Carte £34/108

A/C VISA MC AE D

Tatsuso was among that pioneering wave of Japanese restaurants responsible for introducing Japanese food to inquisitive Londoners. Today it's one of The City's more mature restaurants and remains a favourite, although one that's beginning to slightly show its age.

There is a choice of dining room and, with them, two different dining experiences. On the ground floor it's teppan-yaki, where you sit round the counters and the chefs do their thing in front of you. Prices can rise to fairly lofty heights with some of the set menus, especially if you opt for the Kobe beef.

Downstairs is where you'll find more your traditional Japanese restaurant and prices here are a little more down-to-earth. Service is exceptionally polite and well meaning.

The Larder

Modern European XX

L1

91-93 St John St EC1M 4NU
(020) 7608 1558
Fax (120) 7253 9285
e-mail info@thelarderrestaurant.com
www.thelarderrestaurant.com

⊖ Farringdon
▶ **Plan IX**
Closed 24 December-2 January, Saturday lunch, Sunday and Bank Holidays

Carte £19/39

An appropriate name as there is bounty galore. On one side is the bakery with plenty of artisanal breads and cakes. The restaurant, meanwhile, is one of those large, semi-industrial places with exposed brick and pipes and an open kitchen at the back. This kind of hard-edged space can push up the decibels but that's part of its appeal.

Think modern European comfort food, from moules marinière to roast salmon with pumpkin ravioli, but alongside the halloumi you might find Lancashire cheese and next to the chicken breast with Puy lentils could be a Barnsley chop, so the Union flag is raised occasionally (the owners are from Leeds). A side dish to accompany the main course is recommended and some thought has gone into them.

The White Swan

Modern European XX

K2

108 Fetter Lane EC4A 1ES
(020) 7242 9696
Fax (020) 7404 2250
e-mail info@thewhiteswanlondon.com
www.thewhiteswanlondon.com

⊖ Temple
▶ **Plan VIII**
Closed at Christmas and Bank Holidays

Menu £27 – Carte £26/33

It once went by the name of 'The Mucky Duck' but, in this age of the gastropub, such a name might not necessarily invoke images of culinary expertise. Far better to be thought of as an ugly duckling who was, in fact, a mighty swan.

Drinkers, though, should not despair because the ground floor is still very much a lively bar, with the restaurant found on the first floor. Upstairs it's all very designery and neat and is nicely juxtaposed with the more rustic charms and general clamour of the bar. A clean and bright feel to the room comes courtesy of large picture windows and a rather discombobulating mirrored ceiling.

The menu successfully blends the earthy with the adventurous to appeal to all tastes and degrees of customer adventure.

Saki

L2 **Japanese** XX

4 West Smithfield EC1A 9JX
✆ (020) 7489 7033
Fax (020) 7489 1658
e-mail info@saki-food.com
www.saki-food.com

⊖ Barbican
▶ **Plan VIII**
Closed Christmas-New Year, Sunday and Bank Holidays

Menu £17/58 – Carte £17/45

A/C

VISA
MC
AE

Saki means "happiness" in Japanese, and, when you consider that the Japanese enjoy the longest life expectancy of any country in the world, you can understand the joy. That longevity must be due, in no small part, to a healthy diet. Now, thanks to places like Saki, we can all hopefully live a little longer, and a little better.

It's actually quite easy to miss, with a deli/foodshop on the ground floor, but head downstairs and you'll find yourself in a very sleek and contemporary space. Service is suitably slick. The menu is a combination of the classic and the modern, focusing on seasonality through a mix of kobachi (small plates), carbo (rice or noodles based dishes) and okazu (protein based dishes), all prepared to exacting standards.

Smiths of Smithfield

L2 **Modern European** XX

Top Floor, 67-77 Charterhouse St
EC1M 6HJ
✆ (020) 7251 7950
Fax (020) 7236 5666
e-mail reservations@smithsofsmithfield.co.uk
www.smithsofsmithfield.co.uk

⊖ Barbican
▶ **Plan IX**
Closed 25-26 December, 1 January and Saturday lunch

Carte £32/46

A/C
VISA
MC
AE

If you ever arrange a get-together with a friend here just remember to be a little precise in your meeting spot. Smiths is housed in a vast building where all four of its floors are given over to eating, drinking and general merry making. As a rule of thumb, prices and levels of formality go up the higher up you go yourself.

The ground floor is a relaxed bar with an exposed brick warehouse feel and easy, snacky menu. Then it's the cocktail bar, followed by the large and lively 'dining room' which is actually more a brasserie and finally the 'top floor' which has a more corporate, groomed feel and boasts terrific views of the surrounding rooftops. Cooking is decidedly modern with well sourced meats something of a speciality.

The Clerkenwell Dining Room

French XX

L2

69-73 St John St EC1M 4AN
(020) 7253 9000
Fax (020) 7253 3322
www.theclerkenwell.com

Farringdon
▶ Plan IX
Closed Christmas, Saturday lunch, Sunday dinner and Bank Holidays

Menu £19.50 – Carte £30/40

Its arched windows hark back to a time when this was a pub, but behind its bright red façade there sits a decidedly contemporary restaurant. It's quite capacious inside but the owners, who also run The Chancery, have cleverly divided it up into different sections. The art is abstract and the tables smartly dressed.

Two menus, a de jour and an à la carte, are both offered. The former is competitively priced, no doubt in recognition of the growing number of restaurants available around these parts. The latter menu offers more choice and the kitchen is certainly not shy with flavours, which are predominantly modern French but with the occasional unexpected twist.

Portal

Mediterranean XX

L1

88 St John St EC1M 4EH
(020) 7253 6950
Fax (020) 7490 5836
e-mail reservations@portalrestaurant.com
www.portalrestaurant.com

Farringdon
▶ Plan IX
Closed 23 December - 6 January, Saturday lunch, Sunday and Bank Holidays

Carte £31/56

The sunny Southern Mediterranean is the featured attraction here. In the busy front bar plates of *petiscos* or Portuguese tapas, are the perfect accompaniment to a glass of Sherry, particularly at the end of a hard day, while in the main dining room the menu showcases dishes full of the colours and tastes of Southern France, Spain and Portugal.

Within this Grade II listed building the décor is one of industrial chic, with exposed brick and ventilation shafts and the best place to sit is in the glass walled extension at the back. Service is considerate and thoughtful, as you would expect in a restaurant run by the owner. The small private dining room lined with wine bottles is a particularly attractive space.

Baltic

K4 **East European** XX

74 Blackfriars Rd SE1 8HA ⊖ Southwark
✆ (020) 7928 1111 ▶ **Plan X**
Fax (020) 7928 8487 Closed 25 December and 1 January
e-mail info@balticrestaurant.co.uk **www**.balticrestaurant.co.uk

Menu £17 – Carte £25/30

VISA MC AE

The façade may be a little unprepossessing but persevere and you'll find yourself in a slick bar. If you can resist the tempting array of vodkas, including some appealingly original home-made flavours, then proceed further and you'll end up in the arresting space of the restaurant.

Alcoves around the edge and, above, a wooden trussed ceiling with vaulted glass combine with bright white walls to give this former industrial space a vividly modernist feel. At this point you'll probably expect some sort of pan-Asian fusion thing but fortunately Baltic enjoys the same ownership as Wódka, so the cooking here covers the altogether more muscular cuisines of Eastern Europe and the Baltic states. It is robust, full of flavour and requires an appetite.

Oxo Tower Brasserie

K4 **Modern European** X

(8th floor), Oxo Tower Wharf, Barge House St SE1 9PH ⊖ Southwark
▶ **Plan X**
✆ (020) 7803 3888 **Fax** (020) 7803 3838 Closed 24-26 December
e-mail oxo.reservations@harveynichols.com
www.harveynichols.com

Menu £22 – Carte £26/35

A/C VISA MC AE

The brasserie provides an ideal alternative for those after a less formal and less expensive experience to the Oxo Tower Restaurant, but one that still offers the same commanding setting and impressive vistas. The glass enclosed restaurant, with its open plan kitchen and bustling atmosphere, provides the perfect place in which to entertain those new to the city; the changing light at dusk makes this an ideal period in which to time your arrival, especially if it's warm enough to sit outside on the terrace.

'Brasserie' may describe the room but the dishes on offer are far from what traditionalists would call brasserie classics: the extensive menu is made up of dishes with contemporary, and occasionally Asian, influences.

Blueprint Café

Modern European

N5

Design Museum, Shad Thames,
Butlers Wharf SE1 2YD
(020) 7378 7031
Fax (020) 7357 8810
www.conran.com

⊖ London Bridge
▶ **Plan X**
Closed 25-26 December and Sunday dinner

Carte £26/35

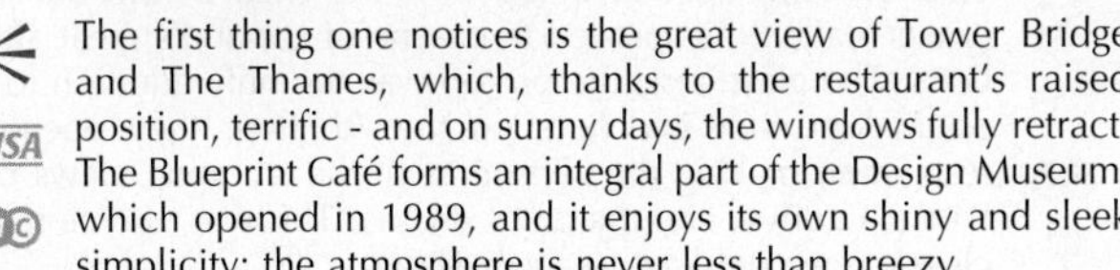

The first thing one notices is the great view of Tower Bridge and The Thames, which, thanks to the restaurant's raised position, terrific - and on sunny days, the windows fully retract. The Blueprint Café forms an integral part of the Design Museum, which opened in 1989, and it enjoys its own shiny and sleek simplicity; the atmosphere is never less than breezy.

The cooking is very much of the no-nonsense, what-you-read-is-what-you-get school and the long-standing chef uses flavours that are pronounced, sunny and seasonal. Dishes from his daily-changing menu, such as smoked eel with horseradish, veal with girolles and lemon posset, come with confident simplicity and, as a result, are easy to eat.

St John

British

L2

26 St John St EC1M 4AY
(020) 7251 0848
Fax (020) 7251 4090
e-mail reservations@stjohnrestaurant.com
www.stjohnrestaurant.com

⊖ Barbican
▶ **Plan IX**
Closed Christmas, Easter, Saturday lunch, Sunday and Bank Holidays

Carte £26/39

A derelict 19c former smokehouse was converted in 1994 into St John, a restaurant which has introduced a new generation to old English recipes, forgotten treats and rediscovered favourites. 'Nose to tail eating' is how they describe themselves, celebrating the British tradition of 'waste not, want not' by using hitherto under-used parts of the animal to challenge our ever more timid palates. Dishes range from the more unusual, such as roast bone marrow, braised mutton or chitterlings with dandelion, to the more comforting, such as Arbroath Smokies or Eccles cake.

The starkly decorated white room provides surroundings that perfectly complement the apparent simplicity of the cooking and clued up staff willingly offer advice to the novice.

Tate Modern (Restaurant)

Modern European

L4

7th Floor, Tate Modern, Bankside
SE1 9LS
(020) 7401 5020
www.tate.org.uk/modern/information/eating.htm

⊖ Southwark
▶ Plan X
Closed 25 December – lunch only and dinner Friday-Saturday

Carte £23/34

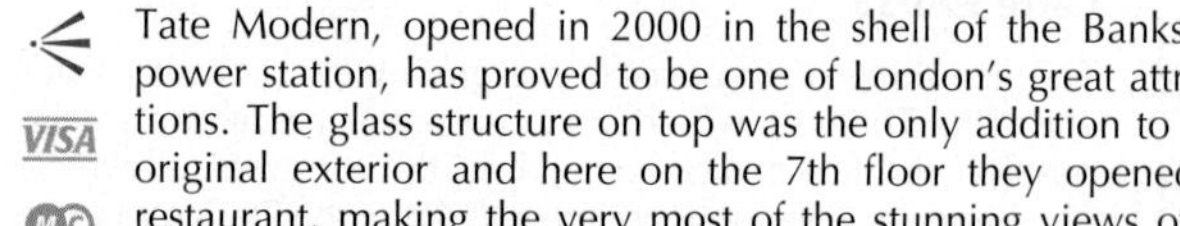

Tate Modern, opened in 2000 in the shell of the Bankside power station, has proved to be one of London's great attractions. The glass structure on top was the only addition to the original exterior and here on the 7th floor they opened a restaurant, making the very most of the stunning views of St Paul's, the river and the city's skyline. This was, therefore, the closest one could get to a sure thing.

Thankfully, they didn't disregard the cooking because the menu offers a varied and sensible choice, ranging from traditionally English to more colourful southern European specialities, as well as providing for those just wanting something light.

Another excuse, if indeed one was ever needed, to head over to Bankside.

Cantina Del Ponte

Italian

N4

36c Shad Thames, Butlers Wharf
SE1 2YE
(020) 7403 5403 **Fax** (020) 7940 1845
www.conran.com

⊖ London Bridge
▶ Plan X
Closed 25-26 December

Menu £14/15 - Carte £25

This is one of those great-after-work sort of places, where you can grab a seat on the terrace under the huge canopy, order a pizza and a bottle of Chianti and admire the view. Even if you don't work in the City, it's still a pretty nice place to spend an evening. As with most restaurants around these streets, it's part of the D&D (formerly Conran) empire but has a more down to earth, rustic feel to it than most of the others which are generally a little shinier. There's plenty of terracotta, a large mural on one wall and a general feeling of openness.

Apart from the pizzas, which are also available for takeaway, the menu offers a comprehensive selection of popular and familiar Italian dishes, from baby octopus to a bowl of penne.

Moro

Mediterranean X

K1

34-36 Exmouth Market EC1R 4QE
✆ (020) 7833 8336
Fax (020) 7833 9338
e-mail info@moro.co.uk
www.moro.co.uk

⊖ Farringdon
▶ **Plan IX**
Closed Christmas, New Year, Sunday and Bank Holidays – booking essential

Carte £26/32

The enduring popularity of Moro is easy to understand because the wholesome, vibrant and flavoursome Moorish food is very appealing, the atmosphere is never less than lively and the place just seems to complement the surroundings and atmosphere of Exmouth Market perfectly.

A zinc bar occupies one side, where tapas can be enjoyed, and the contagious bonhomie generated in the restaurant appears to be reflected in the open kitchen. They certainly make great use of their charcoal grill and wood-burning oven, particularly with the sourdough bread, and the menu changes fully every two weeks. All budding cooks will learn here of the importance of using the freshest produce. If they want to learn any more they can buy the Moro cookbook.

Paternoster Chop House

British X

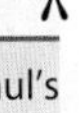
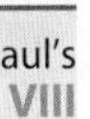
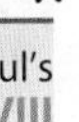
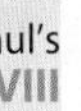
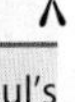

L3

Warwick Court, Paternoster Square
EC4N 7DX
✆ (020) 7029 9400
Fax (020) 7029 9409
e-mail paternosterr@conran-restaurants.co.uk **www**.conran.com

⊖ St Paul's
▶ **Plan VIII**
Closed Sunday dinner and Saturday

Carte £30

Nestling behind St Paul's, in an area celebrated in pre-war days as the best place for ale and chop houses, one now aptly finds the Paternoster Chop House. Being part of the D&D group means the décor was clearly never going to be anything other than bright, light and modern. The menu, however, adopts a formula of back-to-basics. You'll find assorted shellfish, grills and resolutely British classics such as jugged hare, potted shrimps, lamb with mint sauce and Dover sole. This can then be followed by a real pudding, like treacle tart or spotted dick. Even better, all choices come in refreshingly generous portions.

City suits do have a tendency to dominate the room at lunch, but the apron-wearing staff cope with aplomb.

Cantina Vinopolis

L4 **International**

No.1 Bank End SE1 9BU
(020) 7940 8333
Fax (020) 7089 9339
e-mail cantina@vinopolis.co.uk
www.vinopolis.co.uk

London Bridge
▶ Plan X
Closed 23 December-3 January and Sunday dinner

Carte £21/33

Southwark is becoming something of a Utopia for today's gastronauts. Food supplies can be garnered at the wonderful Borough Market and oenologists will find relief and fulfilment at Vinopolis, the wine merchant and museum.

Cantina Vinopolis is the wine attraction's public restaurant and is housed under vast, magnificent Victorian arches that lend a palpable sense of history and atmospherics to the whole place. The exposed kitchen offers a menu that flits between continents and, as one would expect, the wine list offers an interesting and correspondingly diverse selection with many well priced bottles. The styling and comforts are simple and the service is smoothly effective.

Village East

M5 **Modern European**

171 Bermondsey St SE1 3UW
(020) 7357 6082
Fax (020) 7403 3360
e-mail info@villageeast.co.uk **www**.villageeast.co.uk

London Bridge
▶ Plan X
Closed 25-26 December, and 1 January

Menu £15 (lunch) – Carte £24/34

Clever name - sounds a bit downtown Manhattan. But while Bermondsey may not be London's East Village, what Village East does is give this part of town a bit more 'neighbour' and a little less 'hood'.

It's tricky to find so look for the glass façade and you'll find yourself in one of the bars, still wondering if you've come to the right place. Once you've seen the open kitchen you know the dining area's not far away. Wood, brick, vents and large circular lamps give it that warehouse aesthetic. The menu is laid out a little confusingly but what you get are ample portions of familiar bistro style food, as well as some interesting combinations. The separately priced side dishes are not really needed and can push the bill up.

Butlers Wharf Chop House

British

N4

36e Shad Thames, Butlers Wharf
SE1 2YE
(020) 7403 3403 **Fax** (020) 7940 1855
e-mail bwchophouse@dandddlondon.com
www.danddlondon.com

London Bridge
▶ **Plan X**
Closed 1-3 January

Menu £26 - Carte £26/38

The menu at Butlers Wharf Chophouse offers a comprehensive selection of British dishes that range from the classic to the reassuringly familiar. From oysters, dressed crab and prawn cocktails to fish and chips, sausages and roast beef, there are reminders of our own proud culinary heritage.

It is not, therefore, surprising that this roomy and bright chophouse on a converted wharf is always busy, especially at lunchtimes with swarms of suited city workers. The restaurant has the feel of a boathouse and affords terrific views of the river and Tower Bridge, particularly from the very agreeable terrace, while the bar offers a less expensive menu in more relaxed surroundings. The service throughout is diligent and attentive.

Champor-Champor

Asian

M5

62-64 Weston St SE1 3QJ
(020) 7403 4600
e-mail mail@champor-champor.com
www.champor-champor.com

London Bridge
▶ **Plan X**
Closed Easter, Christmas and Sunday – booking essential – dinner only

Carte £28/33

Spirits cannot fail to be lifted as soon as you find yourself in this beguiling restaurant with its exuberant and vibrant decoration; any Malay speakers out there will instantly appreciate the name, which roughly translates as 'mix-and-match'. That certainly applies to the two rooms into which it is divided and where no two tables are the same. The rooms are festooned with everything from Buddha statues to tribal artefacts, from masks to carvings and all with the added exoticism of incense fragrance in the air and flickering candle light.

The cooking also comes with a mix of influences and equal amounts of colour, panache and vitality, and is a fusion of Malaysian and assorted Asian cuisines.

Wright Brothers

L4 Seafood

11 Stoney St, Borough Market
SE1 9AD
(020) 7403 9554
Fax (020) 7403 9558
www.wrightbros.eu.com

London Bridge
▶ **Plan X**
Closed 25-26 December and Sunday

Carte £23/43

This started life as an oyster wholesaler and then developed around the theme of an oyster and porter house – porter, or dark ale, being the traditional accompaniment to oysters.
The range of oysters is huge; they come from all over the world and are served either in their natural state or cooked in a variety of classic ways. Accompanying them is a range of prime shellfish, from winkles and crab to whelks and razor clams, as well as a handful of prepared dishes like fish pie. There's a shellfish barbecue on Saturdays. Don't expect chips or any type of potato – the oyster is the main event and full marks for that. And there's no dessert, except for cheese and truffles.
Decoratively, it's equally no-nonsense and the atmosphere is all the better for it.

Tapas Brindisa

M4 Tapas

18-20 Southwark St, Borough
Market SE1 1TJ
(020) 7357 8880
www.brindisa.com

London Bridge
▶ **Plan X**
Closed Sunday and Bank Holidays
– bookings not accepted

Carte £18/27

A converted potato warehouse on the fringe of Borough Market selling tapas - if that doesn't arouse interest, nothing will. The owners have spent years importing the best Spanish produce, so opening their own place was a logical step.
As in Spain, you have the option of standing or sitting for your tapas. The bar is a great place for a glass of Fino while you watch the acorn-fed Iberian charcuterie being sliced. The full length windows let the light stream in and the tightly packed tables add to the general conviviality.
The list of hot and cold tapas is extensive, from cured fish and speciality cheeses to grilled chorizo and sautéed chicken livers. No reservations are taken so get there early or be prepared to wait.

Vinoteca

Modern European

L2

7 St John St EC1M 4AA
(020) 7253 8786
Fax (020) 7490 4282
e-mail enquiries@vinoteca.co.uk
www.vinoteca.co.uk

⊖ Farringdon
▶ Plan IX
Closed Christmas-New Year, Sunday and Bank Holidays – booking essential at lunch

Carte £20/25

VISA

'Think of a number, double it and add ten' seems to be how most wines are marked up these days. This makes it even more refreshing to find a place like Vinoteca, where the wine comes at realistic and reasonable prices and the choice is both varied and innovative. Vinoteca calls itself a 'Bar, Wine Shop and Kitchen' and it does all three things well.

At dinner you order at the bar from a subtly southern European influenced menu where each dish is paired with a recommended wine; table service is provided at lunch which is a far busier time. But the wine is the king here and those who haven't set foot in anything remotely resembling a 'wine bar' since its apotheosis or nadir (depending on your viewpoint) in the 1980s should think again.

Cicada

Asian 

L1

132-136 St John St EC1V 4JT
(020) 7490 5898
Fax (020) 8608 1551
e-mail reservations@cicada.nu
www.cicada.nu

⊖ Farringdon
▶ Plan IX
Closed 23 December-2 January, Saturday lunch and Sunday

Menu £25/50 – Carte £17/30

VISA

AE

Cicada was the first in Will Ricker's chain of excitable South East Asian restaurants to open and the bustle and buzz of St John Street, with all its bars, pubs and restaurants, now seems an inspired choice.

The principles of the other restaurants were clearly laid down here. Firstly, make the bar an integral part of the operation and add a tempting drinks list. Then make the restaurant equally lively and fun and, finally, ensure that the cooking is far better than anyone expects, with genuine respect for the ingredients and an appreciation of the featured Asian countries.

One of the best things is that you're made just as welcome if you're popping in after work for a quick beer and some noodles or if you're making it an occasion with friends.

Quality Chop House

K1 — **British**

94 Farringdon Rd EC1R 3EA
(020) 7837 5093
Fax (020) 7833 8748
e-mail enquiries@qualitychophouse.co.uk
www.qualitychophouse.co.uk

⊖ Farringdon
▶ **Plan IX**
Closed 25-26 December and Saturday lunch

Carte £19/32

This late 19th century chop house captures perfectly the no-nonsense Victorian approach to eating and the restaurant's stained glass window still proudly proclaims 'Progressive working class caterer'. This theme continues inside with the inimitable furnishings of oak benches, booths and black and white tiled flooring.

Oysters jostle with jellied eels on the starters and the main courses of Cumberland sausage or battered haddock underline the inherent Britishness of the operation, although other choices of a more Gallic persuasion vie for your attention. This culinary democracy comes complete with rows of sauce bottles on each table. After work, pop in for a selection of 'chopas'- a mini version of some menu dishes.

Brew Wharf

M4 — **Traditional**

Brew Wharf Yard, Stoney St
SE1 9AD
(020) 7378 6601 **Fax** (020) 7940 8336
www.vinopolis.co.uk

⊖ London Bridge
▶ **Plan X**
Closed Christmas-New Year

Carte £19/29

Underneath the arches, we can dream our dreams away. With the sound of trains rattling by overhead mixed with the clamour of contented diners, three large brick arches now form the carapace of a bar, an open-plan kitchen, a 90 seater restaurant and, behind a perspex wall, a micro brewery. Welcome to Brew Wharf.

These beers, along with an extensive range of imported bottles, prove to be the main draw for many of the young after-work crowd and the menu, which doubles as a place mat, provides just the right sort of no-nonsense food you'll fancy when you've got a beer in your hand. These include rotisserie dishes such as marinated whole or half chickens, rib-eye steak sandwiches, pints of prawns, choucroute and cassoulet.

Comptoir Gascon

French

K2

61-63 Charterhouse St EC1M 6HJ
(020) 7608 0851
Fax (020) 7608 0871
e-mail info@comptoirgascon.com
www.comptoirgascon.com

Barbican
▶ **Plan IX**
Closed Christmas-New Year, Sunday and Monday

Carte £22/32

Le Comptoir is the baby brother to Club Gascon, found on the other side of Smithfield Market. The deli part of this operation has been reduced slightly as the restaurant section has really taken off, and it's easy to see why. The appealing and very competitively priced menu is divided between 'mer,' 'vegetal' and 'terre,' with daily blackboard specials, starters designed for sharing and plenty of duck. Think cuisine terroir of the South West of France: butch, hearty and satisfying. Desserts are on display in the chilled cabinet and most of the wine is under £25 a bottle. The place does get understandably busy – just ask for a table away from the draughty front door – while the take-home produce is hard to resist.

The Ambassador

Traditional

K1

55 Exmouth Market EC1R 4QL
(020) 7837 0009
e-mail clive@theambassadorcafe.co.uk
www.theambassadorcafe.co.uk

Farringdon
▶ **Plan IX**
Closed 24 December-2 January, Sunday dinner and Bank Holidays

Menu £17 – Carte £19/31

This Ambassador may raise a few eyebrows at the Court of St James's but his thoroughly egalitarian approach to dining sits very easily within the more urban setting of Exmouth Market. Whisper it quietly, but is that lino on the floor? The decorative simplicity to the room actually works well, adding to the generally languorous atmosphere. Staff do their bit by retaining a sense of cool detachment.

Commendably, it's an all day operation, with hangover cures in the morning, followed by satisfyingly continental lunches and seasonally honest and earthy cooking on offer during the more animated evenings. It's pretty evident that all produce has been diligently sourced, from the butter to the coffee, and the wine list pricing is honest and fair.

Medcalf

K1 **Modern European**

40 Exmouth Market EC1R 4QE
(020) 7833 3533
Fax (020) 7833 1321
e-mail mail@medcalfbar.co.uk
www.medcalfbar.co.uk

Farringdon
▶ **Plan IX**
Closed 24 December-2 January and Sunday dinner – booking essential

Carte £22/30

As butchers' shops around the country fall prey to the supermarket behemoths, it is perhaps fitting that here is one former shop that firstly became a bar, but one where the quality of the food turned it from a mainly drinking establishment into a dining destination. Albert Medcalf, who established his original butcher's shop here in 1912, would be proud and his original sign is emblazoned over the window.

The interior strikes the perfect balance between tradition and modern, between ragged and chic, while the staff remain charming and cool, even when under the pressure of large numbers. British and European influenced dishes come with a degree of rustic charm in their presentation, which belies the evident skill and care that goes into their preparation.

Magdalen

M4 **British**

152 Tooley St SE1 2TU
(020) 7403 1342
Fax (020) 7403 9950
e-mail info@magdalenrestaurant.co.uk
www.magdalenrestaurant.co.uk

London Bridge
▶ **Plan X**
Closed 17-31 August, 24-31 December, Saturday lunch, Sunday and Bank Holidays

Carte £25/44

How you pronounce it may depend on your education, but what is certain is that Magdalen is an appealing addition to this part of town. Owned by a triumvirate of chefs, the place is divided between two floors (no bookings are taken on the ground floor) and has the look of a French brasserie about it. The cooking, however, looks closer to home for influence; what you read is, laudably, what you get, and you'll find hugely appealing words like 'roast', 'potted' and 'dripping' appearing regularly. This is all about being fancy-free and full of flavour; there's still the odd Gallic flavour but even the snails come with a nettle soup. There are also dishes made for two, like whole calves kidney or custard tart. Service is pitched just right.

Canteen

British

J4

Southbank Centre, Belvedere Rd
SE1 8XX
(0845) 686 1122
e-mail rth@canteen.co.uk **www**.canteen.co.uk

⊖ Waterloo
▶ **Plan III**

Carte £30/35

A/C · VISA · MC · AE

2007 saw the reopening of the refurbished Royal Festival Hall and, in among the plethora of international chains, room was found for a restaurant celebrating the best of British. It follows the principle of the original Canteen in Spitalfields by being open all day and offering classic British food, from daily roasts to assorted pies, potted shrimps to fish and chips, all at reasonable prices. Desserts may include treacle tart, Eton mess and blackcurrant jelly and that great British institution of breakfast is served all day.

There are booths and shared refectory tables – the former will be a little cramped if you're a party of four. There's also a large terrace, although the place is sadly not on the river side.

The Anchor & Hope 

Gastropub

K4

36 The Cut SE1 8LP
(020) 7928 9898
Fax (020) 7928 4595
e-mail anchorandhope@btconnect.com

⊖ Southwark
▶ **Plan X**

Closed last 2 weeks August, 25 December-1 January, Easter, Sunday dinner and Monday lunch – bookings not accepted

Menu £30 – Carte £20/38

VISA · MC

The Anchor & Hope is always understandably busy, due to some degree to its proximity to both Vic theatres, but mostly because of his culinary reputation. The fact that they don't take reservations means that it's worth getting here early - in fact very early – to secure a table, although if you're willing to share, you'll be seated sooner.

From the tiny kitchen come forth immensely satisfying dishes, in a rustic and earthy style, drawing on influences from St John in Islington, but at prices which make the queuing worth it. Menu descriptions are understated but infinitely appealing: crab on toast, grilled razor clams, rare roast venison with duck fat potato cake, beef on dripping toast and seven hour lamb shoulder.

The Coach & Horses

K1 Gastropub

26-28 Ray St EC1R 3DJ
(020) 7278 8990 **Fax** (020) 7278 1478
e-mail info@thecoachandhorses.com
www.thecoachandhorses.com

⊖ Farringdon
▶ **Plan IX**
Closed 24-27 December, Saturday lunch and Sunday dinner

Carte £19/27

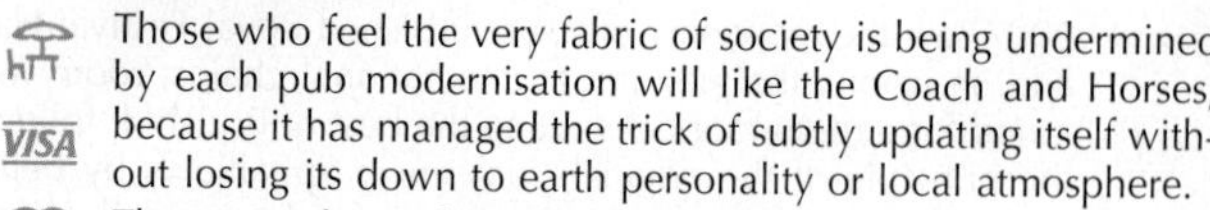

VISA, MC, AE

Those who feel the very fabric of society is being undermined by each pub modernisation will like the Coach and Horses, because it has managed the trick of subtly updating itself without losing its down to earth personality or local atmosphere. The menu also eschews the gastropub standards of sausage and mash or lamb shank and instead has introduced more unusual meats, like pig's ear or ox tongue, as well as using ingredients which are not only fiercely seasonal but all vigorously sourced - traditional reared rare-breed meats are very much the house speciality.

A playful motif of fairy tales and nursery rhymes runs through the operation and there's a charming little terrace for summer's days.

The Hartley

M6 Gastropub

64 Tower Bridge Road SE1 4TR
(020) 7394 7023
e-mail enquries@thehartley.com
www.thehartley.com

⊖ Borough
▶ **Plan X**
Closed 25-26 December, 1 January and Sunday dinner

Carte £16/28

A/C, VISA, MC, AE

There may not be too much local competition to fight off but The Hartley still makes an effort in flying the local gastropub flag. This red-bricked Victorian pub is also doing its bit to remember the diminishing local heritage by honouring, in name and decoration, the Hartley Jam Factory which once stood opposite and is now, predictably, a residential development. There are original posters, black and white photos and even jars of jam scattered around the place. The open plan kitchen produces robust and appetite-satisfying food from the commendably concise menu, supplemented by daily-changing blackboard specials. Service is relaxed and cool-headed.

The locals of this parish are clearly taken with The Hartley.

The Peasant

Gastropub

L1

240 St John St EC1V 4PH
✆ (020) 7336 7726 **Fax** (020) 7490 1089
e-mail gapsbairs@aol.com
www.thepeasant.co.uk

⊖ Farringdon
▶ **Plan IX**
Closed 25 December-3 January – booking essential

Menu £14/18 – Carte £30/35

VISA MC AE

The Peasant continues to set the standard for others to follow and one of its greatest strengths is that it is still very much a 'real' pub. It's bursting with character and atmosphere, with its arched windows, high ceilings and mosaic floor and tiles.
The light bites and tapas served in the bar provide the perfect accompaniment to the range of beers on offer. Upstairs is the less frenetically paced restaurant, decorated with fairground-themed artwork. Here, the words 'pub' and 'traditional' seem less relevant as the cooking is decidedly original and far removed from the usual gastropub staples. The kitchen is not afraid of trying unusual combinations and flavours could be from India one moment, South America the next.

The Well

Gastropub

L1

180 St John St EC1V 4JY
✆ (020) 7251 9363 **Fax** (020) 7253 9683
e-mail drink@downthewell.co.uk
www.downthewell.co.uk

⊖ Farringdon
▶ **Plan IX**
Closed 25 December

Carte £22/29

VISA MC AE

A fairly frenetic atmosphere is guaranteed at The Well as it's quite a small inside and the locals clearly rather like the place. It has built its reputation on giving the menu just the right balance and level of sophistication, so that you can order a pint of prawns or something a little more ambitious like saffron risotto or one of the daily specials.
The sliding screen windows let in the light and the wooden floorboards and exposed brick walls add to the atmosphere of a committed metropolitan pub. The benches outside are popular, particularly with those who don't mind a side order of CO_2 with their beer.
Downstairs you'll find an altogether sexier bar, complete with fish tank, which is available for private hire - the bar, not the tank.

Chelsea · Earl's Court · Hyde Park · Knightsbridge · South Kensington

When London throws a party, the natural choice of summer venue is the city's most expansive central space: **Hyde Park**. The Rolling Stones, Pink Floyd and REM have all rocked out here, as did Live 8's pop Samaritans. But there's another side to this park - a slightly strange fringe element exemplified by the eccentric soapboxers of **Speaker's Corner** and the hardy souls dipping into the **Serpentine** on Christmas morning. Particularly intriguing is the gilded Gothicism of Queen Victoria's monument to love, the **Albert Memorial**. However, for true romance, the adjacent **Royal Albert Hall** offers a more seductive vision and a charismatic spirit that pokes fun at pomp and circumstance on the Last Night of the Proms.

The extent of the area's Victorian endowment becomes clear wandering south, with the museums of **Cromwell Road** preaching enlightenment today with as much conviction as after the Great Exhibition. Once again, frothier pursuits are close by, and in **Knightsbridge** the grand designs are replaced by glitzy designers, with two of the world's most renowned department stores vying for trade - **Harvey Nichols** attracting the pure fashionistas and **Harrods** those who also have a predilection for Egyptian mystique. The crowds here can indeed be madding (particularly during the sales season), but escape up a side street and you'll find lovely lanes of mews cottages, apparently of another place entirely - although no doubt their owners appreciate the glamorous corner shops at the end of the road.

The rest of **South Kensington** settles into a peaceful poshness until you get to the Sloane stomping ground of **Chelsea,** where suddenly the groove changes. It's true that this formerly bohemian enclave is less swinging than it used to be, but the original standard was fabulously high. When Kensington and Chelsea were brought under a single local authority in 1965, the 'Royal Borough' was rather sniffy about its new association with the heart of 'Swinging London', while those in Chelsea were too busy trying on miniskirts to notice, cruising down the **King's Road** straight into Mary Quant's Bazaar. Today, most of the avant-garde boutiques have been replaced by conventional high street chains and gentrified house prices leave little room for punks or hippies; indeed, the Sloane Ranger uniform of Alice band and pearls is much in evidence, worn by yummy mummies, teenage girls and shop mannequins alike. Yet the area's numerous art school students do assert a counter-cultural balance and the basement bar of the **Royal Court Theatre** - the original home of the angry young man - still provides a hang out for bright and engaged talents.

If Chelsea is now more comfortable playing host to its famous flower show than revolutionary flower power, the charm of its riverside streets makes a virtue of steadfastness. Rather than house numbers, **Cheyne Walk** could mark its abodes in the names of eminent ex-residents - Whistler, Rossetti, Brunel - and the historical roll call continues in the well-preserved lanes behind, once home to Thomas Carlyle and Oscar Wilde. By contrast, a skip along the Thames brings you to the unknown face of the future; plans to develop the disused **Lots Road** power station have generated controversy, though modern marina **Chelsea Harbour** perhaps lights the way, providing a pleasant and popular facility.

Of course, to many the name Chelsea begins and ends with foreign signings, friendly roubles and championship trophies - but the district is far too genteel to house its own football stadium and by the time you arrive at **Stamford Bridge**, you're well on your way to the exhibition land of **Earl's Court**. Like Chelsea FC, money has poured into this once rather drab part of town; unlike the football club, many of its foreign players have been forced out. You still see the odd Kiwi or Aussie backpacker making their way to slumming it on a mate's floor - but with house prices almost as high as a star midfielder's transfer fee, the pearls and Alice bands are moving in.

Blickle F. / Bilderberg / StudioX

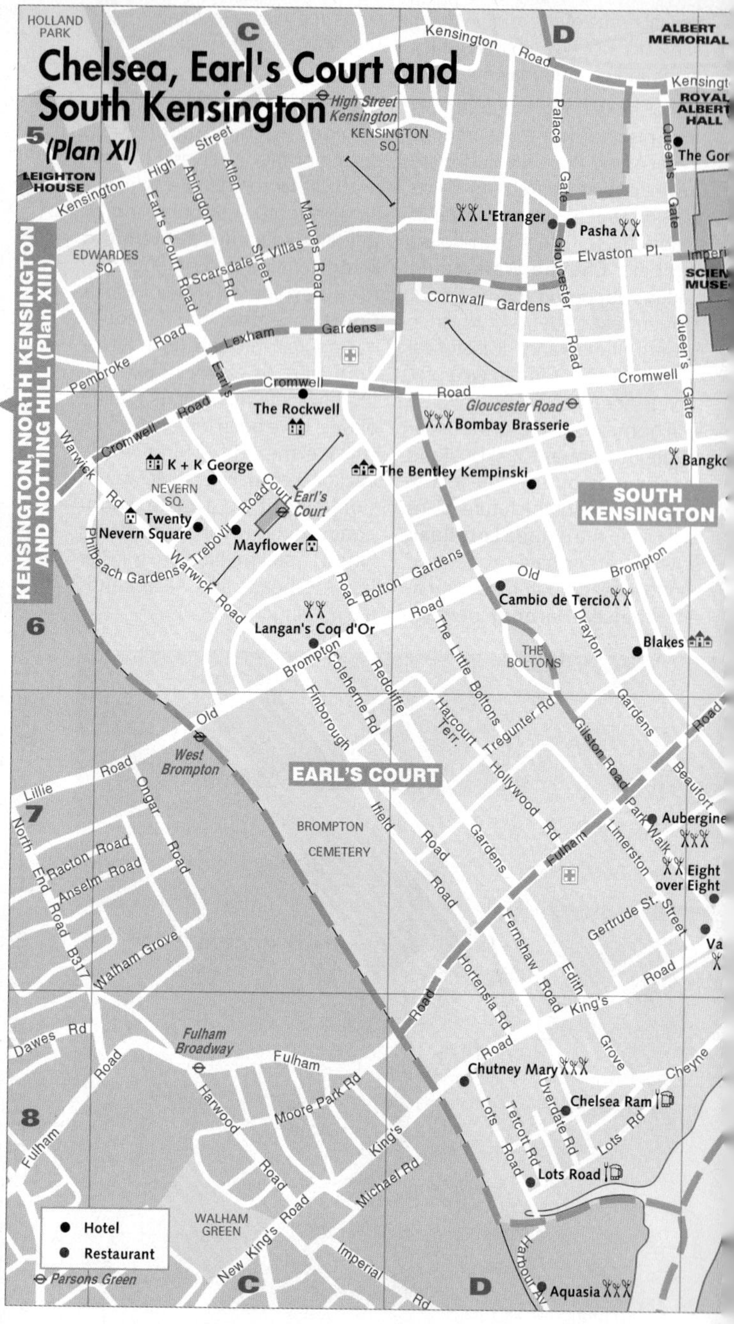
Chelsea, Earl's Court and South Kensington
(Plan XI)
KENSINGTON, NORTH KENSINGTON AND NOTTING HILL (Plan XIII)
HOLLAND PARK
LEIGHTON HOUSE
ALBERT MEMORIAL
ROYAL ALBERT HALL
High Street Kensington
KENSINGTON SQ.
EDWARDES SQ.
NEVERN SQ.
Earl's Court
Gloucester Road
SOUTH KENSINGTON
THE BOLTONS
West Brompton
EARL'S COURT
BROMPTON CEMETERY
Fulham Broadway
WALHAM GREEN
Parsons Green
L'Etranger
Pasha
The Rockwell
Bombay Brasserie
K + K George
The Bentley Kempinski
Twenty Nevern Square
Mayflower
Cambio de Tercio
Langan's Coq d'Or
Blakes
Aubergine
Eight over Eight
Chutney Mary
Chelsea Ram
Lots Road
Aquasia
Hotel
Restaurant

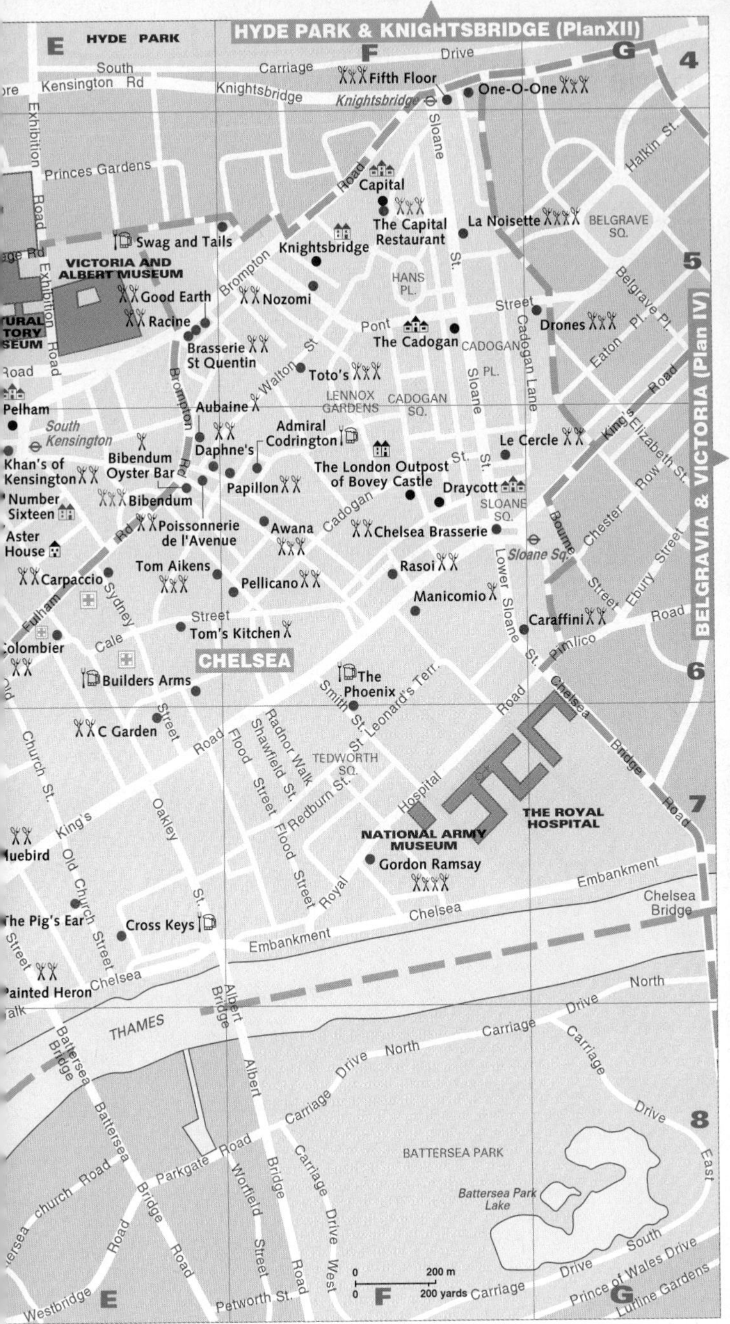
HYDE PARK & KNIGHTSBRIDGE (PlanXII)
HYDE PARK
BELGRAVIA & VICTORIA (Plan IV)
VICTORIA AND ALBERT MUSEUM
CHELSEA
NATIONAL ARMY MUSEUM
THE ROYAL HOSPITAL
BATTERSEA PARK
Battersea Park Lake
THAMES
Fifth Floor
One-O-One
Capital
The Capital Restaurant
La Noisette
Swag and Tails
Knightsbridge
Good Earth
Nozomi
Racine
The Cadogan
Drones
Brasserie St Quentin
Toto's
Pelham
Aubaine
Admiral Codrington
Le Cercle
Daphne's
Khan's of Kensington
Bibendum Oyster Bar
The London Outpost of Bovey Castle
Papillon
Draycott
Number Sixteen
Bibendum
Poissonnerie de l'Avenue
Awana
Chelsea Brasserie
Aster House
Tom Aikens
Rasoi
Carpaccio
Pellicano
Manicomio
Caraffini
Tom's Kitchen
Builders Arms
The Phoenix
C Garden
Gordon Ramsay
The Pig's Ear
Cross Keys
Painted Heron
200 m
200 yards

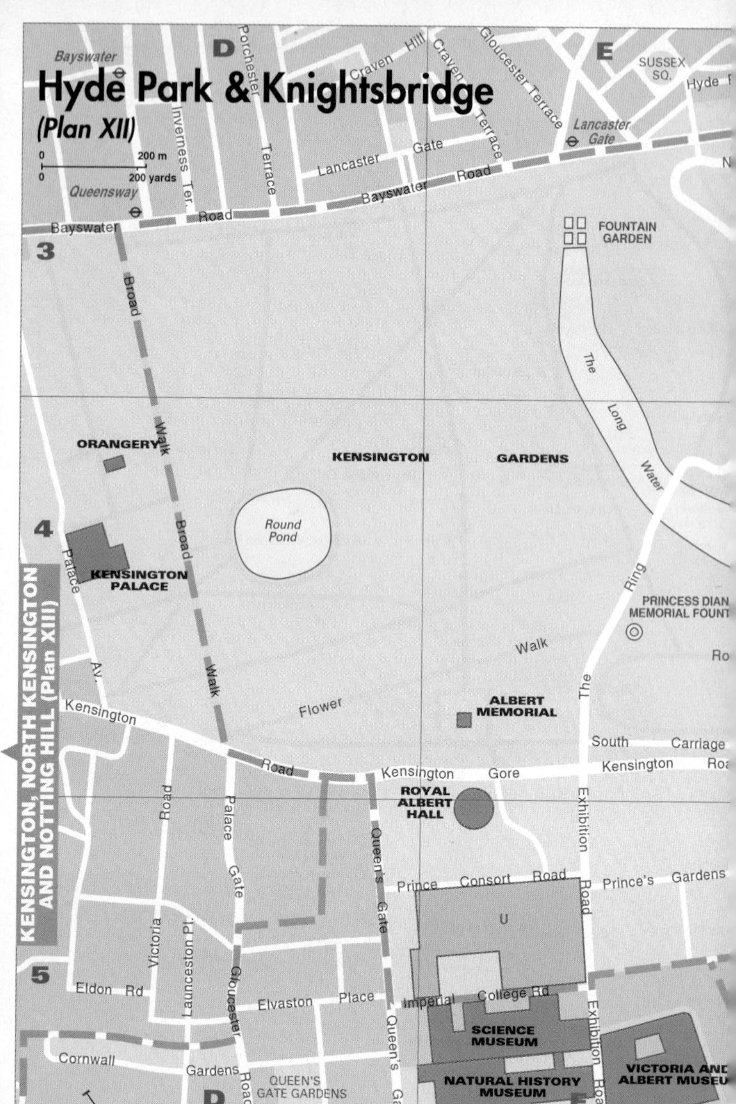
Hyde Park & Knightsbridge
(Plan XII)
0 200 m
0 200 yards
Bayswater
Queensway
Porchester
Inverness Ter.
Terrace
Craven Hill
Craven
Gloucester Terrace
Terrace
Lancaster Gate
Lancaster Gate
Bayswater Road
Bayswater Road
SUSSEX SQ.
FOUNTAIN GARDEN
Broad Walk
The Long Water
ORANGERY
KENSINGTON GARDENS
Round Pond
KENSINGTON PALACE
Palace Av.
The Ring
PRINCESS DIAN
MEMORIAL FOUNT
Flower Walk
ALBERT MEMORIAL
South Carriage
Kensington Road
Kensington Road
Kensington Gore
ROYAL ALBERT HALL
Exhibition Road
Palace Gate
Queen's Gate
Prince Consort Road
Prince's Gardens
U
Imperial College Rd
SCIENCE MUSEUM
NATURAL HISTORY MUSEUM
VICTORIA AND ALBERT MUSEU
Victoria Road
Launceston Pl.
Gloucester Road
Eldon Rd
Elvaston Place
Cornwall Gardens
QUEEN'S GATE GARDENS
KENSINGTON, NORTH KENSINGTON AND NOTTING HILL (Plan XIII)
D
E
3
4
5

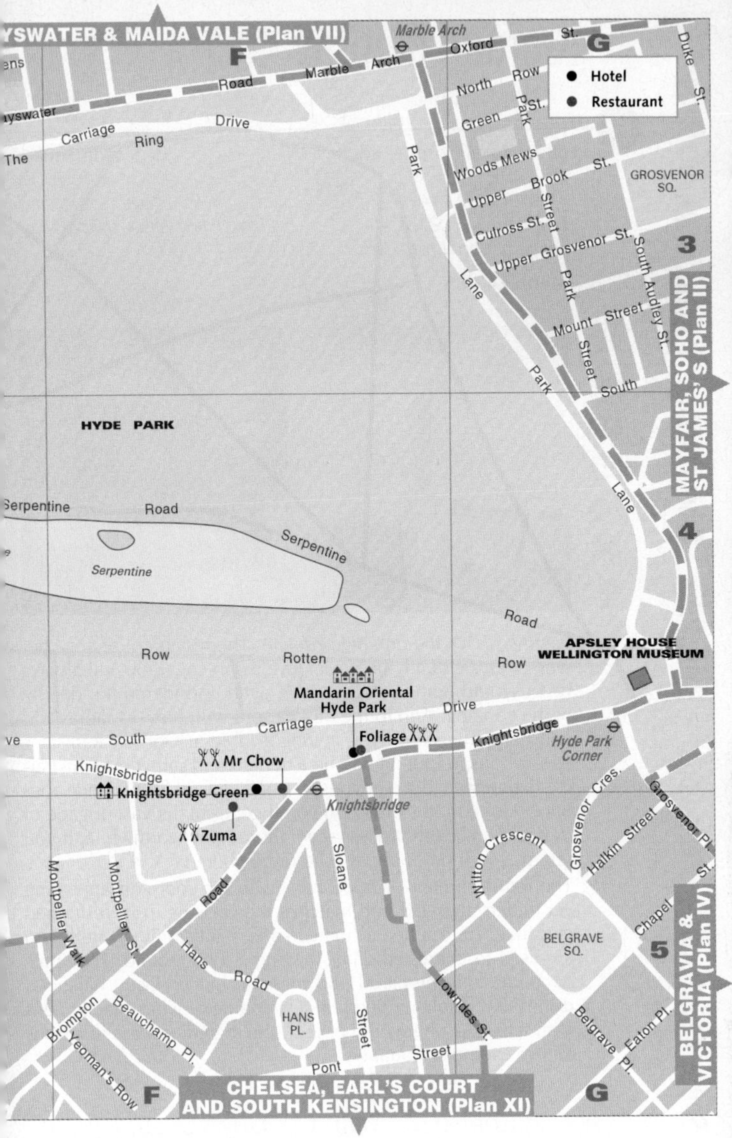
BAYSWATER & MAIDA VALE (Plan VII)
MAYFAIR, SOHO AND ST JAMES'S (Plan II)
BELGRAVIA & VICTORIA (Plan IV)
CHELSEA, EARL'S COURT AND SOUTH KENSINGTON (Plan XI)
Hotel
Restaurant
HYDE PARK
Serpentine
APSLEY HOUSE
WELLINGTON MUSEUM
Mandarin Oriental
Hyde Park
Foliage
Mr Chow
Knightsbridge Green
Zuma
Marble Arch
Hyde Park Corner
Knightsbridge
GROSVENOR SQ.
BELGRAVE SQ.
HANS PL.

Gordon Ramsay ✿✿✿

F7

French XXXX

68-69 Royal Hospital Rd
SW3 4HP
✆ (020) 7352 4441
Fax (020) 7352 3334
www.gordonramsay.com

⊖ Sloane Square
▶ Plan XI
Closed 1 week Christmas, Saturday and Sunday – booking essential

Menu £40/85

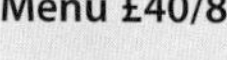

Gordon Ramsay Holdings

Getting in. It's the one big obstacle. The restaurant of any chef who enjoys virtually universal levels of recognition will always be busy and that's before you've even considered the quality of the cooking. Add to the mix a room with only 14 tables and you can understand why getting a table at Gordon Ramsay's eponymous restaurant will be a fraught and sometimes frustrating experience. But smugness is one's reward for patience and, once you're in, the attention you'll get from the vast brigade of staff will make the process seem thoroughly worthwhile; if you return, you'll probably also be remembered.

The refurbishment of 2006 has given the room an appealing yet understated feel and matches the cooking in its restrained elegance. The kitchen is home to a veritable army of chefs who are used to interested diners having a look around. They produce carefully prepared and intricate but perfectly balanced dishes that display a deep understanding of what exactly goes with what. As one would expect, the ingredients are luxurious and of exemplary quality.

First Course

- Pan-fried Scottish scallops with millefeuille of potato, parmesan velouté.
- Loin of tuna with seared veal fillet and artichoke salad.

Main Course

- Roast Bresse pigeon with grilled polenta, baby golden beetroot and date sauce.
- John Dory with Cromer crab, caviar and basil vinaigrette.

Dessert

- Bitter chocolate cylinder with coffee granité and ginger mousse.
- Toffee soufflé with banana ice cream.

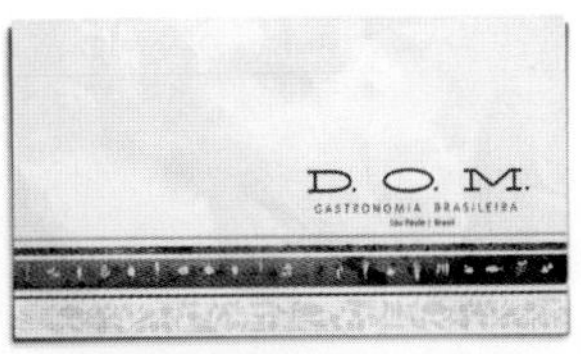

To enhance great foods they choose great waters.

The delicate complex flavours of the finest cuisine are best appreciated by an educated palate. And in the same way that the right wine can release the nuances of a dish, the right water can subtly cleanse the palate, enhancing the pleasure and experience of both. To discover why S.Pellegrino and Acqua Panna are seen on all the best tables, go to WWW.FINEDININGWATERS.COM

ACQUA PANNA AND S.PELLEGRINO. FINE DINING WATERS.

La Noisette ✿

F5

Innovative XXXX

164 Sloane St SW1X 9QB
✆ (020) 7750 5000
Fax (020) 7750 5001
e-mail lanoisette@gordonramsay.com
www.gordonramsay.com

⊖ Knightsbridge
▶ **Plan XI**
Closed Saturday lunch and Sunday

Menu £21/55

A/C
VISA
MC
AE
Ⓓ
🍷

La Noisette

The problem with any restaurant on a first, rather than a ground, floor if that you can't have a reassuring gawp before you go in. You might miss the entrance to La Noisette anyway, situated as it is among some seriously glamorous boutiques. This would be a shame because Bjorn Van der Horst, formerly of the Greenhouse in Mayfair and Picholine in New York, has settled in well here. His seasonal tasting menu showcases the depth and range of his repertoire and may occasionally revolve around one main ingredient, such as a poulet de Bresse which is theatrically carved at the table. The à la carte menu offers equally innovative dishes, with a lexicon that would bamboozle Larousse, but all dishes are exact in their balance and precise in their execution. The lunch price is a positive steal. The room is comfortable without being particularly memorable and the stylish bar upstairs has yet to become the destination it should be. Well informed and personable staff ensure things are kept light, with the emphasis on enjoyment.

First Course

- Seared foie gras with coffee syrup and amaretto foam.
- Almond gazpacho with smoked paprika shrimp.

Main Course

- Spit-roasted chicken from Bresse for two.
- Saddle of lamb with artichoke, sweetbreads and brioche.

Dessert

- White peach soufflé, verbena sorbet and palmito.
- Strawberry millefeuille with olive oil and vanilla.

The Capital Restaurant ✿✿

French XXX

F5

at Capital H.,
22-24 Basil St SW3 1AT
✆ (020) 7589 5171 **Fax** (020) 7225 0011
e-mail caprest@capitalhotel.co.uk

⊖ Knightsbridge
▶ **Plan XI**
Booking essential

Menu £30/55

The Capital

It can take some chefs a while to find the environment that suits them best. Eric Chavot and The Capital hotel seem to be the perfect fit and the fact that he is only the fourth chef since the hotel opened in 1971 says much about the place. He has an original style, a great eye for detail and one can still clearly see he's got a classical French background. He is not, however, afraid of nudging at boundaries but does so in a mischievous manner rather than with the 'look at me' principle adopted by less experienced chefs. He'll deconstruct a 'niçoise' or a 'lasagna' but in a way that demonstrates his understanding of flavours and textures. The wine list boasts impressive depth and range.

The thought of dining in a hotel dining room is anathema to many but here one never feels ensnared in a world of corporate blandness. This feels like a stand-alone restaurant, helped along by the windows overlooking Basil Street. It is comfortable and elegant and serving staff demonstrate an impressive knowledge of the food. They are also enthusiastic and relatively youthful and this, in turn, ensures that the atmosphere avoids stuffiness.

First Course

- Assiette 'Landaise'.
- Crab lasagna with langoustine cappuccino.

Main Course

- Saddle of rabbit with seared calamari and tomato risotto.
- Honey roasted fillet of duck with macaroni gratin and pear jelly.

Dessert

- Iced coffee parfait with chocolate fondant.
- Peanut and salted caramel moelleux, banana and passion fruit sorbet.

Foliage ✿

Innovative XXX

F4

at Mandarin Oriental Hyde Park H.,
66 Knightsbridge SW1X 7LA
⊖ Knightsbridge
▶ Plan XII

✆ (020) 7201 3723 **Fax** (020) 7235 4552
e-mail molon-dine@mohg **www**.mandarinoriental.com

Menu £29/60

A/C VISA MC AE

Mandarin Oriental Hyde Park

The cleverest thing about Adam Tihany's design is that it gives the restaurant a real sense of time and place and lets the seasons outside play a role inside. The large windows of this ground floor restaurant within a luxury international hotel really do let the park in and the earthy colours and foliage motif add a palpable sense of nature.

The cooking, meanwhile, treads a path that owes more to modernity and novelty. The chef has been on his travels recently and has returned with new ideas gleaned from the kitchen of some fairly ground-breaking outposts. His cooking has always been detailed and sophisticated but now it comes with some experimental combinations and unexpected flavours. With all those little extras, you certainly come away feeling you have had an experience and an original one at that. The lighter eater should try the smaller tasting plates available at lunch. The room seats just forty-five and the staff are well-drilled but also positive so there is never any threat of stuffiness pervading the air.

First Course

- Foie gras jelly rolls with smoked duck salad and foie gras ice cream.
- Slow-cooked belly of ham, date marmalade and black pudding.

Main Course

- Lamb with girolles, haricot blanc and jus gras.
- Fillet of sea bass with celeriac, turnips and smoked bacon.

Dessert

- Guava sorbet with raspberry tuile and exotic fruits.
- Walnut cake with kumquats and Assam tea cream.

Tom Aikens ✿

E6 **Innovative** XXX

43 Elystan St SW3 3NT
✆ (020) 7584 2003
Fax (020) 7584 2001
e-mail info@tomaikens.co.uk
www.tomaikens.co.uk

⊖ South Kensington
▶ Plan XI

Closed two weeks August, 10 days Christmas-New Year, Saturday, Sunday and Bank Holidays

Menu £29/65

A/C VISA MC AE

There have been a few changes to Tom Aikens' eponymous restaurant recently: there's a new private dining room, a bigger reception area and a new carpet. However, the most significant change has been in the food. Gone are the 'splats' and 'smears' that may have looked pretty on the plate but detracted somewhat from the dish as a whole. Now, by focusing far more on the main ingredient, his cooking has moved up a level. Dishes still look appetising and the innovative and original touches remain but the extraneous elements have been reined in. He has also rekindled his enthusiasm for traceability, sustainability, seasonality and provenance; he spends time finding the right suppliers, whether that's fish from Newlyn, potatoes from Lincolnshire or salt marsh lamb from Wales.

The room is warm and uncluttered and service continues to be attentive and evenly paced. The professional staff know what they're talking about and the sommelier is understandably passionate about his considerably weighty wine list.

First Course

- Hen's egg with truffled scrambled egg, foie gras mousse and cured duck breast.
- Poached chicken with celeriac fondant and truffle mayonnaise.

Main Course

- Roast pork cutlet with apple purée, baby squid and pork lasagna.
- Roast Salt Marsh lamb with goat's cheese tart and quince purée.

Dessert

- Apple roasted in honey with saffron ice cream.
- Lemon parfait with lemon panna cotta and lemon tapioca.

Aubergine ✿

French XXX

D7

11 Park Walk SW10 0AJ
✆ (020) 7352 3449
Fax (020) 7351 1770
e-mail info@auberginerestaurant.co.uk
www.auberginerestaurant.co.uk

⊖ South Kensington
▶ **Plan XI**
Closed 2 weeks Christmas, Easter, Saturday lunch, Sunday and Bank Holidays – booking essential

Menu £34 (lunch)/64

Aubergine

Aubergine has been quietly going about its business in this unremarkable part of Chelsea for quite some time and William Drabble, the head chef, has held his position since 1998. It is nowhere near anyone's check-list for fashionable dining and the paparazzi never linger outside. But it is this lack of pretentiousness that is the restaurant's trump card and which allows it to concentrate on offering its band of regulars a consistent, all-round experience.

Another thing you won't get is any frightening combinations of flavours or ingredients from the kitchen - Drabble keeps things nicely classical and has an inherent understanding of what goes with what. His cooking is not about throwing expensive ingredients on the plate either – he knows his butchery and excels at creating 'assiettes' by using assorted cuts and contrasting textures. The pricing policy also offers an opportunity to experience the restaurant without breaking the bank, thanks to its decently priced lunch time set menu that comes with a ½ bottle of wine, water and coffee included.

First Course

- Seared scallops with smoked salmon, potatoes and peas.
- Grilled lobster salad with morels and asparagus.

Main Course

- Best end of lamb with braised sweetbreads, tomato and basil.
- Roast John Dory with rosemary butter.

Dessert

- Poached peach jelly and crumble, lemon verbena sorbet.
- Assiette of strawberry.

Bibendum

E6

French XXX

Michelin House, 81 Fulham Rd SW3 6RD
(020) 7581 5817
Fax (020) 7823 7925
e-mail reservations@bibendum.co.uk **www**.bibendum.co.uk

⊖ South Kensington
▶ Plan XI
Closed 25-26 December and 1 January

Menu £29 – Carte £37/60

Dine with the Editor of the Michelin Guide here and he'll go all misty eyed as he remembers when part of the restaurant was once his office. This extraordinarily imaginative building, opened in 1911 and designed by a Michelin employee, anticipated the art deco movement of the 1920s, with its ceramic tiles and stained glass windows, and remained our UK HQ until the mid 1980s.

Named after the Michelin Man, Bibendum proved an instant hit as a restaurant by combining all the elements of style, design, service and carefully prepared food. Today, it remains a favourite by continuing to offer dependably good cooking which, appropriately enough, still retains that French connection, along with professional service and surroundings that never fail to impress.

One-O-One

F4

Seafood XXX

at Sheraton Park Tower H., William St SW1X 7RN
(020) 7290 7101 **Fax** (020) 7235 6196

⊖ Knightsbridge
▶ Plan XI

Menu £19/30 (lunch) – Carte £35/55

A big refurbishment in 2007 not only saw a new and improved decorative style for this spacious restaurant on the ground floor of the Sheraton Park Tower hotel, but also coincided with a change of concept for the food presentation. The Brittany born chef still focuses primarily on seafood, but specialities such as King crab are now more diminutively proportioned as the menu is made up of 'petit plats' for a lighter and more flexible eating experience: four or five per person should leave you feeling fed.

The room is certainly comfortable and has been broken up a little, while the service remains sufficiently dutiful. The unremittingly anodyne background music, though, adds little to the experience.

Drones

G5

Modern European XXX

1 Pont St SW1X 9EJ
✆ (020) 7235 9555
Fax (020) 7235 9566
e-mail sales@whitestarline.org.uk
www.whitestarline.org.uk

⊖ Knightsbridge
▶ **Plan XI**
Closed 26 December, 1 January, Saturday lunch and Sunday dinner

Menu £19 – Carte £32/45

A/C VISA MC AE

Drones is one of those reassuringly timeless restaurants. It has been around since the 1970s, was re-launched by Marco Pierre White in 2000 but the clubby, Chelsea feel has always been maintained. The tables are big enough to spread yourself without fear of trespassing on your companion's territory and the long room, lined with Cornel Lucas photographs of legends of the business they called 'show', has an air of calmness.

The menu is the very definition of the Entente Cordiale. An Englishman could sit on one side having potted shrimps followed by roast pheasant and rice pudding to finish. The Frenchman opposite could enjoy foie gras parfait, followed by poulet chasseur and with crème caramel to end.

Fifth Floor

F4

Modern European XXX

at Harvey Nichols,
Knightsbridge SW1X 7RJ
✆ (020) 7235 5250
www.harveynichols.com

⊖ Knightsbridge
▶ **Plan XI**
Closed Christmas and Sunday dinner

Menu £20/40 – Carte £28/44

A/C VISA MC AE

The ladies who lunch have never had it so good. Harvey Nichol's flagship Knightsbridge store boasts a top floor to satisfy the weariest of shoppers and the most jaded of palates. As well as a food store, sushi bar, café and cocktail bar one finds the strikingly stylish sanctuary of the main restaurant, decorated with a faux skylight and fibre-optic lit walls that change colour periodically. It sets the standards by which all department stores are judged by being so much more than merely an in-store restaurant for there is substance as well as style here.

The express lift from Sloane Street brings more customers up for the light, fresh and balanced dishes of European persuasion; service is polite and efficient and brunch is offered at weekends.

Chutney Mary

Indian XXX

D8

535 King's Rd SW10 0SZ
✆ (020) 7351 3113 **Fax** (020) 7351 7694
e-mail chutneymary@realindianfood.com
www.realindianfood

⊖ Fulham Broadway
▶ **Plan XI**
Dinner only

Carte £34/43

A/C VISA MC AE

Chutney Mary is one of the senior members of the Indian restaurant fraternity but that doesn't mean it has rested on its laurels. In 2002 it was given a head-to-toe revamp which modernised what was already a very comfortable place. The large conservatory is still there but now the room is fringed with storm-lamps and the mood is altogether more seductive and sophisticated. 1840's etchings of Indian life combine with mirrors to add a touch of glamour and the young team provide service that is both conscientious and attentive.

The menu is as interesting as it has always been, with good quality seasonal ingredients and strong presentation. The well chosen wine list challenges those who think only a Kingfisher beer can accompany an Indian meal.

Bombay Brasserie

Indian XXX

D6

Courtfield Rd SW7 4QH
✆ (020) 7370 4040
Fax (020) 7835 1669
e-mail bombay1brasserie@aol.com
www.bombaybrasserielondon.com

⊖ Gloucester Road
▶ **Plan XI**
Closed 25-26 December – buffet lunch

Menu £19 (weekday lunch) – Carte £42/52

A/C VISA MC AE

Bombay Brasserie opened its doors in 1982 and its neon sign and doorman have become established local features. It was one of the first restaurants to prove to Londoners that Indian food merits glamorous surroundings just as much as any other cuisine and succeeds so well in its task that you'll never be able to look flock wallpaper in the eye again. The vast, perpetually busy, dining room is divided into two: the main room with its striking mural of Bombay life and the conservatory extension.

A whole army of staff all know exactly what to do and do so with aplomb. Influences from across India feature, from Kerala to Mughlai, and this includes seafood dishes from Goa and fragrant Parsi fare. The lunchtime buffet is a veritable institution.

Awana

Malaysian XXX

F6

85 Sloane Ave SW3 3DX
(020) 7584 8880
Fax (020) 7584 6188
e-mail info@awana.co.uk **www**.awana.co.uk

⊖ South Kensington
▶ **Plan XI**
Closed 25-26 December and 1 January

Menu £15/40 - Carte £29/41

Malaysia has been one of the few absentees as London embraces the cooking of the world but it is now proudly showcased at this very smart Chelsea restaurant, whose name translates as 'in the clouds'.

Start your meal with a roti canai and order satay from the deftly skilled chef behind the dedicated satay bar. The menu is divided into soups, curries, grills and stir-fry, with the 'Malaysian Journey' tasting menu being a great introduction. The lunch menu is a virtual steal.

A smart bar provides a great spot for one of their original cocktails while the restaurant is designed using traditional elements such as teakwood and batik silk, with stylish glass screens and decorative panels. Very charming Malaysian servers offer sensible advice.

Toto's

Italian XXX

F5

Walton House, Walton St
SW3 2JH
(020) 7589 0075 **Fax** (020) 7581 9668

⊖ Knightsbridge
▶ **Plan XI**
Closed 3 days Christmas

Menu £25 - Carte £35/45

This is a real Chelsea restaurant and one that's been part of local life for many a year. It comes from an era when people went to restaurants to eat rather than to gawp. It's in an attractive period house in a secretive little spot and once you're seated you'll wonder why you don't live in Chelsea yourself (or be glad that you do).

Beyond the bar and small lounge by the entrance, you'll find a smart, marble-floored restaurant that's spread over two floors and is far larger than you're expecting. All the regulars have their own spots and there are various corners and tables for those after added privacy. Service is equally old school and the cooking is traditional and reliable, although it does come at a price. Well, this is Chelsea, after all.

Aquasia

D8 **International** XXX

at Wyndham Grand H.,
Chelsea Harbour SW10 0XG
(020) 7300 8443
www.wyndhamlondon.com

⊖ Fulham Broadway
▶ **Plan XI**

Carte £26/45

The all-suite Conrad Hotel may not be the most accessible place in London if you haven't got a limo, but have lunch on the sun deck of their restaurant Aquasia, overlooking the yachts of Chelsea Harbour, and you'll think you've landed in the Med. The room is shaped like an ocean liner and is all very fresh and light in tone, with a wall of windows that open out on warm days. Most of the tables have a view, although some prefer to gaze inward in case any of the hotel's more famous guests wander in. As the name implies, the cooking blends Mediterranean ingredients with Asian aromatics and techniques to create appealingly refined dishes. On Sundays the champagne brunches have become very popular, helped no doubt by the offer of unlimited champagne.

Daphne's

E6 **Italian** XX

112 Draycott Ave SW3 3AE
(020) 7589 4257
Fax (020) 7225 2766
e-mail reservations@daphnes-restaurant.co.uk
www.daphnes-restaurant.co.uk

⊖ South Kensington
▶ **Plan XI**
Closed 25-26 December – booking essential

Menu £19 – Carte £33/47

Its fortunes may have been mixed since opening in the '60s but today Daphne's is an unequivocally constant blink on the fashionista's radar screen. Lunch is full of ladies weighed down with bags from a hard morning's 'Imeldaring' at Jimmy Choo, while dinner is populated with the tanned and buffed figures of the entertainment world - this is not the place to go when you're not looking your best.

Where the restaurant surprises is in the care and accuracy of the Italian cooking - the kitchen knows what's in season and what goes with what – and the diligence of the service. The front room is where to be seen but if it's privacy you're after then it's best at the back, where there's a retractable roof for summer and a fireplace in winter.

Rasoi ✿

Indian XX

F6

10 Lincoln St SW3 2TS
✆ (020) 7225 1881
Fax (020) 7581 0220
e-mail info@rasoirestaurant.co.uk
www.rasoirestaurant.co.uk

⊖ Sloane Square
▶ Plan XI
Closed 25 -26 December, 1 January, Saturday lunch, Sunday and Bank Holidays

Menu £24 (lunch) – Carte £38/73

A/C VISA MC AE

Rasoi

The Bombay-born chef-owner, Vineet Bhatia, made his name at Star of India and Zaika but moved here to Chelsea in 2004 where he found a fitting environment for his cooking. You ring the doorbell before being ushered into this end of terrace house which retains the feel of a family home, albeit a well travelled family with exotic tastes. On the ground floor, the dining room is L shaped, with a small conservatory area at the back and is decorated with an assortment of ceramics, carvings, face masks and Indian trinkets. The upstairs rooms are often used for private parties and have an equally intimate feel. The staff are a mix of nationalities, from Indian to German.

Vineet has taken Indian cooking and given it a contemporary twist that will make you reassess your preconceptions. His cooking is individual and innovative, spicing is subtle and controlled and the flavours have an impressive clarity. There are plenty of menus on offer; from the Gourmand, which shows off the kitchen's ability the best, to the good value set lunch. Vegetarians are also well looked after.

First Course
- Grilled scallops with asparagus, curry leaf and spinach.
- Tandoori quail with green pea jelly.

Main Course
- Ginger and chilli lobster with curry leaf and spiced cocoa powder.
- Black spiced chicken breast with tomato and cashew nut chutney.

Dessert
- Chocolate samosa with Bailey's ice cream.
- Rasmalai with fresh fruit and cinnamon.

Racine

French XX

239 Brompton Rd SW3 2EP — ⊖ South Kensington
✆ (020) 7584 4477 **Fax** (020) 7584 4900 — ▶ **Plan XI**
Closed 25 December

Menu £18/20 (lunch) – Carte £26/37

Racine is one of those places that just seems right. After six years the French brasserie feel is even more pronounced, as the brown leather now has a more lived-in look, the wood has darkened and the mirrors have gone a smoky opaque. After the departure of Henry Harris, the restaurant is now in the sole hands of Eric Garnier and he continues to run it with a deft touch, which is made easier by the majority of diners being regulars who know how it all works.

There are good value menus for lunch and early dinner, and from the à la carte you can expect a comprehensive selection of bourgeois classics, from tête de veau to steak tartare and crème caramel. That 14½ % service charge, though, can push up the final bill somewhat.

Nozomi

F5

Japanese XX

15 Beauchamp Pl SW3 1NQ — ⊖ Knightsbridge
✆ (020) 7838 1500 **Fax** (020) 7838 1001 — ▶ **Plan XI**
e-mail info@nazomi.co.uk **www**.nazomi.co.uk

Carte £50/65

The fact that there's a liveried doorman standing outside should tell you that this is not your everyday Japanese restaurant, even for Knightsbridge. In fact, you may not even think you're in a restaurant at all because you'll find yourself in a glitzy bar, complete with loud music and a DJ, which sets the tone for the whole place with its dark styling and sleekness. It's up a few steps to the roomy dining area, beneath a large skylight, with a further sushi bar upstairs.

The kitchen attempts to match these fiercely fashionable surroundings with a selection of modern and original creations. A variation on the ubiquitous black cod with miso is there but then so is Genghis Khan Chicken, an altogether more threatening sounding dish.

Bluebird

British XX

E7

350 King's Rd SW3 5UU — ⊖ Sloane Square
✆ (020) 7559 1000 **Fax** (020) 7559 1115 — ▶ **Plan XI**
e-mail enquiries@bluebird-store.co.uk **www**.danddlondon.com

Carte £29/44

Bluebird is a giant brasserie housed in a former garage built in 1923, which was where Malcolm Campbell's famous Bluebird cars were made. The noise of revving engines has now been replaced by the sound of clinking cutlery but, with nearly 200 seats to fill, this place does need to be busy to get going. Its decoration was given a subtle refreshment in 2007 and the bar remains something of a destination in its own right.
Chef Mark Broadbent is making a name for himself as a champion of British produce. His menu offers quite a range, from pies to pasta, but your best bet is to head for the inherently British offerings like Herdwick lamb, Cromer crab or Yorkshire grouse, where the quality of the produce really shines through.

Poissonnerie de l'Avenue

French XX

E6

82 Sloane Ave SW3 3DZ — ⊖ South Kensington
✆ (020) 7589 2457 — ▶ **Plan XI**
Fax (020) 7581 3360 — Closed 24-26 December and Sunday
e-mail info@poissonnerie.co.uk
www.poissonneriedel'avenue.co.uk

Menu £24 - Carte £27/40

This is one of those restaurants that's impossible to walk past without feeling drawn in. The smell of seafood and garlic is enough in itself to arouse your senses and if you peer, like a child, through the window it all looks so warm and inviting inside.
For over forty years this veritable institution has been satisfying the grown ups of Chelsea with its reliably classic seafood and its timeless and well-mannered atmosphere. The wood panelling, nautically themed paintings and the type of waiters they don't make anymore all contribute to the feeling that this is a restaurant that really belongs and one that has a soul. It also has Sole Véronique, to remind us that cooking wasn't invented in the 1990s.

Le Cercle

F6 **French** XX

1 Wilbraham Pl SW1X 9AE
(020) 7901 9999
Fax (020) 7901 9111
e-mail info@lecercle.co.uk

⊖ Sloane Square
▶ **Plan XI**
Closed 24 December-5 January, Sunday and Monday

Menu £15 – Carte £20/32

This offshoot of Club Gascon is housed within what was planned to be the swimming pool of the serviced apartments above so that explains the double height of the ceiling of this basement restaurant. This is a very stylish room, with marble, leather, assorted little nooks and a long bar all divided up by billowing white drapes, lending an air of seduction and secrecy. Lovers should ask for table 24.

The menu comes divided into sections headed *vegetal, marin, fermier, terroirs* and *plaisirs*. Diners should choose three or four dishes – which are delicate little modern French creations - plus a dessert and, as they all come in 'tasting' sizes, now's your chance to order something unfamiliar. The exclusively French wines are thoughtfully paired.

Le Colombier

E6 **French** XX

145 Dovehouse St SW3 6LB
(020) 7351 1155 **Fax** (020) 7351 5124
e-mail lecolombier1998@aol.com
www.lecolombier-sw3.co.uk

⊖ South Kensington
▶ **Plan XI**

Menu £16/19 (lunch) – Carte £28/39

It's a French restaurant in Chelsea but could equally be a Chelsea restaurant in France. The loyalty and regularity of attendance shown by those in the neighbourhood ensures that there's always a cheery atmosphere of familiarity. The restaurant, with a large covered terrace/conservatory at the front, has more than a little feel of a brasserie. It's also quite sizeable but manages to retain a certain intimacy, helped considerably by the presence of the experienced owner who will never knowingly let a face go unrecognised.

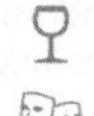

Classic French cooking is the order of the day and it's hearty, stout and generous in size. The munificence of the set price lunch menu is enough in itself to make regulars of us all.

Caraffini

F6 **Italian** XX

61-63 Lower Sloane St
SW1W 8DH
(020) 7259 0235
Fax (020) 7259 0236
e-mail info@caraffini.co.uk **www**.caraffini.co.uk

Sloane Square
▶ **Plan XI**
Closed 25 December, Easter, Sunday and Bank Holidays – booking essential

Carte £24/33

A/C VISA MC AE

One doesn't have to look far to see why Paolo Caraffini's restaurant is always so busy: it has a wonderfully genial host, smooth service, reliably good Italian food and a highly hospitable atmosphere. Just watching the number of regulars Paolo greets as friends, from Chelsea art dealers to King's Road shoppers, will make you want to become a part of the club. Warm and cosy in winter, bright and sunny in summer with pavement tables for alfresco dining, this really is a place for all seasons. Daily specials supplement the already balanced menu that covers many regions of Italy and any requests to veer off-menu are satisfied without fuss or fanfare. Caraffini is proof that good hospitality is very much alive and kicking.

L'Etranger

D5 **Innovative** XX

36 Gloucester Rd SW7 4QT
(020) 7584 1118
Fax (020) 7584 8886
e-mail etranger@etranger.co.uk
www.circagroupltd.co.uk

Gloucester Road
▶ **Plan XI**
Closed 25-26 December, 1 January, Saturday lunch – booking essential

Menu £16.50 – Carte £31/82

A/C VISA MC AE

The accents found within L'Etranger would suggest your classic French restaurant but one coup d'oeil at the menu and you'll see that alongside words like magret and assiette come others like tempura and teppanyaki. Asia exerts quite an influence on the cooking but the kitchen's main selling point is a marriage between the cuisines of France and Japan. So you'll find a delicacy and precision to the food as well as an impressive wine list. This is also a neighbourhood restaurant whose band of sophisticated regulars are a loyal bunch. Their reward is a menu section marked 'favourites' - popular dishes that the chef dare not take off, such as his own take on black cod with miso. The lighting is moody, the music a little loungy and the vibe, friendly.

Langan's Coq d'Or

C6 — Traditional XX

254-260 Old Brompton Rd
SW5 9HR
(020) 7259 2599 **Fax** (020) 7370 7735
e-mail admin@langansrestaurant.co.uk
www.langansrestaurants.co.uk

⊖ Earl's Court
▶ **Plan XI**
Closed Bank Holidays

Menu £23 – Carte £27

The celebrated restaurateur Peter Langan may no longer be with us, but Richard Shepherd has created a restaurant of which his friend would no doubt have approved. He has also named it in honour of the original moniker of Langan's in Stratton Street. It is almost two restaurants in one: the glass enclosed front section goes by the name of the 'bar and grill', is more informal in style and opens out onto the street in summer while beyond is the main restaurant, whose walls are filled with a huge collection of artwork.

The menu is a no-nonsense celebration of the best of British combined with what Europe can offer. So, expect bangers and mash alongside rack of lamb. For the incurably louche, breakfast is served until early evening.

Zuma

F5 — Japanese XX

5 Raphael St SW7 1DL
(020) 7584 1010
Fax (020) 7584 5005
e-mail info@zumarestaurant.com
www.zumarestaurant.com

⊖ Knightsbridge
▶ **Plan XII**
Closed 25 December and 1 January

Carte £30/96

Japanese food meets Contemporary Japanese food at this stylish Knightsbridge restaurant, popular with the glittering and the glitterati and ideally located for those seeking a little respite from the strain of shopping or being photographed doing so. The place is certainly eye-catching in its design, with a plethora of granite, stone, marble and wood creating a restaurant that successfully blends east with west.

Choose from a variety of seating options, from the bustle of the main dining area to the theatre afforded by the sushi counter. The menu offers up an intriguing mix of the traditional with the ultra modern, all expertly crafted and delicately presented. Lovers of sake will find over thirty varieties available.

Mr Chow

Chinese XX

F4

151 Knightsbridge SW1X 7PA
✆ (020) 7589 7347
Fax (020) 7584 5780
e-mail mrchow@aol.com
www.mrchow.com

⊖ Knightsbridge
▶ **Plan XII**
Closed 24-26 December, 1 January and Easter Monday

Menu £25/40 – Carte £38/57

Mr Chow, the self styled Renaissance man, has branches of his Chinese restaurant in various American cities but London was his firstborn, opening its doors in 1968. Over the years it has seen off assorted interlopers and has retained the affections of many. Newcomers should get something clear - this isn't the sort of Chinese restaurant where you plonk yourself down, order a Tsingtao and split your chopsticks in anticipation. Instead, a champagne chariot will be wheeled over to you as you peruse the menu, service is provided by a long standing team of Italian professionals while the room, and the clientele, enjoy a certain timeless elegance.

The Chinese food is reliably good and mixes the traditional with Mr Chow specialities.

Papillon

French XX

F6

96 Draycott Ave SW3 3AD
✆ (020) 7225 2555
Fax (020) 7225 2554
e-mail info@papillonchelsea.co.uk
www.papillonchelsea.co.uk

⊖ South Kensington
▶ **Plan XI**
Closed 24-27 December, 1-4 January

Menu £17 – Carte £26/46

Sometimes you just have to hand it to those designers. Papillon looks as though it has occupied this corner of Draycott Avenue for years but this little butterfly didn't flutter onto the scene until May 2006. From the wood and the mirrors to the lamps and the arched French windows thrown open in summer - everything seems new and old at the same time. It has the feel and the look of a timeless Parisian brasserie and the locals have been flocking in since the doors first opened.

The kitchen, too, does its bit for cross Channel relations by offering a comprehensive selection of Gallic classics, from the robust to the rustic, to appeal to all tastes. Salads from all corners of France remind you that this is also lunching-ladies land.

Pasha

D5 **Moroccan** XX

1 Gloucester Rd SW7 4PP ⊖ Gloucester Road
(020) 7589 7969 ▶ Plan XI
Fax (020) 7581 9996 Closed 25-26 December, and 1 January
e-mail info@pasha-restaurant.co.uk **www**.pasha-restaurant.co.uk

Menu £15/30 – Carte £22/33

Now under the same ownership as Levant restaurant, Pasha has been recharged and refreshed and now represents a fun night out.

The ground floor is given over to the atmospheric cocktail lounge bar, with the exotic scent of hookah pipes and joss-sticks in the air. Downstairs, low tables are strewn with rose petals, light from lanterns and candles bounces off the mosaic floor while the cushions and rich colours add to the seductive feel. As does the belly-dancer.

Moroccan home-style cooking is the feature here, with sharing the key. Lunch is a simpler affair but in the evenings try one of the 'feast' menus. The main menu is divided into tagines, couscous or grills but don't forget Moroccan cooking uses good seafood as well as meats.

Cambio de Tercio

D6 **Spanish** XX

163 Old Brompton Rd ⊖ Gloucester Road
SW5 0LJ ▶ Plan XI
(020) 7244 8970 **Fax** (020) 7373 2359 Closed 2 weeks Christmas
e-mail alusa@btconnect.com **www**.cambiodetercio.co.uk

Carte £27/39

In summer this Spanish restaurant spills out onto the street but still the best tables are right at the back in a cosy little glass-roofed section. The menu is appealing and authentic and the choice extensive. Starters are divided into hot and cold, followed by four meat and four fish dishes which also come in a choice of size, so your best bet is to come with friends and share a load. Spain's proud culinary heritage is there for all to see: Galecian octopus, Serrano and Iberico hams, Manchego cheese, Valencian rice, Segovian suckling pig and crema Catalan all make you wonder why there are not more Spanish restaurants around.

Mustard coloured walls and bright Matador paintings complete the scene. The young owners also have a tapas bar across the road.

Khan's of Kensington

Indian XX

E6

3 Harrington Rd SW7 3ES ⊖ South Kensington
✆ (020) 7584 4114 **Fax** (020) 7581 2900 ▶ **Plan XI**
e-mail info@khansofkensington.co.uk Closed 25 December

Menu £9/17 – Carte £16/27

Virtually opposite South Kensington tube, Khan's of Kensington has been a local feature for quite a few years now and the locals have been resolute in their loyalty. It's really quite contemporary inside and the modern Warhol-esque pictures take you a little by surprise. The size is near perfect: big enough to generate an atmosphere but small enough to create a certain intimacy. The downstairs tables and chairs have been removed and the space has been turned into a comfortable lounge bar.

The menu provides a more modern and, consequently, more interesting selection of dishes, all of which are carefully prepared to a good standard with the emphasis on the North West frontier. A takeaway service is also available.

Pellicano

Italian XX

F6

19-21 Elystan St SW3 3NT ⊖ South Kensington
✆ (020) 7589 3718 **Fax** (020) 7584 1789 ▶ **Plan XI**
e-mail pellicano@btconnect.com **www**.pellicanorestaurant.co.uk

Menu £19 – Carte £22/36

This is another one of those neighbourhood Chelsea restaurants that makes you wonder why your street doesn't look like this. Unless, of course, this is your street. The large blue canopy, with half a dozen tables nestled beneath, highlights the location of this popular local Italian. It has a fresh feel to the interior, with its warm yellows and blues, and the clever use of mirrors makes the place seem bigger than it is. The pelican motif is evident in some of the lively artwork.

It is from Sardinia that the kitchen takes its influence, which is evident as soon as the terrific basket of assorted breads arrives. From the pecorino cheese to the culurgiones (ravioli), the flavours are as bright and aromatic as the island itself.

Brasserie St Quentin

E5 **French traditional** XX

243 Brompton Rd SW3 2EP
(020) 7589 8005 **Fax** (020) 7584 6064
e-mail reservations@brasseriestquentin.co.uk
www.brasseriestquentin.co.uk

Knightsbridge
▶ **Plan XI**
Closed Christmas

Menu £18 – Carte £23/40

A/C, VISA, MC, AE

This was one of the first brasseries to open in the capital and, reassuringly for its clientele of loyal locals and weary shoppers, it is now back under private ownership where places like this really belong.

The success of Brasserie St Quentin is due in no small part to its authentic ambience and confident manner and it feels very much like the genuine article. Mirrors, red leather banquette seating and an ornate bar all fit the brasserie bill perfectly.

The menu is Gallic in essence but many of the ingredients, particularly the meats, come courtesy of some gloriously British estates. The lunchtime and early evening set menus represent excellent value of money, particularly in this neighbourhood.

Chelsea Brasserie

F6 **French** XX

at The Sloane Square H.,
7-12 Sloane Sq. SW1W 8EG
(020) 7881 5999
www.sloanesquarehotel.co.uk

Sloane Square
▶ **Plan XI**
Closed 25 December

Carte £27/37

A/C, VISA, MC, AE

The redevelopment of Sloane Square could be said to have started with the opening of the Sloane Square Hotel. This, their brasserie, occupies a prime spot and the glass doors merely hint at what's inside. It is certainly a stylish and roomy affair with brick walls inlaid with mirrored tiles, smoky green lamps and an army of waiters giving it a Gallic tenor.

The kitchen also looks to France for its influence and classics like filet au poivre, steak tartare or rabbit with Puy lentils fit the bill perfectly and it's nice to see the old favourite of chocolate profiteroles making a comeback. The kitchen is also unafraid of looking occasionally beyond the borders of France for inspiration. The pre-theatre menu represents excellent value.

Painted Heron

Indian XX

E7

112 Cheyne Walk SW10 0DJ
✆ (020) 7351 5232
Fax (020) 7351 5313
www.thepaintedheron.com

⊖ Gloucester Road
▶ **Plan XI**
Closed 25 December, 1 January and Saturday lunch

Carte £25/35

There is hardly a single house on Cheyne Walk without a blue plaque commemorating the literary and artistic talent of a past resident, but one wonders how many of the current occupiers realise they've also got a place like The Painted Heron on their doorstep. The restaurant is immaculately laid out, with pillars dividing it into cosier areas. The simple, fresh décor is enlivened by some contemporary paintings. Stylish leather chairs and neatly dressed tables complete the picture of an undeniably smart neighbourhood Indian restaurant.

The menu is printed daily according to what fresh produce is available and the cooking exhibits an understanding of those ingredients and a degree of originality in their preparation.

Vama

Indian XX

E7

438 King's Rd SW10 0LJ
✆ (020) 7565 8500
Fax (020) 7565 8501
e-mail admin@vama.co.uk
www.vama.co.uk

⊖ Sloane Square
▶ **Plan XI**

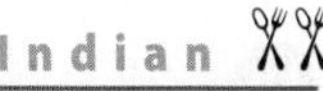

Closed 25-26 December and 1 January – booking essential – dinner only and lunch Saturday-Sunday

Menu £12 (lunch) – Carte £25/45 s

The Northwest Frontier and the Punjab provide inspiration for the cooking at Vama, so vegetarians will find that they have an equal number of dishes to choose from as the carnivores and that there will be an assortment of authentic breads to soak up the creamy sauces.

The brightly lit façade provides a welcoming beacon, particularly on a winter's evening, while inside the place is divided into three. The first section is where the action seems to be; the second area is a narrow tent-like space and this leads into the rear conservatory, ideal for those after a little more intimacy. Teak carvings, oil paintings, Indian stone and pretty crockery all add to the Indian feel and help create very pleasant surroundings.

Carpaccio

E6 — Italian XX

4 Sydney St SW3 6PP
(020) 7352 3435
Fax (020) 7622 8304
e-mail carpacciorest@aol.com
www.carpacciorestaurant.co.uk

⊖ South Kensington
▶ **Plan XI**
closed 25 December, Easter, last 2 weeks August, Sunday and Bank Holidays

Carte £27/33

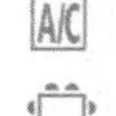

This long, narrow restaurant may be within a pretty Georgian house and fringed with chocolate coloured seating, but the decorative features are more from the testosterone school of interior design – walls come with stills from James Bond films and the owner has displayed his fondness for Formula 1 by hanging the full fibre glass cockpit of an Ayrton Senna racing car.

In this age when every chef is trying to do something different, it can sometimes be reassuring to find a kitchen sticking to the classics. As the name implies, carpaccio is the house speciality with beef, tuna and assorted fish given the treatment. Elsewhere on the menu you'll find familiar but nonetheless carefully prepared Italian classics.

Eight over Eight

E7 — Asian XX

392 King's Rd SW3 5UZ
(020) 7349 9934
Fax (020) 7351 5157
www.rickerrestaurants.com

⊖ Gloucester Road
▶ **Plan XI**
Closed 25-26 December, 1 January and lunch Sunday and Bank Holidays

Carte £26/36

What was once the Man in the Moon pub is now a fiercely fashionable pan-Asian restaurant, proving that the King's Road is not all high street chains and baby shops and can still cut it with the fashionistas.

The menu has a fairly wide remit to cover much of South East Asia with Chinese, Japanese, Malaysian, Korean and Thai influences all featuring and most dishes designed for sharing. Don't hesitate to ask for help from the charming, and alarmingly attractive, staff.

The room is all moody and cool, with a slick bar at the front and the restaurant at the back. Chocolate coloured leather seating and two shades of oak on the walls contrast with the delicate silk parasol styled lamps. Try not to covet the booths too openly.

C Garden

Italian XX

E7

119 Sydney St SW3 6NR — ⊖ South Kensington
✆ (020) 7352 2718 — ▶ **Plan XI**

Closed 25-26 December, 1 January, Good Friday, Sunday dinner and Bank Holidays

Menu £14 (lunch) – Carte £20/35

'Dan's' occupied this site for nearly 25 years but in June 2006 Dan sold up and it became an Italian restaurant. The new owner, Guido Campigotto, not only provided the 'C'in the name but also had the contacts to ensure that business began briskly.

VISA MC AE

Before re-opening it also enjoyed a makeover. The new colour scheme of stone, fawn, light chocolate and cream suits the place well. At the back they've kept the tent-like conservatory and this leads onto the sheltered terrace which is surely one of Chelsea's finest.

Unthreatening, simply prepared and flavoursome Italian food is the order of the day here. However, the final bill can be higher than expected due to the separately priced side orders and the anachronistic cover charge.

Good Earth

Chinese XX

E5

233 Brompton Rd SW3 2EP — ⊖ Knightsbridge
✆ (020) 7584 3658 **Fax** (020) 7823 8769 — ▶ **Plan XI**
e-mail goodearthgroup@aol.com — Closed 22-31 December
www.goodearthgroup.co.uk

Menu £14/30 – Carte £27/32

A/C VISA MC AE

Restaurants, boutiques, shops and salons have all come and gone on Brompton Road but good old Good Earth has outlasted them all, and just keeps on doing its thing. This longevity can be put down to a number of factors: it has been impervious to fashion, its standards are reliable and it gives the punters what they want.

The welcome is guaranteed to be polite and the staff all know what they're doing and do it well. Spread over the ground floor and basement, it wouldn't necessarily win any designs awards but the atmosphere is never less than convivial.

The menu is large without being worryingly vast and performs a clever balancing trick of offering dishes of recognisable popularity alongside others of a more unusual bent.

Tom's Kitchen

E6 French

27 Cale St SW3 3QP
(020) 7349 0202 **Fax** (020) 7823 3652
e-mail info@tomskitchen.co.uk
www.tomskitchen.co.uk

South Kensington
▶ **Plan XI**
Closed 4 days Christmas

Carte £37/49

The Tom is Tom Aikens and this is a simpler but immeasurably worthy addendum to his eponymous restaurant around the corner. What was previously The Blenheim pub now has an industrial-lite feel, with eating on the ground floor, a bar on the second and private dining at the top. Once you've found the right door to get in you'll be welcomed by an enthusiastic team and those without reservations are steered to the counter.

Open from breakfast to very late, the menu offers uncomplicated but carefully prepared comfort food. French is the main influence, with such classics as steak tartare and confit of duck, but Britain supplies the majority of the ingredients as well as the occasional dish, while Italy turns up too with the odd risotto or panna cotta.

Manicomio

F6 Italian

85 Duke of York Sq, King's Rd
SW3 4LY
(020) 7730 3366
Fax (020) 7730 3377
www.manicomio.co.uk

Sloane Square
▶ **Plan XI**
Closed 25-26 December and 1 January

Carte £28/41

The literal translation is 'madhouse', a less than politically correct reference to the building's post-war use as a military asylum. With a large terrace in front and a little deli and café next door, Manicomio dominates this part of the smart redevelopment of the former barracks. The room is divided into two, with a bar on one side. Exposed brick walls, oak flooring and an original fireplace contrast with the flame red seating and modern artwork and create a warm, sophisticated, yet suitably relaxed, atmosphere.

The waiting team are all confidently in control and very charming. The menu concentrates on bright, flavoursome and seasonal Italian cooking. All in all, ideal for those weary from the rigours of shopping.

Aubaine

French

E6

260-262 Brompton Rd
SW3 2AS
(020) 7052 0100 **Fax** (020) 7052 0622
e-mail info@aubaine.co.uk **www**.aubaine.co.uk

South Kensington
▶ **Plan XI**

Carte £28/38

Whether it's a croissant, croque monsieur or coq au vin, Aubaine is among the increasing number of operations of a more fluid nature which recognise that we don't always want to eat three courses at 1pm.

Describing itself as a 'boulangerie, patisserie and restaurant', it opens early morning until late at night and offers a comprehensive choice of French specialities to satisfy all appetites at all times with the location making it especially busy during shopping hours. The breads are baked here and the 'shop' section does a roaring trade. The dining area fuses country and city; dressers, flowers and distressed wooden tables are juxtaposed with the modernity of exposed air-con vents and it all opens out onto the pavement in summer.

Bangkok

Thai

E6

9 Bute St SW7 3EY
(020) 7584 8529

South Kensington
▶ **Plan XI**

Closed Christmas-New Year and Sunday

Carte £20/33

Bangkok was the first Thai restaurant to open in London and is now not too far from celebrating its fortieth birthday. The same owner is still here and can often be seen at the stove.

Dishes may sound rather simple on the menu but the cooking is skilfully executed and the flavours are clear, fresh and nicely balanced.

Don't let the smart canopied façade raise your expectations too high: this is not the most comfortable restaurant around. Basic tables and chairs are close together and on the walls hang simple photographs of Thai life. But the open kitchen gives diners something to look at and there's always a sociable atmosphere. Everyone appears to leave feeling sated and, more unusually these days, with wallets free of burn holes.

Bibendum Oyster Bar

E6 **Seafood**

Michelin House, 81 Fulham Rd SW3 6RD
✆ (020) 7589 1480 **Fax** (020) 7823 7148
e-mail reservations@bibendum.co.uk
www.bibendum.co.uk

⊖ South Kensington
▶ **Plan XI**
Closed 25-26 December and 1 January – bookings not accepted

Carte £20/50

As an alternative to the more formal restaurant upstairs, Bibendum Oyster Bar provides relaxed surroundings in which to enjoy a variety of seafood. It is also just the sort of place we encounter on holiday in France and then ask why we don't have anything like it at home.

The speciality is, as the name suggests, oysters but the plateau de fruits de mer must come a close second. There are also salads, daily specials and plenty of other seafood on the extensive menu. The tiled walls and mosaic floor add to the appeal and the atmosphere is generally convivial. Service from the young team can be a little hit and miss. If you haven't had your fill, you can stock up on more at Bibendum Crustacea, with its counter on the old garage forecourt.

The Admiral Codrington

F6 **Gastropub**

17 Mossop St SW3 2LY
✆ (020) 7581 4005 **Fax** (020) 7589 2452
e-mail admiral-codrington@333holdingsltd.com
www.theadmiralcodrington.com

⊖ South Kensington
▶ **Plan XI**
Closed 24-27 December

Carte £24/31

'The Cod' was perhaps best known in the '80s when it became the unofficial common room of the 'Sloane Ranger'. Twenty years later the pearls and Barbours have long gone and the pub has reinvented itself as a stylish gastropub.

The bar is now a relaxed, easy-going spot for a drink with a short but well chosen menu. The separate long narrow dining room has been transformed into a comfortable and sophisticated space and comes with a clever retractable roof for summer days.

The menu is an appealing balance of erudite restaurant sophistication balanced with dishes of a more comforting and familiar nature. So whether it's foie gras with Muscat jelly or beer battered plaice, there's now something for everyone.

Chelsea Ram

Gastropub

D8

32 Burnaby St SW10 0PL ⊖ Fulham Broadway
(020) 7351 4008 ▶ Plan XI
e-mail bookings@chelsearam.co.uk

Carte £18/24

VISA MC

It's a local pub for local people, albeit Chelsea People. The Ram is a Young's pub, close to Chelsea Harbour, and has seemingly become something of a favourite in this part of the world. It is down to earth – insofar as anything is down to earth in Chelsea - and is one of those places where all the elements just seem to fit well together. It does the pub thing well and holds a weekly pub quiz but it also does proper food for all tastes and appetites, with a regularly changing menu supplemented by daily specials. The wine list isn't bad either.

Its welcoming staff and general atmosphere both play a big part in its success. Those put off by the self-congratulatory smugness of some gastropubs will find this place hard to dislike.

Swag and Tails

Gastropub

E5

10-11 Fairholt St, Knightsbridge ⊖ Knightsbridge
SW7 1EG ▶ Plan XI
(020) 7584 6926 **Fax** (020) 7581 9935 Closed Christmas-New Year
e-mail theswag@swagandtails.com
www.swagandtails.com

Carte £22/33

VISA MC AE

The Swag and Tails is one of the prettier pubs around, with its hanging baskets, log fire, panelling and those swagged and tailed drapes. The dining area is at the rear with a conservatory extension. The kitchen clearly knows its customers and gives them a balanced selection combining modern, Mediterranean-influenced cooking while still satisfying those who just want a decent steak sandwich. There's also a degree of sophistication in that the liver comes with pancetta and the duck is accompanied by pistachios; they also throw in the occasional Asian twist in the form of duck pancakes or spring rolls. Plates of charcuterie or Caesar salads are there for those with lighter appetites. Most of the wine comes in at around £20 a bottle.

Builders Arms

E6 — Gastropub 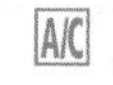

13 Britten St SW3 3TY — ⊖ South Kensington
✆ (020) 7349 9040 — ▶ Plan XI
e-mail buildersarms@geronimo-inns.co.uk — Closed 25-26 December
www.geronimo-inns.co.uk — – bookings not accepted

Carte £20/35

A/C · VISA · MC · AE

They don't take bookings and no orders for food can be placed until 7.15pm, by which time the place is absolutely jumping with locals, so knowing when to arrive is anyone's guess. But at 7.15 precisely the service swings into action like a minor military operation and thereafter is surprisingly helpful and polite. Beyond the bar, those early swarms congregate noisily on sofas, while diners tend to head for the stripped pine tables on the other side. Slightly less frenetic is the glass-roofed area at the back.

Food here mixes gutsy, classic pub cooking with contemporary European dishes, and pies and fish and chips sit happily on the menu alongside salt and pepper squid with chilli dip, or steak with marrow.

The Pig's Ear

E7 — Gastropub 

35 Old Church St SW3 5BS — ⊖ Sloane Square
✆ 020 7352 2908 — ▶ Plan XI
Fax 020 7352 9321 — Closed 25-26 December, 31 December, 1 January
e-mail thepigsear@hotmail.co.uk
www.thepigsear.co.uk

Carte £25/30

VISA · MC · AE

Judging by the scrum of Chelsea's finest packed into the bar every night, some think it's actually a bit of a silk purse. The pub certainly presses all the right buttons, from the chatty staff to the appetite-satisfying food. It has been updated without losing its personality – it's still a real pub - and the porcine-themed decorative touches have added a little quirkiness. The downstairs bar can get a hammering of an evening so, if you want an altogether quieter dinner, merely head upstairs to the rather sweet wood panelled dining room.

The cooking is robust, keeps pace with the seasons by changing daily and is not afraid of offering punters something a little different, from the eponymous deep-fried pig's ears to roast bone marrow.

The Phoenix

F6

Gastropub

23 Smith St SW3 4EE
020 7730 9182
e-mail thephoenix@geronimo-inns.co.uk
www.geronimo-inns.co.uk

Sloane Square
▶ **Plan XI**
Closed 25-26 December

Carte £22/28

More as a result of a comprehensive refurbishment of an existing pub rather than something raised from any ashes, The Phoenix provides the good burghers of Chelsea with another gastropub in which to enjoy modern, robust cooking with a side order of rusticity. It is also confident enough not to simply ape the menus of local restaurants and instead provides just the sort of food locals want to find in their pub.

The front bar, whose modernism is reigned in by the odd retro tweak, is ideal for all those louche local types, while the dining room at the rear provides a slightly more formalised setting, and more comfortable leather chairs. Alfresco dining is such a rare treat in London that the small pavement terrace is hugely popular in summer.

The Cross Keys

E7

Gastropub

1 Lawrence St SW3 5NB
(020) 7349 9111 **Fax** (020) 7349 9333
e-mail xkeys.nicole@hotmail.co.uk
www.thexkeys.co.uk

South Kensington
▶ **Plan XI**
Closed Bank Holidays

Carte £21/30

This may be a pub with a history dating back well over 200 years, but the interior owes more to today's sense of irony and fun. The bar offers plenty of elbow room and its own menu but beyond is the glass-roofed dining room which comes complete with little statues, its own tree and an eye-catching frieze of garden implements.

The kitchen is more conventional in its approach than the surroundings would suggest, with food that is modern in style but robust in flavour and influences are kept largely within old Europe, so expect to find alluring sounding dishes like smoked duck with glazed figs, wild mushroom tart with pesto, lamb cutlets, coq au vin and poached pear in red wine. There are also blackboard specials to supplement the menus.

Lots Road Pub & Dining Room

D8

Gastropub

114 Lots Rd SW10 0RJ
(020) 7352 6645
Fax (020) 7376 4975
e-mail lotsroad@foodandfuel.co.uk
www.lotsroadpub.com

Gloucester Road
▶ **Plan XI**

Carte £35/60

A/C VISA M/C AE

The high windows of this corner building give the impression that it is empty; in reality, the reverse is nearly always true. What keeps the punters, if the Chelsea set could ever be called punters, coming back time and again are the earthy pub dishes such as tasty hamburgers, lamb shanks and belly pork offered on a daily-changing menu, plus the sort of heart-warming puddings that all pubs should do. The sign reads, 'You haven't lived until you've tried our sticky toffee pud,' and its popularity bears witness.

Diligent and friendly young staff stay on the move between table and open kitchen. It calls itself a 'bar and dining room' so drinkers are made welcome and Thursday evenings see regular wine tastings, with bar snacks laid on.

THE WINTER'S TALE

Recent court battles over Granny Smiths may not have gone The Beatles' way, but the life of artist Yoko Ono was definitely changed for the better by an apple she exhibited in her 1966 show at London's Indica Gallery. The installation (appropriately titled 'apple') caught the attention of a certain John Lennon, who plucked it from its plinth and took a bite. At the time, Ono didn't know Lennon from Adam and was cross - but soon forgave him.

C. Barrely / MICHELIN

Kensington · North Kensington · Notting Hill

Kensington, the heart of the 'Royal Borough', has always had something of a regal air about it. When the asthmatic King William III grew tired of choking on 17th Century London's smog, he relocated to the village next door and got his friend Sir Christopher Wren to transform a handsome house at its edge into a royal residence. Today, **Kensington Palace** may be home to only minor royals but, as any proud Kensingtonian will tell you, the area's name itself perhaps derives from the Saxon for 'Kings Town' - with all the wealth, class and ease that implies.

At roughly £1,000 per square foot of property, this is a neighbourhood in which few can afford to live, but that many like to visit. The main thoroughfare, **Kensington High Street**, has a surprisingly down-to-earth array of shops, although the imposing Art Deco edifices of its once-famous department stores ensures it is not totally outdone in the style stakes by its more glamorous Chelsea rival, the King's Road. On top of one of these, high above the hoi polloi, sit the **Kensington Roof Gardens** - a pleasure-dome Kubla Khan would be proud of, appealing to today's urban sophisticates as Vauxhall once did to their Victorian counterparts. But street level has its own retreats and **Holland Park** - which extends a narrow green limb to the shops – is a refined, romantic hideaway of wooded walks, tranquil gardens and peacocks.

With the town hall tucked a few blocks behind the high street, however, the real character of Kensington lies in its residences. Victorian terraces, grand stucco villas and red-brick apartment blocks line streets which in spring are covered by a carpet of blossom. Blue plaques abound and window boxes keep up appearances while keeping out prying eyes – this, after all, is an area as discreet as it is resplendent. The old court buildings of **Kensington Square** evoke an earlier era and became home to such great men as John Stuart Mill and Joseph Addison. These days, London's most exclusive address is the nearby **Kensington Palace Gardens,** a spacious half-mile avenue of magnificent Victorian mansions, housing both embassies and the world's richest individuals.

Walk past security at the avenue's north entrance and things get more relaxed, if not a tad scruffy - **Notting Hill Gate** may not be the best introduction to the neighbourhood glamourised by Richard Curtis's film, but it is unmistakably part of it. In contrast to Kensington's establishment pedigree, this was a place where pigs used to outnumber humans three to one, and which by the 1960s had become known for little more than slums and race riots. Happily, the piggeries disappeared long ago, and the white stuccoed terraces, laid out in the 19th Century, have been restored to their former glory. Now, the area's ethnic diversity is a cause for celebration, with the ebullient **Notting Hill Carnival** calypsoing every August amid steel bands and the smells of jerk chicken.

Although carnival's energy can't be kept up all year, Notting Hill does sustain a hip laid-backness that draws a young(ish) and fashionable crowd. The restaurants and antiquarian art galleries of **Kensington Church Street** here mix with retro clothing stores and second-hand record shops. Former supermodels can be spotted picking the kids up from school, as yesterday's stars of Brit Pop browse designer boutiques. True, rejuvenation has given Notting Hill some middle-aged spread, but it keeps a finger on the pulse with bohemian cafes, period cinemas, the avant-garde **Notting Hill Arts Club** and the daring **Gate Theatre**, while the pubs and market on **Portobello Road** remain as modish as ever. Should you tire of all this cooler-than-thou trendiness, however, a stroll among the pastel town houses and Victorian estates of **Ladbroke Grove** is the perfect antidote. It may not be advisable to do a 'Julia Roberts' and break into the residents-only gardens - but some of these private spaces are open to quite public sightlines, and it's a lovely place to dream.

S. Ollivier / MICHELIN

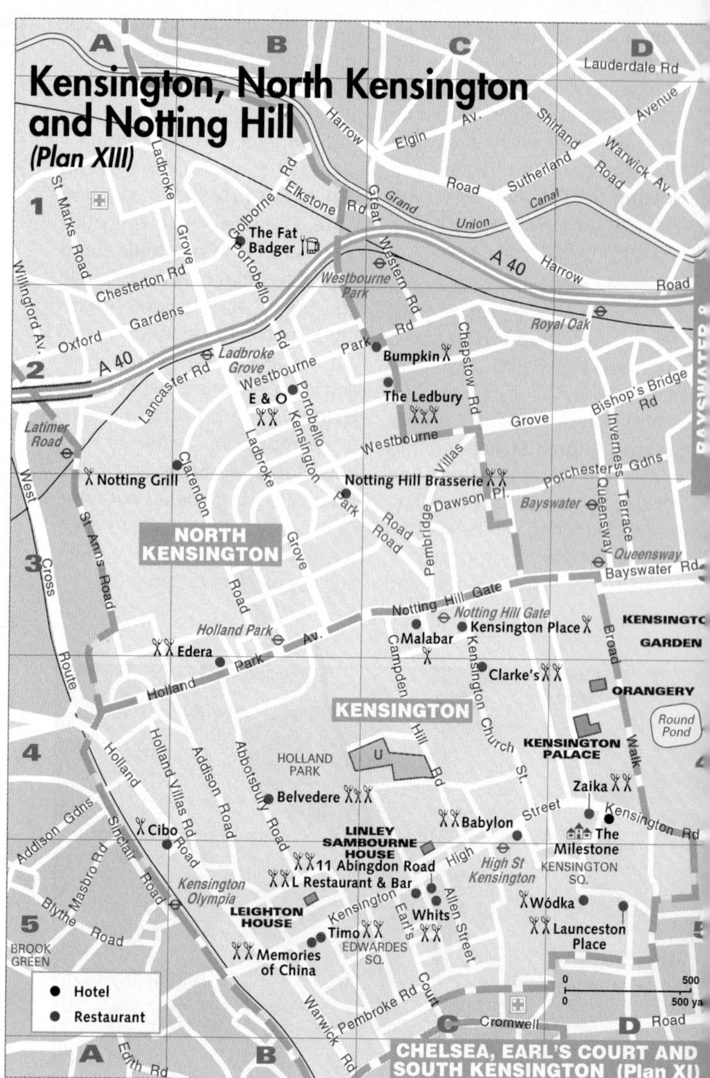
Kensington, North Kensington and Notting Hill
(Plan XIII)
NORTH KENSINGTON
KENSINGTON
HOLLAND PARK
KENSINGTON PALACE
ORANGERY
KENSINGTON GARDEN
Round Pond
LINLEY SAMBOURNE HOUSE
LEIGHTON HOUSE
The Fat Badger
Bumpkin
The Ledbury
E & O
Notting Grill
Notting Hill Brasserie
Malabar
Kensington Place
Clarke's
Edera
Belvedere
Babylon
Zaika
The Milestone
Cibo
11 Abingdon Road
L Restaurant & Bar
Whits
Wódka
Launceston Place
Timo
Memories of China
Hotel
Restaurant
CHELSEA, EARL'S COURT AND SOUTH KENSINGTON (Plan XI)

The Ledbury ✿

French XXX

C2

127 Ledbury Rd W11 2AQ
⊖ Notting Hill Gate
✆ (020) 7792 9090 **Fax** (020) 7792 9191
e-mail info@theledbury.com
www.theledbury.com

Menu £25/50 – Carte £34/47

The Ledbury

Such was the transformation that it's hard to believe this was once a pub. The Ledbury only opened in 2005 but has quickly established itself in this part of town. But then, anywhere that comes from the same stable as The Square is going to get things right. The inside is slick and crisp but still manages to make a bold design statement and the chocolate, cream and leather soften it all up. This is also one of those rare restaurants where there appears to be no bad tables and one that enjoys the support of plenty of locals and is not merely a 'destination'. The seasonal menu is pitched just right: the kitchen adds a subtle but discernible innovative edge to the classical base but never tries to be too clever or off the wall. Flavours are pronounced without ever being overpowering and they display plenty of faith in their ingredients which are superbly sourced. The wine list is an excellent match and as well as having notable variety also has plenty of halves and a balanced selection by the glass.

First Course

- Flame-grilled mackerel with a mackerel tartare, avocado and shiso.
- Seared scallops with pumpkin gnocchi, pumpkin and ginger sauce.

Main Course

- Suckling pig with spring onions, mangosteen, salsify and ham beignet.
- Slow-cooked fillet of beef with smoked bone marrow and girolles.

Dessert

- Date and vanilla tart with cardamom and orange ice cream.
- Citrus and rhubarb terrine with Sauternes custard.

Belvedere

French XXX

B4

Holland House, off Abbotsbury Rd
W8 6LU
(020) 7602 1238 **Fax** (020) 7610 4382
e-mail info@belvedererestaurant.co.uk
www.belvedererestaurant.co.uk

⊖ Holland Park
Closed 26 December, 1 January and Sunday dinner

Menu £18/25 (lunch) – Carte £25/45

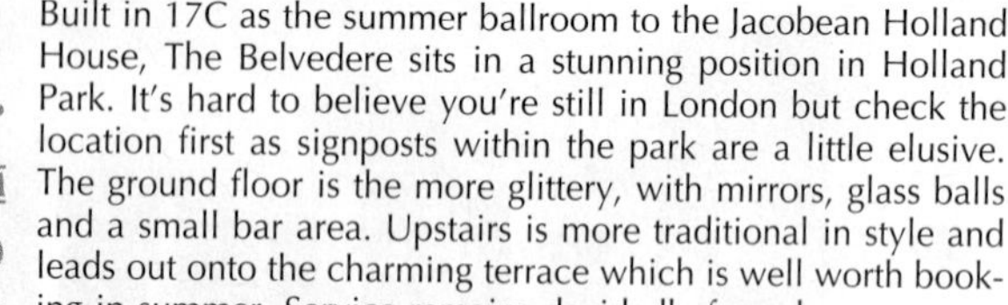

Built in 17C as the summer ballroom to the Jacobean Holland House, The Belvedere sits in a stunning position in Holland Park. It's hard to believe you're still in London but check the location first as signposts within the park are a little elusive. The ground floor is the more glittery, with mirrors, glass balls and a small bar area. Upstairs is more traditional in style and leads out onto the charming terrace which is well worth booking in summer. Service remains decidedly formal.

The menu covers all bases from eggs Benedict to even the occasional Thai but it's worth sticking to the more classical, French dishes as that's where the chef's expertise lies. Produce is well sourced and dishes nicely balanced. France dominates the wine list.

Notting Hill Brasserie

French XX

B3

92 Kensington Park Rd
W11 2PN
(020) 7229 4481 **Fax** (020) 7221 1246
e-mail enquiries@nottinghillbrasserie.com

⊖ Notting Hill Gate
Closed Sunday dinner

Menu £23/30 – Carte £35/45

The name is really only half right. There is certainly no argument over it being in Notting Hill but the service, comforts, styling and cooking are all far beyond what one would expect from a brasserie. One enters into the very pleasant bar where live blues or jazz is played every night between 8pm and midnight. The restaurant is divided into assorted smaller rooms, all with their own character and atmosphere, and decorated with modern or African influenced artwork.

Multinational staff, all dressed in black, provide attentive, structured service. The cooking, too, is as sophisticated as the restaurant; some serious produce is used in fairly intricate dishes that come elaborately presented.

Zaika

Indian XX

D4

1 Kensington High St
W8 5NP
✆ (020) 7795 6533 **Fax** (020) 7937 8854
e-mail info@zaika-restaurant.co.uk **www**.zaika-restaurant.co.uk

⊖ High Street Kensington
Closed 25- December and Sunday lunch

Menu £20 – Carte £20/33

It may be a converted bank but the colourful sign outside appears to draw in countless passers-by to this modern Indian restaurant. The first part of the open-plan room is occupied by the bar and the original wood panelling is juxtaposed with Indian artefacts while a vast ceiling shade scatters warm colours across the room.

One look at the menu tells you that this is no ordinary Indian restaurant. Tasting menus form a major part and dishes are refined and innovative. Spicing is subtle and desserts can be quite ornate. Try specialities such as scallops cooked three different ways or coconut lamb where the richness of the coconut is balanced by mustard seeds and curry leaves. The six course Jugalbandi menu is the ideal introduction and is also available with wine pairings.

Clarke's

Modern European XX

C4

124 Kensington Church St
W8 4BH
✆ (020) 7221 9225
Fax (020) 7229 4564
e-mail restaurant@sallyclarke.com **www**.sallyclarke.com

⊖ Notting Hill Gate
Closed 23 December-8 January, 1 week August, Sunday, Monday dinner and Bank Holidays

Menu £43 – Carte lunch £29

For over twenty years Sally Clarke's eponymous restaurant offered a daily changing no-choice dinner menu until finally, in 2006, bowing to changing habits, she began offering a choice to her customers. The impressive longevity of the restaurant and the fact that she succeeded so long in her particular formula bear testament to her skill in the kitchen and her reputation.

She succeeds through a combination of balanced dishes focusing on the seasonal freshness of ingredients and a lightness of touch in their preparation. It also helps when there's a welcoming atmosphere of intimacy and familiarity which in itself attracts so many loyal customers. Those wishing to take a memento home will find the produce at her next-door deli and bakery hard to resist.

Babylon

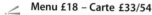

C4 **Modern European** XX

at The Roof Gardens,
99 Kensington High St
(entrance on Derry St) W8 5SA
(020) 7368 3993 **Fax** (020) 7368 3995
e-mail babylon@roofgardens.virgin.co.uk **www**.roofgardens.com

⊖ High Street Kensington
Closed Christmas and Sunday dinner

Menu £18 – Carte £33/54

The challenge is to find the entrance which is secreted on the right as you walk down Derry Street; then it's the lift up to the 7th floor and suddenly you're surrounded by trees.

There's no doubting that this is quite a spot and while the gardens just below may not be 'hanging' they are an understandably appealing place for a party. The restaurant is a long, narrow affair whose contemporary décor reflects the leafy outdoors and the terrace takes some beating in summer. Influences on the menu remain largely within Europe and the cooking shows a degree of perkiness and ambition. The lunch time set menu is priced to appeal to local businesses while the à la carte can get a little expensive. The wine list plants its flag firmly in the New World.

A/C VISA MC AE

Launceston Place

D5 **Modern European** XX

1a Launceston Pl W8 5RL
(020) 7937 6912
Fax (020) 7938 2412
e-mail lpr@egami.co.uk **www**.egami.co.uk

⊖ Gloucester Road
Closed Saturday lunch and Bank Holidays

Menu £15/19 – Carte £25/45

This was once a corner pub, comes shaped like a slice of cake and is one of those places that always looks inviting when you walk past. Decoratively, it has a lived-in, vaguely Victorian look and the skylights and mirrors ensure that there are no dark corners. This country feel is matched by the clientele who are grown up and predominantly English.

The cooking adds some European influence to the mix but does tend to keep things fairly classical. So the choice can be between smoked salmon or langoustine, game or pasta, with a nice balance between fish and meat. Portions are a tad diminutive, although they do seem adequate when you go for the full three courses; there's a set price lunch menu to help in this. The wine list has a pronounced French accent.

A/C VISA MC AE

Edera

Italian XX

B4

148 Holland Park Ave W11 4UE
(020) 7221 6090 **Fax** (020) 7313 9700

⊖ Holland Park
Closed Bank Holidays

Carte £32/49

The bare wood floors, clean lines and muted coloured walls adorned with the odd mirror suggest a rather clinical West End restaurant which somehow landed in the leafier environs of Holland Park. Fortunately, the place is privately owned and the mood is rescued by the locals who need no help in creating their own atmosphere and have a laudable aversion to whispering.

Edera, meaning 'ivy' in Italian, is bigger than you first think and the service, rather like any relationship, improves with time and familiarity. The cooking is earthy, satisfying and flavoursome and there are subtle hints of Sardinia in some of the dishes: the bottarga (grey mullet roe) is a speciality of the house, as is the suckling pig.

B2

14 Blenheim Crescent
W11 1NN
(020) 7229 5454 **Fax** (020) 7229 5522
e-mail eando@rickerrestaurants.com **www**.rickerrestaurants.com

⊖ Ladbroke Grove
Closed 24-26 and 31 December, Sunday and Bank Holidays

Carte £24/38

Once you've sidestepped the full-on bar of this Notting Hill favourite, a step from Portobello Road, you'll find yourself in a moodily sophisticated restaurant packed with the beautiful and the hopeful.

The room is understatedly urbane, with slatted walls, large circular lamps and leather banquettes, while noise levels are at the party end of the auditory index. Waiting staff are obliging, pleasant and often among the prettiest people in the room.

E&O stands for Eastern and Oriental and the menu journeys across numerous Asian countries, dividing itself into assorted headings which include dim sum, salads, tempura, curries and roasts. Individual dishes vary in size and price so sharing, as in life, is often the best option.

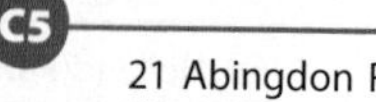

C5 — Modern European XX

21 Abingdon Rd
W8 6AH
✆ (020) 7938 1122
Fax (020) 7937 6121
e-mail eva@whits.co.uk **www**.whits.co.uk

⊖ High Street Kensington
Closed last 2 weeks August, 24-31 December, Sunday dinner and Monday – dinner only

Menu £19/24 – Carte £28/37

A shortened version of the chef owner's name explains the moniker of this enthusiastically run restaurant in a residential street, just off Kensington High Street. As homage to the restaurant's other owner, subtle Hungarian influences can be found in the menu and in certain more robust dishes, but those unfamiliar with Magyar traditions or merely looking for something lighter are more than rewarded with a varied selection of elaborately executed dishes. It is also well worth leaving some trouser space for dessert, as soufflés are very much a house speciality.

The main dining room is in a raised section beyond the bar and is decorated in a fresh, clean style with modern artwork and smartly dressed tables.

11 Abingdon Road

C5 — Mediterranean XX

11 Abingdon Rd
W8 6AH
✆ (020) 7937 0120
e-mail eleven@abingdonroad.co.uk

⊖ High Street Kensington
Closed Bank Holidays

Carte £20/30

Opened late in 2005 and sister restaurant to Sonny's and The Phoenix, 11 Abingdon Road is already attracting quite a following who are helped along, no doubt, by not having to look up the street name and number first. The stylish façade is reflected in the contemporary feel of the clean white lines and lighting of the interior which add to the general feeling of spaciousness. The owners' art collection adorns the walls and the tables are set close together, adding to the atmosphere and general buzz.

The Mediterranean provides most of the influence in the kitchen, with bright, vibrant colours and fresh, clean flavours. There is a good value menu at lunchtimes.

Timo

Italian XX

B5

343 Kensington High St
W8 6NW
(020) 7603 3888 **Fax** (020) 7603 8111
e-mail timorestaurant@fsmail.net **www**.timorestaurant.net

⊖ High Street Kensington
Closed 25-26 December, Easter, Sunday and Bank Holidays

Menu £17 (lunch) – Carte dinner £29/44

At the Olympia end of Kensington High Street sits this warm and inviting Italian restaurant. The colours of cream and beige, matched with summery paintings of garden landscapes, lend a sunny feel, whatever the season outside. The tables are as smartly dressed as the waiters, who provide conscientious service and the suited owner does the rounds and knows his regulars. The set menu comes divided into the typically Italian four courses, although the impressive looking bread basket will test your powers of self-restraint. Daily specials to supplement the menu are temptingly described and the desserts merit particular investigation.

This is a solidly reliable neighbourhood restaurant which sensibly doesn't try to reinvent anything.

Memories of China

Chinese XX

B5

353 Kensington High St
W8 6NW
(020) 7603 6951 **Fax** (020) 7603 0848

⊖ High Street Kensington
Closed Easter and Christmas – booking essential

Carte £22/35

Memories of China is a well established Chinese restaurant which pulls in both the locals, many of whom will never have a bad word said about the place, and those staying in one of the surrounding hotels. As such, it's always busy so it's well worth coming secure in the knowledge that you've made a reservation.

The menu, rather like the room, is relatively compact and keeps things on the straight and narrow by focusing on classic Cantonese and Szechuan cooking. Set menus are available for groups or those who prefer others to make their decisions for them.

The glass façade of this corner restaurant chimes with the bright and modern décor of the interior with Chinese themed murals and calligraphy.

L Restaurant & Bar

C5 **Spanish** XX

2 Abingdon Rd W8 6AF ⊖ High Street Kensington
✆ (020) 7795 6969 **Fax** (020) 7795 6699 Closed Monday lunch
e-mail info@l-restaurant.co.uk **www**.l-restaurant.co.uk

Menu £16 (lunch) – Carte £23/33

A relatively unremarkable façade gives little away but inside they've made great use of light and space to create a vivid and bright Iberian restaurant.

Pass the bar - where you can join the locals in tapas and a glass of champagne - and suddenly it all opens out and you find yourself in a capacious dining room with a sloping glass roof and huge mirrors. It's been decked out in a thoroughly tasteful way, with top notch fixtures and fittings. Ask for a table on, rather than underneath, the mezzanine level.

The menu has an occasional tendency to veer off course into some unusual combinations so the best bet is to stick with the more traditional Spanish dishes and tapas. The wine list is concise but balanced with the emphasis on affordability.

Kensington Place

C3 **Modern European** X

201 Kensington Church St
W8 7LX ⊖ Notting Hill Gate
Closed Christmas and 1 January – booking essential
✆ (020) 7727 3184 **Fax** (020) 7229 2025
e-mail kpr@egami.co.uk **www**.egami.co.uk

Menu £19/25 – Carte £31/40

When Kensington Place opened in 1987, it broke the mould by showing Londoners that good food could be served in a relaxed style and for that we should all be grateful. Now, some twenty or so years later it is gearing up for its new incarnation as something of an elder statesman and is under the ownership of D&D.

Rowley Leigh may also have left but the new kitchen is not reinventing any wheels. The cooking remains unfussy, seasonal and decently proportioned. Classics like foie gras with a sweet corn pancake and scallops with pea purée remain and accompaniments to the main courses are well chosen. The wine list is lengthy and listed by grape variety and style. The acoustics are still terrible but the atmosphere remains great.

Bumpkin

Modern European

C2

209 Westbourne Park Rd W11 1EA
Closed Monday lunch
(020) 7243 9818
www.bumpkinuk.com

Carte £25/40

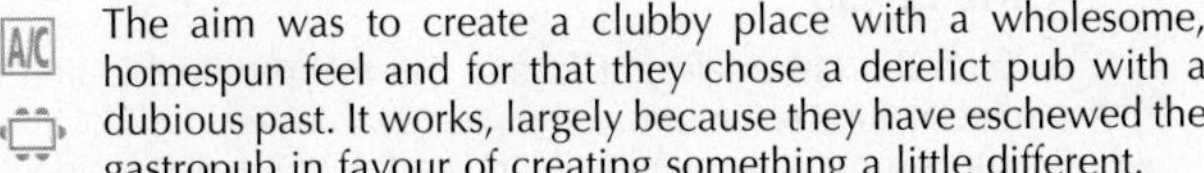

The aim was to create a clubby place with a wholesome, homespun feel and for that they chose a derelict pub with a dubious past. It works, largely because they have eschewed the gastropub in favour of creating something a little different. The ground floor is a brasserie with an appealing menu of light bites, pots, pies and grills with satisfying dishes ranging from macaroni cheese to liver and bacon. Those wanting something equally gutsy for dinner, but slightly more refined, can head to the first floor restaurant for dishes such as osso bucco or wild sea bass. Both kitchens share an emphasis on seasoning, sourcing and buying organic where possible. The other floors are taken up with private dining and whisky tasting.

Malabar

Indian

C3

27 Uxbridge St W8 7TQ
⊖ Notting Hill Gate
(020) 7727 8800
Buffet lunch Sunday
e-mail feedback@malabar-restaurant.co.uk
www.malabar-restaurant.co.uk

Menu £21 – Carte £20/36 s

Malabar celebrates 25 years in 2008 and it is not difficult to see why it has lasted so long: it's tucked away in a residential part of Notting Hill and has a friendly neighbourhood atmosphere; it gets a regular coat of fresh paint; the service is sweet natured and the cooking is both carefully prepared and good value.

The menu is nicely balanced, not too long and focuses on more northerly regions of India. The starters are particularly interesting and vary from succulent marinated chops to tandoori monkfish. Main courses are generously sized, subtly spiced and are served on warm metal thalis; tender lamb dishes are done especially well and the breads are excellent. The buffet lunch on Sunday, when children under 12 go free, is terrific value.

Cibo

A5 **Italian**

3 Russell Gdns W14 8EZ — ⊖ Kensington Olympia
(020) 7371 6271 — Closed Easter, 1 week Christmas, Saturday lunch, Sunday dinner and Bank Holidays
Fax (020) 7602 13,'1
e-mail ciborestaurant@aol.com **www**.ciborestaurant.net

Carte £24/38

VISA MC AE

Behind the rather elegant façade lies this personable and intimate Italian restaurant. Cibo has established itself over the years as something of a local landmark in this smart residential area, due to the mix of refreshingly unabashed and eclectic décor, reliably good Italian food and amiable service. The menu leans towards seafood and the portion size is on the generous side. The wide variety of breads on offer merit full investigation as do the pasta specials.

The place is usually full of locals whose loyalty is such that they appear to exert an influence over the menu content; you're also likely to see one of two local celebrities on any given night. Cibo is one of the best reasons for living in Holland Park.

Notting Grill

B2 **Beef specialities**

123A Clarendon Rd W11 4JG — ⊖ Holland Park
(020) 7229 1500 — Closed 24 December -3 January and Monday lunch
Fax (020) 7229 8889
e-mail nottinggrill@aol.com **www**.awtonline.co.uk

Menu £19 (dinner) – Carte £30

VISA MC AE

From the outside it still looks like the pub it once was, but inside it's gone all soft and spongy. Cushions are everywhere and a mix of pictures, rich colours and exposed brick all give it a warm, rustic yet welcoming feel. It's certainly worth staying downstairs as the room upstairs can't compete on atmosphere and personality.

'Well Bred, Well Fed and Well Hung' proclaims the menu, referring not to the owner, Antony Worrall Thompson, but to the speciality of the house - their well sourced steaks and grilled meats, which explains the dubious pun in the name. Comfort food is very much the order of the day and lovers of the old classics will find much to stir nostalgic thoughts, although those more of the present are not forgotten.

Wódka

Polish

D5

12 St Albans Grove
W8 5PN
⊖ High Street Kensington
Closed lunch Saturday and Sunday
(020) 7937 6513 **Fax** (020) 7937 8621
e-mail info@wodka.co.uk **www**.wodka.co.uk

Menu £17 – Carte £29/35

VISA MC AE

Come to Wódka to celebrate all things Eastern European. Housed in what was once the dairy to Kensington Palace, the décor inside is industrial-lite, where warmth and intimacy soften the sharper edges of the tough minimalism. The robust flavours and classic dishes of Polish and Eastern European cooking are all here, from blinis to pierogi and golabki (stuffed cabbage) to Bigos (Polish Hunters stew). Those who prefer dishes in a lighter, more modern style will find that they haven't been forgotten.

The restaurant has been run by an exclusively Polish team, from a time when that was considered a novelty. With a variety of vodkas available, all served directly from the freezer, no one leaves without their heart a little warmer. Na Zdrowie!

The Fat Badger

Gastropub

B1

310 Portobello Road W10 5TA
⊖ Ladbroke Grove
(020) 8969 4500 **Fax** (020) 8969 6714
Closed 25-26 December
e-mail info@thefatbadger.com **www**.thefatbadger.com

Carte £20/28

VISA MC

What was once The Caernarvon Castle appears to be another pub makeover with the old sofas, church seats and wood floors, but those chandeliers and that intriguing wallpaper hint at something a little different.

Sure enough, one glance at the menu reveals that there is nothing gastropub-formulaic about the cooking. The chef's philosophy is British and seasonal, with a waste-not-want-not approach to butchery. Whole beasts are delivered to the kitchen and they are not afraid of offering unfamiliar cuts; the menu is constantly changing to reflect what the suppliers deem worthy and vegetables reflect what's in season. This is real and earthy cooking. Breakfast and brunch menus also reveal that this is a kitchen with imagination and integrity.

Greater London

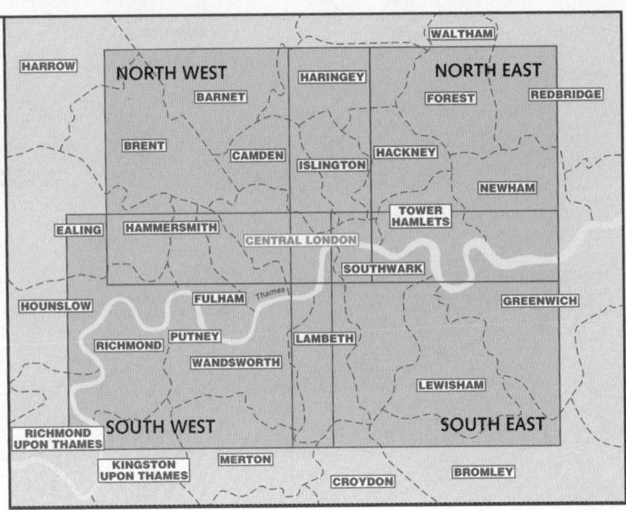

Tips / PHOTONONSTOP

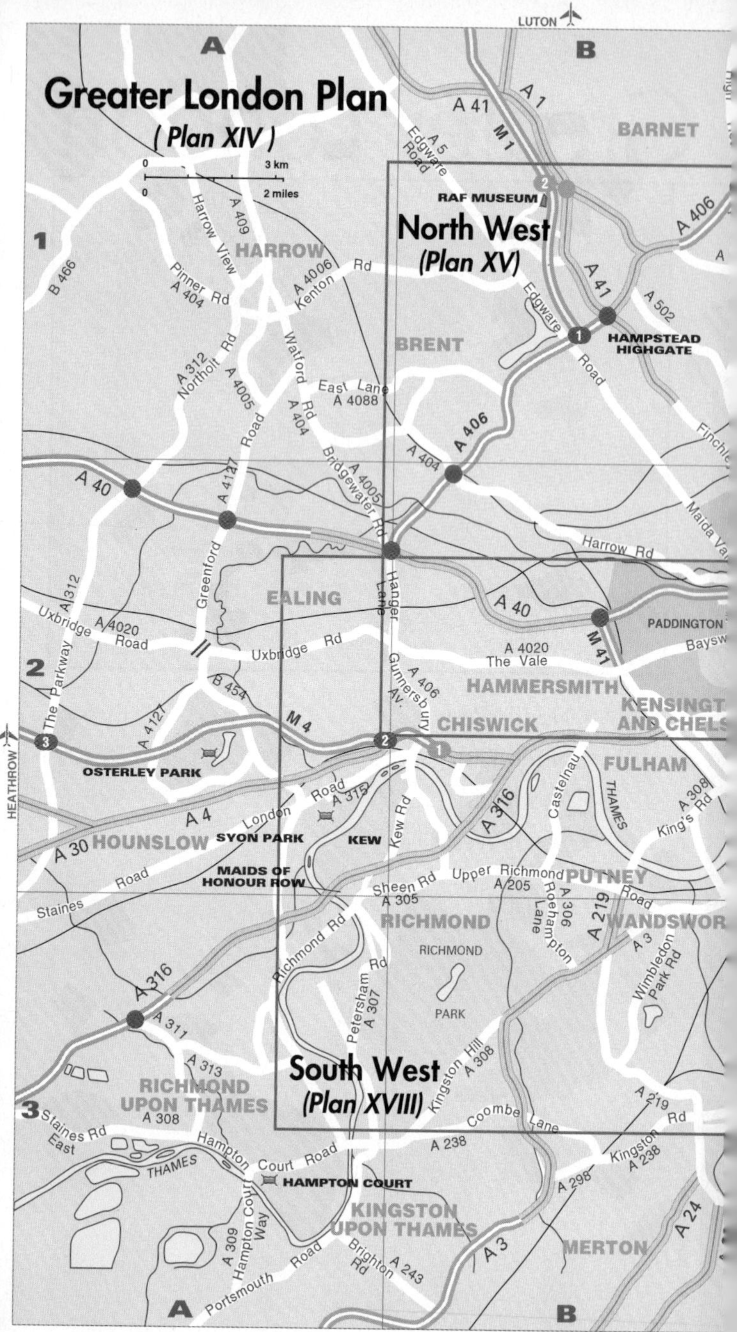
Greater London Plan
(Plan XIV)
North West
(Plan XV)
South West
(Plan XVIII)
LUTON
HEATHROW
BARNET
HARROW
BRENT
RAF MUSEUM
HAMPSTEAD
HIGHGATE
EALING
PADDINGTON
HAMMERSMITH
CHISWICK
KENSINGT
AND CHELS
FULHAM
OSTERLEY PARK
HOUNSLOW
SYON PARK
KEW
MAIDS OF
HONOUR ROW
PUTNEY
WANDSWOR
RICHMOND
RICHMOND
PARK
RICHMOND
UPON THAMES
HAMPTON COURT
KINGSTON
UPON THAMES
MERTON
THAMES
3 km
2 miles

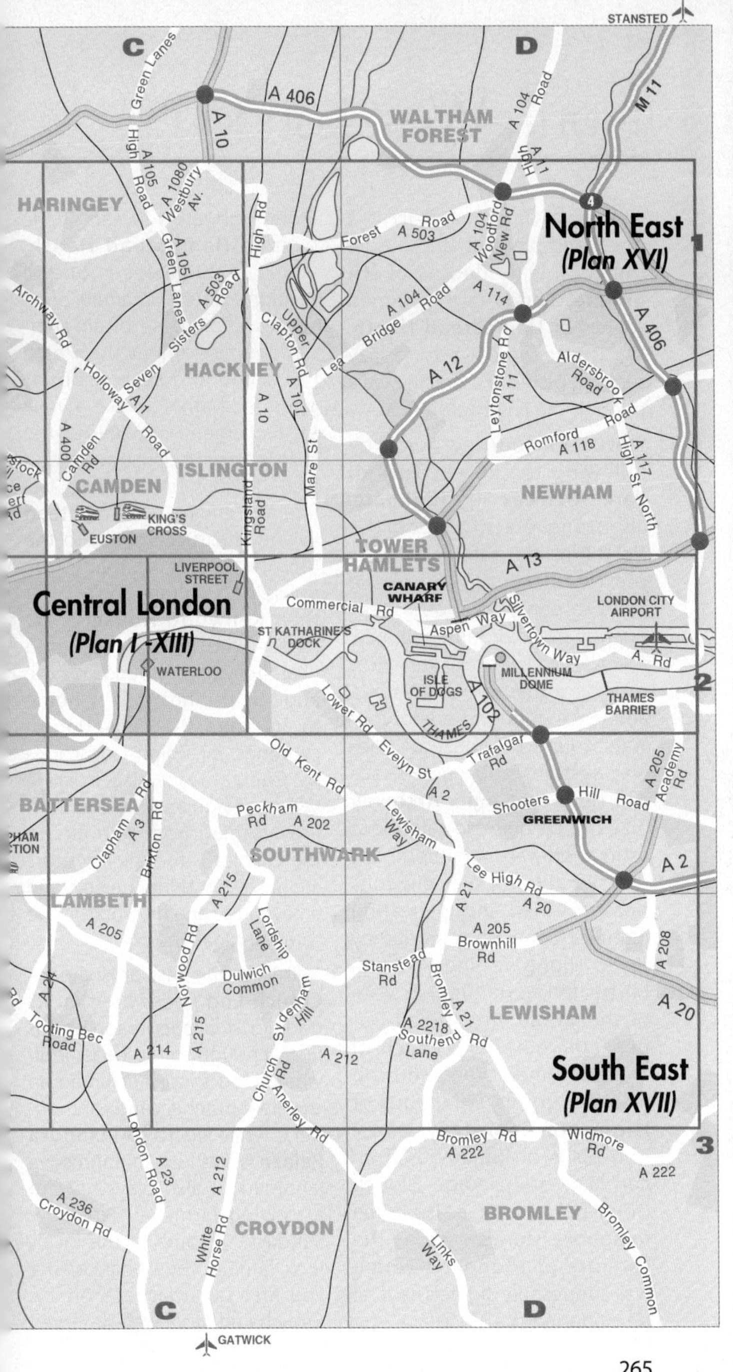
STANSTED
GATWICK
C
D
1
2
3
North East
(Plan XVI)
Central London
(Plan I -XIII)
South East
(Plan XVII)
WALTHAM FOREST
HARINGEY
HACKNEY
ISLINGTON
CAMDEN
TOWER HAMLETS
NEWHAM
BATTERSEA
SOUTHWARK
LAMBETH
LEWISHAM
CROYDON
BROMLEY
GREENWICH
CANARY WHARF
LONDON CITY AIRPORT
MILLENNIUM DOME
THAMES BARRIER
ISLE OF DOGS
THAMES
ST KATHARINE'S DOCK
LIVERPOOL STREET
WATERLOO
EUSTON
KING'S CROSS
A 406
A 10
M 11
A 104 Road
High A 11
Green Lanes
A 105 High Road
A 1080 Westbury Av.
A 105 Green Lanes
A 503 Road
Seven Sisters
High Rd
Forest Road A 503
A 104 Woodford New Rd
A 104 Bridge Road
Lea
A 114
Upper Clapton Rd
A 107
A 10
A 12
Leytonstone Rd A 11
Aldersbrook Road
Romford Road A 118
A 117 High St North
Archway Rd
Holloway Road
A 1
A 400
Camden Rd
Kingsland Road
Mare St
A 13
Commercial Rd
Aspen Way
Silvertown Way
A. Rd
A 102
Lower Rd
Old Kent Rd
Evelyn St
Trafalgar Rd
A 2
Shooters Hill Road
A 205 Academy Rd
Peckham Rd
A 202
Lewisham Way
Clapham A 3 Rd
Brixton Rd
A 215
Lee High Rd
A 20
A 21
A 205 Brownhill Rd
A 208
A 205
Lordship Lane
Norwood Rd
Dulwich Common
Stanstead Rd
Bromley A 21 Rd
Sydenham Hill
A 24
Tooting Bec Road
A 214
A 215
A 2218 Southend Lane
A 212
Church Rd
Anerley Rd
Bromley Rd A 222
Widmore Rd
A 222
London Road
A 23
A 212
White Horse Rd
A 236 Croydon Rd
Links Way
Bromley Common

North-West London

North-west London truly is a green and pleasant land – from the cool, leafy depths of **Highgate Woods** to the rugged spaces of **Hampstead Heath**, NW is just the place for a lazy summer picnic or a bracing walk through the crisp autumn air.

Start your journey north by following the line of **Tufnell Park, Archway** and **Highgate**, all strung prettily along the Northern line. Tufnell Park fits the NW stereotype of peace and prosperity to a tee – designated an 'environmental area' the traffic diverting measures provide a marvellously serene ambience, though finding your way around the maze of one-way-systems and cul-de-sacs can be a challenge. **Archway** may not be quite so salubrious as its moneyed neighbour, but the slightly grubbier environs boast a varied and interesting nightlife. Continue your journey up to Highgate and you will be treated to a stunning vista of the whole city spread out beneath you. For a touch of memento mori, you can drop into the gothic splendour of **Highgate Cemetery** – resting place of luminaries from Karl Marx and George Eliot to Douglas Adams, it is also home to spooky stories such as the Vampire of Highgate, which was supposedly sighted several times during the 1970s.

From Highgate you can amble over to **Hampstead Heath,** which at 791 acres is one of London's largest untamed, open spaces. For those of an energetic temperament the Heath has a lido and several ponds open for bathing. Take a walk up Parliament Hill, one of the highest points in London and justly famous for its views, before descending to **Hampstead** village and succumbing to the temptations of its many fine pubs. If it's culture you're after then **Kenwood House** is the perfect destination. Set amid beautifully kept grounds on the edge of the heath, it is home to an impressive collection of paintings, including landscapes by Constable. It also hosts a series of concerts in summer – everything from pop hits to the classics – to which visitors are invited to bring a picnic and enjoy music and fireworks in the summer gloaming.

A little to the east of Highgate, **Crouch End** prides itself on its traditional village image and is lucky enough still to boast individual food shops, including an excellent butchers and fishmongers, while nearby **Alexandra Palace** is not just an impressive landmark, it also plays host to a thriving farmer's market on Sundays. If some of the locals look familiar then chances are you first saw that face on TV: Crouch End has a well-deserved reputation as a media enclave, beloved by bohemian and arty types. It gets starrier the further west you go, until by **Hampstead, Child's Hill** and **Primrose Hill** you could find yourselves rubbing shoulders with Hollywood A-listers or chart-topping musicians.

The attraction NW holds for artistic types might be explained by a thriving local scene as well as a wealth of historical associations. **Swiss Cottage** is right by **Abbey Road**, home to the legendary recording studio where The Beatles and Pink Floyd, among others, recorded seminal works. The literary cues range from cutting-edge hip – **Willesden Green** was immortalised by Zadie Smith in *White Teeth* – to the dearly departed – William Makepeace Thackery and Anthony Trollope are among those buried at Kensal Green Cemetery in **Kensal Rise**. No surprise that theatre is amply represented too – **Belsize Park** is close to the Roundhouse on **Chalk Farm Road**, while up on **Kilburn High Road** you'll find the Tricycle Theatre along with new music venue, the Luminaire.

S. Ollivier/ MICHELIN

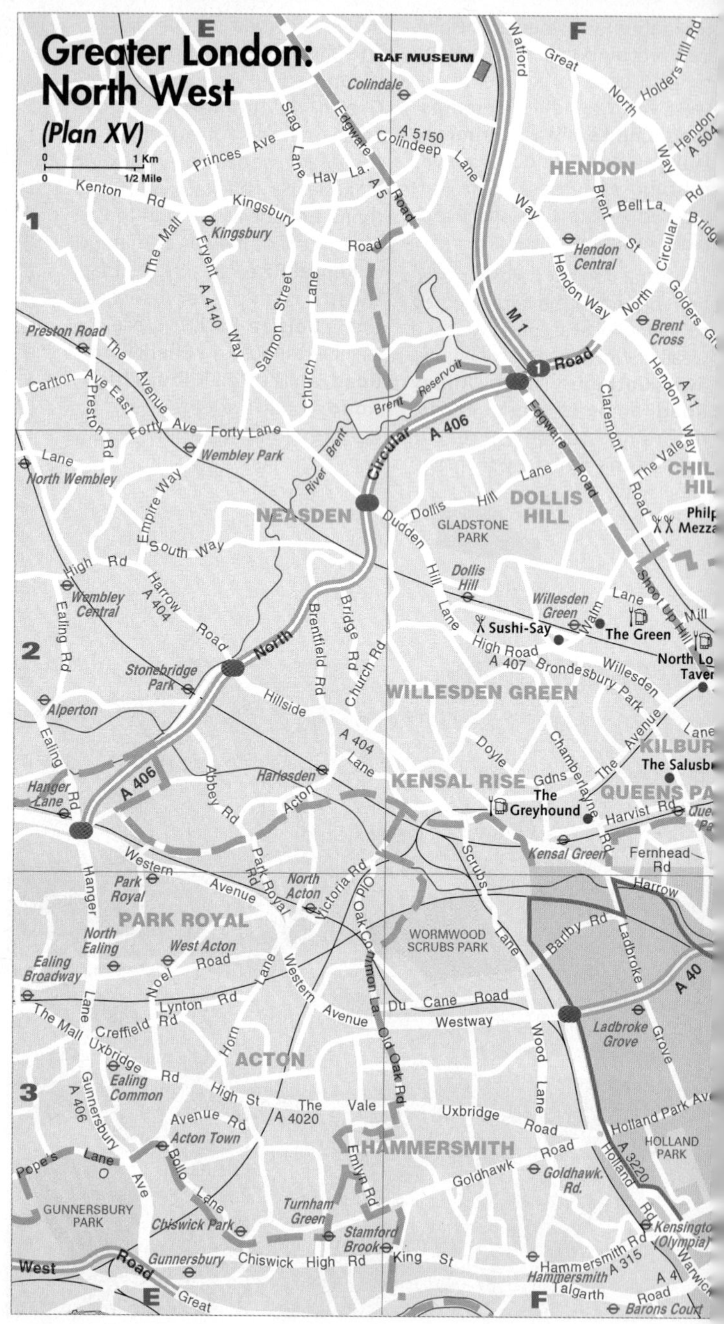
Greater London: North West
(Plan XV)
0 1 Km
0 1/2 Mile
E
F
1
2
3
RAF MUSEUM
Colindale
Watford
Great
North
Holders Hill Rd
Hendon
Way
A 504
HENDON
Brent
Bell La.
Rd
Bridge
Circular
St
Hendon Central
Hendon Way
North
Golders
Brent Cross
Hendon
A 41
Way
Princes Ave
Stag Lane
Hay La.
Edgware Road
A 5
A 5150
Colindeep
Lane
Way
Kenton Rd
Kingsbury
Road
Kingsbury
The Mall
Fryent Way
A 4140
Salmon Street
Church Lane
M 1
1 Road
Brent Reservoir
Preston Road
The Avenue
Carlton Ave East
Preston Rd
Forty Ave
Forty Lane
Wembley Park
Lane
North Wembley
River Brent
Circular
A 406
Edgware Road
Claremont
The Vale
Road
Way
CHIL
HIL
Philp
Mezza
Lane
Dollis Hill
DOLLIS HILL
GLADSTONE PARK
NEASDEN
Dudden Hill Lane
Empire Way
South Way
High Rd
Wembley Central
Ealing Rd
Harrow Road
A 404
Dollis Hill
Willesden Green
Lane
Walm
The Green
Mill
Shoot Up Hill
Sushi-Say
High Road
A 407
Brondesbury Park
Willesden
North Lo
Taver
Stonebridge Park
North
Brentfield Rd
Bridge Rd
Church Rd
Hillside
WILLESDEN GREEN
Alperton
Ealing Rd
A 404
Lane
Harlesden
Acton
Doyle
Gdns
Chamberlayne
The Avenue
Lane
KILBUR
The Salusb
KENSAL RISE
The Greyhound
QUEENS PA
Harvist Rd
Hanger Lane
Rd
A 406
Abbey Rd
Park Royal Rd
Kensal Green
Fernhead Rd
Harrow
Western Avenue
Park Royal
North Acton
Victoria Rd
Old Oak Common La
Scrubs Lane
PARK ROYAL
WORMWOOD SCRUBS PARK
Barlby Rd
Ladbroke
A 40
Hanger Lane
North Ealing
West Acton
Ealing Broadway
Road
Noel
Lane
Western Avenue
Lynton Rd
Du Cane Road
Westway
Ladbroke Grove
Grove
Wood Lane
The Mall
Creffield Rd
Uxbridge Rd
Horn
ACTON
Ealing Common
Gunnersbury
A 406
High St
The Vale
A 4020
Old Oak Rd
Uxbridge Road
Holland Park Ave
HOLLAND PARK
Avenue Rd
Acton Town
Bollo Lane
HAMMERSMITH
Emlyn Rd
Road
Holland Rd
A 3220
Pope's Lane
Ave
GUNNERSBURY PARK
Goldhawk Road
Goldhawk Rd.
Turnham Green
Chiswick Park
Stamford Brook
Kensingto (Olympia)
West Road
Gunnersbury
Chiswick High Rd
King St
Hammersmith Rd
A 315
Hammersmith
A 4
Warwick
Great
Talgarth Road
Barons Court

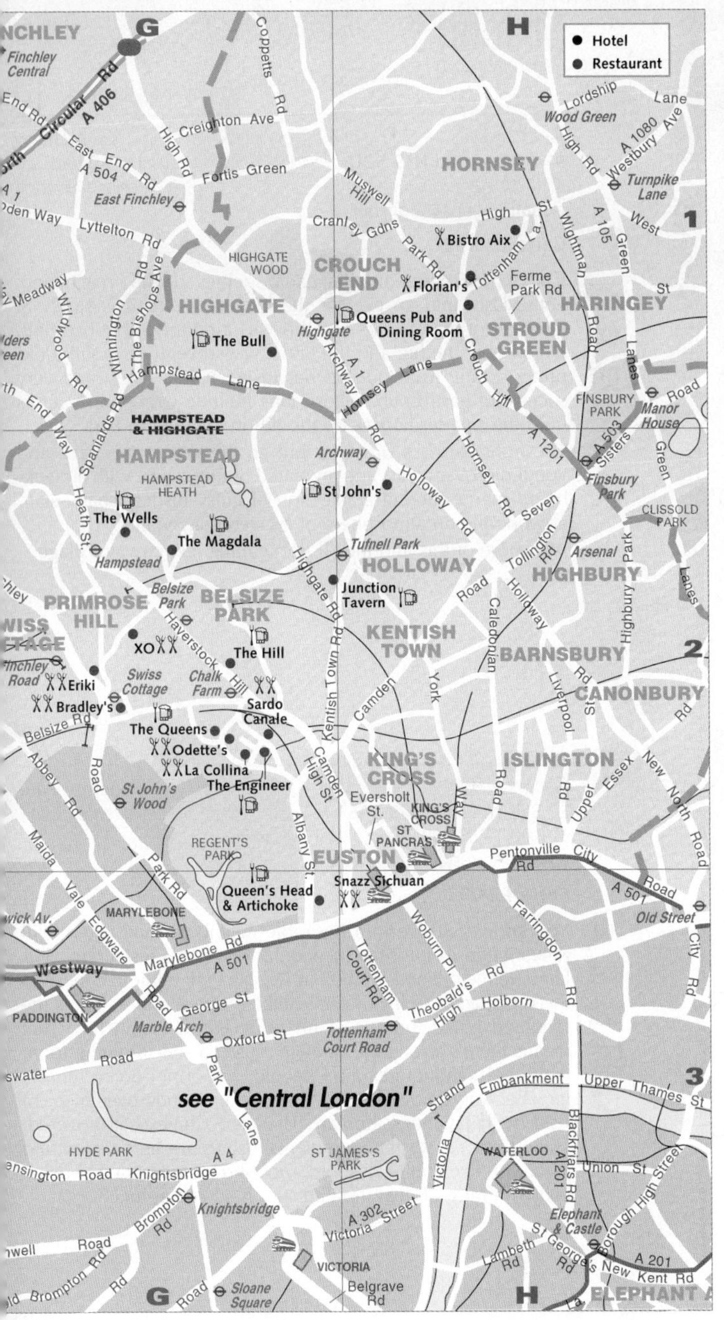

Hotel
Restaurant
Bistro Aix
Florian's
Queens Pub and Dining Room
The Bull
St John's
The Wells
The Magdala
Junction Tavern
XO
The Hill
Eriki
Bradley's
Sardo Canale
The Queens
Odette's
La Collina
The Engineer
Queen's Head & Artichoke
Snazz Sichuan
HORNSEY
CROUCH END
HIGHGATE
HARINGEY
STROUD GREEN
HAMPSTEAD & HIGHGATE
HAMPSTEAD
HAMPSTEAD HEATH
HOLLOWAY
HIGHBURY
PRIMROSE HILL
BELSIZE PARK
KENTISH TOWN
BARNSBURY
CANONBURY
KING'S CROSS
ISLINGTON
EUSTON
MARYLEBONE
PADDINGTON
HYDE PARK
ST JAMES'S PARK
WATERLOO
VICTORIA
REGENT'S PARK
HIGHGATE WOOD
CLISSOLD PARK
FINSBURY PARK
see "Central London"

St John's

Gastropub

H2

Archway

91 Junction Rd N19 5QU

(020) 7272 1587

e-mail st.johns@virgin.net

⊖ Archway

Closed 25-26 December and 1 January – dinner only

Carte £20/32

VISA MC AE

If anywhere represents what can be achieved with imagination, enthusiasm and an eye for the bigger picture it is surely St John's. Not many years ago this was a dodgy old boozer into which only the big and the brave would venture. It still looks pretty scruffy from outside but inside it is a lively and very successful gastro-pub, whose fans include writers and actors from the smarter houses up the hill in Dartmouth Park.

The front half is a busy bar but go through to the back and you'll discover a vast and animated dining room, with a blackboard menu offering a selection of gutsy dishes, chatty staff, artwork and an atmosphere of relaxed conviviality.

Any more of this and they'll start calling it Archway Village.

XO

Asian

G2

Belsize Park

29 Belsize Lane NW3 5AS

(020) 7433 0888 **Fax** (020) 7794 3474

www.rickerrestaurants.com

⊖ Belsize Park

Closed 25-26 December and 1 January

Carte £24/33

A/C VISA MC AE

You know you live in a desirable neighbourhood when Will Ricker chooses it for the location of one of his restaurants. His latest venue opened in 2007 in Belsize Park (although those in Swiss Cottage can legitimately stake a claim) and it adopts the tried-and tested formula of his other London branches. That means there's a long bar, lounge music, a stylish dining room with cool lighting, beautiful people, lots of noise and mirrors for checking hair/make-up. The menu extends over most of Asia, with Japanese, Korean, Thai and Chinese all covered. There's respect for the ingredients, dishes are best shared and favourites like chilli-salt squid, rock shrimp tempura and black cod with miso all feature; dim sum is served at lunch.

Philpott's Mezzaluna

Italian influences XX

F2

Child's Hill

Closed 2 weeks Easter, 25-26 December, 1 January, Saturday lunch and Monday

424 Finchley Rd NW2 2HY
(020) 7794 0455 **Fax** (020) 7794 0452
www.philpotts-mezzaluna.com

Menu £25/30

The eponymous Mr. Philpott has established a loyal local following since opening here in 2000. Most of the heavy traffic has turned off by the time you reach this part of the Finchley Road and it is handily placed to attract customers from across North London. They come here for the robust and unpretentious cooking, which uses assorted influences from across Italy. Menus are priced according to the number of courses you take. The service is undertaken by Mr Philpott's fellow partner in the business who has mastered that relaxed and imperturbable style which helps create a welcoming air. The room mixes a traditional feel with some modern touches. The tiled flooring and colours add to the light and inviting feel.

Florians

Italian X

H1

Crouch End

Closed 25-26 December and 1 January

4 Topsfield Parade, Middle Lane N8 8RP
(020) 8348 8348 **Fax** (020) 8292 2092
www.floriansrestaurant-crouchend.co.uk

Carte £22/28

Don't panic when you first enter - you're in the bar which always seems to be this busy, mostly, apparently, with the same crowd every time. Just head through it and up the few steps and you'll get to the restaurant at the back. Don't, however, sit in the first section which seems a rather disconnected spot betwixt and between bar and restaurant.

The dining room is a bright affair, relaxed and informal, with rough white-washed brick and assorted paintings of varying aptitude available for purchase. The ebullient owner oversees the service, which is undertaken by the young team. The reliable Italian cooking comes in satisfyingly generous portions and the daily changing blackboard specials are always a good option.

Bistro Aix

H1 French

Crouch End

Closed Monday

54 Topsfield Parade, Tottenham Lane N8 8PT
(020) 8340 6346 **Fax** (020) 8348 7236
www.bistroaix.co.uk

Carte £19/36

VISA MC AE

The location may be Crouch End, the chef owner may be American but for a couple of hours this little bistro will whisk you off to the verdant French countryside. The high ceiling, mustard coloured walls, dressers, plants and mirrors all add to that rustic feel, while two specially commissioned paintings of cooks and pastoral scenes tell you this is a place run by, and for, those with a genuine love of food.

Francophiles will find plenty of contentment in the vast majority of the menu, which features all the favourites from classic onion soup or seared foie gras to steak frites or rack of lamb, but there are other dishes whose origins owe more to Italian cooking.

Queens Pub & Dining Room

H1 Gastropub 

Crouch End

26 The Broadway N8 9DE
(020) 8340 2031
e-mail queens@foodandfuel.co.uk

A/C

This classic Victorian pub, with its mahogany panelling and ornate plasterwork, was once known more for the fighting than the food but the 2006 makeover ensures that now the closest thing here to an episode of Eastenders is the occasional presence of a cast member.

The menu changes daily and food is served all day. It's a confident kitchen, offering a mix of modern British with plenty of Mediterranean influence so the sausages that come with the mash may include Toulouse as well as wild boar, and apple crumble might arrive with pistachio ice cream. There's a cocktail of the week and an accessible wine list with plenty available by the glass or carafe; non-drinkers are not ignored either – there's home-made lemonade to stir childhood memories in many.

Snazz Sichuan

Chinese XX

H2

Euston ⊖ Euston

37 Chalton St NW1 1JD

(020) 7388 0808

www.newchinaclub.co.uk

Carte £10/50

The Sichuan Province in the southwest of China is known for its foggy conditions and rare sightings of the sun. To compensate for this lack of heat from the big yellow orb Sichuan cooking provides its own heat in the form of the Sichuan pepper, a fierce and fiery little number. Pork is another speciality and these two elements form a large part of the menu here which is simply split between cold and hot dishes: hot in every sense. Stir-fry is the favoured form of cooking and the meal traditionally ends in rice - so ask if you want it earlier.

Window seats are the best, loudness and laughter are positively encouraged and the restaurant virtually doubles as the Sichuan tourist board as it also houses a gallery and traditional tea room.

The Wells

Gastropub 

G2

Hampstead ⊖ Hampstead Heath

30 Well Walk NW3 1BX Closed 1 January

(020) 7794 3785 **Fax** (020) 7794 6817

e-mail info@thewellshampstead.co.uk

www.thewellshampstead.co.uk

Carte £20/30

Owned by Beth Coventry, sister of restaurant critic Fay Maschler, The Wells lies somewhere in between a restaurant and a pub. But whatever you consider it to be, one thing for sure is that it's in a grand old spot and adds to the mystery of why there are not more places to eat in Hampstead. The ground floor is the pubbier part, with a well chosen menu of the sort of dishes that go well with beer, but it can be a bit of a bun-fight, especially in summer and at weekends. Upstairs is an altogether more composed affair but one that still has considerable charm. Muscular gastropub staples like lamb shank or calf's liver with onion gravy sit alongside dishes whose flavours are more Asian in origin, while others exhibit Italian roots.

The Magdala

G2 — Gastropub

Hampstead
2A South Hill Park NW3 2SB
(020) 7435 2503 **Fax** (020) 7435 6167
e-mail themagdala@hotmail.co.uk

⊖ Belsize Park
Closed 25 December

Carte £17/27

VISA MC AE

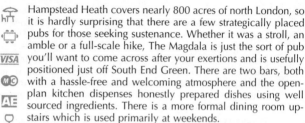

Hampstead Heath covers nearly 800 acres of north London, so it is hardly surprising that there are a few strategically placed pubs for those seeking sustenance. Whether it was a stroll, an amble or a full-scale hike, The Magdala is just the sort of pub you'll want to come across after your exertions and is usefully positioned just off South End Green. There are two bars, both with a hassle-free and welcoming atmosphere and the open-plan kitchen dispenses honestly prepared dishes using well sourced ingredients. There is a more formal dining room upstairs which is used primarily at weekends.

All great pubs should have a secret and The Magdala was where Ruth Ellis, the last woman to be hanged in Britain, shot her lover in 1955.

The Bull

G1 — Gastropub

Highgate
13 North Hill N6 4AB
(0845) 456 5033 **Fax** (0845) 456 5034
e-mail info@inthebull.biz **www**.inthebull.biz

⊖ Highgate

Carte £30/45

VISA MC AE

Up and over the top of Highgate brings you to The Bull, a good-looking pub spread over two floors with a large front terrace.

Apparently there's been a pub here since 1765 but its current incarnation, with the emphasis firmly on the food, very much captures the zeitgeist. Cream walls, wood flooring, modern art and mix of furnishings give it an urbane and uncomplicated feel.

There's a self assured swagger about the service and equal confidence about the menu which tells you the people behind this pub (and their other place, The House) have gained experience at some fairly lofty establishments. The cooking cleverly combines classical French with British, so you can have your Sunday roast but also your foie gras parfait beforehand.

The Greyhound

Gastropub

F2

Kensal Rise ⊖ Kensal Green

64-66 Chamberlayne Road
NW10 3JJ

Closed 25-26 December, 1 January, Sunday dinner and Monday

✆ (020) 8969 8080 **Fax** (020) 8969 8081
e-mail thegreyhound@needtoeat.co.uk

Carte £18/25

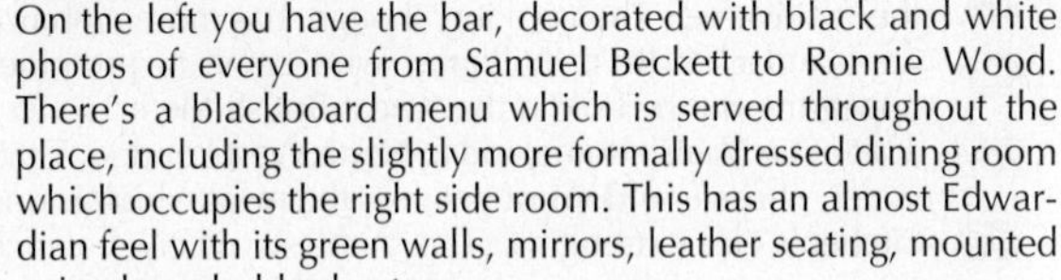

On the left you have the bar, decorated with black and white photos of everyone from Samuel Beckett to Ronnie Wood. There's a blackboard menu which is served throughout the place, including the slightly more formally dressed dining room which occupies the right side room. This has an almost Edwardian feel with its green walls, mirrors, leather seating, mounted animals and old adverts.

The menu covers all points, from the burger, steak or haddock in an Adnam's beer batter to dishes where a lighter touch is required such as sea bass with lentils. Pâtés are robust and come with homemade piccalilli, the chicken is free range, fish comes daily from Cornwall and vegetarians are well looked after (if they can avert their eyes from the taxidermy).

North London Tavern

Gastropub

F2

Kilburn

375 Kilburn High Rd NW6 7QB
✆ (020) 7625 6634 **Fax** (020) 7625 6635
e-mail northlondontavern@realpubs.co.uk **www**.realpubs.co.uk

Carte £20/24

Its Johnny-Cash-black exterior is a clue that here's an imposing former railway inn that's been given the makeover. The large bar pulls in the punters while the dining room at the back is half separated by glass panelling and operates at a gentler pace. Here, old church seats, large candles, glass chandeliers and high ceilings add a hint of Gothic moodiness.

The cooking is satisfyingly full-bodied. Crusty bread is delivered in sizeable slices, while dishes come fully dressed so there is none of that side-dish paraphernalia. Along with the robust stuff like rib-eye, duck and tagines you'll find some Iberian influences which suit the pub environment well. This is also the sort of place where you find puddings rather than desserts and these come in man-size portions.

Odette's

Modern European XX

G2

Primrose Hill
130 Regent's Park Rd NW1 8XL
(020) 7586 8569 **Fax** (020) 7586 8362
e-mail odettes@vpmg.net

⊖ Chalk Farm
Closed Christmas, Sunday dinner and Monday

Menu £18 (lunch) – Carte £40

A/C VISA MC AE

Odette's has long been a part of Primrose Hill, sitting pretty in the main street. The cooking, though, has more ambition these days and chef Bryn Williams, who came to prominence by appearing on the box in the 'Great British Menu' series, brings a bit of his Welsh homeland to North West London. That means water, cheeses and, most notably, the meat which is one of the kitchen's clear strengths. The menu is nicely balanced and continues to evolve, whilst keeping things quite classical, and dishes pull back from ever being over-worked.

The downstairs bar may not yet have reached the fashionable set but the restaurant itself is warm, smart and inviting. The locals are the ones still wondering where all the old mirrors went.

Sardo Canale

Italian XX

G2

Primrose Hill
42 Gloucester Ave NW1 8JD
(020) 7722 2800 **Fax** (020) 7722 0802
e-mail info@sardocanale.com **www**.sardocanale.com

⊖ Chalk Farm
Closed 25-26 December and Monday lunch

Carte £23/33

A/C VISA MC AE

Baby sister to Sardo's near Warren Street, Sardo Canale is a relaxed, neighbourhood Italian restaurant boasting a warm and familiar ambience which acts as something of a counterpoint to the recent racy reputation afforded to Primrose Hill, thanks to the exploits of its more recognisable locals.

The place is divided into four different rooms, as well as the summer terrace, three of which are contemporary in style with the fourth being the most interesting place for star crossed lovers and which was originally an access tunnel to the canal. The cooking is appetisingly rustic, with a proud Sardinian theme running through the menu that's supplemented by daily changing specials. Post-prandial strolls along the canal are optional.

La Collina

Italian XX

G2

Primrose Hill ⊖ Camden Town

17 Princess Rd NW1 8JR — Closed Bank Holidays – dinner only

✆ (020) 7483 0192

e-mail lacollinanw1@aol.com

Menu £24

"The Hill" arrived in early 2006 to continue the trend of there being an Italian restaurant at this address. It comes divided between the ground floor and the basement, with the former brighter and the latter more intimate. Decorated in a suitably rustic style, with its artwork for sale, it has a pleasant little garden terrace at the back. Service makes up in efficiency what it may lack in personality.

The chef hails from Piedmont, so expect some hearty specialities from this region to feature on the menu of Northern Italian cooking. There's ample choice, the portions come sensibly sized and it's all good value – being priced per course, the more you eat the cheaper it seems. The exclusively Italian wine list is also commendably affordable.

The Queens

G2

Primrose Hill ⊖ Chalk Farm

49 Regent's Park Rd NW1 8XD — Closed 25 December and Sunday dinner

✆ (020) 7586 0408 **Fax** (020) 7586 5677

e-mail thequeens@geronimo-inns.co.uk

www.geronimo-inns.co.uk

Carte £15/25

The Queens will have a place in the annals of gastropub history, as it was one of the pioneers in bringing decent food into an environment hitherto resistant to change and proved that a local with good food was not a contradiction.

Its location on the main drag and alongside the Hill is clearly another attraction and the balcony terrace is a sought after summer spot. The whole place was stripped down and done up in 2006.

The narrow bar remains an established local meeting point, with the footie on the TV on the corner, but head upstairs and you'll find a warm and welcoming dining room. Here, gutsy gastropub staples are on offer; main courses come with a good choice of side dishes and there's a daily special for two to share.

The Engineer

Gastropub

G2

Primrose Hill
65 Gloucester Ave NW1 8JH
(020) 7722 0950 **Fax** (020) 7483 0592
e-mail info@the-engineer.com **www**.the-engineer.com

⊖ Chalk Farm
Closed 3 days at Christmas

Carte £18/45

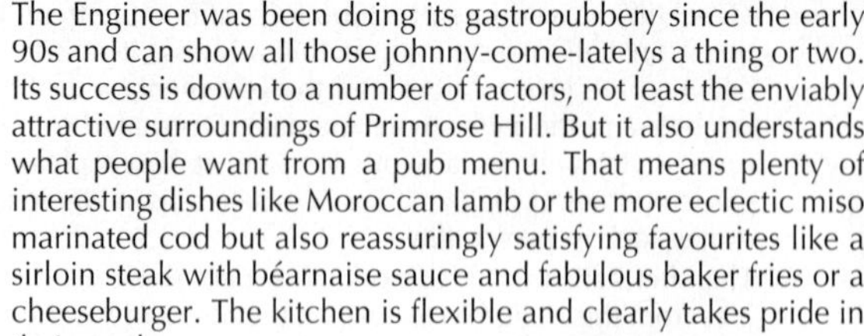

The Engineer was been doing its gastropubbery since the early 90s and can show all those johnny-come-latelys a thing or two. Its success is down to a number of factors, not least the enviably attractive surroundings of Primrose Hill. But it also understands what people want from a pub menu. That means plenty of interesting dishes like Moroccan lamb or the more eclectic miso marinated cod but also reassuringly satisfying favourites like a sirloin steak with béarnaise sauce and fabulous baker fries or a cheeseburger. The kitchen is flexible and clearly takes pride in their work.

It's all open all day, the dining room spills out onto the delightful terrace and staff prove that looking good and being friendly are not mutually exclusive.

The Salusbury

Gastropub

F2

Queens Park
50-52 Salusbury Road NW6 6NN
(020) 7328 3286
e-mail info@thesalusbury.com

Closed Monday lunch

Carte £24/32

Salusbury Road is becoming quite a foodie quarter. There's a Sunday farmers' market up the road, plenty of local cafés and The Salusbury Pub & Dining Room, complete with its own food store a couple of doors down. It's divided down the middle and is half pub, half dining room although you have to fight through the former to get to the latter. The style is pleasantly higgledy and the occasional shared table contributes to the bonhomie.

The cooking, though, is more restaurant than pub and comes with a distinct Italian accent. Quality bread and olive oil set things off and the various pasta dishes come as either starters or mains. Flavours are pronounced, ingredients good and portions generous. It's also well worth leaving trouser space for dessert.

Bradley's

Modern European XX

G2

Swiss Cottage
25 Winchester Rd NW3 3NR
(020) 7722 3457 **Fax** (020) 7435 1392
e-mail ssjbradleys@aol.com **www**.bradleysnw3.co.uk

⊖ Swiss Cottage
Closed 1 week Christmas, Sunday dinner, Monday

Menu £15/22 – Carte £24/37

A number of menus are available from which to choose dishes that come neatly presented and with a decidedly classical base. There is an 'early bird' for those who missed lunch, a pre-theatre for attendees at the nearby Hampstead Theatre and a full à la carte for diners under no time or dietary restraints. The eponymous owner, who supervises the cooking, runs a smooth operation and is helped out by a young but efficient team, all smartly kitted out in black.

The room is sophisticated and contemporary in its tone but without the impersonal feel one often encounters in the West End. Extra warmth comes courtesy of the high count of loyal locals, who all seem to know one another, and the genuine neighbourhood feel that this generates.

Eriki

Indian XX

G2

Swiss Cottage
4-6 Northways Parade, Finchley Rd NW3 5EN
(020) 7722 0606 **Fax** (020) 7722 8866
e-mail info@eriki.co.uk **www**.eriki.co.uk

⊖ Swiss Cottage
Closed Christmas, 1 January, Saturday lunch and lunch on Bank Holidays

Carte £23/26

You'll see it just at the moment you realise you're in the wrong lane. Eriki's location may not be the greatest, bang on the permanently busy Finchley Road, but once seated all is calm and the traffic outside gets quickly forgotten. The decoration certainly helps in this regard - the vivid red and orange walls, carved wooden screens and smart table setting make the room smart yet unstuffy and the cutlery, imported from Rajasthan, is certainly original. Furthermore, the conscientious and obliging waiters, all in smart tunics, ensure that everyone is attended to. The menu takes diners on a culinary trail around India and the carefully prepared dishes come with a level of refinement usually associated with more expensive establishments.

Junction Tavern

G2 — Gastropub

Tufnell Park
101 Fortess Rd NW5 1AG
(020) 7485 9400 **Fax** (020) 7485 9401
www.junctiontavern.co.uk

⊖ Tufnell Park
Closed 24-26 December and 1 January

Carte £20/28

With its brass cock glinting in the sun, you can't miss The Junction, and nor would you want to. Just as impressive inside, it's painted ox blood red, with rich wood panelling. With a conservatory, dining room and terrace as well as the bar, there's also plenty of space to accommodate the youthful regulars.

The choice on the daily-changing menu is as eclectic as the range of cookbooks propped up at one end of the open kitchen. Wholesome and bold, choices might include wild mushroom and spinach crepes or dukkah crusted tofu - and the chunky chips deserve a special mention. An ale pub at heart, the weekly-changing selection boasts a menu all of its own and enthusiasts gather several times a year for a beer festival.

Sushi-Say

F2 — Japanese

Willesden Green
33B Walm Lane NW2 5SH
(020) 8459 2971
Fax (020) 8907 3229

⊖ Willesden Green
Closed 25-26 December, 1 January, 1 week August and Monday – dinner only and lunch Saturday and Sunday

Carte £15/38

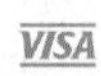

It's been given a little makeover and now the tinted windows make it look really quite inviting. Sushi-Say is an authentic neighbourhood Japanese restaurant and the perfect antidote to those restaurants that deem Japanese food ripe for reinterpretation. This is all about tradition and the care taken in the preparation of the dishes is clear.

The layout remains the same: the owner stands, complete with his head band, behind his sushi counter and this is the favoured spot of the regulars and, as the name suggests, the house speciality. Otherwise, it's through to the simply furnished little dining room. There's a surprisingly large number of staff and plenty of set menus which deliver a good all round experience.

The Green

Gastropub

F2

Willesden Green

⊖ Willesden Green

110 Walm Lane NW2 4RS

Closed 25 December and 1 January

✆ (020) 8452 0171 **Fax** (020) 8452 0774

e-mail info@thegreennw2.com **www**.thegreennw2.com

Menu £18 – Carte £16/28

VISA

MC

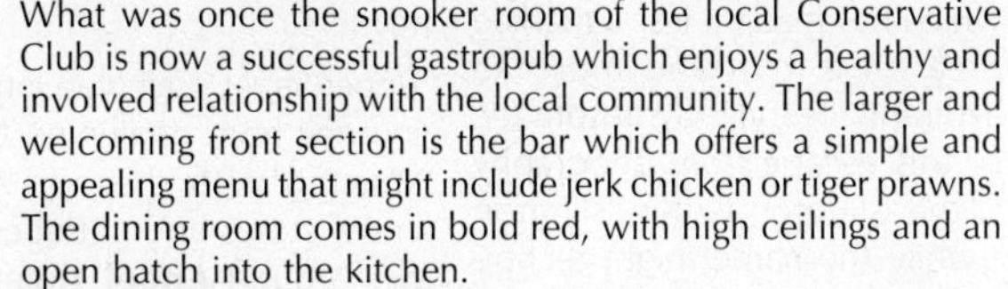

What was once the snooker room of the local Conservative Club is now a successful gastropub which enjoys a healthy and involved relationship with the local community. The larger and welcoming front section is the bar which offers a simple and appealing menu that might include jerk chicken or tiger prawns. The dining room comes in bold red, with high ceilings and an open hatch into the kitchen.

That kitchen sends forth dishes that are both robust in flavour and generous in size, whether that's a bowl of mussels, a vegetarian risotto or more sophisticated restaurant-style food like foie gras terrine. The wine list is concise but inexpensive and there's an equally satisfying brunch menu available at weekends.

THE WINTER'S TALE

Conspiracy theorists still like to claim that 17C man of letters Sir Francis Bacon wrote Shakespeare's plays, but more startling (and true) is the fact that Bacon lost his life in the furtherance of culinary science. The Highgate resident tried to prove that meat could be preserved by freezing. Unfortunately, while putting this to the test by stuffing a dead chicken with snow he caught a chill, which eventually killed him.

North-East London

A wellspring of champagne socialism, **Islington** enjoyed a rejuvenation in the late 1980s which has made it less a marked area on a map and more an aspirant lifestyle. Symptomatic of this escape from geography is the Islington within Islington - while the name might technically encompass an entire London borough, it is the gentrified Georgian enclave around **Upper Street's** irrepressible liveliness which has made it synonymous with fashionable theatre crowds, media darling dinner parties and hanging out in bars, looking like you really can't help being that cool.

Although Islington's half-suburban homeliness prevents it from being part of central London proper, it is the district's habit to suggest that it can match anything the rest of the capital cares to offer - indeed, that real London is to be found in N1, not Westminster or the West End. To an extent, it has a point; after all, it was in an Upper Street restaurant that Blair and Brown made their infamous power-sharing pact, while the scene-stealing **Almeida Theatre** frequently eclipses more central venues in combining artistic daring with glamour and commercial success. What is more, this is where many of British society's powerhouses live, as well as play. Shopping in the Sainsbury's Local by **St Mary's Church** can require you to steer your basket round a who's who of popular comedians and television news readers.

Upper Street itself is an intriguing journey from beginning to end, starting with the odd mix of chain stores and antiques arcades around **Angel**, going past the cosmopolitan headiness of **Islington Green**, before reaching the esoteric music venues, lounge bars and furniture sellers closer to **Highbury Corner**. To the west lie the handsome squares of **Barnsbury**, where an imaginative one-way system leaves strollers to enjoy the streets in peace - though many prefer to duck into some of the most atmospheric old-man pubs in zone one. To the east, **Canonbury** is even prettier, with some drinking taverns boasting that most prized of urban assets: a beer garden. Head north and the lovely leafy space of **Highbury Fields** leads on to the Victorian cosiness of **Highbury** itself, where the arresting Art Deco of the old **Arsenal Stadium** has now been superseded by the Gunners' new space-age ground at **Ashburton Grove.**

But if the gentrification of Islington's slums would have appeared remarkable to bygone residents like George Orwell, who turned **Canonbury Square** into the squalid Victory Mansions in *Nineteen Eighty-Four,* neighbouring **Hackney's** turnaround seems properly in the realm of science fiction. Up against decades of neglect, parts of Hackney are beginning to blossom - literally, in the case of the **Columbia Road Flower Market.**

Some of this is overspill from Islington's success, with first-time buyers forced further out, moulding **Stoke Newington's Church Street** into a calmer, slightly more bohemian version of Upper Street. In general, however, Hackney's rise has a flavour all of its own. **Shoreditch** became London's edgiest clubland, where mainstreamers still don't quite fit in and some venues open only after dawn begins to break. Meanwhile, nearby **Hoxton** was invaded by the Young British Artists, shocking the establishment with unmade beds and sharks pickled in formaldehyde. Soon, City financiers were also moving in, with derelict warehouses converted into luxury loft apartments, alongside the garrets and studios.

Now the boundaries of trendy living are being pushed ever northwards, up **Kingsland Road** and right into **Dalston**. The area is likely to be one of the big winners when the Olympics come to town, close to the main venues. What's more, the underground is extending into Hackney - a sure sign of London's own estimation of this district's rising star.

C. Eymenier / MICHELIN

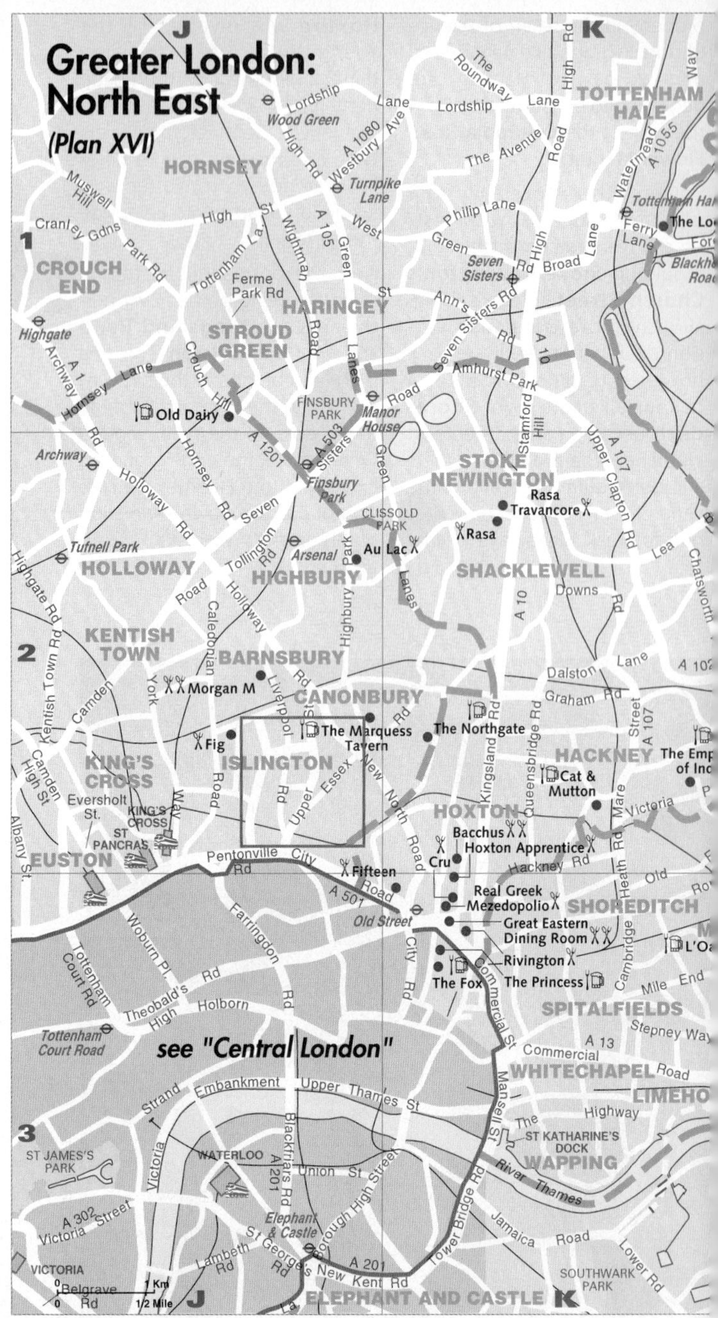

Greater London: North East
(Plan XVI)
HORNSEY
CROUCH END
HARINGEY
STROUD GREEN
TOTTENHAM HALE
FINSBURY PARK
STOKE NEWINGTON
HOLLOWAY
HIGHBURY
SHACKLEWELL
KENTISH TOWN
BARNSBURY
CANONBURY
ISLINGTON
KING'S CROSS
HACKNEY
HOXTON
EUSTON
SHOREDITCH
SPITALFIELDS
WHITECHAPEL
ST KATHARINE'S DOCK
WAPPING
ELEPHANT AND CASTLE
Old Dairy
Rasa Travancore
Rasa
Au Lac
Morgan M
The Marquess Tavern
The Northgate
Fig
Cat & Mutton
Bacchus
Hoxton Apprentice
Cru
Fifteen
Real Greek Mezedopolio
Great Eastern Dining Room
Rivington
The Fox
The Princess
see "Central London"

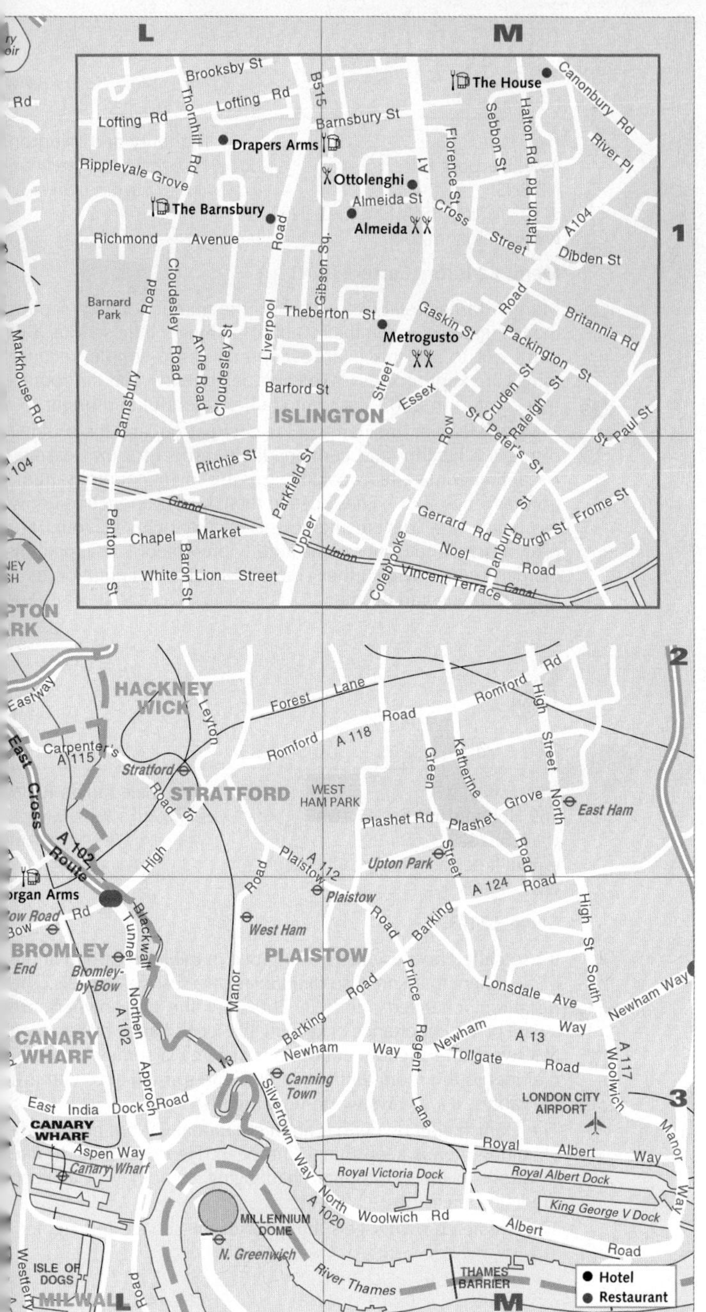

L
M
The House
Drapers Arms
Ottolenghi
The Barnsbury
Almeida
Metrogusto
ISLINGTON
HACKNEY WICK
STRATFORD
WEST HAM PARK
PLAISTOW
BROMLEY
CANARY WHARF
LONDON CITY AIRPORT
MILLENNIUM DOME
THAMES BARRIER
ISLE OF DOGS
Royal Victoria Dock
Royal Albert Dock
King George V Dock
River Thames
Hotel
Restaurant

Morgan M

J2 — French XX

Barnsbury
489 Liverpool Rd
N7 8NS
(020) 7609 3560 **Fax** (020) 8292 5699
www.morganm.com

⊖ Highbury and Islington
Closed 24-30 December, lunch Tuesday and Saturday, Sunday dinner and Monday

Menu £24/36 – Carte £36/41

A/C VISA MC

Morgan M has established itself as the number one choice for the Islington set when they want something a little serious. But that's not to say this is an overformal gastro-temple because things are kept nicely relaxed and neighbourly and the room - redecorated in 2007 - is comfortable, colourful and bright.

M is for Meunier, the name of the chef-patron, and his cooking displays a healthy and commendable respect for the seasons. As a Frenchman, his cooking uses his own country's traditions as a base but he has been in the UK long enough to know we have some decent ingredients of our own. Flavours are pronounced and dishes come artfully presented. The appealing Garden menus will further cement Islington's reputation as a hotbed of vegetarianism.

Fig

J2 — Modern European X

Barnsbury
169 Hemingford Rd N1 1DA
(020) 7609 3009
e-mail figrestaurant@btconnect.com
www.fig-restaurant.co.uk

⊖ Caledonian Road
Closed 2 weeks Christmas - New Year, 1 week Easter, 2 weeks summer and Monday – dinner only

Carte £21/32

VISA MC AE

It's so called because there's a fig tree in the little garden at the back, where there are also four tables on a first come basis. The restaurant changed hands in 2006 but the new owners are aware of the importance of keeping the locals happy by retaining the sweet and friendly atmosphere. There's a somewhat colonial feel to the room, enlivened by some spirited art. With just ten tables, it's always worth booking first.

The Danish chef owner has an international CV but his weekly changing menus keep things European. He does, though, like to throw in the occasional challenging combination to keep diners on their toes.

The Aussie co-owner gets the tenor of the service just right.

The Morgan Arms

Gastropub

L3

Bow

43 Morgan St E3 5AA

(020) 8980 6389

e-mail morgan@arms.fsworld.co.uk **www**.geronimo-inns.co.uk

⊖ Bow Road

Closed Sunday dinner – bookings not accepted

The eponymous Mr Morgan owned all the land around these parts in the 1800s and he would, no doubt, be flattered to see this characterful pub in what is now a smart residential area. Shabby chic is the order of the day, with an appealing mismatch of furniture, although the partially separated dining room is marginally quieter than the raucous bar.

The menu is always appealing and constantly evolving. Regular trips to Billingsgate are in evidence and the kitchen is not afraid of offering different things like pig's cheeks or oxtail ravioli; there's even a helpful glossary to explain some of the more unusual ingredients. This is robust, filling and full-on cooking, entirely appropriate for what was formerly a spit and sawdust boozer.

The House

Gastropub

M1

Canonbury

63-69 Canonbury Rd
N1 2DG

(020) 7704 7410 **Fax** (020) 7704 9388

e-mail info@inthehouse.biz **www**.inthehouse.biz

⊖ Highbury and Islington

Closed 24-26 December and Monday lunch

Carte £30/45

VISA

When Islingtonians arrange to meet you back at 'the house', more than likely they mean at this coolly sophisticated pub, tucked away in a residential part of the borough. It effortlessly combines a laid back vibe at the bar, which adjoins a triangular shaped terrace at the front, with a more urbane atmosphere found in the nattily attired dining room.

Just reading the menu provides evidence that The House has loftier culinary ambitions than many a gastropub. Indeed, a number of the kitchen's carefully composed dishes would not look out of place in restaurants sporting a much higher brow and a more prosperous postcode. Pleasingly, it also remembers its roots and still knows how to do a decent shepherd's pie.

The Marquess Tavern

British

J2

Canonbury
⊖ Highbury and Islington
32 Canonbury Street N1 2TB
Closed 25 December
✆ 020 7354 2975
e-mail info@marquesstavern.co.uk **www**.marquesstavern.co.uk

Menu £15 – Carte £22/30

This Marquess is a handsome fellow standing proudly in his cosy corner spot. The Victorian character is still there but it's all been sympathetically updated for our age. The dining room is at the far end, although the blackboard menu can be enjoyed anywhere.

The cooking is resolutely and laudably British and suits the place perfectly. Sourcing and traceability are taken seriously, with small, independent suppliers used. The cooking is satisfying and hearty, with some of the meat dishes such as lamb shoulder designed for sharing. The wine list continues the British theme by offering some bottles from Cornwall and Kent; beer and whisky are given equal billing and there's even mead and Pomona on offer. Business is booming so it's worth booking.

Cat & Mutton

Gastropub

K2

Hackney
⊖ Bethnal Green
76 Broadway Market E8 4QJ
Closed 25-26 December and 1 January
✆ 020 7254 5599
e-mail catandmutton@yahoo.co.uk **www**.catandmutton.co.uk

Menu £15 – Carte £23/30

Standing outside the Cat and Mutton you'd think nothing much has changed here over the years. The large sign, the Victorian façade and the huge windows etched with "Toby and Carrington" convey a certain tradition but, when inside, it's the one single huge space of the room which seems so striking.

Exposed brick, panelled ceiling, wood top tables and old school chairs account for the decoration, with the large windows on two sides making it all seem so open. The daily changing menu is chalked on a slate board, with snackier items at lunch and gutsier fare for the evening, with an admirable selection of wines available by the glass.

A DJ plays on Sunday evenings - information which will either attract you in or frighten you off.

The Empress of India

Gastropub

K2

Hackney

⊖ Mile End

130 Lauriston Rd, Victoria Park E9 7LH
(020) 8533 5123 **Fax** (020) 8533 4483
e-mail info@theempressofindia.com
www.theempressofindia.com

The building dates from the 1880s and has enjoyed various past incarnations as a nightclub and a floristry training school. Now a smart, open plan pub with the emphasis firmly on dining, it's brightly lit with high ceilings, mosaic flooring, red leather banquettes and eye-catching murals picturing Indian scenes.
The seasonally-evolving menu is classically based with some Mediterranean influences, and blends the robust with the more refined. The patrons use rare breeds for their meats and poultry, and these can often be temptingly seen and smelt cooking on the rotisserie. It's also open all day, with the Empress Afternoon Tea accompanied by an interesting selection of leaf teas. Kids have their own menu that they can colour in.

Au Lac

Vietnamese 

J2

Highbury

⊖ Arsenal
Dinner only

82 Highbury Park N5 2XE
(020) 7704 9187 **Fax** (020) 7704 9187

Carte £8/21

On a busy road boasting a number of dining options, several of them Vietnamese and some of questionable quality, Au Lac manages to stand out from the crowd and pull in plenty of regulars. Its draw is perhaps not in its decoration, which has a simple but curiously comforting modesty about it, but in the tangy Vietnamese cooking and the extensive choice available. The brothers who run the place are eager to please and the charming nature of the staff helps guide those unfamiliar with the zesty delicacies. Vegetarians will find many appealing dishes and there are set menus available for larger parties. Perhaps best of all, the generous pricing allows for unabashed experimentation and unselfish sharing.

Great Eastern Dining Room

South East Asian XX

K3

Hoxton

54 Great Eastern St EC2A 3QR

✆ (020) 7613 4545 **Fax** (020) 7613 4137

www.greateastern-restaurant.com

⊖ Old Street

Closed Christmas and Sunday

Carte £24/37

A/C VISA MC AE Diners

Will Ricker's flourishing group of hip restaurants came into its own here in Great Eastern Street and coincided with Hoxton's own emergence onto the fashion radar.

The format here is similar to the others in the group: the bar, given equal billing as the restaurant, occupies most of the front section and it's usually so packed a sardine would think twice. The noise spills into the restaurant, adding a lively vibe to the place. It's all great fun. The kitchen's influences spill across South East Asia, with dim sum, curries, roasts and tempura all carefully prepared. Helpfully, the reverse of the menu carries a glossary of Asian culinary terms. The serving team are a sassy and well-informed bunch.

Bacchus

Innovative XX

K2

Hoxton

177 Hoxton St N1 6PJ

✆ (020) 7613 0477 **Fax** (020) 7100 1704

e-mail bookings@bacchus-restaurant.co.uk

www.bacchus-restaurant.co.uk

⊖ Old Street

Closed Saturday lunch and Sunday

A/C

It's an early 19C pub but that's pretty much the only traditional thing about the place. It has been buffed and bleached and turned into a restaurant for Hoxton's fashionistas. There are some retro-styled lounges upstairs and the high decimal levels suit it perfectly. But it's the menu where we witness the biggest innovation and to say it's ambitious is only half the story. There are ingredients you haven't heard of, words used like 'paint' 'bubble' and 'spray,' and some adventurous flavour combinations using influences from Portuguese to Japan. It may not always work but it's an exhilarating ride and the slow-cooked meat is a speciality. There are chosen wines by the glass to match the food; something that's sure to have pleased Dionysus.

Fifteen London

K3 **Italian**

Hoxton ⊖ Old Street
13 Westland Pl N1 7LP Closed 25 December and 1 January
(0871) 3301 515 **Fax** (020) 7251 2749
www.fifteen.net

Menu £25 (weekday lunch)/60 – Carte £38/60

A/C VISA AE

Jamie Oliver's rise to sainthood began in earnest in 2002 with 'Jamie's Kitchen', a TV programme which followed the traumas and ultimate triumphs of setting up a training kitchen and restaurant for disadvantaged youngsters. Fifteen is that established restaurant, with other branches of this most laudable charitable foundation now appearing elsewhere.

There are two dining options: the downstairs restaurant, with its open plan kitchen, where you can watch the chefs prepare dishes with Italian and Mediterranean influences using carefully sourced ingredients, and the ground floor Trattoria which offers a more relaxed and less expensive dining option. If you're undecided whether to have that third course, remember that all profits go to the foundation.

Cru

K3 **Mediterranean**

Hoxton ⊖ Old Street
2-4 Rufus St N1 6PE Closed 25-30 December and Monday
(020) 7729 5252 **Fax** (020) 7729 1070
e-mail info@cru.uk.com **www**.cru.uk.com

Carte £23

VISA AE

The flowering of a neighbourhood can often be put down to the seeds planted by pioneering local restaurants and artistic endeavours. Virtually opposite The White Cube Gallery, you'll find the restaurant Cru.

Great use has been made of the 19th century warehouse in which it is housed. At the front there's a bar and small all-day deli. The restaurant is at the back, divided by the open kitchen. The vibe is animated and the service relaxed but in control.

The Mediterranean provides the influence to the menu and the sunny colours clearly suit the place. Many of the dishes are designed for sharing. Smaller, lesser-known vineyards are a feature of the interesting wine list and many unfamiliar wines are also available by the glass.

Hoxton Apprentice

Modern European

K2

Hoxton

⊖ Old Street

Closed Monday

16 Hoxton Sq N1 6NT

(020) 7749 2828

e-mail info@hoxtonapprentice.com **www**.hoxtonapprentice.com

Carte £23/34

Despite the severe parking restrictions, Hoxton Square has become quite a dining quarter and Hoxton Apprentice stands out from others for two reasons. Firstly, it was set up by a charity, Training for Life, to give opportunities to the unemployed or homeless with all the profits going back into the charity and, secondly, the cooking is rather good.

This is not merely a restaurant for the community minded - the restaurant stands up in its own right. The apprentices work alongside pros and the kitchen uses decent, seasonal ingredients; the wine is competitively priced and the service is both conscientious and considerate.

Housed in a former Victorian school, the room retains a relaxed and easy feel, with French windows opening out onto the terrace.

Real Greek Mezedopolio

Greek

K3

Hoxton

⊖ Old Street

15 Hoxton Market N1 6HG

Closed 25-26 December, 1 January, Sunday and Bank Holidays – bookings not accepted

(020) 7739 8212

Fax (020) 7739 4910

e-mail admin@therealgreek.demon.co.uk

www.therealgreek.co.uk

Carte £10/16

What were previously two distinct neighbouring restaurants, the Real Greek and Mezedopolio, are now one, which focuses on providing a very relaxed environment, where the emphasis is on an unstructured, shared eating experience. The menu is divided between cold and hot meze, souvlaki and large plates for 'sharers', which could be fish, meat or vegetarian, and it's all very fresh and healthy. The idea is to chat, drink and order a few plates – like barrel-aged feta, flatbread, grilled kalamari or loukaniko sausage – then have a few more drinks, followed by more chat and more ordering.

It's all housed within a 1913 Christian Mission, with the large marble bar the best place to sit if you're just in for a quick bite after work.

Almeida

French XX

M1

Islington ⊖ Angel

30 Almeida St N1 1AD
✆ (020) 7354 4777 **Fax** (020) 7354 2777
e-mail sharonw@danddlondon.com
www.almeida-restaurant.co.uk

Menu £24/29

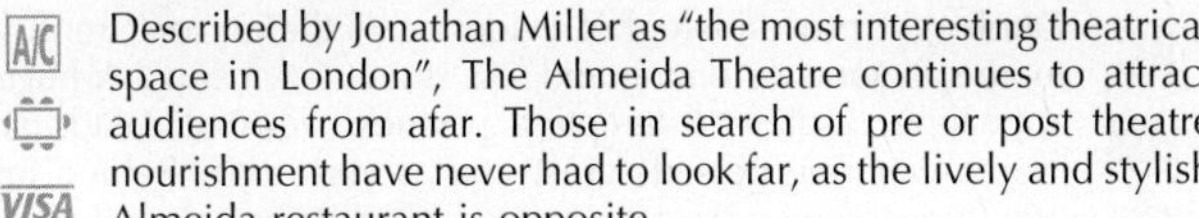

Described by Jonathan Miller as "the most interesting theatrical space in London", The Almeida Theatre continues to attract audiences from afar. Those in search of pre or post theatre nourishment have never had to look far, as the lively and stylish Almeida restaurant is opposite.

Now, thanks to the more down to earth prices of its main menu, diners flock here without so much as glancing at watches. Despite the odd detour, the best bet is to stick to the classic French dishes. The terrines, pâtés and rillettes from the trolley are a good way of kicking things off and the main courses may include rump of lamb or halibut with pomme purée. Finish as you started, with another trolley – this time filled with tarts.

Metrogusto

Italian XX

M1

Islington ⊖ Angel

13 Theberton St N1 0QY
✆ (020) 7226 9400
Fax (020) 7226 9400
www.metrogusto.co.uk

Closed 1 January, Easter, Sunday dinner and Bank Holidays – dinner only

Menu £19 (lunch) – Carte £25/31

Just looking in the window tells you that this is no ordinary Italian restaurant. One rarely sees interesting artwork in local restaurants - maybe some chefs feel threatened by the presence of someone else's creativity - but Metrogusto shows that having interesting pieces of art can, at the very least, provide diners with a conversation piece. The menu, too, shows an unwillingness to merely go with the flow and offers four courses of carefully prepared dishes, where the vitality of the ingredients is very much to the fore and where hints of originality are subtle and well judged.

The pricing structure sensibly allows those who have come for an occasion or for a simple, quick bite to do so without breaking the bank.

Ottolenghi

M1 International

Islington
287 Upper St N1 2TZ
(020) 7288 1454
Fax (020) 7704 1456
e-mail upper@ottolenghi.co.uk **www**.ottolenghi.co.uk

⊖ Highbury and Islington
Closed 25-26 December, 1 January and Sunday dinner

Menu £15 (lunch) – Carte £25/31

A/C VISA MC AE

Ottolenghi provides further evidence of the current trend for more spontaneous dining and less structured menus. A hugely appealing display of tempting pastries, unusual salads and mouth-watering desserts greet you as you enter. Behind this, one finds the restaurant, decorated as white as celestial purity, where two long communal tables dominate. Waiting staff will explain the 'concept' which involves ordering an assortment of small dishes, some of which display certain Mediterranean leanings while others may exhibit subtle Eastern spicing. The breads and puddings are particularly good.

Takeaway is a large part of the business and lunch is an altogether simpler affair, with mostly salads and quiches.

The Drapers Arms

L1 Gastropub

Islington
44 Barnsbury St N1 1ER
(020) 7619 0348 **Fax** (020) 7619 0413
e-mail info@thedrapersarms.co.uk **www**.thedrapersarms.co.uk

⊖ Highbury and Islington
Closed 24-27 December,

Carte £23/30

VISA MC AE

This battleship grey Victorian pub in an oasis of leafy residential splendour must be good, because all the access streets have speed humps. Its secret appears to be in its sincerity – it just feels like a proper pub, albeit one with decent food. Granted, there's a more formal dining room upstairs, but the same menu is served throughout so stay downstairs for the banter in the bar, decorated with assorted drapery-themed photos. Dishes are British in their frankness or Mediterranean in their inclination, so choose between chips and couscous, steak and risotto, and Eton mess and crème brûlée. The catch of the day can be three different fish, flavours are pronounced and natural, and dishes are heartening in their lack of pretension.

The Northgate

K2

Islington ⊖ Highbury and Islington
113 Southgate Rd
N1 3JS
✆ (020) 7359 7392

Closed 25-26 December, and 1 January – dinner only and lunch Saturday and Sunday

Carte £19/30

VISA

MC

The Northgate is a large, square Victorian pub located on a corner of, paradoxically, Southgate Road. It may look fairly unremarkable from the outside but it was one of the first of many Islington pubs to blossom into a gastropub. There's an honesty about the place which engenders a relaxed and welcoming vibe, even when it is full-on busy which appears to be most evenings.

The front section comes decked out with the gastropub uniform of mismatched furniture, modern art and a large central bar. There's a separate dining room at the back with a skylight and the terrace is a big draw.

From the blackboard menu come liberally sized plates of satisfying wholesome gastropub staples, like tiger prawns and lamb shank.

The Barnsbury

L1

Islington ⊖ Highbury and Islington
209-211 Liverpool Rd
N1 1LX
✆ (020) 7607 5519 **Fax** (020) 7607 3256
e-mail info@thebarnsbury.co.uk **www**.thebarnsbury.co.uk

Closed 25-26 December, 1 January

Carte £23/33

VISA

AE

It may have been spruced up a few years back but The Barnsbury is still your proper local. Hence, you'll find it on down-to-earth Liverpool Road rather than glossier Upper Street which runs parallel.

The more traditional features of restored wood panelling and a large central counter contrast with contemporary touches, such as the chandeliers made from crystal wine glasses and the regularly changing local artwork. It's all very relaxed and the young staff are helpful and competent.

The owner, an acolyte of the Conran empire, clearly knows what he is doing. The menu will satisfy the appetites of both those who like to see recognisable British ingredients, as well as those who prefer more of an Italian connection to their food.

L'Oasis

K3

Mile End

⊖ Stepney Green

237 Mile End Rd, Stepney Green E1 4AA
(020) 7702 7051
e-mail info@loasisstepney.co.uk **www**.loasisstepney.co.uk

Fully confident in his chef's abilities, the owner of the-pub-formerly-known-as-The-Three-Crowns decided that the new name L'Oasis would perfectly reflect its role in the culinary desert that is Stepney Green. Although it looks more like a bar than a modern dining pub, the inside is cavernous and bright, with original features including a delightful ornamental Victorian ceiling and decorative glazed tiles.

Upstairs, a bright yellow function room copes with any overflow, service is friendly and efficient and food delivery is prompt even when they are busy. Concise menus offer hearty, rustic cooking with influences from all over the world, and what dishes may lack in finesse, they more than make up for in flavour and size.

Rivington

British

K3

Shoreditch

⊖ Old St

28-30 Rivington St EC2A 3DZ
(020) 7729 7053
e-mail shoreditch@rivingtongrill.co.uk
www.rivingtongrill.co.uk

Closed 25-26 December 1 January and August Bank Holiday

Carte £22/51

Well judged English cooking is the draw here, using oft forgotten ingredients to make Mrs Beeton proud, such as haslet, mutton, turnips and pilchards, all prepared with today's lighter and more nimble touch.

The converted warehouse, with its well worn floorboards, paper menu-as-placemats, school chairs and playful 'neon-art' embellishments, provides the coolly contemporary backdrop for this everyman fare. It attracts all manner of customer, from business-type to local - even the odd hoodie has been known to venture over the threshold.

Serving staff all have their skates on, particularly at lunch when delivery from the kitchen is swift, but those in more of a hurry can grab something from the next door deli.

The Princess

Gastropub

K3

Shoreditch ▸ Plan XVI
76-78 Paul St EC2A 4NE
✆ (020) 7729 9270
e-mail theeaston@btconnect.com

⊖ Old Street
Closed 24 December-8 January and Saturday lunch

Carte £22/27

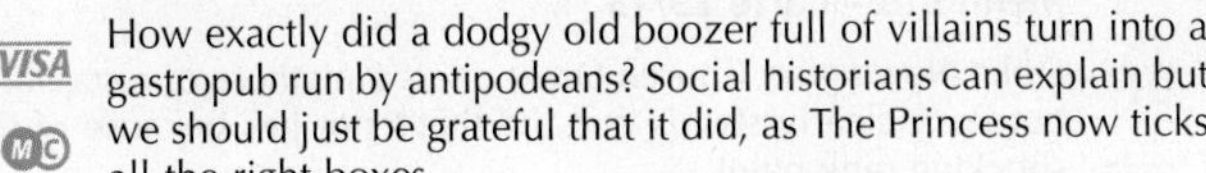

VISA MC AE

How exactly did a dodgy old boozer full of villains turn into a gastropub run by antipodeans? Social historians can explain but we should just be grateful that it did, as The Princess now ticks all the right boxes.

The downstairs remains loyal to its Victorian roots, except with better food, but ascend the spiral staircase and you'll find yourself in an unexpectedly stylish dining room. A little art deco, oil paintings, floral wallpaper, mirrors and a fireplace all set the tone. The kitchen is skilled at producing flavoursome and robust dishes of assorted influences, but with a pronounced seasonality.

The name of the place is not, sadly, in honour of East End vernacular but is a shortened version of the original, The Princess Royal.

The Fox

Gastropub

K3

Shoreditch
28 Paul St EC2A 4LB
✆ (020) 7729 5708
e-mail thefoxpublichouse@thefoxpublichouse.com
www.thefoxpublichouse.com

⊖ Old Street
Closed lunch Saturday and dinner Sunday – booking essential

Carte £23/26

VISA MC AE

Friday lunchtime and it'll be like a rugby scrum at the bar, but head upstairs for the contrasting serenity of the first floor dining room, where you'll also find a delightful roof terrace.

Four choices per course form the set menu, although there's no pressure exerted to have the full three-courser. Dish descriptions are refreshingly concise and this no-nonsense simplicity is reflected in the rustic cooking with specialities of either a British or Mediterranean persuasion.

The dining room boasts an appealingly thrown-together quality and, in between their constant sprints up and down the stairs from the kitchen, the waiting staff pitch the tone of service perfectly.

Rasa

K2 — Indian

Stoke Newington
55 Stoke Newington Church St
N16 0AR
(020) 7249 0344 **Fax** (020) 7637 0224
www.rasarestaurants.com

Closed 24-26 December, and 1 January – booking essential – dinner only

Menu £16 - Carte £9/13

A/C VISA MC AE

Stoke Newington Church Street offers a plethora of restaurants but Rasa clearly stands out and that's not just because of the shocking pink paint.

The locals are drawn here for both the satisfying cooking and the munificence of the pricing. Kerala and the south west coast of India provide the influence for the cooking which is vegetarian and full of flavour. The pickles and chutneys tell you straight off that this is somewhere different and the spicing is added with a sure hand. Specialities include deep-fried patties and dosa pancakes and Kerala's great produce such as bananas, coconut, cardamom and cashew also feature in the desserts which are well worth trying. Try getting a table in the back as it offers a little more room.

Rasa Travancore

K2 — Indian

Stoke Newington
56 Stoke Newington Church St N16 0NB
(020) 7249 1340
www.rasarestaurants.com

Closed 23-30 December – dinner only

Carte £12

A/C VISA MC AE

Virtually opposite Rasa is its sister Rasa Travancore. It also offers specialities from the Kerala region of India, but this time carnivores are catered for as it celebrates the unique cooking found within the Christian Syrian communities. Meat and fish play a large part and the menu offers a balanced selection, from steamed prawns to chicken stews and lamb curries. Despite having a basement kitchen, the dishes arrive piping hot and portions are in manageable sizes, so be sure to try some of the pre-meal snacks.

Ornamentation within the two dining rooms is relatively limited but the delightful and charming service more than compensates. Everyone involved in the restaurant hails from Kerala and they're all rightly proud of their cuisine.

The Old Dairy

Gastropub

J1

Stroud Green

Closed 25 December

1-3 Crouch Hill N4 4EP

(020) 7263 3337

Carte £19/25

Of all the new pub conversions around, there can be few as characterful as The Old Dairy. Dating from 1890, the picture panels among the original red bricks and steel girders illustrate the listed building's former use when owned by Friern Manor Dairy Company. Despite the renovation and the locale's increasing gentrification, the pub has kept itself at the heart of the community by investing as much effort in the bar – which occupies quite a space – as it has in the dining room.

The cooking is bold and honest and how nice it is that dishes arrive exactly as described. It's modern British with a hint of Europe. The crisp sourdough gets you started and the portions are well judged and confidently flavoured. Weekend brunches are a real hit.

The Lock

Mediterranean

K1

Tottenham

⊖ Tottenham Hale

Closed Monday

Heron House, Hale Wharf,
Ferry Lane N17 9NF

(020) 8885 2829 **Fax** (020) 8885 1618

e-mail thelock06@btconnect.com **www**.thelock-diningbar.com

Menu £12 - Carte £18/32

Full marks to The Lock for opening in Tottenham and doing their bit for the regeneration of this part of London. It's in the big yellow industrial looking building on your left as you approach from the west and, while the address may hint at a rather charming lock-side setting, the Norfolk Broads it ain't.

It is, though, a very sweetly run place, with two keen young owners. The room's quite spacious, with a bar and sofas on one side and the restaurant, with its mismatched tables and chairs, on the other. With much of the produce coming from Walthamstow market, the open kitchen offers up a menu of French and Italian influences, with the odd idiosyncratic twist, and several vegetarian choices.

South-East London

The rest of the world may once have relied on **Greenwich** to keep the clocks ticking, but down in the historic centre, you'd be forgiven for thinking time had stopped. Greenwich has succeeded in the miraculous trick of preserving its heritage without becoming just a museum piece. There are museums, of course, the **Royal Observatory** and the **National Maritime Museum** among them. But despite Greenwich's designation as a World Heritage Site, life carries on in the pubs and the playhouse, the tea rooms and the market, albeit at a steady pace.

Naval gazing

Visitors are well advised to maintain that relaxed speed as they scale the heights of **Greenwich Park** in the direction of neighbouring **Blackheath,** one of the most pleasant examples of London's village-suburbs. You may be tempted immediately to cross the heath towards the striking **All Saints Church** and the lovely hanging-basketed streets behind. But turn around and the view could change your mind - for beyond the picture-postcard perfection of Wren's **Naval College** you'll see the glistening towers of **Canary Wharf**, with the rest of the **Docklands** spread out like a toy town below. The scale of the project to redevelop London's derelict dockyards really hits you from this vantage point, but its success is even more overwhelming down among the glass canyons.

There was a time - until really quite recently in fact - when Londoners looked on this crystal and chrome landscape with little but suspicion, as if the CBD of a second-tier North American city had been plonked in the capital. Yes, these office buildings reaching for the sky, reflected in the water, were all very impressive. But where was the life? And where was London?

Towers of London

Today, Canary Wharf is not only an established fixture of the skyline, but also - with the Tube whisking you to **Westminster** in roughly 10 minutes - an integrated part of the city. With that, it's found the confidence to develop its own personality. There's still something of the Toronto about it, but funky quayside bars, signature bridges, subterranean shopping malls and surprising vistas of the **Gherkin** and the **Dome** all give character. Sure, the place is quieter at the weekends, when the financiers, journalists and advertisers go home - but since many now live in the plush residential developments nearby, the beat goes on.

And on we go too, to **Wapping**, which - although part of the Docklands - has been revitalised in a different way. Here, after an initial stage of demolishing warehouses and filling in docks, the decision was made to try to pursue projects that were in sympathy with the existing architecture. The result is a rather high-class Dickensian feel - appropriate enough since the great man was a regular in some of the local pubs.

Pushing the Boat Out

Still, it was **St Katherines Dock** on Wapping's edge which was the initial showpiece and proved that redevelopment could produce atmosphere where most original buildings had been destroyed. The marina might now be more St Tropez than smugglers' den, but somehow it still evokes the mastmakers, victuallers and pirates of the not too distant past.

But for dark undercurrents, you can't beat the adjacent **Whitechapel**, with its Jack the Rippers, Elephant Men and general East End edginess. Emerging from the relatively clean-cut Docklands, the gothic vibe is actually rather refreshing. What's more, the gigs here are great and the pubs nicely bohemian. Local markets such as **Spitalfields**, meanwhile, tread the line the area also walks: between lovably tatty and madly hip.

C. Eymenier / MICHELIN

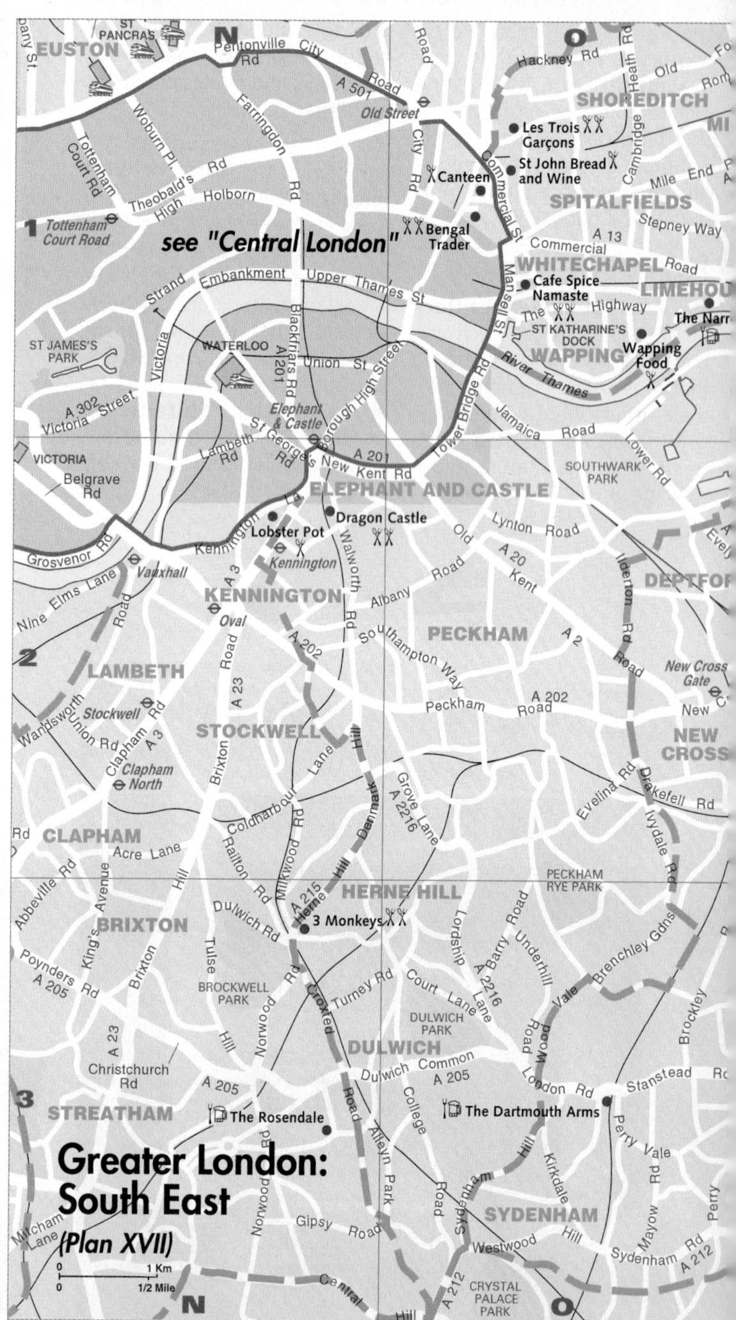
Greater London: South East
(Plan XVII)
see "Central London"
Les Trois Garçons
St John Bread and Wine
Canteen
Bengal Trader
Cafe Spice Namaste
The Narrow
Wapping Food
Lobster Pot
Dragon Castle
3 Monkeys
The Rosendale
The Dartmouth Arms
EUSTON
ST PANCRAS
SHOREDITCH
SPITALFIELDS
WHITECHAPEL
WAPPING
ST KATHARINE'S DOCK
WATERLOO
VICTORIA
ST JAMES'S PARK
SOUTHWARK PARK
ELEPHANT AND CASTLE
KENNINGTON
PECKHAM
LAMBETH
STOCKWELL
NEW CROSS
CLAPHAM
HERNE HILL
BRIXTON
PECKHAM RYE PARK
BROCKWELL PARK
DULWICH PARK
DULWICH
STREATHAM
SYDENHAM
CRYSTAL PALACE PARK
River Thames
0 1 Km
0 1/2 Mile

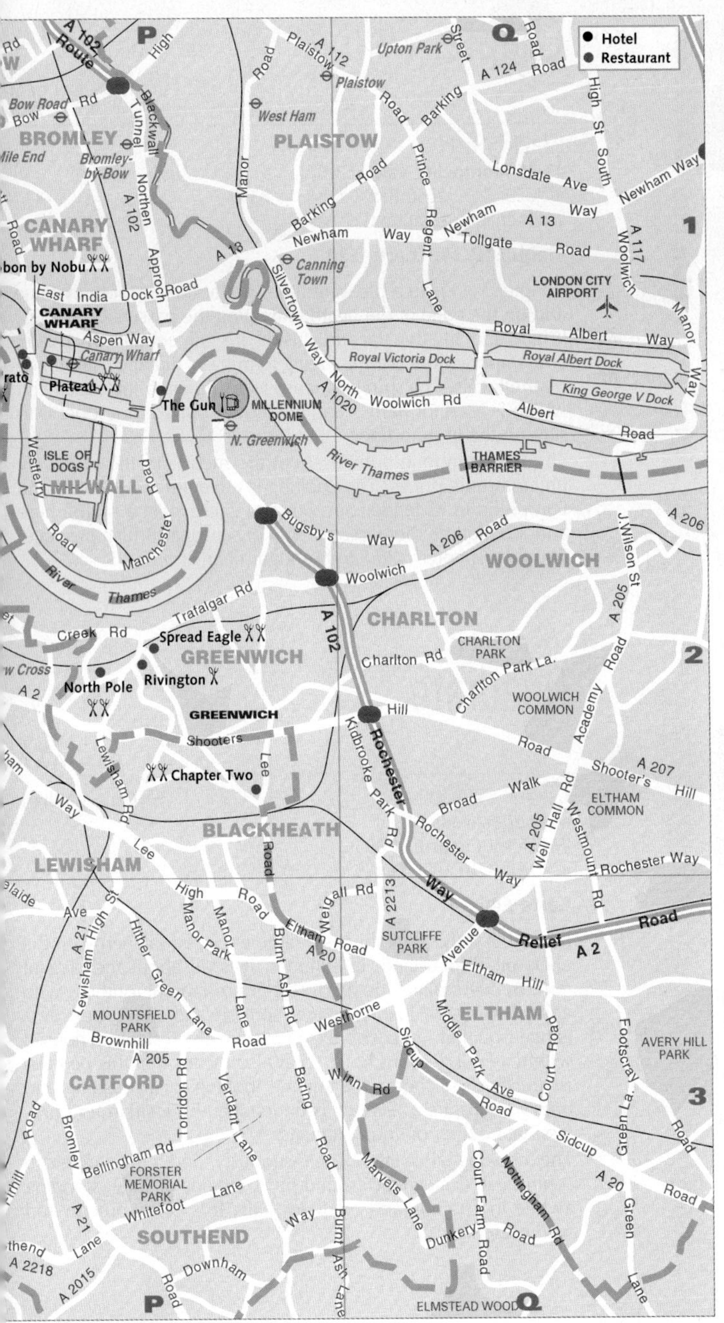
Hotel
Restaurant
BROMLEY
CANARY WHARF
PLAISTOW
WOOLWICH
CHARLTON
GREENWICH
BLACKHEATH
LEWISHAM
ELTHAM
CATFORD
SOUTHEND
LONDON CITY AIRPORT
Royal Victoria Dock
Royal Albert Dock
King George V Dock
MILLENNIUM DOME
THAMES BARRIER
ISLE OF DOGS
MILWALL
River Thames
bon by Nobu
Plateau
The Gun
Spread Eagle
North Pole
Rivington
Chapter Two
CHARLTON PARK
WOOLWICH COMMON
ELTHAM COMMON
SUTCLIFFE PARK
MOUNTSFIELD PARK
FORSTER MEMORIAL PARK
AVERY HILL PARK
ELMSTEAD WOOD
1
2
3
P
Q

Chapter Two

P2 — Modern European XX

Blackheath

43-45 Montpelier Vale SE3 0TJ
(020) 8333 2666 **Fax** (020) 8355 8399
www.chapterrestaurants.co.uk

Menu £19/24 – Carte £24

A/C VISA MC AE

Chapter Two is in a pleasant little spot at the top of the village and on the edge of the heath, attracting the passers-by with its bright and inviting façade. Inside it's all equally vivid and contemporary but without being terminally hip and frightening off the locals. The spiral staircase leads down to the basement, which is used for parties and overflows, but your best bet is to stay on the ground floor.

The first thing one notices about the menu are the positively philanthropic prices. The cooking is adventurous, spirited and Europhilic in its tendencies. So, you can expect a ravioli here and a ballottine there, plus plenty of seasonal British produce. The first Chapter is in Farnborough, near Bromley.

Quadrato

P1 — Italian XXX

Canary Wharf

⊖ Canary Wharf

at Four Seasons H.,
Westferry Circus E14 8RS
(020) 7510 1999 **Fax** (020) 7510 1998

Carte £46/54

A/C VISA MC AE

Instead of a fish tank there's a large enclosed kitchen with the chefs on display and, in summer, it is all about the elegant terrace, overlooking the river. This is a restaurant for those who enjoy feelings of luxury, space, comfort and general extravagance – qualities one would expect from any restaurant housed within a Four Seasons hotel. That also means that this perhaps is not the first choice for anyone looking for a bustling and buzzy atmosphere. Service is undertaken by a smart and professional bunch of young Italians.

The cooking also takes itself seriously and offers diners a sophisticated meander around most regions of Italy, stopping awhile in Tuscany and Northern Italy. It is clear, precise and well presented.

Ubon by Nobu

Japanese XX

P1

Canary Wharf
34 Westferry Circus E14 8RR
(020) 7719 7800
Fax (020) 7719 7801
e-mail ubon@noburestaurants.com **www**.noburestaurants.com

⊖ Canary Wharf
Closed Saturday lunch, Sunday and Bank Holidays – booking essential

Carte £38/54

The Mayfair Nobu's may be hard to get into but at least they're easy to find. Ubon, more of a cousin than a sister branch, doesn't share the cachet but its challenging location, in a high rise in Canary Wharf, does ensure that diners feel a similar sense of pride in actually getting in. Then, when you leave, you find yourself facing a Holmes Place fitness centre and feeling guilty about all that tempura you've just had.

The menu is not that different: the same Japanese favourites like rock shrimp tempura and plenty of sushi plus other more robust dishes to satisfy the greater appetites of your average business exec. The pace is frenetic and noise levels high. Look out for the terrific views, day or night, as well as the 15% service charge.

A/C VISA MC AE

Plateau

Modern European XX

P1

Canary Wharf
(4th floor) Canada Place, Canada Square E14 5ER
(020) 7715 7100 **Fax** (020) 7715 7110

⊖ Canary Wharf
Closed 25-26 December, 1 January and Sunday dinner

Carte £30/47

London's own Masters of the Universe gather here at Plateau, the closest thing London has to the Manhattan skyline. It's certainly an impressive open-plan space and the dramatic glass walls and ceilings make the surrounding monolithic office blocks look strangely appealing. The striking 1970s retro design also seems to fit perfectly.

There are two choices: the Grill where, as the name suggests, the choice is from rotisserie meats and classic grilled dishes, or the more formal restaurant beyond with its more comfortable surroundings. Here, the range is more eclectic and dishes are constructed with more global influences. They also come in ample sizes, though, so ignore the enthusiastic selling of the side dishes.

A/C VISA MC AE

The Gun

P1 — Gastropub

Canary Wharf — ⊖ Blackwall (DLR)
27 Coldharbour E14 9NS — Closed 25 December
(020) 7515 5222
e-mail info@thegundocklands.com **www**.thegundocklands.com

Carte £27/32

The Gun is glorious proof that not everything in this part of London is big, new and shiny. Dating back to the 18th century, the pub's history is entwined with that of the surrounding docks and it was here where Lord Nelson conducted his trysts with Lady Emma Hamilton.

Today, painstakingly restored after a fire, The Gun has been brought up to date, but without compromising its colourful heritage. The charming decked terrace looks over the Dome while the interior is warm and inviting, with separate areas for drinkers and eaters. With specials on the blackboard and much of the fish from Billingsgate, the cooking is contemporary in style and exact in execution. The only thing missing is a room full of dockers and smugglers.

VISA MC AE

Dragon Castle

N2 — Chinese XX

Elephant and Castle — ⊖ Elephant and Castle
114 Walworth Rd SE17 1JL
(020) 7277 3388
e-mail dragoncastle@hotmail.com **www**.dragoncastle.co.uk

Carte £15/30

Those unused to searching for restaurants around the Elephant and Castle should look out for a large blue building and a red studded door. The Dragon Castle is a huge and decoratively understated Chinese restaurant that may well represent the first phase of the area's planned rebirth. The staff are all enthusiastic, obliging and seemingly impervious to their unflattering uniforms.

The cooking is Cantonese and, if you're a little more adventurous and want something different from the usual crowd pleasers, then go for what the Chinese clientele are having. This way you'll find yourself with very generously sized plates of authentic and enticing specialities, such as eel or hotpots of pork. The daytime dim sum is proving very popular.

A/C VISA MC AE

The Dartmouth Arms

O3 Gastropub

Forest Hill — Closed 25-26 December, 1 January

7 Dartmouth Road SE23 3HN
✆ (020) 8488 3117 **Fax** (020) 7771 7230
e-mail info@thedartmoutharms.com
www.thedartmoutharms.com

Menu £18 - Carte £21/28

The Dartmouth Arms' position opposite Forest Hill train station meant that this was once the sort of pub whose main selling point was as somewhere to dive into for a swift one on the way home. Since its makeover in 2004 it is now the sort of place in which to spend the evening. The couple running the show know what their customers want and the menu offers an appealing mix of dishes. Many have more of a restaurant pedigree than your average pub grub, but there's commendable Britishness in evidence here, as well as a healthy regard for seasonality. So expect to see Barnsley chops, asparagus, samphire and Jersey Royals at certain times of the year. There's also some invention so you'll find the black pudding in a risotto and crab beignets with chilli jam.

VISA · MC · AE

North Pole

P2 Modern European

Greenwich — ⊖ New Cross — Dinner only

131 Greenwich High Rd SE10 8JA
✆ (020) 8853 3020 **Fax** (020) 8853 3501
e-mail north-pole@btconnect.com
www.northpolegreenwich.com

Menu £20 - Carte £25/34

North Pole sits on the summit of a converted pub, above a hip bar, but has its own street entrance for those not wishing to expose their corduroy to the fashion police downstairs.

It's divided into two rooms and has a cosy feel and a twinkly warmth to it. There's a fireplace in the smaller of the two rooms, while those in the larger, airier room have the benefit of a nightly playing pianist to accompany their dinner and add to the general bonhomie. The tables are all neatly laid, the candlelight supplies extra intimacy and the service is well organised. The cooking is modern with a fairly classical base to it. Dishes come with unfussy and straightforward presentation, allowing the quality of the ingredients to come to the fore.

VISA · MC · AE

Spread Eagle

P2 French XX

Greenwich
1-2 Stockwell St SE10 9JN
(020) 8853 2333 **Fax** (020) 8293 1024
www.spreadeaglerestaurant.com

New Cross
Closed 1 January

Menu £20/31 s

Forming part of a 17th century coaching inn, the Spread Eagle in its current incarnation has been part of the Greenwich dining scene since 1966 and, in that time, has remained proudly impervious to changing design and decorative tastes.

There are a number of different sitting areas, the best being the two semi-private booths on the ground floor, but the more able-bodied should try upstairs, via the original spiral staircase. On a winter's night the place really comes into its own with its log fire, panelling, antiques and dim lighting all adding to the well-mannered atmosphere.

The kitchen attempts a modern interpretation of rustic French cooking and offers tasting menus, one of which is a vegetarian, accompanied by chosen wines.

Rivington

P2 British X

Greenwich
178 Greenwich High Rd SE10 8NN
(020) 8293 9270
e-mail office@rivingtongrill.co.uk **www**.rivingtongrill.co.uk

New Cross
Closed 25-26 December and 1 January, Monday, lunch Tuesday and Wednesday

Carte £21/38

Perhaps all independent cinemas should have an adjacent restaurant so that the Pavlovian effect of watching 'Babette's Feast' or 'Big Night' (but perhaps not 'Life is Sweet') can be satisfied by nipping next door after the credits. Rivington, sister to the original Shoreditch branch, takes this further by offering cinema-goers an extra 10% discount.

The menu features classic British dishes using classic British ingredients but executed in more contemporary style. Meanwhile, the dining room, with a galleried level overlooking the bar, sets the right tone with its hassle-free atmosphere.

Service is switched on and the place is open early for appealing breakfasts and also offers a set lunch menu at a compassionate price.

3 Monkeys

Indian XX

N3

Herne Hill

Closed 25 December

136-140 Herne Hill SE24 9QH
(020) 7738 5500 **Fax** (020) 7738 5505
e-mail info@3monkeysrestaurant.com
www.3monkeysrestaurant.com

Menu £8/13 s – Carte £22/29 s

There's seating for about 140 in this Indian restaurant set on a busy main road, but gallons of white emulsion does little to create any personality and the atmosphere is usually generated by the larger tables. There is an unusual entrance, where one walks over a bridge with the bar below, but this is undoubtedly one of those restaurants where it's all about the food.

The menu leaves behind the usual old suspects and opts instead for more interesting offerings, while still respecting classic flavours and combinations. The selection of tandoor or char-grilled kebabs is worth trying and there's plenty on offer for vegetarians. Portions are generous and there's a lightness of touch to the preparation. Locals can take advantage of the take-away service.

Lobster Pot

French X

N2

Kennington

⊖ Kennington
Closed Sunday, Monday and Saturday Lunch

3 Kennington Lane SE11 4RG
(020) 7582 5556
www.lobsterpotrestaurant.co.uk

Menu £22/40 – Carte £26/45

Kennington Lane may not necessarily evoke scenes of seafaring adventure and fishermen's catches - and there is certainly little in the way of salty sea air around the Elephant and Castle - but come to the Lobster Pot and you'll be instantly transported to a Breton fishing village, complete with the sound of seagulls. Portholes, fishing nets, shells and aquariums complete a scene so nautical you'll need to find your sea legs before ordering.

There is, however, much more to this place that its highly eccentric but undeniably endearing décor. The husband and wife team know what they're doing and serve authentic and expertly timed French accented seafood, supplemented by the daily specials depending on the day's catch.

The Narrow

01 **British**

Limehouse ⊖ Limehouse (DLR)
Narrow Street E14 8DP Booking essential
(020) 7592 7950 **Fax** (020) 7592 1603
e-mail thenarrow@gordonramsay.com **www**.gordonramsay.com

Carte £17/26

Gordon Ramsay's world domination (or, at the very least, London domination) continues with his first foray into the world of the gastropub and it appears he's cracked it already. For a start, he's found a handsome pub in a grand spot – a Grade II listed former dockmaster's house on the river. But the real skill and experience is there to see on the menu; expect British classics alongside dishes that will stir childhood memories for many. You'll find potted crabs, sardines on toast, salt beef, monkfish and chips and proper puddings, not fancy desserts. As you would expect, the kitchen knows what it's doing and what's more, the prices are competitive, although too many of the tempting but individually priced side dishes can push up the final bill.

Bengal Trader

01 **Indian**

Spitalfields ▶ Plan XVII ⊖ Liverpool Street
44 Artillery Lane E1 7NA Closed Sunday
(020) 7375 0072 **Fax** (020) 7247 1002
e-mail mail@bengalclipper.co.uk **www**.bengalclipper.co.uk

Carte £16/21

The renewal of this part of town continues apace, but you'll find the Bengal Trader down a little lane that's positively Dickensian in its character.

Sister restaurant to the Bengal Clipper in Butler's Wharf, the Trader comes divided into two, with ten tables on the ground floor but the main event is the cavernous downstairs area, where larger parties are entertained.

The place may be lacking a little in personality but regulars seem to appreciate the consistency of the cooking and the earnest service. The menu journeys across India, from Goa to the Bay of Bengal and those who never like to stray too far from more traditional Anglo-Indian dishes will also find many recognisable favourites, to which the kitchen has added its own touches.

Les Trois Garcons

French XX

01

Spitalfields ▶ Plan XVII ⊖ Shoreditch

1 Club Row E1 6JX

Closed 23 December-8 January, Sunday, and Bank Holidays – dinner only

(020) 7631 1924

Fax (020) 7613 1924

e-mail info@lestroisgarcons.com **www**.lestroisgarcons.com

Menu £29 - Carte £36/51

The decoration is so gloriously theatrical and eccentric, you can't fail to feel just a little bit better about life. The three friends who own the place have antique shops and the room is practically bursting with everything from stuffed and mounted animals to elaborate chandeliers and beads - even a display of evening handbags hang from the gold coloured ceiling. Despite being a converted pub, it also has something of the French brasserie about it, with waiters kitted out in the traditional style. The cooking is not as unconventional as the menu suggests and there is clear ability in the kitchen but at prices which are certainly high for the area so there should be. There is, though, a less expensive set menu on offer early in the week.

Canteen

01

Spitalfields ▶ Plan XVII ⊖ Liverpool Street

2 Crispin Pl E1 6DW

Closed 25 December

(0845) 6861 122

e-mail info@canteen.co.uk **www**.canteen.co.uk

Carte £17/29

This glass enclosed modern cube, juxtaposed next to the old Spitalfield market, has come up with a terrific idea which, like all great concepts, leaves you wondering why no one else thought of it before. The clue's in the name.

It has adopted the all-day menu and shared refectory table look but then serves well priced, decidedly British food. So, whether it's a morning bacon sarnie, a lunchtime pie or an evening stew, there's something for everyone and every appetite. The daily roasts and fish are favourites but all flavours are natural and all produce conscientiously sourced.

If you're a team of four you may snag one of the outer tables with cushioned seats. Otherwise, just hunker down with your fellow man and rediscover some classics.

St John Bread and Wine

01 British

Spitalfields ▶ **Plan XVII**
94-96 Commercial St E1 6LZ
(020) 7251 0848
Fax (020) 7247 8924
e-mail reservations@stjohnbreadandwine.com
www.stjohnbreadandwine.com

⊖ Shoreditch
Closed Christmas-New Year and Bank Holidays

Carte £22/26

A/C VISA MC AE

Son of the Smithfield St John but with more of a local feel. It's in a perfect position for this type of restaurant, with Spitalfields opposite. As the name implies, bread and French wines are a large part of the business, the latter with excellent take-home prices but there's also a 50 seater casual restaurant where the menu is changed twice daily. It's also centred around time: 9am for breakfast and bacon sandwiches, 11am for cakes and, come midday, an array of English classics with blackboard specials. It's best to share and order a selection, from smoked sprats and sand eels to grilled plaice or smoked Old Spot. Arrive around 7pm for the roast just out of the oven and, for dessert, try some warm Madeleines or British cheeses.

Wapping Food

01 Modern European

Wapping
Wapping Wall E1W 3ST
(020) 7680 2080
www.thewappingproject.com

⊖ Wapping
Closed 23 December-3 January, Sunday dinner and Bank Holidays

Carte £27/32

VISA MC AE

Tate Modern isn't the only former industrial edifice put to good use. The Wapping Project also opened in 2000 and is an art and restaurant complex housed within an 1890's hydraulic power station.
The vast industrial space looks remarkably unchanged, from the rough brick walls to the pumps and machinery. There are exhibitions, an outside cinema, assorted performances and this most unique of restaurants. If you want to see all the action, ask for a table on the 'plinth'. As expected, the cooking has its own vitality and comes with a mostly European feel, with the odd Asian accent. In deference to the owner's homeland, the wine list is exclusively Australian.
For those after something a little different, Wapping Food certainly fits the bill.

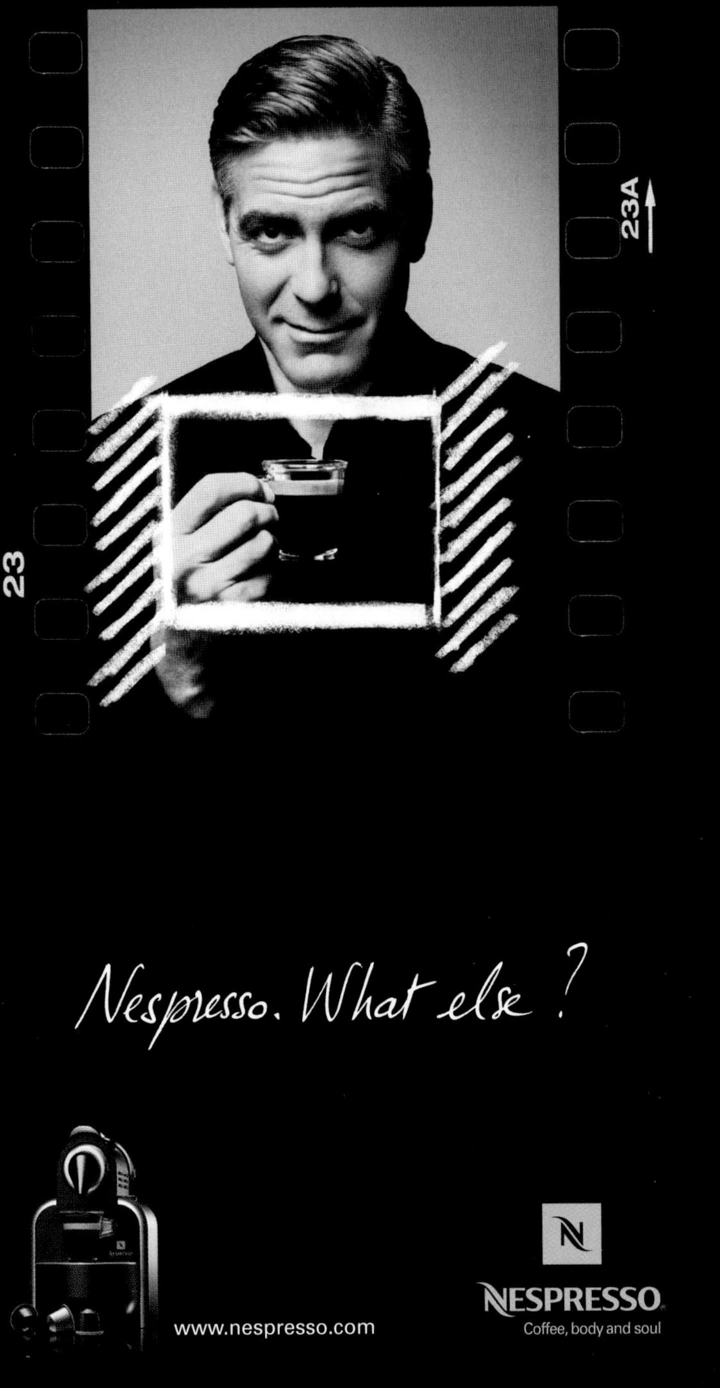
23A
23
Nespresso. What else ?
www.nespresso.com
NESPRESSO
Coffee, body and soul

The Rosendale

Gastropub

N3

West Dulwich

65 Rosendale Rd SE21 8EZ
(020) 8670 0812
e-mail dine@therosendale.co.uk
www.therosendale.co.uk

Carte £26/45

Included among the many things that stand out about The Rosendale are that they make their own butter as well as their own bread and have a wine list that is remarkable in its breadth, depth and affordability. This vast former coaching inn dates from the 1820s and has a soaring ceiling and plenty of original features. There are two menus - the front bar has a grill menu, with more of your typical pub food. Go through to the dining room at the back and the menu there is of a more ambitious nature. It can appear even more complicated on the plate but there is no denying the quality of the ingredients and sourcing is clearly taken seriously. Fish is delivered daily from Cornwall; they hang their own meat and smoke their own fish.

Cafe Spice Namaste

Indian

O1

Whitechapel ▶ **Plan XVII** — Tower Hill

16 Prescot St E1 8AZ — Closed Christmas-New Year, Saturday lunch, Sunday and Bank Holidays
(020) 7488 9242
Fax (020) 7481 0508
e-mail info@cafespice.co.uk **www**.cafespice.co.uk

Menu £30 - Carte £24/32

This red bricked Victorian building was once a magistrate's court. That information hardly prepares you for the sheer vivaciousness of the interior. Cyrus Todiwala's vibrant and ebullient restaurant has been going strong now for over a decade, having been at the vanguard of the new wave of Indian restaurants.

It comes divided into two large, high-ceilinged rooms separated by the bar. If there is a colour that hasn't been used in the fabrics or on the walls it's because it hasn't yet been created. Don't be surprised to see game and other classic British ingredients on the menu - the cooking here has moments of real innovation. All dishes come fragrantly spiced and nicely balanced, but look out for the Parsee specialities.

South-West London

South West London is perhaps best defined by the Thames, which coils through the districts and former villages that make up the outer reaches of the metropolis. However, although the river is central to SW – from sleepy pubs dappled with shifting light to the cries of birds and the hum of insects at the London Wetland Centre in Barnes – it's not the only thing the area has to offer.

If you're of a sporting bent you can catch national and international rugby union matches at **Twickenham**, while football-mad **Fulham** is home to Premiership rivals Fulham FC and Chelsea FC. The University Boat Race takes place on the river in spring, starting at **Putney Bridge** and ending up at **Mortlake**: spectators line the banks to cheer on the light and dark blues. As summer ripens, sports fans head down to **Wimbledon** for strawberries and cream, and world-class tennis.

Lavender Mill Mob

For those who prefer their entertainment to come with a little less physical exertion, SW is equally rich in television and film associations. **Ealing** not only gave its name to the film comedies, most of which are set in the area, but the studios have played a part in the making of films from *Star Wars* to *The Importance of Being Earnest*. BBC Television Centre is a stone's throw away from **Hammersmith** and a great place for a free evening's entertainment: check out the website for the chance to be part of a studio audience. Down the road **Earl's Court Olympia** not only holds exhibitions such as the Ideal Home Show, it's also one of London's top concert venues. **Battersea Arts Centre** already offers an eclectic programme of theatre and music, however, it could soon be joined by a local rival: Sir Giles Gilbert Scott's **Battersea Power Station** is being redeveloped as a residential and creative hub.

Having a Field Day

For the obligatory London green spaces and historical ambience, head down to the magnificent botanic gardens at **Kew** and the deer park at **Richmond**. If this leaves you feeling a little out of the loop then check out **King Henry VIII Mound**, where a specially protected sight line offers a clear view all the way to **St Paul's Cathedral**. However, tranquil appearances can be deceptive: **Bushy Park** in **Teddington** may seem serene, but it was General Eisnehower's base when he planned the D-day invasion in 1944. All in all SW has seen its fair share of less happy times – from the all too real bombings of the blitz to the Martian destruction of **Sheen**, chillingly imagined by HG Wells in *The War of the Worlds*.

Sound of the suburbs

Today SW is particularly popular as a home for City workers and the influx of money has resulted in a roaring night life in **Clapham** and **Tooting**, with pubs, bars and restaurants lining the streets: although there's plenty to choose from it can be difficult to find a seat on a weekend night. Alternatively head over to **Chiswick**, where discerning residents throng to the smorgasbord of dedicated foodie shops. **Wandsworth** has long been a fan of letting the good times roll: it's home to Young's Brewery where beer has been brewed on the same site since the 16C. Neighbouring Smithfields has a more sober history: an abstinence law prevented pubs from being built in the so-called grid until it was repealed in the 1990s. Perhaps it's only fitting that SW's mixture of creative talent and suburban surrounds has resulted in some genuine rock'n'roll legends: Pete Townshend was born and bred in **Acton**; John Lydon, formerly Jonny Rotten, comes from Fulham; while the ill-fated Marc Bolan was born in **Putney** and met his untimely end in Barnes.

D. Chapuis / MICHELIN

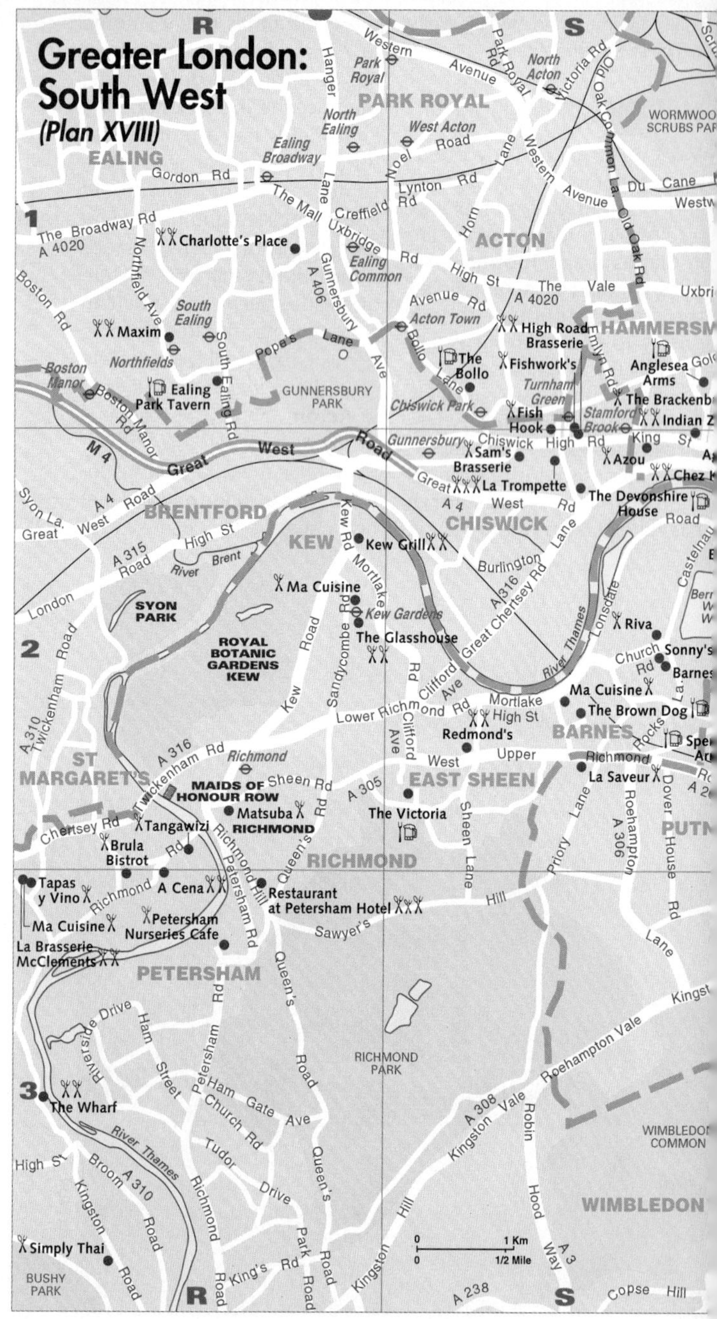
Greater London: South West
(Plan XVIII)
Charlotte's Place
Maxim
Ealing Park Tavern
The Bollo
High Road Brasserie
Fishwork's
Fish Hook
Anglesea Arms
The Brackenbury
Indian Zing
Sam's Brasserie
Azou
La Trompette
Chez Kristof
The Devonshire House
Kew Grill
Ma Cuisine
The Glasshouse
Riva
Sonny's
Ma Cuisine
The Brown Dog
Redmond's
La Saveur
Matsuba
Tangawizi
Brula Bistrot
The Victoria
Tapas y Vino
A Cena
Restaurant at Petersham Hotel
Ma Cuisine
Petersham Nurseries Cafe
La Brasserie McClements
The Wharf
Simply Thai
EALING
PARK ROYAL
ACTON
BRENTFORD
KEW
CHISWICK
BARNES
EAST SHEEN
RICHMOND
PETERSHAM
ST MARGARET'S
WIMBLEDON
GUNNERSBURY PARK
SYON PARK
ROYAL BOTANIC GARDENS KEW
MAIDS OF HONOUR ROW
RICHMOND PARK
WIMBLEDON COMMON
BUSHY PARK
River Thames
0 1 Km
0 1/2 Mile

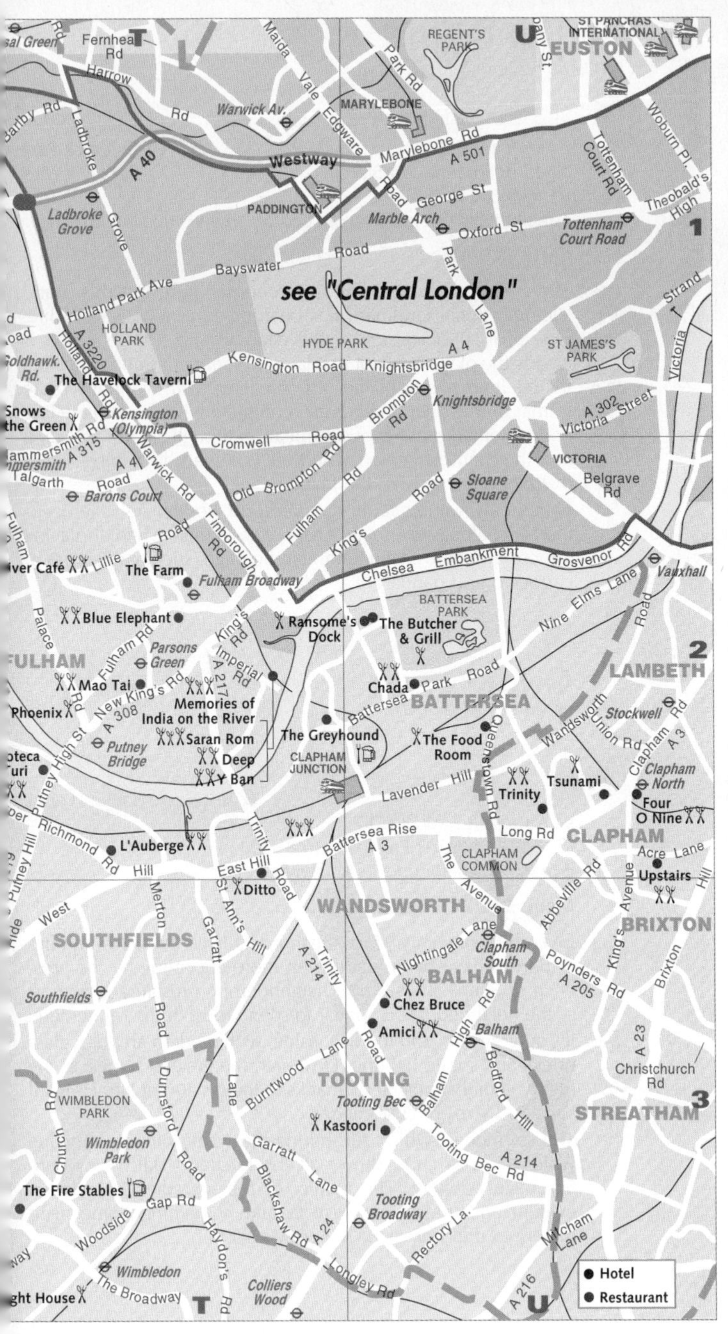
see "Central London"
REGENT'S PARK
EUSTON
ST PANCRAS INTERNATIONAL
MARYLEBONE
PADDINGTON
Westway
Marylebone Rd
A 501
George St
Marble Arch
Oxford St
Tottenham Court Road
Tottenham Court Rd
Woburn Pl.
Theobald's
High
Bayswater Road
Park Lane
HYDE PARK
HOLLAND PARK
Holland Park Ave
Ladbroke Grove
Warwick Av.
Kensington Road
Knightsbridge
A 4
ST JAMES'S PARK
Strand
Victoria
Brompton Rd
Cromwell Road
A 302
Victoria Street
VICTORIA
Belgrave Rd
Sloane Square
Old Brompton Rd
Fulham Rd
King's Road
Chelsea Embankment
Grosvenor Rd
Vauxhall
The Havelock Tavern
Kensington (Olympia)
Snows the Green
Hammersmith Rd
A 315
Talgarth Road
Barons Court
Warwick Rd
Finborough Rd
Lillie Road
River Café
The Farm
Fulham Broadway
Blue Elephant
Parsons Green
Ransome's Dock
The Butcher & Grill
BATTERSEA PARK
Nine Elms Lane
LAMBETH
FULHAM
Mao Tai
Imperial Rd
A 217
New King's Rd
A 308
Memories of India on the River
Saran Rom
Deep
Ban
Phoenix
Putney Bridge
Chada
Park Road
BATTERSEA
Battersea
The Greyhound
CLAPHAM JUNCTION
The Food Room
Queenstown Rd
Wandsworth
Union Rd
Stockwell
Clapham Rd
A 3
Clapham North
Tsunami
Trinity
Four O Nine
Lavender Hill
Long Rd
CLAPHAM
Richmond Rd
L'Auberge
Battersea Rise
A 3
East Hill
Ditto
Trinity Road
CLAPHAM COMMON
The Avenue
Acre Lane
Upstairs
Abbeville Rd
King's Avenue
BRIXTON
WANDSWORTH
SOUTHFIELDS
Merton Road
Garratt
St Ann's Hill
A 214
Nightingale Lane
Clapham South
BALHAM
Poynders Rd
A 205
Brixton
Southfields
Chez Bruce
Amici
Balham
Balham High Rd
Bedford Hill
A 23
Christchurch Rd
TOOTING
Burntwood Lane
Tooting Bec
Kastoori
STREATHAM
WIMBLEDON PARK
Wimbledon Park
Church Rd
Durnsford Road
Lane
Garratt Lane
Blackshaw Rd
A 24
Tooting Bec Rd
A 214
The Fire Stables
Gap Rd
Woodside
Tooting Broadway
Rectory La.
Mitcham Lane
A 216
Wimbledon
The Broadway
Haydon's Rd
Colliers Wood
Longley Rd
Light House
Hotel
Restaurant
1
2
3

The Bollo

Gastropub

S1

Acton Green
13-15 Bollo Lane W4 5LR
(020) 8994 6037
e-mail thebollohousel@btconnect.com **www**.thebollohouse.co.uk

⊖ Chiswick Park
Closed 25 December

Carte £20/45

The Bollo is a large, handsome corner pub and this grand Victorian local landmark has been given a new lease of life. One of its best features is the wrap-around terrace which is clearly the place to be for that languid summer's Sunday. Inside, it's retained plenty of the old character, with a slightly more formal dining area at the back, complete with wood panelling and a domed glass roof. Hospitality, though, is the key here and the menu is served wherever you want it, adding to the overall conviviality of the place.

That menu features fairly standard pub workhorses, like deep-fried brie, alongside others of a more gastro nature and displaying a more ambitious Mediterranean heritage, such as sea bass al cartoccio and panna cotta.

Sonny's

Modern European

S2

Barnes
94 Church Rd SW13 0DQ
(020) 8748 0393 **Fax** (020) 8748 2698
e-mail manager@sonnys.co.uk **www**.sonnys.co.uk

Closed Sunday dinner and Bank Holidays

Menu £16/22 – Carte £23/32

Over the last twenty years, the thoroughly genteel surroundings of Barnes have been made even more appealing by the presence of Sonny's. It's a true neighbourhood restaurant as most of the neighbourhood appear to spend most of their time here. It's all very light and modish inside, with modern artwork, glass bricks and subtle lighting. However, the greatest appeal is the highly genial atmosphere, thanks to the restaurant attracting all sorts and sizes of customer.

The set menus, which run during the week, offer great value while the à la carte shows off the kitchen's skill in modern European cooking. The quality of the ingredients is clearly evident and those who wish to take something home need merely to pop next door to Sonny's shop.

Riva

S2

Italian

Barnes
169 Church Rd SW13 9HR
(020) 8748 0434
Fax (020) 8748 0434

Closed last 2 weeks August, 24 December-4 January, Saturday lunch and Bank Holidays

Carte £30/42

Apparently the menus outside keep getting stolen but, as this is Barnes, it probably just means the local villains are after some new recipes. What they will find themselves with is a collection of rustic, satisfying and comforting Italian dishes, with a nod towards more northerly parts and plenty of pasta. What they will miss is the highly personable owner within, describing the half dozen daily specials which are usually the popular choice. Few proprietors exert as much influence on their establishments as Andrea Riva and his charm and personality ensure that the place is so full of regulars that you feel you've gate-crashed a private party. Many will let him choose the wine or sometimes even the whole meal.

Barnes Grill

S2

Barnes
2-3 Rocks Lane SW13 0DB
(020) 8878 4488
www.awtonline.co.uk

Closed Monday lunch – booking essential

Carte £22/45

There are a number of rather affluent suburbs around the edges of London wholly devoid of decent restaurants. Barnes is not one of them because here the locals have always been very supportive of any local endeavours and it only takes one good restaurant to succeed for others to follow.

Barnes Grill is a relative new boy but comes with an established format which was developed in Notting Hill and Kew and comes courtesy of Antony Worrall Thompson, TV chef and champion restaurant-opener.

That format is relatively simple: bright and casual surroundings with a few eye-catching decorative touches and a generally relaxed atmosphere coupled with an appealing menu of classic British dishes, with the emphasis on well hung steaks.

Ma Cuisine

S2 French

Barnes

7 White Hart Lane SW13 0PX

(020) 8878 4092

www.macuisinegroup.co.uk

Menu £16 (lunch) – Carte £21/27

VISA MC

John McClements appears to have hit on a winning formula with his little group of Ma Cuisine restaurants. That formula involves warm and welcoming service and earthy and satisfying French bourgeois classics like coq au vin, cassoulet and pig's trotter, with plenty of wine available by the large glass. Added to the mix is affordability; prices are positively philanthropic when one considers the quality of ingredients and for this it certainly helps that the owner also has his own fishmongers. It's a long narrow room, split into two, with a bit of gingham here and some tiling there to add some more Gallic flavour. This is one of those places we'd all want at the end of our street, for casual local dining.

The Brown Dog

S2 Gastropub

Barnes

Closed Sunday dinner

28 Cross St SW13 0AP

(020) 8392 2200

VISA MC AE

Tucked away down a veritable labyrinth of residential streets, you may feel you need a ball of string to help find your way back from The Brown Dog but the locals can count themselves lucky. The décor is charming - cast iron fireplaces and antique furniture, eclectic artwork, and space age lamps. Set around a horseshoe bar, seating is split into snug lounge and separate dining area.

The daily-changing, seasonal menu mixes traditional with modern to produce moreish dishes like winter fish stew, lamb shank with root veg or cauliflower soup with truffle oil. Why the *Brown* Dog? Well, when a Geordie claims, "I'm taking the dog for a walk," what he really means is, "I'm off down the pub for a bottle of Newcastle Brown Ale." So now you know.

The Bridge

Gastropub

S2

Barnes

Closed 25 December

204 Castelnau SW13 9DW
(020) 8563 9811

Carte £25/40

A short stroll from Hammersmith (and not Barnes) Bridge will bring you to the Bridge at Barnes. Got that? However you arrive, you'll find an attractively refitted Victorian pub where the front bar is a real delight and offers semi-private booth seating. Go through the second bar to reach the neatly laid dining room which opens out onto the decked terrace.

The menu is all encompassing and global in its influences. There are plenty of salads, both big and small, which is something you don't often see in a pub and there are also dishes such as plates of charcuterie which are designed for sharing – an activity that should be positively encouraged in all pubs. There's a weekend brunch and a good value menu for those who like to dine early evening.

A/C VISA MC AE

Chada

Thai

U2

Battersea

Closed Sunday and Bank Holidays – dinner only

208-210 Battersea Park Rd SW11 4ND
(020) 7622 2209 **Fax** (020) 7924 2178
e-mail enquiry@chadathai.com
www.chadathai.com

Carte £15/29

It may have been around for over twenty years but Chada has been given a makeover and looks positively resplendent, although there isn't much in the way of competition along Battersea Park Road these days. It may never be the busiest restaurant around but the welcome is always warm, the service polite and endearing and the Thai cooking satisfying and keenly priced.

The menu is still a very long affair but it's easy to navigate. Several dishes, such as tom kha soup and phad prik, are available with a choice of meat, prawn or vegetables. Flavours are clean and fresh and efforts are made to make dishes look appetising. There are plans afoot to simplify the choice and introduce some fish dishes.

A/C VISA MC AE

Ransome's Dock

U2 — Modern European

Battersea
35-37 Parkgate Rd SW11 4NP
(020) 7223 1611 **Fax** (020) 7924 2614
e-mail chef@ransomesdock.co.uk
www.ransomesdock.co.uk

Closed Christmas, August Bank Holiday and Sunday dinner

Carte £21/37

VISA, MC, AE

It may never have had a full river view but these days Ransome's Dock, a converted warehouse, is somewhat dwarfed by the new apartment buildings that hug the south side of the river. Inside, though, still has a freshness and something of a 'by the sea' feel. The real clues to the owner's great passion are in the wine-themed prints: his wine list is thoughtful, extensive, reasonably priced and ripe for exploration. It also provides easy matches for the food, where ingredients are thoughtfully paired, like foie gras rillettes with caper berries; or altogether more classic and down to earth, such as liver and bacon with bubble and squeak. Name-checked suppliers ensure those ingredients are fresh and seasonal.

The Butcher & Grill

U2 — Traditional

Battersea
39-41 Parkgate Rd SW11 4NP
(020) 7924 3999 **Fax** (020) 7223 7977
e-mail info@thebutcherandgrill.com **www**.thebutcherandgrill.com

Closed 25-26 December, Easter, Sunday dinner and Bank Holidays

Menu £15 (lunch) – Carte £24/35

A/C, VISA, MC, AE

The name really says everything - this is all about carnivores and all about meat. What better way is there of providing customers with provenance assurance than by having your own butcher's shop, complete with a Master Butcher, forming part of your restaurant? Simply pick your meat of choice, get it grilled to your liking, decide what 'stuff on the side' you want and tuck in with your Rambo hunting knife. Even the napkins are man-sized tea towels.

A converted warehouse provides just the right surroundings for this clever concept, with everything exposed and spread over two levels. Prices are kept realistic, while the atmosphere is contagiously enthusiastic. There is one fish dish available for those who came by accident.

The Food Room

Mediterranean

U2

Battersea

123 Queenstown Rd SW8 3RH

Closed 1-3 January, 25-26 December, Sunday and Monday – dinner only

(020) 7622 0555 **Fax** (020) 7627 5440

e-mail info@thefoodroom.com **www**.thefoodroom.com

Menu £26

This is one of those proper neighbourhood restaurants – it's in a residential area and equally as welcoming to small parties, starry-eyed couples or those just wanting a quick bite after work. Redecoration in early 2007 has given the room a more relaxed feel and the artwork and mirrors keep it bright.

The chef-owner's cooking is informed by the wider Mediterranean. There's an appealingly sunny aspect to dishes such as artichoke tart with goat cheese, and an earthiness to main courses like rump of lamb with polenta. The well-balanced menu is priced per course, changes every 3 to 4 weeks and is supplemented by daily-changing specials. The female team provide cheery and informed service and know all their regulars.

The Greyhound at Battersea

Gastropub

T2

Battersea

136 Battersea High St SW11 3JR

Closed 24 December-2 January, Sunday dinner and Monday

(020) 7978 7021 **Fax** (020) 7978 0599

e-mail sam@sampubs.com **www**.thegreyhoundatbattersea.co.uk

Menu £31 - Carte £16/30

There was a time when the only wine served in pubs was warm, probably corked and invariably German. When the current owner took over The Greyhound he brought with him his passion and knowledge of wine gained from his previous career as a sommelier and now this attractive pub boasts a terrific list with great breadth of choice and super prices. The pub's not bad too.

The bar is quite a stylish little number and, behind it, sits the restaurant which continues the theme of being casual yet contemporary. It, in turn, opens out onto a courtyard. The kitchen does its bit to compete with the wines. The set price dinner menu (with the more limited lunchtime choice) reads like a gastropub manifesto, with influences aplenty.

Upstairs

U2 — Modern European XX

Brixton
89b Acre Lane SW2 5TN
(020) 7733 8855
www.upstairslondon.com

⊖ Clapham North
Closed 24 December-7 January, 18 August-1 September, Sunday dinner and Monday except November-December – dinner only

Menu £27/35

VISA

Look out for the Opus Coffee shop because upstairs is Upstairs but the only clue is a non-descript door and entry buzzer. Once you're in and up the narrow stairs you'll find a bar on the first floor and the restaurant on the second. It's a cosy affair with seating for 26; turquoise is the favoured colour and there's plenty of natural light.

The menu comes on a single sheet of A4; there are three starters, mains and desserts at a set price, although there are usually also a couple of supplements. The cooking is neat, accurate and things are kept simple. The style is a mix of French and English so alongside the potted shrimps may be a foie gras parfait and you could follow the Guinea fowl with apple crumble or chocolate millefeuille.

High Road Brasserie

S2 — Mediterranean XX

Chiswick
162 Chiswick High Rd W4 1PR
(020) 8742 7474
www.highroadhouse.co.uk

⊖ Turnham Green

Carte £28/36

A/C

VISA

AE

The name says it all. It's a brasserie and it's on the High Road. With French windows opening onto a terrace, mirrors, pewter topped tables, leather seats and tiled flooring, all the ingredients are in place to create that genuine brasserie feel. But it also manages to avoid being an art nouveau Parisian pastiche - there's not an Alphonse Mucha poster to be seen.

Chiswickians have clearly taken to the place because there's often a snake of people queuing to get in. Maybe they should consider staggering their arrival times, because it all starts at breakfast, the menu is served all day and weekend brunches are a big hit. The menu will float everyone's boat, with classics like potted shrimp and eggs Benedict to casseroles, grills and salads.

La Trompette ✿

S2

French XXX

5-7 Devonshire Rd W4 2EU
✆ (020) 8747 1836
Fax (020) 8995 8097
e-mail reception@latrompette.co.uk **www**.latrompette.co.uk

⊖ Turnham Green
Closed 24-27 December and 1 January – booking essential

Menu £24/35 s

La Trompette

It's on one of those charming side streets that make Chiswick so appealing, and the pretty terrace at the front deserves a few sunny days. La Trompette, rather like its sibling Chez Bruce in Wandsworth, is a genuine neighbourhood restaurant, albeit with neighbours who are nicely scrubbed and polished. But here the service really comes into play because the young team are a great strength and are very well organised; they also get the tone just right to take the edge off any formality that may threaten to engulf the room. That room is comfortable and elegant but with tables close enough to lend some community spirit. The kitchen has also now found the right level of consistency. It takes classical French food and gives it the occasional tweak but there are no unusual combinations or pointless garnishes. It relies chiefly on the freshness of the ingredients and the flavours are pronounced and satisfying. The wine list is also exceptional, for its breadth and originality. Even more satisfying is the final bill, which would be considerably higher if the W of the postcode were followed by a 1 rather than a 4.

First Course

- Steamed paupiette of sea bass and crab with mussels.
- Foie gras and chicken liver parfait with toasted brioche.

Main Course

- Rump of lamb with globe artichoke and cassoulet of beans, bacon and lamb breast.
- Roast fillet of halibut with asparagus and Jersey Royals.

Dessert

- Crème brûlée with plum compote.
- Pear and almond tart with Jersey cream.

Sam's Brasserie

S2 — Mediterranean

Chiswick — ⊖ Turnham Green

11 Barley Mow Passage
W4 4PH — Closed 24-26 December

(020) 8987 0555 **Fax** (020) 8987 7389

e-mail info@samsbrasserie.co.uk **www**.samsbrasserie.co.uk

Menu £15 – Carte £20/32

A/C · VISA · MC · AE

Sam and his brasserie continue to pull in the crowds, thanks to a combination of lively surroundings and appealing menus to suit everyone. The Barley Mow Centre was once a paper mill and this semi-industrial space provides the ideal backdrop for this busy restaurant, where the locals can just drop in at any time. Noise levels are at the party end of the spectrum and the staff keep things moving along nicely.

There are all sorts of menus available, from Brunch and Early Evening deals to something for the kids, and the kitchen knows what brasserie food is all about. That means satisfying and easy-to-eat dishes for whatever hour, such as omelettes and bowls of pasta or more adventurous offerings like sea bass with sauce *vierge* or shin of veal.

Fish Hook

S1 — Seafood

Chiswick — ⊖ Turnham Green

6-8 Elliott Rd W4 1PE — Closed 23 - 26 December

(020) 8742 0766 **Fax** (020) 8742 3374

e-mail info@fishhook.co.uk **www**.fishhook.co.uk

Menu £14 – Carte £30/47

A/C · VISA · MC · AE

What was previously a South African restaurant called Fish Hoek became the more straightforward Fish Hook in the end of 2005 and it's been pulling in the locals from day one.

It has kept the unusual device adopted by the previous owner whereby virtually every dish is available as either a starter or a main course – it's merely a matter of size. This works to a degree, although some dishes just sound more of one course than the other. Nevertheless, there is plenty of choice available; the chef-owner clearly has ability and he handles his fish with dextrous aplomb.

The room's simply dressed with wood-backed banquettes, mirrors and black and white photos. It has a cheery atmosphere, thanks to the closely set tables.

Fishworks

S1

Seafood

Chiswick
6 Turnham Green Terrace
W4 1QP
(020) 8994 0086 **Fax** (020) 8994 0778
e-mail chiswick@fishworks.co.uk **www**.fishworks.co.uk

⊖ Turnham Green
Closed 25 - 28 December and 1 January – booking essential

Menu £14 (lunch) - Carte £26/38

VISA

The Chiswick branch of this burgeoning chain was the first to open in London and you can see why there are others now popping up everywhere. The formula is wonderfully simple: an open fishmonger on the street level (although the passing traffic rather spoils the scent of the sea), then up a few steps into a bright, sunny restaurant.

AE

On warm days head straight for the charming decked terrace at the back, where diesel belching buses seem a world away. Freshness is the key here and all the fish is delivered daily, mostly from Devon or Cornwall. The choice is considerable, from shellfish platters to fisherman's stew, but there can be few things in life more pleasing that a simply grilled piece of fish with some hollandaise on the side.

The Devonshire House

S2

Gastropub

Chiswick
126 Devonshire Rd W4 2JJ
(020) 8987 2626 **Fax** (020) 8995 0152
e-mail info@thedevonshirehouse.co.uk
www.thedevonshirehouse.co.uk

⊖ Turnham Green
Closed 23 December-3 January and Monday

Menu £14/19 - Carte £20/27

Strolling from the high street, past the pretty terrace houses of Devonshire Road, and just when you're wondering if there's anything down here, you'll come across The Devonshire, with its tell-tale modern lettering.

VISA

This has been a good foodie pub for a while but, as we go to print, it is shortly to open under the auspices of the Gordon Ramsay empire - the place is currently being redecorated and the French polisher is hard at work. The menu will be devised and overseen by Mark Sargeant, who is the head chef of Claridge's but also a very local resident. It will follow the principles of The Narrow, which was their successful first foray into the world of the gastropub, by offering plenty of robust British classics and down-to-earth favourites.

AE

Four O Nine

U2 — Modern European XX

Clapham
entrance on Landor Rd, 409
Clapham Rd SW9 9BT
(020) 7737 0722
www.fouronine.co.uk

⊖ Clapham North
Closed 25-27 December and 1 January – dinner only

Carte £25/32

A/C VISA MC AE

If anyone's watching you from their car on Clapham Road they'll see you ring the bell before being let in and think something nefarious is afoot. However, the shabby staircase and secretive entrance pay dividends by somehow adding to the intimacy of this surprisingly smart first floor restaurant.

The chef is an acolyte of Chez Bruce and his set menus share the philosophy of crisp, appetisingly presented food, free from unnecessary over-elaboration and with natural flavours to the fore. The influences are predominantly French but occasionally there are dishes or ingredients derived from over the Italian border such as a linguini, risotto or some excellent prosciutto. The wine list is less predictable than many.

Trinity

U2 — Innovative XX

Clapham
4 The Polygon SW4 0JG
(020) 7622 1199 **Fax** (020) 7622 1166
e-mail dine@trinityrestaurant.co.uk
www.trinityrestaurant.co.uk

⊖ Clapham Common
Closed 25-26 December, 1 January and Monday lunch

Menu £20 (lunch) – Carte dinner £34/45

A/C VISA MC AE

Judging by the scarcity of empty tables, Clapham gastronauts are rather taken with Trinity. It's a light and bright room, with a modern feel and a real sense of place; service is well meaning and avoids being too ceremonial, while the chef has always enjoyed a good local reputation. His menu is appealingly laid out; each dish is titled by the three main components such as Squid-Skate-Chorizo, with the supporting cast of ingredients listed below. There's plenty of originality, the plates are artfully presented and, despite a slight tendency to over-elaborate, his know-how, gathered by working in some serious places, is apparent. A lighter menu is available at lunch, while the atmosphere remains appealingly local and relaxed.

Tsunami

Japanese

U2

Clapham

Unit 3, 5-7 Voltaire Rd
SW4 6DQ

⊖ Clapham North

Closed 25-26 December and Easter – dinner only and Saturday-Sunday lunch

(020) 7978 1610 **Fax** (020) 7978 1591

www.tsunamijapaneserestaurant.co.uk

Carte £30

The restaurant certainly doesn't make life easy for itself. We all now understand the name and the location is on the uninspiring side but, thanks to this Japanese restaurant's coolly minimalist interior, you'll forget soon enough where you are.

Tsunami attracts a younger clientele and proves that one doesn't have to be in the West End to sample good food in stylish surroundings. While the menu will easily satisfy the more traditionally minded, it is those willing to try the more exotic specialities and original combinations who will get most out of the experience. Indeed, the knowledgeable staff positively encourage you to try something different. Dishes arrive from the kitchen as and when they are ready, so sharing is encouraged

Maxim

Chinese

R1

Ealing

153-155 Northfield Ave W13 9QT

⊖ Northfields

Closed 25-28 December and Sunday lunch

(020) 8567 1719 **Fax** (020) 8932 0717

Menu £10/20 – Carte £17/30

Loyalty is a two-way street which is why you'll find Mr Chow doing the rounds in his restaurant, greeting his guests and keeping them happy. Those guests include a high proportion of regulars who have made Maxim a local favourite for over thirty years. The service is never less than attentive and the suited managers are all equally personable. The restaurant itself is also more comfortable than the norm and is broken up into different areas, with splashes of colour coming from the huge vases and dragon costume.

Mrs Chow runs the kitchen with the same level of reliable enthusiasm. You'll find all the favourites as well as specialities from Peking and the best bet is to go for one of the four good value set menus.

Charlotte's Place

R1 **Modern European**

Ealing
16 St Matthew's Rd W5 3JT
(020) 8567 7541
www.charlottes.co.uk

⊖ Ealing Common
Closed 1-2 January, 26-30 December and lunch Monday

Carte £24/35

VISA

Charlotte may have long gone but the restaurant still exudes the feel of a friendly, neighbourhood restaurant. Ealing's most noted feature, the Common, is right outside the door and the large windows and mirrors ensure there's plenty of light. The ground floor seats twenty and is more fun than the somewhat soulless basement area which is used as an overflow or for larger parties.

The menu combines modern Euro food, like sea bass with crushed new potatoes, with brasserie classics such as Caesar salad and fishcakes. British and Irish cheeses are a feature and there's a good value set menu for lunch and early-in-the-week dinners. The wine list is largely Old World and what it lacks in depth it more than makes up in its affordability.

The Ealing Park Tavern

R1 **Gastropub**

Ealing
222 South Ealing Rd W5 4RL
(020) 8758 1879 **Fax** (020) 8560 5269

⊖ South Ealing
Closed 25-26 December, 1 January and Monday lunch

Carte £24/28

VISA

AE

This impressive Arts and Crafts property was built in 1886 and extended in 1939, when the cavernous 'hall' area was added. Now used for dining, light streams in and were it not for the open plan kitchen spanning the back walls, with its high ceilings and wood panelling, this could well be a schoolroom. Fittingly, the daily-changing menu is written on a huge blackboard above the kitchen. No nonsense, decent sized dishes made with quality ingredients are mainly British, with some French and Italian influences. Some tapas type dishes are also available in the bar, although this is primarily a space for drinkers.

At lunchtimes businessmen from nearby offices come in to eat, but the buzzy atmosphere in the evening is down to the locals.

Redmond's

Modern European XX

S2

East Sheen
170 Upper Richmond Road West
SW14 8AW
(020) 8878 1922
e-mail pippa@redmonds.org.uk **www**.redmonds.org.uk

Closed 3 days Christmas, Sunday and Bank Holidays – dinner only

Menu £27/32

Redmond's and East Sheen appear to be the perfect coupling because the restaurant celebrated its tenth anniversary last year. Not only is that good for the local burghers, who have done all the supporting over those years, but it's also encouraging news for anyone considering going into business with one's spouse. Redmond does the cooking here and for that he relies on his innate understanding of what-goes-with-what and an appreciation of what the seasons bring. His cooking is crisp yet satisfying. Pippa is in charge of the service and to this she brings her comprehensive knowledge of what happens to the ingredients in the kitchen as well as an appreciation of her regulars. The next ten years look like they're in the bag.

La Saveur

French X

S2

East Sheen
201 Upper Richmond Road West SW14 8QT
(020) 8876 0644
e-mail info@brula.co.uk **www**.brula.co.uk

Closed 25-26 December and 1 January

Menu £15/17 - Carte £20/36

From the stable that brought you Brula – you just know that anywhere this French must be the brainchild of Brits - comes La Saveur; not only a restaurant but also a salon de thé. That means that in between coming in for escargots, steak frites or coquilles St Jacques you can pop round for a little petit dejeuner first thing or while away the après midi with a café and the tarte de jour. It all works well because they keep everything classic, the food is satisfying and delivers what the menu promises. The prix fixe menus are good value and you can bring your own wine for a corkage fee.

A bit of art nouveau, wood panelling and mirrors gives the room something of a French bistro feel; the nonchalance of the service adds extra authenticity.

The Victoria

S2 — Gastropub

East Sheen — Closed 24-27 December

10 West Temple Sheen SW14 7RT
(020) 8876 4238 **Fax** (020) 8878 3464
e-mail reservations@thevictoria.net **www**.thevictoria.net

Carte £19/25

Fresh, seasonal produce is the appeal here, with a mix of British cooking alongside splashes of continental colour from the more southerly parts of Europe. Helpful menu notes are a lesson for all those chefs who try to bamboozle their diners with the muddled lexicon of modern cookery. So, expect a bit of pasta, fish soup, sweetbreads or sardines and the best UK produce such as asparagus, Jersey royals and samphire. The wines come in largely under £30 a bottle and are also accompanied by informative text.

It's a sizeable pub, with a roomy bar and a terrific conservatory. Children are positively encouraged, by virtue of the play area and the coffee-and-cake mornings which have proved a hit with local mothers.

Saran Rom

T2 — Thai

Fulham — ⊖ Fulham Broadway

The Boulevard, Imperial Wharf,
Townmead Rd SW6 2UB
(020) 7751 3111
e-mail info@saranrom.com **www**.saranrom.com

Carte £29/38

Imperial Wharf is giving Chelsea Harbour a run for its money. In February 2006 Saran Rom opened, with a look based on a Thai Royal summer palace. It's so impressive you think you're gazing across the Chao Phraya River rather than The Thames. Elaborately decorated with carved teak, it's divided into a series of large rooms, including a very attractive bar and pretty terrace, but it still manages to feel quite intimate, despite its size.

The menu prudently treads a traditional path and does so with aplomb, with the cooking executed with care and attention. The charming girls are reminders of how nothing beats sweet and eager service and how can you not love a place which has tuk-tuks on hand outside to ferry you to the local station?

Memories of India on the River

Indian XXX

T2

Fulham
7 The Boulevard, Imperial Wharf SW6 2UB
(020) 7736 0077 **Fax** (020) 7731 5222
www.memoriesofindiaontheriver.co.uk

Fulham Broadway
Closed 25 December

Carte £31/48

No restaurant development is complete without Indian representation and so it is that, in among all the matching façades on the boulevard of Imperial Wharf, one finds Memories of India (originally called Memsaab).

It occupies the same amount of square footage as its neighbours. A love of white emulsion paint has been thoughtfully balanced by colourful silks and large pictures of spice baskets, and the room is certainly light and open in its feel. Larger parties should try for one of the four booths beneath the central palm tree. There's ample choice on the menu, with the nucleus exhibiting a fair degree of originality and impressive presentation, although those who prefer more familiar dishes are not forgotten.A takeaway service is available for locals.

Yi-Ban

Chinese XX

T2

Fulham
The Boulevard, Imperial Wharf SW6 2UB
(020) 7731 6606 **Fax** (020) 7731 7584
www.yi-ban.co.uk

Fulham Broadway
Closed Sunday – dinner only

Menu £15/40 – Carte £30/60

Yi-Ban completes the roll call of international cuisines found at Imperial Wharf by offering Chinese cooking. The decorative style is seductively nocturnal - appropriate as the restaurant does not open at lunchtime - with billowing sheer drapes, moody lighting and dark, polished tables. The menu comes clearly laid out and covers a number of bases by offering contemporary dishes alongside more traditional specialities and, curiously, some Japanese sushi. Efforts are made with the presentation, portion size is creditably generous and service comes courtesy of a young team in traditionally inspired outfits.

It's divided into three main areas: a smart cocktail bar, a grill and sushi counter and the main dining area.

Deep

T2 — Seafood XX

Fulham
The Boulevard, Imperial Wharf SW6 2UB
✆ (020) 7736 3337
Fax (020) 7736 7578
e-mail info@deeplondon.co.uk **www**.deeplondon.co.uk

⊖ Fulham Broadway
Closed 2 weeks Christmas - New Year, 1 week August, Monday, Sunday dinner, Saturday lunch and Bank Holidays

Menu £20 – Carte £25/43

Apart from pavement terraces clouded with exhaust fumes, the choice of where to eat on a summer's day is not altogether overwhelming. Fortunately, Deep is at hand. It not only has a great terrace but also offers river views from its spot on this revived riverside wharf. Inside it's all very slick and contemporary, with immaculate napery and comfortable armchairs making it a relaxing experience. It is also very big, which is presumably why it was used as the setting for Gordon Ramsay's 'F Word' TV programme.

The bar is quite an attraction. It has its own terrace and the UK's largest selection of Aquavit. Seafood is the speciality of the house and comes with a delicate Scandinavian touch, reflecting the owners' nationality.

Blue Elephant

T2 — Thai XX

Fulham
4-6 Fulham Broadway
SW6 1AA
✆ (020) 7385 6595 **Fax** (020) 7386 7665
e-mail london@blueelephant.com **www**.blueelephant.com

⊖ Fulham Broadway
Closed Christmas and Saturday lunch – booking essential

Menu £15/35 – Carte £27/44

There are now Blue Elephants stretching from Dubai to Moscow but the Fulham branch has had a twenty year head start and is still as busy as ever. The façade gives nothing away but, then again, no façade could do justice to what's going on inside. It's a cross between a tropical forest and a film-set with a decent budget. There are plants and flowers, water gardens, streams, bridges, barges and pergolas. No, really, it's a jungle in there. Fortunately, they realise that the surroundings won't distract the diners forever and put just as much effort into the cooking. Those relatively unfamiliar with Thai could do worse than head for the Royal Banquet menu, while the main menu offers an intriguing mix of the familiar and the more original.

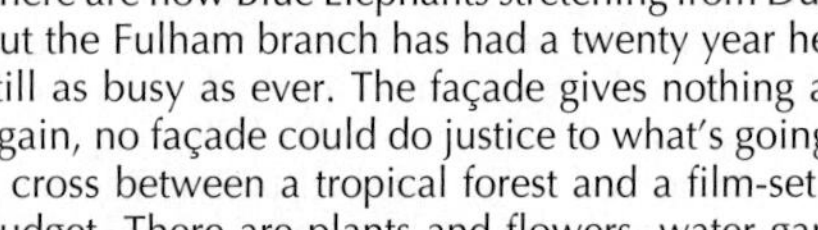

Mao Tai

Chinese XX

T2

Fulham

⊖ Parsons Green

58 New Kings Rd, Parsons Green
SW6 4LS

Closed 25-26 December

(020) 7731 2520

e-mail info@maotai.co.uk **www**.maotai.co.uk

Carte £28/43

Apart from the hint in the name, there is little to suggest, to the casual observer, that this is a Chinese restaurant - the plush new cocktail bar is a stylish and popular spot while the main dining room, split between two levels, is a moodily lit affair.
Mao Tai does appear to have been invigorated by its new image, both in the enthusiastic service and in the cooking. An appealing dim sum menu is served until 8pm, while the à la carte offers a comprehensive mix of modern and more traditional dishes, with a subtle nod towards more fiery Szechuan specialities; it's also unafraid of throwing in the occasional Thai or even Japanese influence. The beef is particularly tender and there's a fresh zing to the seafood dishes.

The Farm

Gastropub

T2

Fulham

⊖ Fulham Broadway

18 Farm Lane SW6 1PP

Closed 25 December

(020) 7381 3331

e-mail info@thefarmfulham.co.uk **www**.thefarmfulham.co.uk

Menu £25/29 – Carte £20/45

Style and sophistication are words not usually associated with the pub, but then The Farm is not your typical pub, gastro or otherwise. It certainly does what pubs usually do, with a large bar and a separate dining room at the back, but this one comes with a higher degree of class and, through its use of woods, leathers, glass and thoughtful lighting, a greater appreciation of comfort and design.

The kitchen also assumes some degree of sophistication on the part of the customer by offering a modern take on brasserie favourites, combined with a certain amount of Mediterranean vibrancy.

Lovers of spit-and-sawdust may cry foul, but The Farm highlights the resourcefulness and potential of the modern city pub.

River Café ✿

Italian XX

T2

Thames Wharf, Rainville Rd
W6 9HA
✆ (020) 7386 4200
Fax (020) 7386 4201
e-mail info@rivercafe.co.uk **www**.rivercafe.co.uk

⊖ Barons Court
Closed Christmas-New Year and Sunday dinner – booking essential

Carte £42/65

Ian Heide

Twenty years may not seem long but in restaurant years it's a lifetime, which is why the River Café has become an institution. It has also become something of a training school with its latest alumnus being Theo Randall, who flew the nest to open his own restaurant. The change in the kitchen has been seamless, however, because this place seemingly runs itself. Seasonality and top quality produce are the cornerstones of the cooking and the owners, Rose Gray and Ruth Rogers, still spend plenty of time in Italy sourcing the finest ingredients. This is clearly evident on the plate; dishes are forthright and honest and come with a seeming simplicity that belies the work that went into their creation.

The serving team are an equally enthusiastic bunch and all spent time in the kitchen familiarising themselves with ingredients and the make-up of the dishes. This enthusiasm is contagious and ensures that customers find themselves diving headlong into the menu. The shelf laden with cakes and tarts has the desired Pavlovian effect.

First Course

- Chargrilled squid with rocket and red chilli.
- Split and wood-roasted langoustines with oregano, chilli and lemon.

Main Course

- Wood-roasted turbot with capers, spinach and marjoram.
- Chargrilled leg of lamb marinated in garlic and rosemary with red peppers.

Dessert

- Chocolate 'Nemesis'.
- White peach sorbet.

Indian Zing

S1

Indian XX

Hammersmith ⊖ Ravenscourt Park

236 King St W6 0RF

✆ (020) 8748 5959 **Fax** (020) 8748 2332

e-mail indianzing@aol.com **www**.indianzing.co.uk

Menu £16/27 – Carte £20/33

As the name implies, this is a sophisticated and urbane Indian restaurant, which opened in 2005. The kitchen presents a selection of the more traditional and recognisable fare one usually expects from an Indian restaurant but accompanying this are dishes of an altogether more vibrant and modern persuasion. It is these dishes, such as jumbo prawns in pomegranate seeds and dill, which make a visit to Indian Zing worthwhile and show the kitchen's creativity alongside its respect for the traditions and craft of Indian cooking.

The interior is appropriately bright and crisp, with assorted pictures of life on the subcontinent mixed with some striking architectural pieces, such as elaborately carved doors. The service is thoughtful and efficient.

Chez Kristof

S1

French XX

Hammersmith ⊖ Hammersmith

111 Hammersmith Grove, Brook Green W6 0NQ

Closed Christmas

✆ (020) 8741 1177

e-mail info@chezkristof.co.uk **www**.chezkristof.co.uk

Menu £17 – Carte £23/30

From the people who brought you the Eastern European restaurants, Baltic and Wódka, comes Chez Kristof, a restaurant so celebratory in its Frenchness that it could only be the brainchild of a non-Frenchman. You'll find all the classics on the menu and, in this age where culinary identities are becoming interestingly blurred, that can be a reassuring sight. So, if your favourites include such standards as escargots, steak tartare or pot au chocolat you've come to the right spot.

The place really comes into its own in the summer with its large, appropriately French, windows opening onto a bamboo framed terrace.

Snows on the Green

Mediterranean

T1

Hammersmith
166 Shepherd's Bush Rd, Brook Green W6 7PB
(020) 7603 2142 **Fax** (020) 7602 7553
e-mail info@snowsonthegreen.co.uk
www.snowsonthegreen.co.uk

⊖ Hammersmith
Closed Christmas, Saturday lunch, Sunday and Bank Holidays

Menu £17 – Carte £24/27

A/C VISA MC AE

The eponymous Mr Snow was one of the first of a troupe of chefs who decided to pitch their culinary tent in greener and leafier surroundings than Central London. Neighbourhood restaurants are the lifeblood of a healthy eating-out scene and Snows on the Green has now been doing its bit in this part of town for over 15 years. This part of town is Brook Green and the locals appear pleased to have this place in their armoury when jousting with their Notting Hill neighbours.

It has a fresh and sunny feel and the undeniable challenges of being a neighbourhood joint are reflected in the varyingly priced menus available. The constant is the cooking which embraces both France and the Med. It's fresh, flavoursome and executed with care.

The Brackenbury

Modern European

S1

Hammersmith
129-131 Brackenbury Rd
W6 0BQ
(020) 8748 0107 **Fax** (020) 8748 6159
www.thebrackenbury.co.uk

⊖ Ravenscourt Park
Closed last 2 weeks August, 25-26 December and Sunday dinner

Menu £15 – Carte £25/32

VISA MC AE

Local estate agents may still insist on calling the area Brackenbury Village but, for most of us, it's just the place we looked up in the A-Z to find The Brackenbury restaurant all those years ago. It's changed hands a couple of times over the years but for many it remains a firm favourite and is still the type of place we'd all like on our own street.

It's simply furnished but adequately comfy and comes divided into two rooms with a bold colour scheme. There's a popular heated terrace at the front.

The daily changing menu focuses on primary ingredients, in dishes ranging from the modern and eclectic to more traditional European and British. It still gets busy and the lively atmosphere remains one of the attractions.

Azou

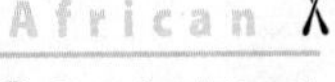

S2

Hammersmith
375 King St W6 9NJ
(020) 8563 7266 **Fax** (020) 8741 1425
e-mail info@azou.co.uk **www**.azou.co.uk

⊖ Stamford Brook
Closed 25 December, 1 January, Bank Holidays

Carte £15/26

Morocco, Tunisia and Algeria are the countries whose cooking features most at this sweet little neighbourhood restaurant, although other North African and Middle Eastern influences occasionally find themselves on the menu.

The husband and wife team run a cosy little place with only ten tables and the room is simply but decoratively furnished with draped silks and Moroccan lanterns. Specialities of the house include brik, rich tagines and assorted couscous dishes which will all satisfy the heartiest of appetites. It is certainly worth leaving room to sample the gloriously sweet pastries, especially when accompanied by mint tea, although they do also offer a well chosen selection of wines and beers.

Agni

Indian

S2

Hammersmith
160 King St W6 0QU
(020) 8846 9191
e-mail info@agnirestaurant.com
www.agnirestaurant.com

⊖ Ravenscourt Park
Closed 25 December and 1 January

Menu £13/14 – Carte £14/18

Many of us have found ourselves getting used to the ghee based dishes of traditional Indian restaurants, but Agni makes its pitch by offering a consciously healthy angle to their cooking, by using natural ingredients of dietary importance. Here, you can sip on a colourful fresh juice and choose from the exotic and original temptations on the menu, from Hyderabad biryani pots to the nutritional balanced thalis. The philosophy is captured by the desserts which include 'paan' kulfi - home made betel leaf ice cream which is a natural digestive and blood purifier. The room is long and narrow, with further space available upstairs; the service is helpful and conscientious and, most commendably, the prices are wallet-friendly.

Anglesea Arms

S1 Gastropub

Hammersmith
35 Wingate Rd W6 0UR
✆ (020) 8749 1291 **Fax** (020) 8749 1254

⊖ Ravenscourt Park
Closed Christmas week
– bookings not accepted

Carte £24/35

The best thing about the Anglesea Arms is that it's a proper pub. Granted, it was one of the pioneers of the gastropub movement, but it has managed to retain the looks, feel and atmosphere of a corner local and is all the more popular for that. This popularity does have a downside: if you have come to eat then take note that reservations for tables are not taken, so be prepared to wait. Fortunately the bar is a welcoming spot at which to pass the time.

Another reason for the pub's continuing prosperity is the food. The open kitchen offers a decent selection of robust and full flavoured fare and at prices that remain on the right side of reasonable. Service makes up in endeavour what it lacks in alacrity.

The Havelock Tavern

T1 Gastropub

Hammersmith
57 Masbro Rd, Brook Green W14 0LS
✆ (020) 7603 5374
e-mail info@thehavelocktavern.co.uk
www.thehavenlocktavern.co.uk

⊖ Kensington Olympia
Closed 22-26 December, Easter Sunday and second Monday in August
– bookings not accepted

Carte £19/25

Despite being reborn after a fire in 2006, The Havelock Tavern has stuck firmly to its roots as a 'proper' pub, just one that happens to do decent food. Don't bother booking: it is all done on a strictly first-come-first-served basis and you can leave your plastic at home – they only take the readies, although irritatingly that means paying at the bar with each order. However, it's all about the food which is good enough and well-priced enough to overlook these inconveniences. The daily changing blackboard menu lobs up a selection of balanced, hearty dishes, in portions so generous you'll be hard pressed to manage the full three courses. The influences range across the board from modern European to the occasional touch of Thailand.

The Glasshouse ✿

Modern European XX

R2

14 Station Parade TW9 3PZ
⊖ Kew Gardens
(020) 8940 6777
Closed 24-26 December and 1 January
Fax (020) 8940 3833
e-mail info@glasshouserestaurant.co.uk
www.glasshouserestaurant.co.uk

Menu £24/35 s

A/C
VISA
MC
AE

The Glasshouse

As a nation that seemingly favours the reliability of recognisable brand names, the fact that The Glasshouse comes from the same team as Chez Bruce and La Trompette should be reassurance aplenty. What that guarantees is a decently priced set menu and buckets of choice from a comprehensive list of dishes displaying modern European characteristics with Francophilic tendencies. The kitchen knows what the habitués of Kew like, which appears to be earthy and honest dishes, involving recognisable ingredients with a proven track record of harmonious union. In other words, things go together, whether that's scallops with a pea purée, pork belly with apple or sticky toffee pudding with vanilla ice cream. The wine list also has great range, with plenty by the glass.

The place may not be quite as bright as the name suggests but there are two walls of glass and it clearly falls into the more contemporary category of restaurant, free from ceremonial service and overly ornate surroundings. This is a proper neighbourhood restaurant: relaxed in tone and frequented by those who look as though they walked here.

First Course

- Foie gras, smoked chicken and artichoke terrine with lentils.
- Warm salad of wood pigeon with deep-fried truffled egg.

Main Course

- Rump of lamb with olive oil crushed potatoes and Niçoise jus.
- Roast fillet of cod with mussels, chorizo and chick peas.

Dessert

- Champagne and raspberry trifle.
- Hot chocolate mousse with milk chocolate sorbet.

Kew Grill

R2 — Beef specialities XX

Kew — ⊖ Kew Gardens

10b Kew Green TW9 3BH

Closed 24-26 December and Monday lunch – booking essential

☎ (020) 8948 4433

Fax (020) 8605 3532

e-mail kewgrill@aol.com **www**.awtonline.co.uk

Menu £15 (lunch) - Carte £25/43

A/C VISA MC AE

This was the second branch of Antony Worrall Thompson's burgeoning restaurant empire to open and follows the same guiding principles as the original in Notting Hill. It offers diners plenty of choice with the emphasis on classic dishes from prawn cocktail to beef Stroganoff and with a special feature on steaks, which are all Prime Aberdeen Angus and aged for 35 days.

The restaurant is on the eastern side of Kew Green and boasts a relaxed and friendly neighbourhood feel, helped along by some personable service. Sturdy tables line the exposed brick walls, brightened by large photos and the exposed kitchen adds a little theatre to the operation. Booking is necessary as capacity isn't as large as the apparent demand.

Ma Cuisine

R2 — French X

Kew — ⊖ Kew Gardens

The Old Post Office, 9 Station Approach TW9 3QB

☎ (020) 8332 1923

www.macuisine.kew.co.uk

Menu £16 - Carte £18/24

VISA MC

This informal French bistro, set in a red bricked former post office, certainly delivers the goods for a neighbourhood restaurant - the prices are fair, the service friendly and the cooking rustic and regional. The French theme is hard to avoid, from the period posters and pictures to the gingham tablecloths, while the menu offers a comprehensive selection of robust dishes from across France, including some of the classics. A blackboard marks that day's seasonal special, while those without much time can take advantage of the lunchtime menu rapide.

Staff all welcome their regulars by name and, as it's quite a small place, it fills very quickly, particularly at weekends. There's another branch in nearby Twickenham.

L'Auberge

French XX

T2

Putney
22 Upper Richmond Rd
SW15 2RX
✆ (020) 8874 3593
www.ardillys.com

Closed 2 weeks Summer, 2 weeks Winter, Sunday and Monday – dinner only

Menu £16 – Carte £23/30

This is what those of a certain maturity would call a 'proper' restaurant - it's run by a husband and wife team, provides authentic and traditionally prepared French cuisine and is decorated in a rustic and homely style which makes the countryside feel that little bit closer. The L-shaped dining room comes with yellow walls of heavily textured artex, tiled flooring and even Edith Piaf makes the odd appearance on the soundtrack to add to the Gallic character.

The owners provide service that is reassuringly gracious and warm hearted while the menu is decidedly old fashioned but in the very best sense. Just make sure you leave room for a dessert, the speciality of the house, as the chef owner originally trained as a patissier.

Enoteca Turi

Italian XX

T2

Putney
28 Putney High St SW15 1SQ
✆ (020) 8785 4449
Fax (020) 8780 5409
e-mail enoteca@tiscali.co.uk **www**.enotecaturi.com

⊖ Putney Bridge
Closed 25-26 December, 1 January, Sunday and lunch Bank Holidays

Menu £18 – Carte £30/36

Along with the river, Giuseppe Turi is one of Putney's greatest assets. The High Street may have adopted the bland façade of unthreateningly familiar chains, but Enoteca Turi still proudly stands there in the middle, waving the flag for individuality and bringing something wholly lacking from nearly every High Street – a sense of pleasure.

This Italian restaurant boasts enthusiastic and well organised service, a bounteous selection of regional dishes all using well-sourced ingredients and, thanks to a full refurbishment a couple of years back, a bright and sunny spot in which to enjoy it all. Evenings are particularly busy and the mood is always contagiously friendly. So why can't every high street have a place like this?

The Phoenix

T2 — Italian influences

Putney

Closed Bank Holidays

Pentlow St SW15 1LY
(020) 8780 3131 **Fax** (020) 8780 1114
e-mail thephoenix@sonnys.co.uk **www**.sonnys.co.uk

Menu £16 – Carte £19/35

A/C VISA MC AE

Just look out for the twinkling lights wrapped round the shrubs in front. Monthly-changing art for sale adorns the white walls of the two adjoining rooms, while in summer the charming terrace has a screen to hide the traffic but, sadly, not the noise. There's a great value set menu, although it's not available on Friday and Saturday nights. Like the tower in Pisa, the menu has Italian leanings; there's lots of flavour and a certain perkiness to the cooking. This being a neighbourhood restaurant means you can just pop in for a plate of San Daniele ham with figs, a bowl of risotto or rabbit with porcini mushrooms. There are also contributions from Blighty, like potted shrimps or apple crumble; over fifteen wines are available by the glass.

The Spencer Arms

S2 — Gastropub

Putney

Closed 25 December, 1 January

237 Lower Richmond Road SW15 1HJ
(020) 8788 0640 **Fax** (020) 8780 2216
e-mail info@thespencerarms.co.uk **www**.thespencerarms.co.uk

Carte £23/29

A/C VISA MC

This Victorian pub sits on the edge of Putney Common and is close to the river which is exactly where you'd want to find a gastropub. It even has a pavement terrace for summer days. Etched glass and a lick of paint have brightened the exterior, while the inside has been sympathetically updated and divided into two. On your left as you enter is an area with leather sofas, a fireplace and plenty of books and games, while on the other side you'll find a rustic bar-cum-restaurant, with the ubiquitous hardwood floor, pine scrubbed tables and mix and match chairs.

The semi open-plan kitchen delivers a well-balanced menu of dishes that are as hearty as they are heart warming, from a blackboard menu which focuses on seasonality and changes daily.

The Restaurant at The Petersham

French XXX

R3

Richmond — Closed 25-26 December

Nightingale Lane TW9 6UZ
(020) 8939 1084 **Fax** (020) 8939 1002

Carte £35/48

From its vantage point on Richmond Hill, the Petersham Hotel, built in 1865, offers wonderfully unspoilt vistas of the Thames at its most majestic and, thanks to its large windows, diners at virtually all the tables in its restaurant can enjoy this great view. The advantages of dining within a hotel include the considerable elbow and leg-room: tables are well spaced for added privacy and there's a comfortable lounge and bar, with its own terrace. Those understandably hesitant about dining within a hotel can rest assured that the room does have its own personality. The cooking displays a classical French education, but will also please those who prefer their culinary ambitions to be a little closer to home.

Matsuba

Japanese 

R2

Richmond — Closed 25-26 December, 1 January and Sunday

10 Red Lion St TW9 1RW
(020) 8605 3513
e-mail matsuba10@hotmail.com **www**.matsuba.co.uk

Carte £35

The sleek and contemporary interior of this Japanese restaurant on the High Street, with its panelled walls, polished tables and high-backed leather chairs, provides a perfectly comfortable environment in which to enjoy their delicately prepared specialities. However, with only eight tables in the restaurant, those without reservations may find themselves having to wait.

It's family run which adds to the relaxed and friendly mood. A small counter is also on hand from where an impressive selection of sushi and sashimi is offered. Lunchtime visitors will find particularly good value Bento Boxes in assorted variations, as well as various 'rice bowl' options which come with appetiser, soup, pickles and fruit.

Petersham Nurseries Café

R3 — Italian influences X

Richmond — Closed Monday – lunch only

Church Lane (off Petersham Rd) TW10 7AG
(020) 8605 3627
e-mail info@petershamnurseries.com
www.petershamnurseries.com

Carte £27/65

It's just as the name suggests, which is why it's only open for lunch. The locals may be a bit sniffy about the place but dig in and don't panic if your wobbly chair falls back into the greenery. If the sun's out, the café's on the terrace, otherwise it's in a greenhouse - either way this is a charming spot with engaging service.

But it's also all about the food which matches its setting by being natural, earthy and full of goodness. Ingredients are very well sourced and seasonal and there's an Italian accent to many dishes, such as roasted wild salmon with fennel, spinach and rocket or beetroot with buffalo mozzarella and rainbow chard. The prices may not be quite so down to earth but who can resist somewhere serving jugs of real lemonade?

VISA AE

The Wharf

R3 — Modern European XX

Teddington — Closed 25-26 December, 1 January, Sunday dinner and Monday

22 Manor Rd TW11 8BG
(020) 8977 6333 **Fax** (020) 8977 9444
e-mail the.wharf@walk-on-water.co.uk **www**.walk-on-water.co.uk

Menu £14/16 - Carte £28/35

The Wharf is a delightful converted boathouse on the banks of the Thames, overlooking Teddington Lock, and reminds us how little we sometimes make of this great river. On warm summer days the whole place becomes one vast terrace and many will leave a July lunch wishing they had a little something to navigate towards the landing stage next time.

Weekends and Twickenham match days are naturally the busy periods and the upstairs floor is ideal for private parties. Those coming during the weekdays are rewarded with keenly priced menus.

The chef owner, a protégé of Anton Mosimann, offers modern European cuisine, coupled with some Asian touches. Waiting staff catch the mood with their competence and courtesy.

A/C VISA AE

Simply Thai

R3 **Thai**

Teddington
196 Kingston Rd TW11 9JD
(020) 8943 9747
e-mail simplythai1@yahoo.co.uk **www**.simplythai-restaurant.co.uk

Booking essential at lunch

Menu £16 – Carte £16/21

Disguised by a fairly unremarkable façade, Simply Thai is a friendly little Thai restaurant with a popular local following. The thoroughly engaging owner does the cooking and credits her aunt for her culinary education. She certainly displays an absolute understanding of the harmony and balance that underpins Thai cooking; seafood is her speciality, from crispy red snapper with sweet tamarind to grilled sea bass with ginger. Curries cooked without coconut and light, crisp stir-fry dishes provide healthy options and the menus also feature regional dishes, especially from the north eastern parts of Thailand.
It all happens in a narrow room with just eleven tables but a modern feel. Service is authentically polite and obliging.

Kastoori

U3 **Indian**

Tooting
188 Upper Tooting Rd SW17 7EJ
(020) 8767 7027

Tooting Bec
Closed 25-26 December and lunch Monday and Tuesday

Carte £13/17

Proof that one should never judge a restaurant by its appearance comes in the form of Kastoori. An unremarkable façade is matched by a fairly modest interior but this is all about the owners, the Thanki family, celebrating their East African and Gujarati heritage through their cooking, and the pride they have in their restaurant is obvious to everyone.

All dishes here are vegetarian and prepared to order; if a certain vegetable is unavailable then the dish isn't on. The cooking is assured, vibrant and invigorating – Kastoori means 'fragrant'- but it is also philanthropically priced, hence a need to book at weekends. They even make their own garam masala to a secret recipe involving the roasting of over 24 spices.

A Cena

R3 — Italian XX

Twickenham
418 Richmond Rd TW1 2EB
(020) 8288 0108
Fax (020) 8940 5346
www.acena.co.uk

⊖ Richmond
Closed Sunday dinner and Monday lunch

Carte £27/33

A/C VISA MC AE

Just as Italy is now an established participant in the Six Nations Rugby, so it is appropriate that an Italian restaurant, A Cena, has built a reputation among the assorted dining options available in the vicinity of Twickenham, home of English rugby. Italian for 'to eat', A Cena succeeds by combining flavoursome cooking, a well chosen all-Italian wine list, grown-up service and calming, stress-free surroundings. Decorated with church pew style chairs and scrubbed floorboards, with large mirrors adding to the feel of light and space, the room also benefits from having a stylish bar offering an extensive cocktail list to those making it more of an occasion.
Odds on an English restaurant opening in Rome remain long.

Brula Bistrot

R3 — French X

Twickenham
43 Crown Rd, St Margarets TW1 3EJ
(020) 8892 0602 **Fax** (020) 8892 7727
e-mail info@brulabistrot.com

Closed 25-26 December and 1 January – booking essential

Menu £15/17 – Carte £20/36

VISA MC AE

No, you haven't forgotten your school French – Brula is not a real word but an amalgam of the owners' names, Bruce and Lawrence. They have created an authentic little French bistro out of a corner Victorian building that has been a pub and a butchers. It's a charming place with a genuine neighbourly feel and the owners regularly put in an appearance. It's also one in the eye for all those who've bored friends with tales of finding that inexpensive little gem whilst driving through the Dordogne. The fixed price menus are a positive steal and are available all week and early evening during weekends. It covers all the classics, from moules to mousse and even the à la carte will have your bank manager's blessing.

Ma Cuisine

French

R3

Twickenham

Closed Sunday

6 Whitton Rd TW1 1BJ
(020) 8607 9849
www.macuisinetw1.co.uk

Menu £16 – Carte £18/24

Londoners have always appreciated that dining out should be part of every day living. This does, in turn, call for plenty of affordable restaurants and here Ma Cuisine fits the bill nicely. By keeping prices low, it has proved a real local draw and makes us wish we had one of these at the end of our street.

For starters, it's a bistro, with the sort of informality that makes dining out a relaxing, stress-busting experience. Secondly, it serves reassuringly rustic and recognisable French classics like onion soup, coq au vin and lemon tart. The French theme continues in the decoration, in the posters and the music, gingham table covers and plenty of cries of "bon appétit" from the staff. You get all this without breaking the banque.

Tangawizi

Indian

R2

Twickenham

Richmond

Closed 25-26 December and 1 January – dinner only

406 Richmond Rd, Richmond Bridge
TW1 2EB
(020) 8891 3737 **Fax** (020) 8891 3737
e-mail tangawizi-richmond@hotmail.com

Carte £14/28

Rich in colour and vitality, Tangawizi - meaning 'ginger' in Swahili – is another in the new breed of Indian restaurants. That means thoughtful design with clever use of silks and saris, attentive and elegant staff but, above all, cooking that is original, fresh and carefully prepared.

North India provides much of the influence and although the à la carte menu offers plenty of 'safe' options, there are gems such as the roasted then stir-fried 'liptey' chicken. Diners should, however, head for the 'specials' section where the ambition of the kitchen is more evident. Lamb is another house speciality and is marinated to ensure it arrives extremely tender. For cooking this good, the prices are more than fair.

Tapas y Vino

R3 — Mediterranean X

Twickenham — Closed Sunday

111 London Rd TW1 1EE
(020) 8892 5417
e-mail info@tapasyvino.co.uk **www**.tapasyvino.co.uk

Menu £20 (dinner) – Carte £12/20

VISA MC

The name almost says it all – the only thing missing is mention of the low prices. This is a couple of doors down from Ma Cuisine and under the same ownership; it's simply done out in a pseudo Spanish style, but what's attracting the locals is the carefully judged and satisfying tapas. Not exclusively Spanish tapas, however, - the influences stretch across the Med, taking in Morocco and Greece. The menu divides itself into traditional hot, cold and speciality tapas and this final section is where you find the interesting stuff, like tagine, snails with Jabugo ham, roast suckling pig or morcilla black puddings with quince. Unless you've come straight from the rugby ground, four plates per person should be sufficient.

Amici

U3 — Italian XX

Wandsworth — ⊖ Balham

35 Bellevue Rd SW17 7EF
(020) 8672 5888 **Fax** (020) 8672 8856
e-mail info@amiciitalian.co.uk **www**.amiciitalian.co.uk

Carte £19/30

A/C VISA MC AE

To be called a genuine 'neighbourhood' restaurant requires more than just a leafy location – the restaurant has to be part of the local community. Amici does its bit by holding cookery demonstrations, courtesy of local resident and cookery writer Valentina Harris who is the consultant here. The fact that some of those classes are for kids and teenagers is proof than local families make up an important part of the clientele here.

It's a brightly decorated place, with an appealing and easy-going charm, relaxing and informal service. The Italian cooking is equally uncomplicated and unfussy, and comes with a slight Tuscan influence.

The attractive bar at the front, overlooking the Common, is open all day and offers up its own snack menu.

Chez Bruce ✿

French XX

U3

2 Bellevue Rd SW17 7EG
✆ (020) 8672 0114
Fax (020) 8767 6648
e-mail enquiries@chezbruce.co.uk **www**.chezbruce.co.uk

⊖ Tooting Bec
Closed 24-26 December and 1 January – booking essential

Menu £24/38

A/C VISA MC AE

Chez Bruce

SOUTH-WEST ▶ Plan XVIII

Good cooking, like good singing, is more about what you leave out – it's not about showing your range but about creating something appealing, and if anywhere understands the maxim 'less is more' then it is Chez Bruce. There are no fancy pictures on the plates, no funny foams and nothing sticking out at a strange angle. Here in Wandsworth the menu is reprinted for every service and the cooking is all about confident flavours and combinations of ingredients that are tried and tested, like beef with béarnaise, halibut with artichoke and lamb with olives. The kitchen keeps things classical; mostly French but with a touch of the Mediterranean and the set price format works to everyone's satisfaction.

Subsequently, it's easy to spot the locals –they're the ones looking decidedly smug – and anyone who has travelled from afar, or merely over a bridge, will feel a little like an interloper. Fortunately the staff are sufficiently well organised and sympathetic to ensure the same levels of attention for everyone and, as with all shared activities, the atmosphere is always animated and appreciative.

First Course

- Cornish crab and saffron tart.
- Foie gras and chicken liver parfait with toasted brioche.

Main Course

- Roast cod with olive oil mash, roast tomato and grilled courgette.
- Rump and shoulder of lamb with broad beans and olives.

Dessert

- Hot chocolate pudding with praline parfait.
- Steamed pear and almond pudding with vanilla ice cream.

Ditto

T2 Mediterranean

Wandsworth

Closed 26-30 December

55-57 East Hill SW18 2QE

(020) 8877 0110 **Fax** (020) 8875 0110

e-mail will@doditto.co.uk **www**.doditto.co.uk

Menu £26 (dinner) – Carte £18/26

VISA MC AE

Wandsworth's one-way system appears to have been designed to bamboozle the out-of-towner, so it's hardly surprising that Ditto enjoys a lively, and very local, atmosphere. It comes divided into two, with a roomy bar down one side with assorted sofas, and an informal restaurant on the other. The menu jumps around, from Spain to Italy via France, but it all works well; there's something for everyone, including small snacks for sharing like tempura and some original touches like dessert cocktails. Meals can be taken in the bar or restaurant and the serving team are all helpful and obliging.

How can you not take to a place that turns its private dining room into a crèche to encourage mums to meet up for lunch?

Light House

T3 International

Wimbledon

⊖ Wimbledon

75-77 Ridgway SW19 4ST

Closed 25-26 December, 1 January and Sunday dinner

(020) 8944 6338 **Fax** (020) 8946 4440

e-mail info@lighthousewimbledon.com

www.lighthousewimbledon.com

Menu £17 – Carte £25/30

VISA MC AE

Those expecting a tall, tubular building with a light on the top will be disappointed. The name refers to the time when this was a shop selling lights and light fittings. Nowadays it provides an illuminating insight into our more adventurous dining habits by offering cooking unfettered by national boundaries. On any one day you may find influences ranging from a bit of Italian, Greek or Tunisian to the odd Asian twist. The fact that it seems to work speaks volumes for the quality of the ingredients. The pricing is also eminently sensible, especially for the set lunch menu.

The restaurant itself is a relatively simple affair, with plenty of light wood, a semi-open kitchen and a roomy bar area. The atmosphere is one of contented bonhomie.

The Fire Stables

Gastropub

T3

Wimbledon ⊖ Wimbledon

27-29 Church Rd SW19 5DQ
(020) 8946 3197
Fax (020) 8946 1101
e-mail thefirestables@youngs.co.uk

Menu £16/20 - Carte £25/32

This may have originally been where the horses to pull the old fire engines were stabled but nowadays it calls itself a 'pub and dining room' and is modish in style without being threateningly trendy. It is also the nearest place to eat when leaving the well-known local tennis courts. Whatever it is, it seems to work. You'll find a separate bar area with its own snackier menu and a long dining room at the back overlooking the garden. Lunch times appear popular with mothers with young children, while noise levels become more boisterously adult in the evenings. The menu covers all bases, from Caesar salads and burgers to more adventurous choices such as game in season and rack of lamb. Puddings are full-bodied and satisfying.

ROLL OUT THE BARREL

Horatio Nelson is celebrated by one of London's best-known landmarks; however he was not always treated with such respect. When he fell at the Battle of Trafalgar in 1805, his body was transported back to England preserved in rum or brandy. The story goes that when the ship arrived home the crew had drunk half the spirits from the barrel: although of dubious truth, the tale has given rise to the slang 'tapping the Admiral', for illicit drinking.

Where to **stay**
Köster C. / Picture Press / STUDIO X

Alphabetical list of Hotels

Dorchester

Park Lane W1A 2HJ ⊖ Hyde Park Corner
✆ (020) 7629 8888 **Fax** (020) 7629 8080
e-mail info@thedorchester.com **www**.thedorchester.com

200 rm – 🚹£323/664 🚹🚹£611/734, ☕ £25.50 – 49 suites
China Tang *(See restaurant listing)*

The Dorchester

Continually evolving and improving, The Dorchester has been a byword for glamour and luxury since opening in 1931. Indeed, its guest list would read like a veritable who's who of the rich and famous, although the hotel is far too discreet to actually let anyone read it. It certainly occupies a commanding position looking over the park, but the reason its reputation remains as high as ever is that it anticipates the expectations and needs of its clients. The bedrooms are undoubtedly one of its great strengths and its suites some of the most sought after rooms in London. Standards of housekeeping are exemplary, as one would expect, and the bathrooms are particularly luxurious.

The Promenade, famed for its light meals and afternoon tea, is the most recognisable feature of the hotel; The Grill Room has been given an exuberant makeover, with acres of tartan and vast murals of dancing Highlanders. Those seeking a glamorous and stylish Chinese restaurant can head downstairs to China Tang. As we went to print Alain Ducasse was about to open another in his series of worldwide restaurants in the hotel.

The Ritz

H4

150 Piccadilly W1J 9BR ⊖ Green Park
(020) 7493 8181 **Fax** (020) 7493 2687
e-mail enquire@theritzlondon.com **www.**theritzlondon.com

116 rm – £306/494 £423/470, £30 – 17 suites

The Ritz Restaurant *(See restaurant listing)*

VISA

AE

The Ritz

In the style of a French chateau, with Louis XVI furnishings, The Ritz has always been more than just a byword for glamour and luxury: it has set the standards by which other hotels are judged and its roll-call of admirers includes the good and the great of the last century. Its position on Piccadilly, overlooking the Park, also makes it one of the city's great landmarks.

Afternoon tea in the magnificent surroundings of the Palm Court is as much a London institution as the Changing of the Guard. It is also so popular that it reinterprets the word 'afternoon' by starting at 11.30am and not finishing until 9pm. The Ritz Restaurant is unquestionably the most opulent dining room in the country and the Rivoli Bar rightly celebrates its art deco origins. The private dining rooms are also unrivalled in the richness of their decoration.

Peach, pink, blue and yellow are the distinctive Ritz colours used in the bedrooms. Antique furniture and gold leaf enhance the Louis XVI feel and the elegance and size of the suites makes them highly desirable; the Royal Suite has a secret door to the bedroom and the Prince of Wales Suite is vast. New bedrooms are being added in 2008.

Mandarin Oriental Hyde Park

66 Knightsbridge SW1X 7LA — ⊖ Knightsbridge
✆ (020) 7235 2000 **Fax** (020) 7235 2001
e-mail molon-info@mohg.com
www.mandarinoriental.com/london

173 rm – ♦£417 ♦♦£476, ☕ £28 – 25 suites
Foliage *(See restaurant listing)*

Mandarin Oriental Hyde Park

The building of the new Richard Rogers designed serviced apartments next door will ensure that traffic around here stays jammed for a couple more years and, while it's bound to make someone nostalgic for Bowater House, it does mean that the Mandarin Oriental Hyde Park will dominate this part of Knightsbridge to an even greater extent. But then, with a façade as impressive as this, maybe they deserve to. Built in 1889 and once a Gentleman's Club, the hotel has considerably more personality than one would expect from a member of an international hotel chain - and there are few hotels so intertwined with Hyde Park. There are two restaurants and you can watch the Household Cavalry ride past from either. Foliage is all about the fancy end of gastronomy while the Park is more informal and crowd-pleasing in its menu. The spa must be one of the best in the city and bedrooms are elegantly decorated and extremely comfortable. They blend a British lack of showiness with touches of Asian gracefulness. Floor managers are still a feature and staff-guest ratios highly impressive.

Claridge's

G3

Brook St W1A 2JQ ⊖ Bond Street
(020) 7629 8860 **Fax** (020) 7499 2210
e-mail guest@claridges.co.uk
www.claridges.co.uk

143 rm – £563/633 ££739, £26 – 60 suites
Gordon Ramsay at Claridge's *(See restaurant listing)*

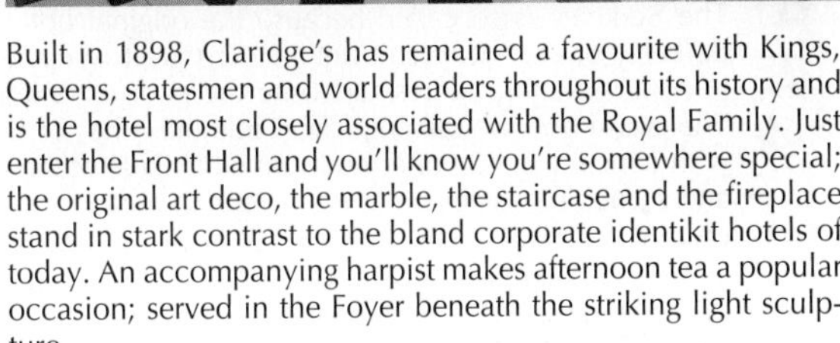
Claridge's

Built in 1898, Claridge's has remained a favourite with Kings, Queens, statesmen and world leaders throughout its history and is the hotel most closely associated with the Royal Family. Just enter the Front Hall and you'll know you're somewhere special; the original art deco, the marble, the staircase and the fireplace stand in stark contrast to the bland corporate identikit hotels of today. An accompanying harpist makes afternoon tea a popular occasion; served in the Foyer beneath the striking light sculpture.

Into such genteel surroundings came the more bullish figure of Gordon Ramsay, but he has managed to update and improve the restaurant while still respecting its traditions. The bar shows how to skilfully add contemporary glamour to complement the original art deco design. This updating of the traditional continues in the bedrooms; the Brook Penthouse suite retains its 1930s fittings and features, yet still feels fresh and vibrant. All mod cons are there but are discreetly concealed, and liveried staff all know exactly what they're doing.

The Berkeley

Wilton Pl SW1X 7RL ⊖ Knightsbridge
(020) 7235 6000 **Fax** (020) 7235 4330
e-mail info@the-berkeley.co.uk **www**.the-berkeley.co.uk

189 rm – £539 £598, £29 – 25 suites
Pétrus *(See restaurant listing)*

The Berkeley

VISA

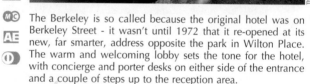

The Berkeley is so called because the original hotel was on Berkeley Street - it wasn't until 1972 that it re-opened at its new, far smarter, address opposite the park in Wilton Place. The warm and welcoming lobby sets the tone for the hotel, with concierge and porter desks on either side of the entrance and a couple of steps up to the reception area.

One of the hotel's most striking features is the rooftop swimming pool, complete with a retractable roof and terrific views of Hyde Park. Those who prefer more spirit-based relaxation should head for the ice cool Blue Bar, which has become one of the most fashionable destination bars in London.

New bedrooms have been seamlessly added to the hotel in recent years which are more contemporary in their styling, but all the rooms are very smart and extremely comfortable; the first to get snapped up are the conservatory suites which all have their own outside terrace. Boxwood Café, located to the side of the hotel, has a relaxed and breezy feel and a menu to match. For some seriously indulgent dining, make reservations at Marcus Wareing's opulent restaurant, Pétrus.

The Lanesborough

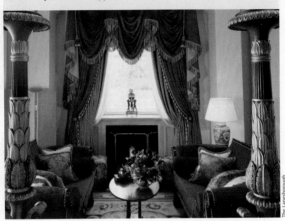

Hyde Park Corner SW1X 7TA ⊖ Hyde Park Corner
✆ (020) 7259 5599 **Fax** (020) 7259 5606
e-mail info@lanesborough.com
www.lanesborough.com

86 rm – 🚹£393/417 🚹🚹£652/675, ☕ £28 – 9 suites

The Lanesborough

VISA

As one of the city's premier luxury hotels, The Lanesborough dominates this part of Hyde Park Corner with its strikingly bright exterior. No doubt some of its more health conscious guests benefit as much from the fresh air of the park as did the patients many years ago when this was a hospital, dating from the early 18C.

All the bedrooms are decorated with a bold Regency opulence and technological mod cons have been incorporated in an unobtrusive manner. Travelling corporate types will appreciate the mobile phone and business cards printed on arrival. All guests enjoy the services of a butler, and will wonder how they ever managed without one; the hotel also has ten cars and its own chauffeurs. The Royal Suite must surely be one of the most lavish and luxurious suites in London. The ornate glass-roofed Conservatory restaurant currently has a Chinoiserie theme but there are plans for a complete overhaul in the early part of 2008. The Library Bar holds some impressive vintage cognacs.

Four Seasons

Hamilton Pl, Park Lane
W1A 1AZ
⊖ Hyde Park Corner

✆ (020) 7499 0888 **Fax** (020) 7493 1895
e-mail fsh.london@fourseasons.com **www**.fourseasons.com

193 rm – †£411/446 ††£493, ☕ £27 – 26 suites

Four Seasons

VISA AE

For the many years this was the only Four Seasons hotel in Europe and, in an understandable bid for independence and individuality, went by the name of the 'Inn on the Park'. Nowadays, in our world of brands and 'corporate identity', it falls more into line among the international portfolio of hotels that cover a considerable number of the major cities around the world. Purpose built over thirty years ago, what it may lack in architectural character it makes up for in space and size - the bedrooms are on average 430 square foot, which is considerably larger than most in the city.

A majority of the suites have balconies or little terraces and the corner suites are particularly capacious. The lobby is overseen by separate concierge and reception areas, while the lounge at the far end of the ground floor is a popular spot for snacks and afternoon tea. Upstairs on the first floor one finds 'Lanes', the hotel dining room which is colourfully decorated with plenty of glass and has an easy, appetising menu. Overlooking the park, it occupies a pleasant spot, as does the clubby bar adjacent.

Landmark London

222 Marylebone Rd NW1 6JQ — ⊖ Baker Street
(020) 7631 8000 **Fax** (020) 7631 8080
e-mail reservations@thelandmark.co.uk
www.landmarklondon.co.uk

290 rm – †£211/340 ††£246/376, □ £28 – 9 suites

Those Victorians certainly knew how to build hotels. The Landmark was originally called the Great Central and was one of the last of the great railway hotels; the façade today still reflects the architectural style of that age. Once inside, however, you quickly realise you're in the company of an international hotel corporation, where size, comfort and facilities fit the exacting standards demanded by your average 21st century traveller.

The most striking feature of the hotel is the vast glass-roofed atrium, under which the Winter Garden restaurant serves breakfast and an international menu at lunch and dinner. Those after something a little more traditional should head downstairs to the wood panelled Cellar Bar, while the Mirror Bar is an altogether more sophisticated spot for cocktail hour.

The bedrooms, many of which face inwards into the atrium, are all generously proportioned and have every mod con you need. Bathrooms are also a good size and the majority have separate showers and double washbasins. Those looking for even greater levels of relaxation will be more than happy with the well equipped Health Club.

The Goring

15 Beeston Pl, Grosvenor Gdns ⊖ Victoria
SW1W 0JW
(020) 7396 9000 **Fax** (020) 7834 4393
e-mail reception@goringhotel.co.uk **www**.goringhotel.co.uk

65 rm – †£327/393 ††£386/434, ☕ £23 – 6 suites

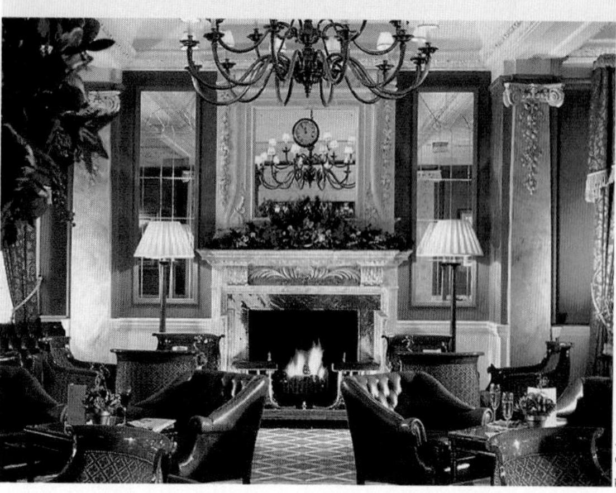

The Goring

The Goring celebrates proper old school hospitality and is all the more admirable for that. It opened in 1910, when it could proudly boast of being London's first hotel to offer private bathrooms and central heating in all its bedrooms, an achievement of uncommon innovation at that time. Today, it is one of the few hotels that have stayed in private hands. Even more remarkable is that those hands all belong to the same family, as it is now being overseen by the fourth generation of the Goring family.

The style is very much English country house in the city (it even has a garden) and the housekeeping standards are never less than exemplary. The atmosphere is discreet and thoroughly courteous.

The Goring, commendably, never merely rests on its considerable laurels but still looks for ways of improving and developing; the restaurant was recently redesigned by David Linley in an understated yet contemporary way which perfectly complements the proudly British fare on offer.

If you see someone in morning dress in the lobby don't assume they're the manager - they're just as likely to be one of the guests about to pop over the road to collect a gong.

One Aldwych

J3

1 Aldwych WC2B 4RH ⊖ Covent Garden
(020) 7300 1000 **Fax** (020) 7300 1001
e-mail sales@onealdwych.com **www**.onealdwych.com

96 rm – †£447 ††£447, ☕ £29.50 – 9 suites

Axis *(See restaurant listing)*

One Aldwych

In 2008 One Aldwych celebrates ten years as one of London's more fashionable addresses. Not only is the location still just so but the contemporary styling within this converted 19C bank and former home to the Morning Post remains fresh and vibrant. There are over 400 pieces of artwork and sculpture scattered throughout the hotel and they start in the enormous lobby which doubles as a bar – a concept that may sound strange but one that works surprisingly well. The bedrooms are very comfortable, with an unfussy and discreet style but one still exuding plenty of warmth. Expect to find all the extras and more. There are two restaurants - Indigo is on the mezzanine level, looking down on the lobby bar, and is the place for salads and lighter fare. Axis has more of a personality as a stand-alone restaurant with its own bar and more ambitious cooking. The leisure facilities have to be good to compete with the attractions outside the front door - and they certainly are. Staff are enthusiastic and committed.

Brown's

Albemarle St W1S 4BP ⊖ Green Park
✆ (020) 7493 6020 **Fax** (020) 7493 9381
e-mail reservations.browns@roccofortecollection.com
www.roccofortecollection.com

105 rm – 🚹£415/575 🚹🚹£540/725, ☕ £27 – 12 suites
🍴 **The Grill** *(See restaurant listing)*

Brown's

Brown's is one of the most English of hotels and comes steeped in history. Opened in 1837 by James Brown, Lord Byron's butler, and extended by the Ford family later that century, it quickly established itself as the favoured choice of the gentry, nobility and royalty. It was here that Alexander Graham Bell first demonstrated his telephone.

The hotel reopened at the end of 2005, having spent a million pounds for every one of the 20 months it was closed for refurbishment. The new look respects both the building and the heritage of the hotel, but also considers the greater expectations of the modern traveller. Books and magazines add character to the bedrooms, which are smart, well equipped and come with some generously proportioned bathrooms. Afternoon tea remains something of an institution but avoids being too quaint or affected. The Donovan Bar, named after the celebrated photographer Terence Donovan, is a contemporary addition and attracts a more youthful clientele. For classic British cooking and a traditional style of service, it's worth booking a table at The Grill restaurant.

The Soho

13

4 Richmond Mews ⊖ Tottenham Court Road
W1D 3DH
✆ (020) 7559 3000 **Fax** (020) 7559 3003
e-mail soho@firmdale.com
www.sohohotel.com

83 rm – †£300 ††£370, ☕ £18.50 – 2 suites

The Soho

A/C SAT VISA MC AE

Amazing what you can do with an old NCP car park, imagination, and an eye for detail and design. The Soho opened late 2004 and the ten foot bronze cat by the entrance tells you this is no ordinary hotel.

For one thing, it proves that style need not compromise comfort and that size does sometimes matter - the bedrooms here are more than generously proportioned and the Penthouse and Soho suites are both handsome and vast. Modern art and sculptures are found throughout the rooms and no detail has been overlooked in their design.

'Refuel' is half bar, half restaurant, with an enormous mural paying ironic homage to this site's former life as one of those architectural carbuncles known as multi-storey car parks. The menu treads a sunny path through warmer climes and offers something for everyone. The adjoining bar will be a welcoming sight after a long day, as will the two sitting rooms which both have a soothing and relaxed quality about them.

The young staff are confident and knowledgeable about their hotel. Even with Soho just outside the door and a youthful clientele, the bedrooms somehow manage to be relatively quiet.

Soho ▶ Plan II

Andaz Liverpool Street

Liverpool St EC2M 7QN ⊖ Liverpool Street
✆ (020) 7961 1234 **Fax** (020) 7961 1235
e-mail info.londonliv@andaz.com
www.london.liverpoolstreet.andaz.com

264 rm – ♀£487/511 ♀♀£546 – 3 suites
Aurora *(See restaurant listing)*

Andaz Liverpool Street

A/C SAT VISA AE

This shows what you can do with a Victorian railway hotel. The red brick exterior may look quite traditional but inside it's all quite funky and individual, with enough restaurants to satisfy the most capricious of diner; there's a pub, a formal and very grand dining room, a Japanese restaurant and one specialising in fish and seafood, as well as several bars.

Originally opened by Sir Terence Conran as the Great Eastern, it now flies under the Hyatt flag and they have done what big corporations do: they have 're-branded' it, in this case with the Andaz name, which apparently means 'special and personal'. The good news is that these hotels are more about individuality and their specific locality and less about corporate identity. This makes sense as this hotel is difficult to pigeonhole, especially when one has seen the gloriously atmospheric Masonic lodge that is available for hire or the mezzanine that looks like something from Frank Lloyd Wright. Bedrooms, too, display an individuality and sense of irony that sets the hotel apart.

Sofitel St James London

6 Waterloo Pl SW1Y 4AN ⊖ Piccadilly Circus
(020) 7747 2200
Fax (020) 7747 2210
www.sofitelstjames.com

179 rm – £161/252 £280/400, £21 – 7 suites
Brasserie Roux *(See restaurant listing)*

Sofitel St James London

Another hotel with a great location, this one overlooking the John Nash designed Waterloo Place, on the corner with Pall Mall and within strolling distance of many of the city's most familiar attractions. It is housed, commendably discreetly, within the sensitively restored Grade II listed former home of the Cox and Kings Company and was built in 1923.

The hotel opened as a Sofitel in 2002 and offers the level of comfort one associates with today's more demanding international traveller; the bedrooms come with all the communication gadgets we now expect, there's a choice of colour schemes and the general style is one of sleek, contemporary design lines, refreshingly free from chintz.

Yin and yang come courtesy of the bar and lounge; the bar is a decidedly masculine room, furnished with plenty of wood and leather and with a decidedly clubby atmosphere, while the Lounge is an altogether more florid affair, which exuberantly celebrates the rose in all its splendour and serves that altogether more genteel event: afternoon tea. For classic French specialities head to Brasserie Roux, found in the former banking hall.

Haymarket

1 Suffolk Place SW1Y 4BP ⊖ Piccadilly Circus
(020) 7470 4000 **Fax** (020) 7470 4004
e-mail haymarket@firmdale.com
www.haymarkethotel.com

47 rm – £288 £364, £18.50 – 3 suites

Firmdale Hotels

The latest hotel from Tim & Kit Kemp opened in May 2007 and once again they've created a stylish, hip place, refreshingly free from any bland corporate appurtenances. They have converted a grand John Nash Regency building that had been a gentleman's club and an office before the interior was destroyed in a fire. Now colours, art and an eclectic collection of furniture run through it; the lobby, conservatory and library of the ground floor are immaculately dressed and set the tone for the hotel. Individually styled bedrooms come with dressed mannequins - the motif of the Kemp's hotels – and custom-made furniture. They are all light, bright and calming with a subtle English feel. For extra quietness ask for one overlooking the inner decked courtyard. Brumus is the restaurant – named in honour of the owner's hound- and offers easy Italian food in spacious surroundings.

The location couldn't be better for those coming 'up west'. Theatre-land is literally just outside – indeed, the hotel adjoins the Haymarket theatre – and is a short stroll away from all that London offers, from galleries and parks to shops and squares. If that isn't enough, there's a very cool swimming pool downstairs.

The Waldorf Hilton

Aldwych WC2B 4DD ⊖ Covent Garden
(020) 7836 2400 **Fax** (020) 7836 4648
e-mail enquiry.waldorflondon@hilton.com
www.hilton.co.uk/waldorf

289 rm – £198/421 £198/421, £22 – 10 suites

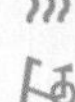

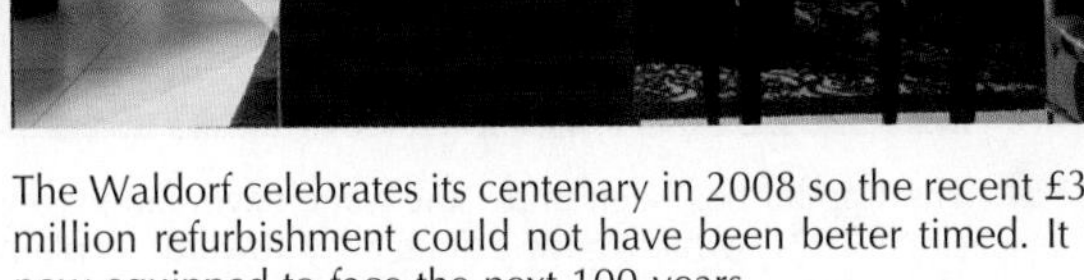

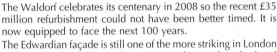

The Waldorf Hilton

The Waldorf celebrates its centenary in 2008 so the recent £35 million refurbishment could not have been better timed. It is now equipped to face the next 100 years.

The Edwardian façade is still one of the more striking in London and, inside, the designers have managed to update the hotel while still respecting its traditions. The bedrooms certainly have a more contemporary look and the branded corporate identity is kept to a minimum so perhaps they were conscious the Waldorf name is more interesting than the name of the owners. It is just a shame that the Palm Court, once one of London's most famous spots for afternoon tea dances, is now just used for private parties.

Homage is the all-encompassing name for the food and drink part of the operation. This includes the Grand Salon, a large pillared restaurant with changing artwork for sale and a Mediterranean influenced menu. The patisserie morphs into a Champagne bar as night falls. Those who prefer to spend their free time in more physical pursuits will find impressively spacious leisure facilities, especially when one considers the price per square footage in this part of town.

Capital

F5

22-24 Basil St SW3 1AT ⊖ Knightsbridge
✆ (020) 7589 5171 **Fax** (020) 7225 0011
e-mail reservations@capitalhotel.co.uk **www**.capitalhotel.co.uk

49 rm – ♦£206/335 ♦♦£394/429, ☐ £18.50

The Capital Restaurant *(See restaurant listing)*

Capital

A/C

SAT

VISA

AE

The Capital has been under the same Levin family ownership since 1971, which goes a long way towards explaining the atmosphere found within. Staying here is like staying at a quintessentially British country house hotel, albeit one that's in the centre of London and yards from some of the capital's world famous emporia. The hotel has always understood the importance of a good welcome and the one thing guaranteed here is that you will not be able to just sidle in unnoticed; the little lobby is sandwiched between concierge and reception desks and an acknowledgment is a sure-thing. Public areas are quite limited in size but that just seems to add to the sense of discretion. They include a charming little sitting room for afternoon tea and an elegant little bar which adjoins the restaurant. Bedrooms have all recently been refurbished but have retained their sense of Britishness in look and personality. Paintings from the owner's own collection feature throughout and one can tick off all the luxury features: hand-made mattresses, Egyptian cotton sheets, control consoles and luxury marbled bathrooms.

Charlotte Street

12

15 Charlotte St W1T 1RJ ⊖ Goodge Street
✆ (020) 7806 2000 **Fax** (020) 7806 2002
e-mail charlotte@firmdale.com **www**.charlottestreethotel.co.uk

44 rm – 🚹£247/282 🚹🚹£347, ☕ £19 – 8 suites
🍴 **Oscar** *(See restaurant listing)*

VISA

AE

Charlotte Street

It's not just the location, within strolling distance of Soho, or that the hotel has its own private screening room that attracts the media types, film industry sorts and arty souls who have made this hotel their own, but the stimulating way in which it has been decorated and the prevailing vibe.

This one-time dental warehouse has been deftly transformed into a very chic hotel and proves that comfort and design can be equal bed fellows and that something good has come from British dentistry. Using a combination of abstract art, sculpture and paintings from artists of the neighbouring Bloomsbury set, the hotel manages to be also quite English in tone. The drawing rooms are tranquil, stress-free areas, in contrast to the bustle of the bar and Oscar restaurant.

Dotted among the bedrooms are one-off pieces of furniture combined with top drawer fabrics and fittings, all supported by a maintenance programme of virtually constant refurbishment. Staff all appear to be enthusiastic and confident. The loft and penthouse suites will stir emotions of envy and desire or, if you've got one, glee.

The Halkin

5 Halkin St SW1X 7DJ ⊖ Hyde Park Corner
(020) 7333 1000 **Fax** (020) 7333 1100
e-mail res@halkin.como.bz **www**.halkin.como.bz

35 rm – £458 ££558, £25 – 6 suites
Nahm *(See restaurant listing)*

SAT VISA AE

The Halkin

The Halkin was one of the first places in London to call itself a 'townhouse hotel' before any of us really knew what that meant. It recognised that design and aesthetics were as important as the number of TV channels on offer and that fewer rooms ensured more personal service and a more intimate atmosphere. Today, through constant refurbishment and refreshment, it remains one of the city's most chic addresses, offering understated English elegance matched with Italian design flair, while effortlessly complementing the very charming Georgian surroundings of Belgravia. You know you're somewhere pretty glamorous when even the staff are wearing Giorgio Armani.
The lobby is a relatively discreet affair, with gossamer drapes dividing it from the bar. Nahm, also on the ground floor, offers artful Thai cuisine. The accommodation, spread over five floors, offers guests all the latest hi-tech facilities at the tap of a touch-pad. Rooms are uncluttered and unfussy, with white the predominant colour, and the bathrooms are very luxurious.

Covent Garden

13

10 Monmouth St WC2H 9HB ⊖ Covent Garden

✆ (020) 7806 1000 **Fax** (020) 7806 1100
e-mail covent@firmdale.com
www.coventgardenhotel.co.uk

56 rm – ♂£264/323 ♂♂£376, ☕ £19.50 – 2 suites

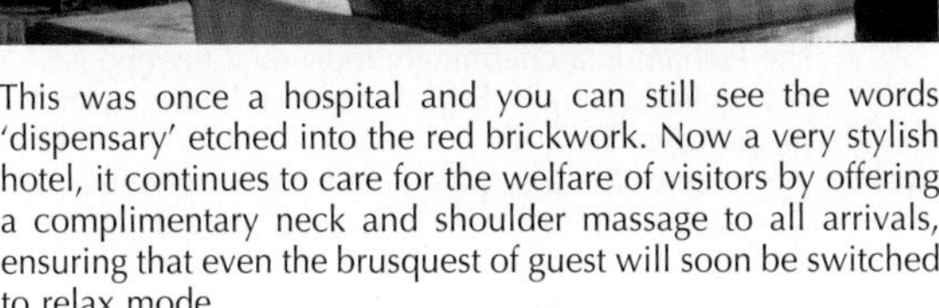

Covent Garden

This was once a hospital and you can still see the words 'dispensary' etched into the red brickwork. Now a very stylish hotel, it continues to care for the welfare of visitors by offering a complimentary neck and shoulder massage to all arrivals, ensuring that even the brusquest of guest will soon be switched to relax mode.

To the right of the entrance one finds Brasserie Max, a casual, easy restaurant that boasts plenty of local followers and offers an extensive selection of modern dishes with European influences, as well as doubling as the breakfast room. It's upstairs to the charming wood panelled drawing room, open only to residents, which offers a calming oasis when not being used for a photo shoot.

Those whose pastime or profession involves cinema can arrange a private viewing in the hotel's own screening room, with its soft Italian leather seats. Bedrooms continue the theme of understated elegance and thoughtful design and are all very comfortable and individual. Those on the Monmouth Street side tend to benefit from larger windows and of the two top floor suites, one has its own library, the other its own terrace.

The Pelham

E6 

15 Cromwell Pl SW7 2LA ⊖ South Kensington
✆ (020) 7589 8288 **Fax** (020) 7584 8444
e-mail pelham@firmdale.com **www**.pelhamhotel.co.uk

50 rm – 🛉£200/223 🛉🛉£305, ☕ £21 – 2 suites

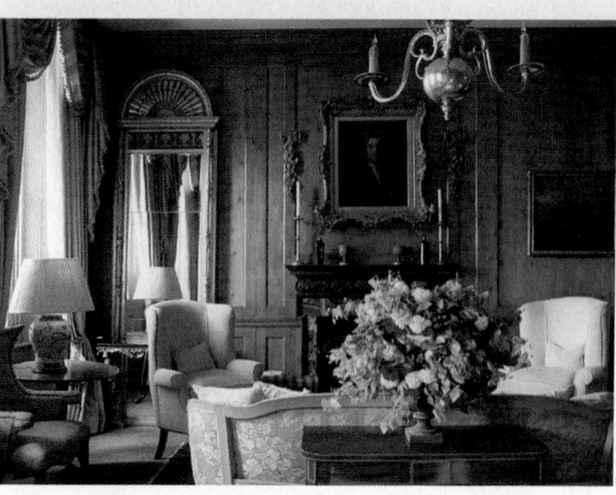

The Pelham

The Pelham is a charmingly individual townhouse, decorated in a quintessentially English country house style. The period feel surrounds you the minute you enter and the two drawing rooms, one with pine panelling the other with mahogany lined bookcases and both with fireplaces, are a delight.

Downstairs you'll find Kemps, the cosy restaurant decorated with original works of art which becomes a very romantic spot in the evenings. The menu offers a satisfying selection of dishes with either a British or Mediterranean bent.

All the bedrooms are individually decorated and continue the theme of a country house in the city. Those on the first and second floors benefit from higher ceilings and many share some of the original features of the house. Techno-extras are discreetly blended into the decoration to ensure that business types have all the facilities they require, without the feeling of sleeping in an office. South Kensington tube station is literally across the road so, if the plethora of attractions nearby is not enough, reaching those around the city could not be easier.

Blakes

D6

33 Roland Gdns SW7 3PF ⊖ Gloucester Road
✆ (020) 7370 6701 **Fax** (020) 7373 0442
e-mail blakes@blakeshotels.com **www**.blakeshotels.com

40 rm – †£205/315 ††£440, ☕ £25 – 12 suites

Blakes

Before they applied to hotels like Blakes, words like "daring" and "dramatic" were mostly used to describe the more eccentric of guest, when the poor loves had nowhere to stay that really understood them. The opening by Anouska Hempel of Blakes in 1981 not only provided London with its first strikingly theatrical hotel, it also blazed a trail in hotel design in which all subsequent boutique hotels and townhouses were to follow.

The lobby sets the tone with oriental boxes, bamboo, birdcages and idiosyncratic little design touches, which all tell you this is no ordinary hotel. The Chinese room and bar, which adjoin the basement restaurant, have become popular nightspots and this fusion of east meets west continues in the specialities on the menu.

It is in the bedrooms where the sheer individuality is most evident. Stencils, shutters, prints, period furniture, ethereal drapes and *trompe d'oeils* make every room a true original. Suite 007 is one of the most striking bedrooms in London. Many hotels boast of not having two rooms alike, but few can really claim to boast of differences as conspicuous as Blakes.

The Milestone

D4

1-2 Kensington Court ⊖ High Street Kensington
W8 5DL
(020) 7917 1000 **Fax** (020) 7917 1010
e-mail bookms@rchmail.com **www**.milestonehotel.com

52 rm – £376 ££376, £25 – 5 suites

R.Burr/Michelin

It may be on quite a busy road, but the location of this charming Victorian hotel is pretty impressive as it's opposite Kensington Palace and allows great views across Kensington Gardens. Inside, it's much bigger than one realises but it still manages to retain a sense of intimacy and affability.

Afternoon tea is served in the Park Lounge, a charming wood panelled room with comfy sofas, while Cheneston's is the sweet little dining room, offering a menu which balances contemporary dishes with the more traditional. If you're a bigger group try booking the Orangery, a cosy area attached to the restaurant, which was originally the prayer room of the house. The bar is at the back of the house and is called Stables - this was where the original owner of the house kept his horses and the equine theme is continued with the paintings and collection of jockey silks.

Bedrooms are all attractively furnished, have a discernible sense of individuality and all offer plenty of modern extras. The suites are particularly charming; some are split level and several have four poster beds.

Stafford

16-18 St James's Pl SW1A 1NJ ⊖ Green Park
(020) 7493 0111 **Fax** (020) 7493 7121
e-mail information@thestaffordhotel.co.uk
www.thestaffordhotel.co.uk

73 rm – †£317/352 ††£411/440, ☕ £23 – 32 suites

Stafford

Tradition without progress usually means just worn-out. The Stafford has managed the dual task of respecting its heritage as a quintessentially English hotel while, at the same time, renewing itself by constantly refurbishing and improving. 2007 saw the opening of their new Mews suites and the existing rooms, decorated with the best of British fabrics and fittings, are regularly given a facelift.

The hotel enjoys one of the best locations in London – bang in the middle but shielded from the general clamour of merry-making. Its lounges are areas of quiet repose punctuated by the clinking of tea cups while the dining room, where men are still required to don a jacket, offers the classic cuisine combination of Britain and France, so that, alongside the Dover Sole and game, you'll find terrines and soufflés. Furthermore, there aren't many restaurants left where things are carved and flambéed at your table.

It's not just the clientele that has proved their loyalty: there are so many long-standing members of staff that any member who has been at the hotel for less than 10 years is considered to be just settling in.

The Hempel

D3

31-35 Craven Hill Gdns W2 3EA — Queensway
(020) 7298 9000 **Fax** (020) 7402 4666 — Closed 25 December
e-mail hotel@the-hempel.co.uk **www**.the-hempel.co.uk

42 rm – £346/370 ££370, £19.75 – 5 suites

The Hempel

Anyone whose idea of a hotel is a trouser-press, a kettle and those little capsules of UHT milk will just not get The Hempel, for here is a hotel all about aesthetics, symmetry and style. Designed by Anouska Hempel and now owned and run by Irishman Michael McBride, the hotel was like nowhere else when it opened a decade ago. All monochrome and minimalist, anyone wishing for privacy needed only to wear white and they would disappear, chameleon-like, into the surroundings. Today, the place remains just as crisp and uncluttered but the new owner has softened things up with the addition of a little colour and the occasional spot of whimsy. It is also now more fashionable than ever.

I Thai is the downstairs restaurant that ploughs its own culinary furrow by blending the cuisines of Thailand, Japan and Italy but it's the bedrooms that are the main event here. They are idiosyncratic, chic and original. Room 107 must have one of the highest ceilings in London, there's a suspended bed in 110 and those who like black should ask for 405.

Bayswater • Maida Vale ▶ Page VII

Sanderson

H2

50 Berners St W1T 3NG ⊖ Oxford Circus
✆ (020) 7300 1400 **Fax** (020) 7300 1401
e-mail sanderson@morganshotelgroup.com
www.morganshotelgroup.com

150 rm – †£264/441 ††£294/499, ☕ £21.50

Sanderson

Oil paintings of pastoral scenes hang in all the bedrooms. The difference is that at The Sanderson they hang on the ceiling. Welcome to the world of Philippe Starck.

The celebrated French designer's touch is evident everywhere, reflecting his love of the playful, the whimsical, the clean and the uncluttered. The dream-like style of the lobby alone sets the tone for this most fashionable hotel, which takes its name from the building's previous incarnation as HQ of the famous wallpaper company.

The Purple Bar is as exclusive as it gets and uses fabrics of every shade of purple to create a theatrical and mysterious vibe. In contrast, the Long Bar rejoices in light and freshness. Suka is the name of the new black and marble restaurant, where Malaysian dishes designed for sharing are cooked in an open kitchen. Agua is draped with white and offers some serious pampering, while those who prefer more active therapy should head to the billiard room, with its striking John Piper stained glass.

Modernity and originality continue in the bedrooms which come with glass enclosed bathrooms, sleigh beds, bright white walls and sheer drapes.

Draycott

F6

26 Cadogan Gdns SW3 2RP ⊖ Sloane Square
(020) 7730 6466 **Fax** (020) 7730 0236
e-mail reservations@draycotthotel.com
www.draycotthotel.com

31 rm – †£159/347 ††£219/347, ☕ £19.95 – 4 suites

A/C

VISA

MC

AE

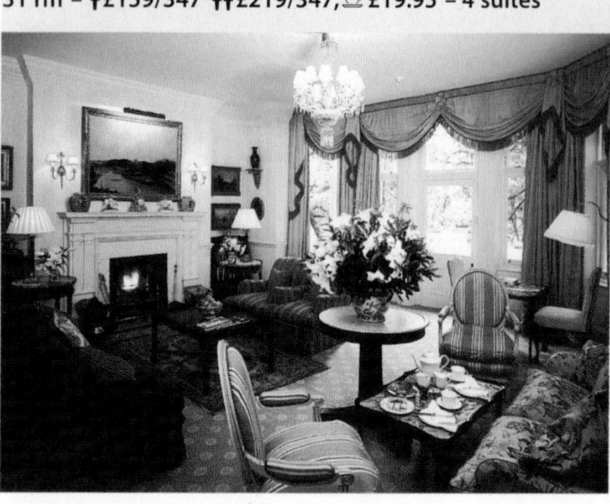

Draycott

The Draycott is actually three Edwardian houses (numbers 22, 24 and 26) knocked together, and occupies an enviable spot just yards from Sloane Square. The drawing room is one of the hotel's most charming features and looks out over the communal gardens. It is here where complimentary afternoon tea is served, as well as early evening drinks, giving the more sociably inclined the opportunity of meeting one's fellow guests.

All the rooms are named after writers or actors, although whoever decided that Peter O'Toole would be an appropriate name for the breakfast room is clearly unfamiliar with the great man's reputation.

Bedrooms are all individual in their size and styling; those in house number 22 tend to be slightly bigger and first floor rooms have higher ceilings. There are nice little touches, like a teddy bear in each room and a memento, such as a book or photograph, relating to the person after whom the bedroom is named and some of the rooms have a fireplace. There is no dining room but a room service menu provides an adequate selection for those not wishing to venture outside.

The Metropolitan

Old Park Lane W1K 1LB ⊖ Hyde Park Corner
(020) 7447 1000 **Fax** (020) 7447 1100
e-mail res.lon@metropolitan.como.bz **www**.metropolitan.como.bz

147 rm - £440 £440/763, £25 - 3 suites
Nobu *(See restaurant listing)*

The Metropolitan

Welcome to the world of the beautiful people. If you've seen paparazzi shots of a star – of the real or reality firmament - leaving a bar in a tired and emotional state then more than likely those snaps were taken outside the Met Bar, a nightspot considerably smaller in size than in reputation. For some, getting guaranteed access to the Met Bar is, in itself, reason enough to check into the Metropolitan Hotel but this is more than just a hang out for the achingly trendy.

The rooms are chic in an understated way and come with the full range of technological gizmos. For those staying in rooms at the front of the hotel, the large windows frame the wonderful views of Hyde Park and the penthouse suite – and its wonderful shower - is certainly one of the most striking in the city. All this and you've got Nobu on the first floor.

As one would expect, this is a popular hotel with the music and film businesses and those who use words like agent, stylist and wardrobe. So look carefully, because the seemingly confused troglodyte sharing the lift with you may well be someone who brushes up exceedingly well.

Westbury

H3

Bond St W1S 2YF ⊖ Bond Street
(020) 7629 7755 **Fax** (020) 7495 1163
e-mail sales@westburymayfair.com **www**.westburymayfair.com

230 rm – £468 ££515, £20.95 – 19 suites

Westbury

The Westbury was built in 1955 and the Polo bar caused quite a stir at the time with its confident American swagger. Today the bar remains one of the best spots in Mayfair for satisfying any number of needs, whether they be post-shopping restorative refreshment, afternoon tea with out-of-towners or pre-prandial cocktails in the evening.

With the ever fashionable Bond Street outside the front door, The Westbury could not be better placed for those who enjoy shopping at the loftier end of the retail world. The hotel itself has also been spending money at a furious pace, with a recently completed programme of comprehensive refurbishment and redecoration. The bedrooms have all been done up to a good standard; flat screen TVs and all the mod cons have been installed but they have retained a sense of Englishness and Mayfair understatement so nothing is too brash or designery; those rooms with front facing balconies provide a real sense of time and place. The smart new restaurant on the ground floor is all fawns and muted colours, with a modern and quite elaborate European menu.

The Cadogan

75 Sloane St SW1X 9SG ⊖ Knightsbridge
✆ (020) 7235 7141 **Fax** (020) 7245 0994
e-mail cadogan@thesteingroup.com **www**.cadogan.com

63 rm – 🚹£300/347 🚹🚹£347, ☕ £20 – 2 suites

The Cadogan

The Cadogan owes much of its lasting fame to two of its most renowned residents; Lillie Langtry, actress and royal mistress, and Oscar Wilde, who was famously arrested here in 1895 (it was in room 118, which is, in reality, quite a lot smaller than it was depicted on stage in *The Judas Kiss*).

120 years after its opening, the hotel still has a very English, even Edwardian, feel, while managing to offer the comforts and standards expected by today's traveller. The bedrooms are divided roughly half and half between a contemporary and a more traditional style, both with their own appeal. All the rooms are reached via a wonderful old-fashioned lift which, no doubt, causes palpitations for your average Health and Safety inspector.

The ground floor wood panelled drawing room is a charming place for afternoon tea or afternoon napping, and leads into the clubby bar. The restaurant is a fairly intimate affair, popular with local groups and societies, and offers a menu of assorted international influences.

Outside, one of the city's most exclusive shopping streets awaits your credit card.

The Bentley Kempinski

27-33 Harrington Gdns ⊖ Gloucester Road
SW7 4JX
✆ (020) 7244 5555 **Fax** (020) 7244 5566
e-mail info@thebentley-hotel.com **www**.thebentley-hotel.com

52 rm – †£353 ††£470, ☕ £22.50 – 12 suites

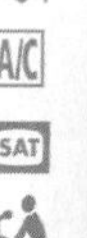

The Bentley Kempinski

A series of white stuccoed buildings were knocked together in 2003 to create the hotel and if the liberal use of gold leaf is anything to go by, it wasn't done on the cheap. Apparently over 600 tonnes of marble were also imported and much of that is evident in the public areas. It's there too in the bedrooms which all occupy a decent amount of acreage. The Imperial Suite is the biggest and best and should satisfy your average corporate big-wig. Bathrooms are where the designers were clearly given free rein to spend the owner's money and understated there are not.

There are two restaurants, with Peridot being the brighter and more attractive of the two. This is where breakfast and the occasional lunch are served while dinner is offered downstairs in the 1880 restaurant, named after the date of the building. Tables are so far apart that they may be in different time zones and the room does need customers to create an atmosphere. The kitchen has ambition and serves highly elaborate cooking that's a tad overworked. Malachite, the bar opposite, is a very snazzy affair.

Knightsbridge

F5

10 Beaufort Gdns SW3 1PT ⊖ Knightsbridge
✆ (020) 7584 6300 **Fax** (020) 7584 6355
e-mail knightsbridge@firmdale.com
www.knightsbridgehotel.com

44 rm – ♂£188/229 ♂♂£280/329, ☕ £16.50

Knightsbridge

The assertion "whoever said money can't buy happiness simply didn't know where to shop" has been attributed to several people, but whoever it was would love the Knightsbridge Hotel. Being so close to all the great shops, department stores and boutiques of London it's hardly surprising that every guest returning to the hotel late in the day appears weighed down with shopping bags. The hotel re-opened in 2002, was originally converted from a row of Victorian terrace houses and the pretty little cul-de-sac provides relatively quiet surroundings considering the central location.

Featured in the centre of the lobby is an original sculpture resembling a stalagmite of slate and you'll find further artwork in the drawing room, summing up the general style of the place. There's a library which, surprisingly for a hotel, actually contains books, as well as an honesty bar for residents. There is no restaurant but breakfast and a 24 hour menu are served in the rooms.

The bedrooms themselves offer the perfect balance between style and practicability, with the three junior suites being particularly attractive. This is a cool and altogether rather sophisticated London address.

The Zetter

St John's Square, 86-88 Clerkenwell Rd EC1M 5RJ — ⊖ Farringdon

✆ (020) 7324 4444 **Fax** (020) 7324 4445

e-mail sales@thezetter.com **www**.thezetter.com

59 rm – ♦£182 ♦♦£182, ☕ £16.95

VISA

MC

AE

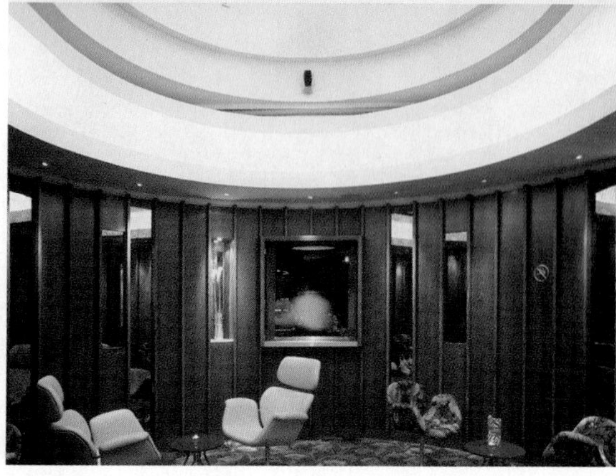

The Zetter

Housed in a converted 19th century warehouse and with a reputation for style, design and laid-back urban chic, The Zetter mirrors the fashionable reputation of its Clerkenwell surroundings. The building's origins are evident in the exposed brick walls but there are also a number of original design aspects to set this hotel apart, from the striking atrium to the 7 studio bedrooms with their own patios.

Within the subtly lit bedrooms you'll find modern techno services, such as LCD televisions with a vast library of music tracks available, have been nicely juxtaposed with homely touches, such as a selection of classic Penguin paperbacks. Vending machines on each floor provide anything from disposable cameras to champagne and the building's air conditioning uses water pumped from the hotels own bore-hole.

The general carefree vibe of the crescent-shaped restaurant, with its large sash windows overlooking the cobbled St John's Square, also bears little resemblance to a typical hotel dining room. Here the cooking is Italian in influence, with a welcome flexibility in both menu and opening hours to suit all comers.

Number Sixteen

16 Sumner Pl SW7 3EG ⊖ South Kensington
✆ (020) 7589 5232 **Fax** (020) 7584 8615
e-mail sixteen@firmdale.com
www.numbersixteenhotel.co.uk

42 rm – 🚹£130/217 🚹🚹£311, ☕ £19.50

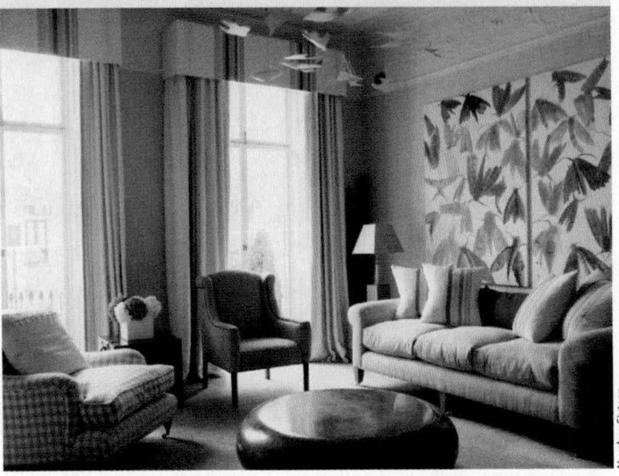

Number Sixteen

Actually, it's numbers 14 – 17 but whose counting? Anyway, Number Sixteen is a snappier name. The hotel is made up of four lustrously bright white houses in a mid Victorian terrace, located in a very charming street with all the museums, shops and restaurants you'll need within walking distance. Unlike many a recent conversion from private house to intimate hotel, this one has ensured that everyone has plenty of room. On the ground floor there are two delightful drawing rooms, overlooking Sumner Place and decorated with interesting modern British artwork.

The conservatory breakfast room leads out into a pretty private garden, which is surprisingly large given the South Kensington location, and indeed four of the bedrooms open out onto this very restful space.

All the bedrooms combine a sense of Englishness with a modern freshness and vitality. Roberts radios are in all the rooms, along with granite bathrooms and top of the range fabrics and the housekeeping department is clearly on top of its game. This is one of those hotels which doesn't feel too much like a hotel and is all the more special for that.

Durrants

26-32 George St W1H 5BJ ⊖ Bond Street
(020) 7935 8131 **Fax** (020) 7487 3510
e-mail enquiries@durrantshotel.co.uk **www**.durrantshotel.co.uk

89 rm – £120 £175, £14.50 – 3 suites

Durrants

Durrants is as English as warm beer and understatement and has been under the same family ownership for over eighty years. You'll find liveried staff polishing the brass in the lobby and what looks like your Great Aunt taking afternoon tea in surroundings resembling a country house. The timeless feel is particularly evident in the bar which is divided into two rooms and has muskets hanging on the walls and above the fireplace.

The wood panelled dining room offers a full range of classics, supplemented by the daily changing dishes on the trolley, although there are nods to more contemporary cuisine. A separate dining room is used exclusively for breakfast which is served until a highly commendable midday.

Traditionalists and technophobes will be pleased to know that bedrooms are still opened by an actual key. The housekeeper, who has been here over twenty years, keeps the rooms spotless and they are furnished in a traditionally English style. The quietest are at the back and have air conditioning. The rooms themselves are also traditionally English in a simple and unassuming style.

Dorset Square

39-40 Dorset Sq NW1 6QN ⊖ Marylebone
✆ (020) 7723 7874 **Fax** (020) 7724 3328 Closed 1 week Christmas
e-mail reservations@dorsetsquare.co.uk **www**.dorsetsquare.co.uk

37 rm – †£176 ††£282, ☕ £14

Dorset Square

Dorset Square is one of those ideal locations; within walking distance of many attractions but one removed from the great bustle and din of the metropolis. The hotel is a pretty Regency house and the square opposite was where Thomas Lord laid out his ground in 1787, before it moved up the road in 1814 to what is now Lord's. His memory lives on during Test matches; just check out the number of guests sporting the MCC club colours of egg-and-bacon. They all stay here not just because of the ease of travel but for the very Englishness of the hotel and the effusive welcome. There's an honesty bar in the drawing room and the Potting Shed restaurant downstairs is as delightful as the name suggests. Here, the cricket theme continues, thanks to the large mural, and the menu offers a balanced selection of modern European food, with the occasional live jazz accompaniment. The bedrooms reflect the age of the house which means a mix of sizes and some sloping lintels - but they all share fine country style fabrics and bags of charm.

K + K George

C6

1-15 Templeton Pl SW5 9NB ⊖ Earl's Court
(020) 7598 8700 **Fax** (020) 7370 2285
e-mail hotelgeorge@kkhotels.co.uk **www**.kkhotels.com

154 rm – £200 ££235

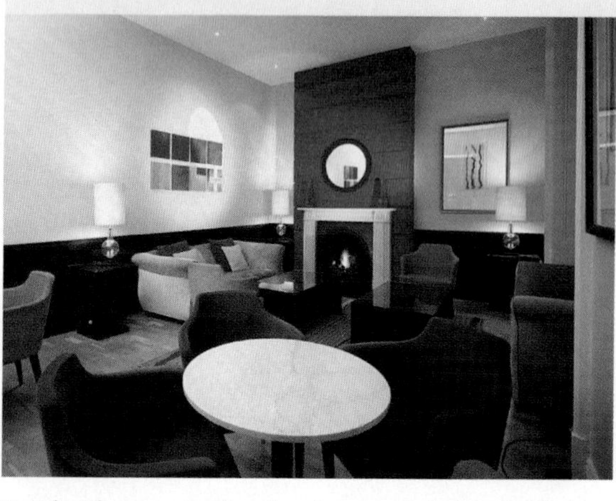

K&K George

K+K hotels are a small, privately owned chain, all of whose hotels seem to blend seamlessly into the fabric of the assorted European cities in which they are located. London is no exception, as the K+K George is set within an imposing stucco fronted and luminously white Georgian terrace and is in a useful location for both tourists and attendees of exhibition halls and trade fairs nearby.

In contrast to the period façade, the hotel's interior is colourfully contemporary in style, with clean lines and a refreshing lack of chintz. Those who struggle to lift their mood first thing in the day will appreciate the bright and comfortable breakfast room as it looks out onto the hotel's own private garden - a charming and, considering the location, surprisingly large space.

A simple bistro style menu is served in the friendly and less structured surroundings of the bar while corporate guests will find all the kit they need for any homework. Bedrooms all come in relatively decent dimensions and have a certain Scandinavian feel and freshness about them.

The Gore

D5

190 Queen's Gate SW7 5EX ⊖ Gloucester Road
✆ (020) 7584 6601 **Fax** (020) 7589 8127
e-mail reservations@gorehotel.com **www**.gorehotel.com

50 rm – †£330 ††£340/520, ☕ £16.95

The Gore

The Gore feels considerably smaller and more intimate than its number of bedrooms suggests, has considerable idiosyncratic charm and its location, in a pleasant tree lined avenue within walking distance of so much, cannot be faulted. The tone is set by the charming hallway and reception, where the walls are covered with pictures and paintings of Queen Victoria, highly appropriate considering this is a late Victorian building and the neighbourhood is so closely linked to her reign.

The restaurant lies somewhere between a bistro and a brasserie and is a fun and lively spot, with a Euro friendly menu. The wood panelled bar opposite has proven to be a destination in itself (and benefits from being the nearest one to the Albert Hall).

An on-going refurbishment programme ensures that the rooms and bathrooms are kept up to scratch, although there has been a reduction recently in the vast number of paintings and pictures which once covered virtually every space. The style of the bedrooms remains theatrical, original and, at times, mildly eccentric with many a story behind the furniture: the Venus Room boasts Judy Garland's old bed.

The London Outpost

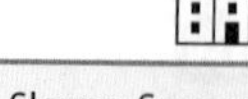

F6

69 Cadogan Gdns SW3 2RB
⊖ Sloane Square
(020) 7589 7333 **Fax** (020) 7581 4958
Closed 23-27 December
e-mail info@londonoutpost.co.uk **www**.londonoutpost.co.uk

11 rm – 🚹£235 🚹🚹£273/387, ☕ £16.95

A/C VISA MC AE

R.Burr/Michelin

Until recently the full moniker was 'The London Outpost of Bovey Castle' but when the owner, Peter de Savary, sold off his hotel in deepest Devon the name of his London hotel changed to its current shorter version.

The London Outpost is his charming little townhouse hotel with just eleven bedrooms, all of which are named after writers or artists who have some local connection to this part of Chelsea. 'Turner' is the best room, with a four poster bed, high ceiling and a fireplace, but all the bedrooms are individual in character, with busts, antiques and prints adding to the period feel.

Being so small, the hotel encourages a certain house-party mood and guests are invited each evening to share a glass of champagne with the manager and get a chance to meet fellow guests in the very charming drawing room. Afternoon tea is served in the downstairs library, as are an extensive selection of malt whiskies later in the day.

The hotel will also supply a key for access to the gardens opposite and will willingly organise a picnic on summer's days.

22 Jermyn Street

22 Jermyn St SW1Y 6HL ⊖ Piccadilly Circus
(020) 7734 2353 **Fax** (020) 7734 0750
e-mail office@22jermyn.com **www**.22jermyn.com

5 rm – ♂£258 ♂♂£258 – 13 suites

22 Jermyn St

A hotel for the man about town. Running between Regent and St James's Streets, Jermyn Street dates back to 1664 and is one of London's most celebrated, thanks to the roll call of familiar names providing all manner of sartorial finery to the well dressed gentleman. Number 22 was reconstructed at the turn of the 19C and has been in the Togna family since 1915, with Henry Togna, the current owner, responsible for transforming it into the luxury townhouse it is today.

While there are no public areas to the hotel, the bedrooms are of sufficient size for this not to matter; of the 18 rooms, 13 are suites and who can complain when breakfast in bed is the only option? A full 24-hour room service menu is also available but this is a hotel for the sort of person who knows their way around town; there are innumerable dining options within walking distance and assorted hostelries within staggering distance. All the rooms are elegantly decorated, with additional sofa beds in the suites and plenty of extras, from DVD players to bathrobes.

Knightsbridge Green

159 Knightsbridge SW1X 7PD
(020) 7584 6274 **Fax** (020) 7225 1635
e-mail reservations@thekghotel.com
www.thekghotel.com

⊖ Knightsbridge
Closed Christmas

16 rm – £135/206 ££176/206, £12 – 12 suites

VISA

Knightsbridge Green

Those who enjoy shopping, jogging or sightseeing, or indeed all three, will find little wrong with Knightsbridge Green's location: it's on the doorstep of all the best shops, a road-crossing away from Hyde Park and a short bus ride away from all the attractions.

Spread over six floors, it offers clean and comfortable accommodation at a price that must be thought reasonable when one considers the position and the neighbourhood. Decoration is inoffensively neutral and unfussy, with decently sized single rooms found on the top floor. Bedrooms 34 and 24 are perhaps the pick of the rooms in terms of size and are also quieter than most.

What makes Knightsbridge Green stand out is the care shown to customers, consequence of it being relatively small and privately owned. It also helps that many of the staff, from manager to maid, have been with the hotel for many years so regulars are recognised and any special requests catered for.

Complimentary teas and coffees are provided throughout the day and breakfast is served in the bedrooms until 10am for those impervious to the attractions of early morning exercise.

The Rockwell

C5

181-183 Cromwell Rd SW5 0SF
(020) 7244 2000 **Fax** (020) 7244 2001
e-mail enquiries@therockwell.com
www.therockwell.com

40 rm – £120/160 £180/200, £12.50

The Rockwell

The Rockwell brings a little contemporary styling to the less glamorous 'Australian' end of Cromwell Road. Owned by a family of builders, they have knocked together two large Victorian houses and have created a hotel with a sense of individuality and freshness. The lobby/reception is an open-plan affair with a fireplace and plenty of reading material and this leads through into the small dining room and bar which offer an easy menu of modern European staples. This, in turn, looks out over what is one of the most appealing features of the hotel – the secluded and stylishly lit south-facing garden terrace.

Bedrooms come with plenty of oak and are decorated in bold, warm colours. Flat screen TVs, mini-bars and Egyptian cotton sheets are standard features. Bathrooms are a little on the small size but more than make up for the lack of footage with the quality of the toiletries and the fittings. Room sizes vary, reflecting the age and character of the house; Garden Rooms all have their own patios and Room 107 is a quiet room with a high ceiling.

The Rookery

12 Peters Lane, Cowcross St ⊖ Barbican
EC1M 6DS
(020) 7336 0931 **Fax** (020) 7336 0932
e-mail reservations@rookery.co.uk **www**.rookeryhotel.com

32 rm – ♦£206/241 ♦♦£241, ☕ £9.75 – 1 suite

VISA

The Rookery

For an area of London so obviously steeped in history, it is entirely fitting to find a hotel that positively exudes character and whose very name was used colloquially to describe the surrounding streets once known for their rather raffish reputation. The Rookery is a hotel housed in a row of restored 18C houses and is decorated with a unique blend of period furniture, ranging from the restored Victorian bathrooms - whose grandeur gives meaning to the expression "sitting on the throne" - to wood panelling, stone flag flooring, oil paintings and open fireplaces. Bedrooms are named after those who have lived at the address over the last 250 years and the fact that no two of the 33 bedrooms are the same can go without saying. What appeals most is the cosy and seductively secretive atmosphere that prevails, which is aeons away from the modern purpose-built bed factories that seemingly spring up overnight. This is a place for those who wish to feel like a genuine Londoner and you spent half your time expecting a camera crew to turn up to start filming a period drama.

Hazlitt's

13

6 Frith St W1D 3JA ⊖ Tottenham Court Road
✆ (020) 7434 1771 **Fax** (020) 7439 1524
e-mail reservations@hazlitts.co.uk
www.hazlittshotel.com

22 rm – 🚹£206 🚹🚹£241, ☕ £9.75 – 1 suite

Hazlitt's

Named after the essayist and critic William Hazlitt who lived and died here in 1830, Hazlitt's is a delightfully idiosyncratic little hotel made up of three adjoining town houses dating from 1718. The 23 bedrooms are spread over three floors (there are no lifts) and are all named after writers from the 18th and 19th century who were either residents or visitors to the house. Today, the hotel is still attracting its fair share of writers, artists and those of a bohemian bent. Each room is full of character, from everything from wood panelling, busts and antique beds to Victorian bathroom fittings and fixtures.

The Earl of Willoughby is the largest room and comes with a small sitting room. The ground floor sitting room is the only communal area and breakfast is served in the bedrooms as there's no restaurant. Being in very heart of Soho, however, means that if you can't find a restaurant here then you really shouldn't be allowed out.

The staff match their surroundings in their wit and self-assurance which clearly comes from having pride in their hotel. As Hazlitt himself said "the art of pleasing consists in being pleased".

Soho ▶ Plan II

Miller's

C2

111A Westbourne Grove
(entrance on Hereford Rd) W2 4UW
(020) 7243 1024 **Fax** (020) 7243 1064
e-mail enquiries@millersuk.com **www**.millersuk.com

⊖ Bayswater

8 rm – †£176 ††£217/270

AE

Miller's

Just look out for the red door as the only sign that tells you that this is indeed a little hotel is a discreet brass plaque. The clue lies in the name: this 18th century house is owned by Martin Miller, he of Miller's Antique Guide and his stock appears to be scattered all over the house. Ring the bell, climb the stairs and you'll find yourself in a charming drawing room chock-a-block with antiques, pictures, baubles, candles and assorted objets d'art. This is the only communal area in the hotel - and the heart of the house. It is also where breakfast is served – on a single large table. You'll find an honesty bar here as well as bowls of fruit and chocolate bars scattered around.

The seven bedrooms are on the first and second floors and are all named after Romantic poets; highly appropriate as they are all quite theatrical and imaginative in their decoration. Wordsworth is big enough to let you wander; Keats is a thing of beauty and book Blake for when you want sleep to come hither. Miller's greatest selling point as a hotel is that it doesn't feel anything like a hotel.

Twenty Nevern Square

Nevern Sq SW5 9PD ⊖ Earl's Court
✆ (020) 7565 9555 **Fax** (020) 7565 9444
e-mail hotel@twentynevernsquare.co.uk
www.twentynevernsquare.co.uk

20 rm – ♂£89/140 ♂♂£110/175, ☕ £13

VISA

AE

R.Burr/Michelin

There can be few things more irritating for hoteliers who have spent buckets of money on marketing than to read their hotel being described as a "well kept secret" but Twenty Nevern Square is just that. It's part of a very charming red bricked Victorian Square, overlooking gardens, with comes with a palpable sense of neighbourhood.

Through the arched entrance you'll find they've made the best of the available space with a small but cosy little lounge area which leads into the light of the conservatory breakfast room. Ten of the bedrooms overlook the gardens and that includes Room 5, the Pasha Suite, which is the best room in the house, with an elaborately carved four poster and is own private terrace. Indeed, much of the furniture comes hand-carved from Indonesia which adds to the slight exoticism of the hotel when combined with the elaborately draped curtains. Bathrooms all come with a clever light sensor which turns itself on when movement is detected. The regular guests all seem to know one another and the small number of rooms makes for a general air of friendliness.

Aster House

3 Sumner Pl SW7 3EE ⊖ South Kensington
(020) 7581 5888 **Fax** (020) 7584 4925
e-mail asterhouse@btinternet.com **www**.asterhouse.com

13 rm – £146 £177/211

A/C

VISA

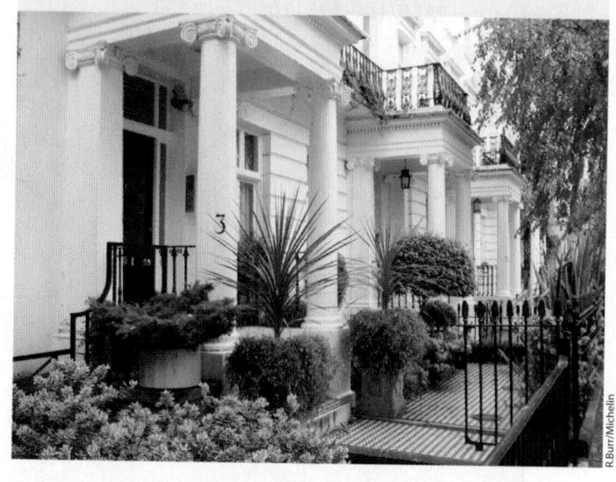

R.Burr/Michelin

Sadly, but realistically, few of us will ever be able to afford to buy a huge Victorian house, spread over four floors, in the Elysian Fields known as South Kensington. So staying in a Bed and Breakfast in a delightful and typically Kensington street, with restaurants, shops and attractions all within walking distance, is a great opportunity to live the dream.

Like all B&B's you get the distinct feeling you are staying in someone's house, particularly when you have to ring the doorbell to be let in. But it's not just in regards to its location where Aster House scores heavily; the house is immaculately kept, offers sizeable rooms and comes with rates that are a little more down to earth than many.

Three of the thirteen rooms are classified as "superior", including the particularly popular Garden Room which, as the name suggests, leads out onto a small garden. Breakfast is served in a very charming conservatory on the first floor which doubles as a bright and comfortable sitting room, overlooking Sumner Place and your fellow Kensington residents below.

Mayflower

26-28 Trebovir Rd SW5 9NJ ⊖ Earl's Court
(020) 7370 0991 **Fax** (020) 7370 0994
e-mail info@mayflower-group.co.uk **www**.mayflowerhotel.co.uk

46 rm – £69/99 £95/135, £9

Mayflower

A few years back if you mentioned you were staying in a hotel in Earl's Court everyone would have assumed you were sharing a leaky room with half a dozen Aussie backpackers. Just as the area is smartening itself up, so is the accommodation on offer. The Mayflower has had a lot of money spent on it and now provides both comfort and style; it's also accessible and affordable. The reception area is quite swish and adjoining it is a little juice bar for the health conscious. Following the wholly understandable trend these days, there is no restaurant in the hotel but a decent and sustaining breakfast can be had in the basement room.

The bedrooms have been nicely done up, with some personal design touches lending a sense of individuality. Hand carved bed heads and wardrobes, along with ceiling fans, add a subtle Eastern note, while the bathrooms are well lit and attractive. Some of the rooms can be a little on the small size but bear in mind the prices charged. Five of the rooms are on the ground floor and several on the first floor have their own balcony.

B + B Belgravia

64-66 Ebury St SW1W 9QD ⊖ Victoria
✆ (020) 7259 8570 **Fax** (020) 7259 8591
e-mail info@bb-belgravia.com **www**.bb-belgravia.com
17 rm ☕ – **👤£97/107 👥£107**

R.Burr/Michelin

Affordable accommodation in London is rarer than hen's teeth so when B&B Belgravia opened in 2004 it proved to be an instant hit. The formula is straightforward: clean, simple but very well priced bedrooms in the heart of the city. The downside of this success is that, with only seventeen rooms, actually getting one of those rooms can be challenging.

The entrance is quite discreet which adds to the feeling that you're staying with friends rather than in a faceless edifice in hoteldom. Don't, though, let the name confuse you: this is not your Mrs Miggins type of B&B with candlewick bedspreads and a pervading smell of soup but an altogether rather stylish and contemporary place.

Two terrace houses have been knocked together and there is a welcoming lounge on the ground floor decorated in black and white with a complimentary coffee machine available all day, as well as local information and DVDs. Breakfast is served in a bright and sunny room which overlooks the little garden terrace.

Bedrooms have a Scandinavian freshness and simplicity and provide perfectly comfortable accommodation.

Hart House

51 Gloucester Pl W1U 8JF ⊖ Marble Arch
(020) 7935 2288 **Fax** (020) 7935 8516
e-mail reservations@harthouse.co.uk **www**.harthouse.co.uk

15 rm ☐ – †£65/95 ††£95/125

R.Burr/Michelin

Gloucester Place is a street made up almost entirely of large Georgian terrace houses, many of which are given over to the provision of accommodation of a budgetary nature and questionable standard. Hart House bucks the trend by proving that you can offer bedrooms that are clean, spacious and still competitively priced for those travelling on a budget or those looking for something a little less impersonal than your average overpriced city centre bed factory.

Run by the same family for over thirty-five years, Hart House has its bedrooms spread over three floors where the ceilings get lower the higher you climb, reflecting the time when the house's staff had their quarters at the top of the house. Rooms at the front of the house benefit from the large windows and they're fitted with double glazing which keeps the traffic noise outside at bay, so maybe those salesmen were telling the truth after all. Four of the fifteen rooms are decently priced single rooms and there are family rooms also available. There are no communal areas except for the small basement room where breakfast is served.

Index of maps

Maps & plans

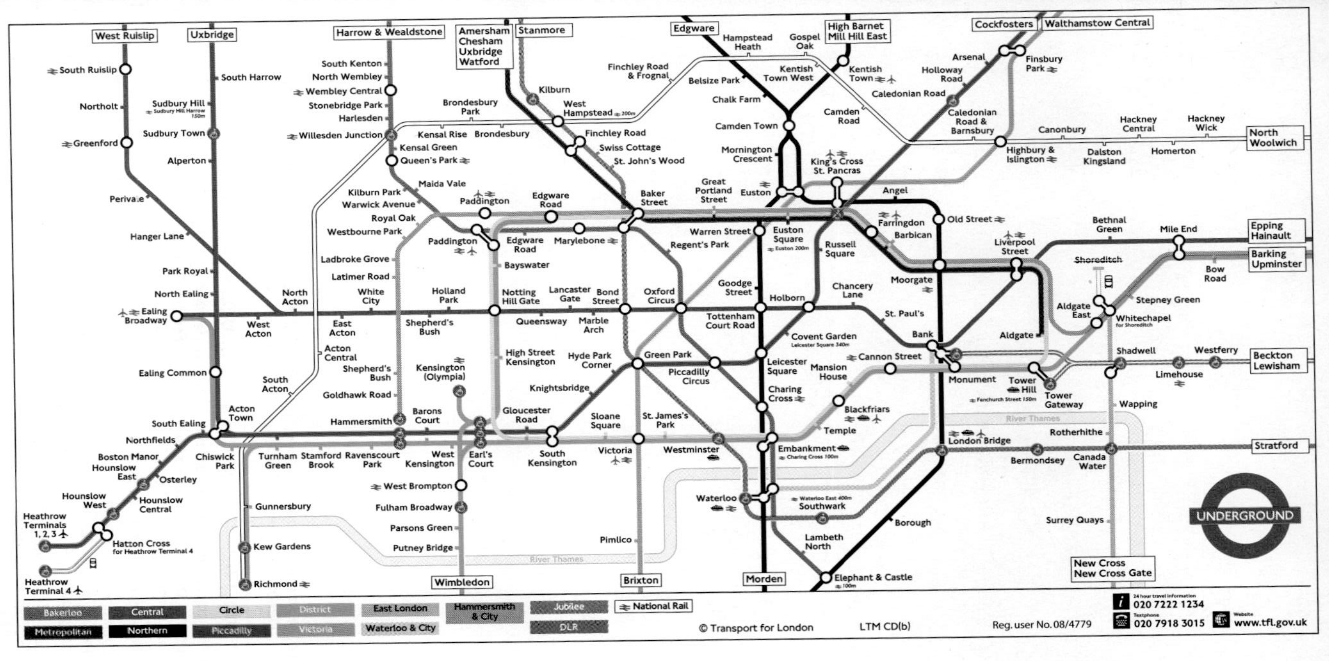

West Ruislip
Uxbridge
Harrow & Wealdstone
Amersham
Chesham
Uxbridge
Watford
Stanmore
Edgware
High Barnet
Mill Hill East
Cockfosters
Walthamstow Central
South Ruislip
South Harrow
Northolt
Sudbury Hill
Sudbury Town
Greenford
Alperton
Perivale
Hanger Lane
Park Royal
North Ealing
Ealing Broadway
Ealing Common
South Ealing
Northfields
Boston Manor
Hounslow East
Osterley
Hounslow West
Hounslow Central
Heathrow Terminals 1, 2, 3
Hatton Cross
for Heathrow Terminal 4
Heathrow Terminal 4
South Kenton
North Wembley
Wembley Central
Stonebridge Park
Harlesden
Willesden Junction
Kensal Green
Queen's Park
Kensal Rise
Brondesbury
Brondesbury Park
Kilburn
West Hampstead
Finchley Road & Frognal
Finchley Road
Swiss Cottage
St. John's Wood
Maida Vale
Kilburn Park
Warwick Avenue
Royal Oak
Westbourne Park
Ladbroke Grove
Latimer Road
North Acton
West Acton
White City
East Acton
Acton Central
South Acton
Acton Town
Chiswick Park
Turnham Green
Stamford Brook
Ravenscourt Park
Hammersmith
Goldhawk Road
Shepherd's Bush
Kensington (Olympia)
Holland Park
Barons Court
West Kensington
Earl's Court
West Brompton
Fulham Broadway
Parsons Green
Putney Bridge
Wimbledon
Gunnersbury
Kew Gardens
Richmond
Paddington
Edgware Road
Marylebone
Bayswater
Notting Hill Gate
Queensway
Lancaster Gate
Marble Arch
Bond Street
High Street Kensington
Gloucester Road
South Kensington
Knightsbridge
Hyde Park Corner
Sloane Square
Victoria
Pimlico
Brixton
Baker Street
Great Portland Street
Regent's Park
Oxford Circus
Green Park
St. James's Park
Westminster
Hampstead Heath
Gospel Oak
Belsize Park
Chalk Farm
Kentish Town West
Kentish Town
Camden Town
Camden Road
Mornington Crescent
Euston
Warren Street
Euston Square
Euston 200m
Goodge Street
Tottenham Court Road
Holborn
Piccadilly Circus
Leicester Square
Covent Garden
Leicester Square 340m
Charing Cross
Embankment
Charing Cross 100m
Waterloo
Waterloo East 400m
Southwark
Lambeth North
Elephant & Castle
Morden
King's Cross St. Pancras
Russell Square
Angel
Farringdon
Barbican
Old Street
Moorgate
Chancery Lane
St. Paul's
Bank
Mansion House
Cannon Street
Blackfriars
Temple
Monument
Tower Hill
Fenchurch Street 150m
Tower Gateway
London Bridge
Borough
Bermondsey
Canada Water
Rotherhithe
Surrey Quays
New Cross
New Cross Gate
Arsenal
Holloway Road
Caledonian Road
Caledonian Road & Barnsbury
Finsbury Park
Highbury & Islington
Canonbury
Dalston Kingsland
Hackney Central
Hackney Wick
Homerton
North Woolwich
Liverpool Street
Bethnal Green
Mile End
Epping
Hainault
Barking
Upminster
Bow Road
Shoreditch
Stepney Green
Aldgate East
Whitechapel
for Shoreditch
Aldgate
Shadwell
Wapping
Westferry
Limehouse
Beckton
Lewisham
Stratford
River Thames
UNDERGROUND
Bakerloo
Central
Circle
District
East London
Hammersmith & City
Jubilee
Metropolitan
Northern
Piccadilly
Victoria
Waterloo & City
DLR
National Rail
© Transport for London
LTM CD(b)
Reg. user No. 08/4779
24 hour travel information
020 7222 1234
Textphone
020 7918 3015
Website
www.tfl.gov.uk

Maps & plans

Manufacture française des pneumatiques Michelin

Société en commandite par actions au capital de 304 000 000 EUR
Place des Carmes-Déchaux – 63000 Clermont-Ferrand (France)
R.C.S. Clermont-Fd B 855 200 507

Dépot légal janvier 2008
Printed in France : 12-07
Compogravure : APS à Tours – Impression et brochage : AUBIN, Ligugé